SB003574
C

Galdós

MODERN LITERATURES IN PERSPECTIVE

General Editor:

SEÁN HAND, University College of Wales, Aberystwyth

Published Titles:

LILIAN R. FURST, *Realism*

JO LABANYI, *Galdós*

Galdós

Edited and Introduced by

Jo Labanyi

Longman
London and New York

Longman Group UK Limited,
Longman House, Burnt Mill,
Harlow, Essex CM20 2JE, England
and Associated Companies throughout the world.

Published in the United States of America
by Longman Publishing, New York

First published 1993

ISBN 0 582 08529 2 CSD
ISBN 0 582 08530 6 PPR

British Library Cataloguing-in-Publication Data

A catalogue record for this book is
available from the British Library

Library of Congress Cataloging-in-Publication Data

Galdós / edited and introduced by Jo Labanyi.
p. cm. — (Modern literatures in perspective)
Includes bibliographical references and index.
ISBN 0-582-08529-2. — ISBN 0-582-08530-6 (pbk)
1. Pérez Galdós, Benito, 1843-1920—Criticism and interpretation.
I. Labanyi, Jo. II. Series.
PQ6555.Z5G25 1992
863.5—dc20 92-12957
CIP

Set 9k in 9/11.5 Palatino
Produced by Longman Singapore Publishers (Pte) Ltd.
Printed in Singapore

Contents

General Editor's Preface

Modern Literatures in Perspective is a series of collected critical essays on post-1800 European-language authors, works or concepts. It is designed to help the reader study these literatures in isolation and in context by selecting and presenting the most representative and inspiring reactions to the works in question from the time of their first appearance to the present day.

A crucial feature of the series' approach is its open recognition of the critical revolution which has taken place this century and in particular in the last thirty years. Marxist, structuralist, psychoanalytical, deconstructionist and feminist theories have utterly transformed our assessment of literature. *Modern Literatures in Perspective* takes full account of the general issues raised by the revolution in theory, together with the practical effects which these theories have on the reading of the literary canon.

Recognizing the need for direction within this plural field of perspectives, each volume offers a high degree of critical guidance and advice in addition to presenting its subject in a methodical and accessible manner.

A substantial introduction outlines the historical and cultural contexts within which the literature in question was produced. It explores and explains the conflicting critical reactions to the literature in perspective and suggests ways in which these critical differences may be put to work. Each essay is prefaced by an introductory headnote setting forth the significance of the piece. A glossary of critical terms and cultural references provides further background information.

Modern Literatures in Perspective offers much more than textual analysis, therefore. It openly examines the relationship between literature and a range of wider issues. At the same time, its approach is more concrete than any history of literature. Rather than impose a synthesis or single methodology, the volumes in this series bring the reader into the heart of a crucial critical debate.

New critical insights, teaching practices and reading publics continue to transform our view of modern European-language writings. *Modern Literatures in Perspective* aims to contribute to this continuous transformation by disseminating and analysing the best modern criticism on the best modern literatures.

Acknowledgements

We are grateful to the following for permission to reproduce copyright material:

The Director, *Anales Galdosianos* for the articles 'Reality and Fiction in the Novels of Galdós' by Gerald Gillespie in *Anales Galdosianos* **1** (1966) 11–31, 'Galdós and the nineteenth-century novel: The need for an interdisciplinary approach' by Peter B. Goldman in *Anales Galdosianos* **10** (1975) 5–18 and '*El amigo Manso* and the Game of Fictive Autonomy' by John W. Kronik in *Anales Galdosianos* **12** (1977) 71–94; the Editor, *Crítica Hispánica* for the article 'Galdos's *Gloria*: A re-vision' by Catherine A. Jagoe in *Crítica Hispánica* **13** (March 1991) 31–43; Dovehouse Editions Inc., 322 Glen Ave, Ottawa K1S 2Z7 for the article 'Silencios y cambios de rumbo: Sobre la determinación histórica de las ficciones de Galdós' by Carlos Blanco Aguinaga in *Galdós y la historia* ed. Peter Bly (Ottowa: Dove House Editions, 1988) pp. 187–206; Circulation Manager *Hispanic Review* and the Author, Professor Diane F. Urey for her article 'Identities and differences in the *Torquemada* Novels of Galdós' in *Hispanic Review* **53** (1985) 41–66; General Editor, *Modern Language Review* and the Author, Professor Peter A. Bly for his article 'The use of distance in Galdós's *La de Bringas*' in *Modern Language Review* **69** (1974) 88–97; the Director, *Nueva Revista de Filología Hispánica* for the article 'La palabra hablada y *Fortunata y Jacinta*' by Stephen Gilman in *Nueva Revista de Filología Hispánica* **3–4** (1961) 542–60; The Hispanic Institute of Columbia University for the article '*Angel Guerra* o la novela monstruo' by Noël M. Valis in *Revista Hispánica Moderna* **41.1** (June, 1988) 31–43; Támesis Books Ltd for the article 'Individual, class and society in *Fortunata y Jacinta*' by John H. Sinnigen in *Galdós Studies* II, ed. Robert J. Weber (London: Támesis Books, 1974) pp. 49–68.

Articles and quotations translated from the Spanish by Nick Caistor, 1991.

Introduction

Galdós and the modern reader

This is the first critical anthology in English that aims to give an overview of Galdós's novels. It is designed for two kinds of reader. First, students of European literature who do not have a knowledge of Spanish but are interested in establishing cultural connections across national boundaries. Second, specialists in Spanish literature wanting an introduction to Galdós's novelistic output and to the range of critical writing on his work. I am assuming both kinds of reader will be interested in critical theory, by which I mean an understanding of the premises underlying criticism of the past as well as an awareness of recent theoretical developments. My main motivation for putting this collection together has been an increasing discomfort at what seems to me a general conservatism in Spanish studies, when compared with the adventurousness of criticism in the English field, or even that of Latin America. The essays included here are intended to trace the historical development of criticism on Galdós, and to bring readers' attention to the ways in which recent scholars have applied the insights of critical theory to his work. I hope this book may play a role in stimulating new approaches to Galdós's work, both by providing models that suggest possibilities for further research, and by indicating areas still to be explored.

While compiling this volume I have been mindful of the current trend towards comparative and interdisciplinary study, and the need to ensure that Spanish culture is not, as so often in the past, left out in the cold. Now that Galdós's novels are at last becoming available in English translation, his work is likely to be represented increasingly on courses in the European novel, in gender studies (for which they are especially suited), and perhaps (given **Buñuel**'s versions of *Nazarín* and *Tristana*) in film studies. This book does not limit itself to novels that have been translated but gives all quotations in English, in order to make the inclusion of Galdós's work in such courses possible. The titles of his novels are given in English where translations are available (with the exception of *La de Bringas*, whose English title *The Spendthrifts* does not readily identify it); I have given my own translations of other titles, on first mention only. Bibliographical references are also to works in English. I have not included essays or bibliographical references on the historical novels (***National episodes***, as Galdós titled them) and drama, since these are neither available in translation nor widely studied. Names and terms printed in bold type (e.g. **Buñuel**, p. 1), are explained in the Glossary at the end of this volume for the benefit of readers unfamiliar with Spanish culture.

My experience of teaching Galdós on interdisciplinary courses has been that students who know little or nothing of Spanish literature are consistently impressed by the quality and interest of his work, and surprised that they have not encountered it before. My own explorations of the European nineteenth-century novel as a result of teaching on such courses has confirmed my belief that Galdós's novels possess a scope and inventiveness rarely found in their English, or even French, counterparts. Indeed, while remaining anchored within his late nineteenth-century Spanish bourgeois context, Galdós is in many ways an extraordinarily modern writer. The articles in this anthology reveal aspects of his work that do not fit easily with what is usually understood by nineteenth-century realism. This is partly because we need to get away from the representational definitions of realism that have prevailed from the nineteenth century until recently, misleadingly suggesting that the fictional text 'copies' a pre-existing reality, rather than – as most critics would now prefer to put it – constructing a model of human relationships that passes itself off as 'reality' in the mind of its readers. (The 1991 *Concise OED* still defines realism as 'fidelity to nature in representation; the showing of life, etc. as it is in fact'.) But, more importantly, Galdós's 'difference' is due to the particular circumstances in which the realist novel developed in Spain. Paradoxically, it is Spain's backwardness with regard to Europe that gives his work its modernity.

The Spanish cultural context

In the first half of the nineteenth century, Spain was intellectually isolated from Europe (the Inquisition was abolished only in 1834; until the 1850s there were restrictions on Spaniards studying abroad), torn by civil and military dissension (the majority of coups d'état were the work of liberals), and still largely untouched by industrialization and urbanization (in 1864, out of an estimated workforce of three million, 2,390,000 were peasants). The highly politicized Romantic writers of the 1830s were succeeded by a nostalgic cultural conservatism, whose chief exponents were the woman writer Fernán **Caballero** and Ramón de **Mesonero Romanos**. Fernán Caballero's novels of rural Andalusia punish those, especially women, who transgress against the traditional class structure; Mesonero Romanos's immensely popular 'cuadros de costumbres' (sketches of popular customs) give a folkloric depiction of low-life urban types threatened by the beginnings of capitalist social organization. The genre of '**costumbrismo**' to which Mesonero Romanos's writings gave rise was an antecedent of the realist novel in its attention to city life (Galdós and Mesonero Romanos met in 1867, and had a lengthy correspondence), but its focus on the picturesque aspects of the urban populace betrays its fundamentally romantic view of the people as the repository of national tradition. The middle of the century also produced a corpus of female **conduct literature**, largely written by women; and a stream of **melodramas** in which lower-class heroines defend their virtue against the predations of male members of the upper classes: both of these genres have been shown to have influenced Galdós's work.

It was only with the Revolution of 1868 – in which a group of liberal generals overthrew the Bourbon monarchy, driving Isabel II into exile – that Spain was opened up to the outside world and to new ideas (and capital). The period from 1870 (the date of Galdós's first novel) to the mid-1890s saw a remarkable outpouring of novelistic activity, with writers such as Benito Pérez Galdós (to give his full name), Leopoldo **Alas**, Emilia **Pardo Bazán**, Juan **Valera**, José María de **Pereda**, Armando **Palacio Valdés**. The **regional novel** remains a strong current, for it was not until the 1960s that Spain was to become a predominantly industrial nation. But Alas (1884–5, *La Regenta*; 1984, Penguin, Harmondsworth) and Pardo Bazán (1886, *Los pazos de Ulloa*; 1990, *The House of Ulloa*, Penguin, Harmondsworth) construct provincial scenarios that dramatize the contemporary conflict between scientific and religious discourse, and current concerns about the role of women. Galdós is the one novelist whose work is overwhelmingly urban, both in setting and outlook: after coming to study at Madrid University in 1862 at the age of nineteen, he lived in the capital for the rest of his life, returning to his native Canary Islands only once after 1869; Madrid was to be the location of all his novels from 1878–89, and of the majority of his contemporary novels overall. And, unlike the Madrid of Mesonero Romanos, this was a city of commerce, rapid social change and class mobility; a city where, in accordance with the new capitalist economy based on exchange value, everything is in circulation. The link between changing economic relations and changing social structures underpins the whole of Galdós's writing.

The fact that the Spanish realist novel was a late developer can be seen as an advantage, for two reasons. First, because it meant that the Spanish novelists had a knowledge of earlier French, English and Russian realist writers (Balzac, Zola, Dickens and Tolstoy in the case of Galdós; Flaubert in the case of Alas), which gives their work a conscious self-reflexivity rarely found in the nineteenth-century novel outside Spain (with the exception of Flaubert, himself a second-generation realist). In the work of Galdós, this **metafictional** dimension is reinforced by explicit recourse to his Cervantine heritage. Just as **Cervantes**'s irony founds the realist novel while at the same time undermining its premises, so Galdós's exploitation of the ironic possibilities of the self-reflexive novel foregrounds the constructed nature of the fictional world he simultaneously persuades us to believe in. This playful metafictionality makes Galdós in some ways closer to Sterne and to the twentieth-century avant-garde than to his English contemporaries, whose work – for all its brilliance – seems by comparison one-dimensional.

The second reason why the lateness of the Spanish realist novel was advantageous is that the Spanish novelists started to write at a time when the ideological premises of realism – based (as Zola made explicit) on a medical prototype of knowledge, in which underlying causes can be logically deduced from the empirical observation of surface symptoms – were beginning to be challenged. In other words, Spain started to discover bourgeois **rationalism** and **positivism** at a time when they were starting to become obsolescent. This time-lag allows Spanish writers to have a double focus, placing them simultaneously inside and outside realism. The result in the case of Galdós (and Alas) is again an ironic vision, whereby the texts question the underlying tenets that make them possible in the first place. A comparison could be drawn with the ways in which recent Latin American writers have taken advantage of their position inside and outside a dominant Western discourse to produce a literature that is multifocal. Writing from a position of 'backwardness' (or perhaps, to use a term current in Latin American studies, one should say 'uneven development') can be a source of strength. Some of Galdós's most interesting novels (certainly the strangest) were written in the 1890s – for example *Angel Guerra* (1890–1; 1990, Edwin Mellen Press, Lampeter), *Nazarín* (1895; [in press] Oxford University Press, Oxford), *Misericordia* (1897, Charity) – when science had been declared 'bankrupt' and the Catholic Revival, combined with a vogue for orientalism, produced a new interest in mysticism and esoteric religions. What is disconcerting about these novels is the way they apply realist techniques to a description of subjects overtly in conflict with the empiricist tenets of realism. I have made a point in this anthology of including some discussion of the novels of the 1890s, which are sometimes neglected; I am sorry there was not space for more.

There are many reasons why the 1868 Revolution (otherwise known as the September Revolution or 'la Gloriosa') should have ushered in a period of novelistic creativity. The parliamentary debates on the 1869 constitution created a climate of intellectual ferment by calling into question the traditional Catholic basis of Spanish society, proposing freedom of worship (this article of the constitution was the one most hotly contested; Galdós's anticlerical novels of the 1870s would be his all-time best-sellers) and discussing divorce (not approved till 1931 under the Second Spanish Republic; something called 'divorcio' was permitted, but it was in effect legal separation). The leading intellectual supporters of the Revolution were adherents to a philosophical movement known as **Krausism**, which roughly speaking was a secular alternative to religion (some of its leading thinkers were former priests), which allowed Spanish progressives to oppose the Catholic establishment without opting for a materialist position. The Krausists were banned from their teaching posts at Madrid University in 1867 for refusing to swear allegiance to Queen and Church; reinstated after the 1868 Revolution (in the early 1870s they held seven out of twelve chairs in the Faculty of Arts); dismissed again in 1875 after the Restoration of the Monarchy, whereupon the following year they founded an alternative educational establishment, the Institución Libre de Enseñanza (Institute of Free Education), that would educate a large number of future progressive intellectuals; and in 1881, with the liberal government of Sagasta, once more reinstated. Galdós was taught by the Krausist Professor of History, Fernando de Castro, at Madrid University during his brief studies there in 1862–3, and had many Krausist friends; the protagonists of his novels *La familia de León Roch* (1878; The Family of León Roch) and *El amigo Manso* (1882; 1987, *Our Friend Manso*, Columbia University Press, New York) are critical versions of the Krausist intellectual. The Krausists were important not only because of their project of constructing a secular society, but also because they put women's rights, and particularly women's education, on the political agenda (I shall come back to this later). It was also Krausist intellectuals who founded the study of psychology in Spain in the late 1870s and 1880s, coinciding with the boom period of the Spanish realist novel.

Arnold Hauser has suggested that the realist novel in France was the outcome of the loss of political idealism following the establishment of the July Monarchy in 1830 and the failure of the 1848 Revolution.[1] A similar case could be made in relation to Spain. The 1868 Revolution produced a flurry of novel writing but it was only in the 1880s, after the betrayal of that revolution with the Restoration of the Bourbon monarchy in 1875, that the realist novel as such became established. The novels of the 1870s, at the time called 'thesis novels', are dominated by ideological – largely religious – conflicts that threaten to turn the plot into an allegorical struggle between good and evil. But by 1881 it was no longer possible to differentiate clearly between opposing camps. The 1869 constitution drew back from declaring Spain a republic, nominated the republican general Serrano – a leader of the 1868 Revolution – Regent, and sent letters to various members of the European royalty inviting them to occupy the throne. After a number of refusals, Amadeo of Savoy was finally 'elected' King of Spain in 1870, only to resign in 1873, leaving Spain a republic by default and Spaniards somewhat flattened by the rebuff. From this point on, Spanish intellectuals became convinced that Spain was ungovernable: a myth that was repeatedly exploited by the military (notably Franco in 1936) as an excuse for seizing power. This belief seemed to be confirmed by the First Spanish Republic of 1873–4, which had four presidents in less than a year, and saw the north-west of Spain fall to traditionalist Carlist rebels (see **Carlism**), while parts of Andalusia and the south-east declared themselves independent cantons, having taken literally the federalist rhetoric of Republican politicians. The latter reacted by sending in troops to quell their supporters' uprisings in the south, and the right-wing General Pavía highjacked parliament to restore law and order in January 1874; a second military coup in December proclaimed the deposed Isabel II's son, Alfonso XII, King. So many U-turns led to a cynicism about political distinctions, which would be compounded under the Restoration by the 'turno pacífico' (peaceful rota): a gentleman's agreement between the Conservative and Liberal Parties, led by Cánovas del Castillo and Sagasta respectively, to rig the elections so as to alternate in power. The full title of Sagasta's party – the Liberal Dynastic Party – itself suggests something of the political contradictions of the period. This sense of blurring of distinctions translates itself in fictional terms from 1881 onwards as a complex, ambiguous vision of a world in flux, where the key mood is disillusionment. Many of Galdós's novels – particularly *La desheredada* (1881; The Disinherited), *La de Bringas* (1884; 1951, *The Spendthrifts*, Weidenfeld and Nicolson, London), *Fortunata y Jacinta* (1886–7; 1988, *Fortunata and Jacinta*, Penguin, Harmondsworth) – incorporate political events of the period 1868–76 into their plots; in every case the impression given is of a chaotic lack of direction, in which change turns out to mean more of the same.

The 'turno pacífico' affected the development of the novel also by engineering a political stability that allowed the first real economic boom in modern Spanish history to take place. The decade from 1876–86 was one of capitalist enterprise and speculation, foreign investment, industrial expansion (especially in the Basque mining and Catalan textile industries), and urbanization (when Galdós first arrived in Madrid in 1862, it had a population of 300,000; by 1900 it had virtually doubled): all of which belatedly consolidated the power of the Spanish middle classes. The resulting commodification of human relations was to be a constant theme in Galdós's novels of the 1880s. This economic boom created an affluent class with sufficient leisure to form a significant reading public, and the economic infrastructure for the newspaper and publishing industries to turn themselves into commercial operations. The boom period of the Spanish realist novel, beginning in 1881, would come to an end some three to five years after the economic crisis of 1892; it was in 1892 that Galdós would take up writing for the stage to obtain an alternative source of income.

The press, publishing and the reading public

All Spain's leading novelists were also journalists. Galdós started his career in 1865 as a writer for the progressive paper *La Nación*; in September 1868 he became parliamentary correspondent for the daily *Las Cortes*; in 1870 he joined the newly founded *Revista de España*; in 1871 he became editor of the liberal *El Debate*, leaving this post in 1872 to take up editorship of *Revista de España*; in 1873 he gave up full-time journalistic work to concentrate on writing novels, but continued to write for the press freelance throughout his career; in addition, from 1883–93 he was European correspondent for the Buenos Aires paper *La Prensa*. This journalistic apprenticeship was fundamental in steering Galdós towards a kind of fiction based on reportage and documentation: his first novels, with the exception of the psychological fantasy *La sombra* (1870; 1980, *The Shadow*, Ohio University Press, Columbus), were historical works, a genre he would continue to cultivate with the 46 volumes of his *National episodes* (1873–9, 1898–1912). In his **contemporary novels**, the narrator constantly refers to himself as a historian or chronicler (though there is often a Cervantine irony here). Since his arrival in Madrid in 1862, Galdós had made a point of touring the working-class districts, on one occasion accompanying a tenement rent-collector on his rounds. From 1881 onwards he would systematically research his contemporary novels, visiting the lunatic asylum at Leganés for *La desheredada*, and getting permission to inspect the rented quarters of the Royal Palace for *La de Bringas* (for the research done for *Fortunata and Jacinta* and *Misericordia*, see Chapter 3). Galdós also contributed to women's magazines, including *La Guirnalda* whose editor became his publisher from 1873–97, when Galdós sued him and won exclusive rights to his work (as his own publisher from 1897 onwards he was not a success). Whether as crime reporter or out of personal interest, he was a frequent attender at the law courts, often interviewing witnesses and the accused, as in the notorious 1888–9 Calle Fuencarral murder trial which gave rise to the novels *La incógnita* (1888–9; 1991, *The Unknown*, Edwin Mellen Press, Lampeter; the title is reminiscent of a detective novel) and *Realidad* (1889; Reality). This interest in crime is particularly interesting given Carlo Ginzburg's observation that late nineteenth-century psychological theories of identity go hand in hand with the birth of the detective novel and the development of techniques of police identification.[2] In the mid-1890s Galdós would, like many Spaniards, become interested in the theories of the Italian criminologist Cesare Lombroso, whose works, newly translated into Spanish, postulated a connection between disparate forms of deviance such as criminality, anarchism, genius and madness.

Without this growth of the newspaper and publishing industries, a major novelistic project like that of Galdós (46 *National episodes*, plus another 31 novels of – mostly – contemporary life, several of which run to 600–800 pages and various volumes) could never have got off the ground. The process was aided by the relaxation of censorship laws, abolished by the 1868 Revolution, and reinstated with the Restoration but in a relatively mild form, particularly in periods of liberal government. (It is salutary to compare the reaction to Zola in Spain and England: in Spain, Zola's works were from 1880 all translated, some of them several times, with a good deal of scandal but without incident; Zola's English translator was jailed and died in prison.) That so much print (fictional and journalistic) was produced in Spain during the post-1868 period is remarkable when one considers that the census of 1877 gives an illiteracy rate of 67 per cent; it has been suggested that, given the underestimate of the total population, this figure should in fact read 75 per cent. By 1900, this had dropped by only 5–7 per cent to 68–70 per cent (if one excludes children under school age, 63 per cent). Figures for 1887 – the year of completion of Galdós's major novel *Fortunata and Jacinta* – give an average illiteracy rate of 71.4 per cent: 61.5 per cent for men and 81.2 per cent for women. So who, one asks, was reading novels? It is estimated that, from the publication of his first novel in 1870 to his death in 1920, Galdós sold some 1,700,000 volumes (1,250,000 corresponding to the *National episodes* and 450,000 to the contemporary novels), averaging nearly 35,000 volumes a year over his fifty-year career. Over the same period, with only twenty novels to his credit, Zola sold 2,549,000 copies of his works. Despite being outshone by Zola, Galdós's sales success is astonishing given such illiteracy figures for Spain.

Curiously, contemporary Spanish writers and critics all conjure up an image of the typical reader of fiction as female: with a female illiteracy rate of 81.2 per cent it seems unlikely that most of Galdós's readers were women. In her brilliant book *Desire and Domestic Fiction: A Political History of the Novel*, Nancy Armstrong argues that the English realist novel posits a feminine sensibility, not because it was addressed primarily to women, but as part of a political project to 'feminize' British culture by encouraging readers to identify with the depoliticized, private sphere of the home and the emotions.[3] One suspects that Spanish writers, when they posit a female reader, may have been engaged on a similar project. Critics have praised Galdós for depicting national history in terms of the private life of individuals (what Unamuno was later to call 'intrahistory'), attributing this to a social concern with the common people. An alternative view might be to see Galdós's adoption of the role of 'historian of private life' (to borrow Balzac's phrase) as a strategy for 'feminizing' his readership by presenting what are political issues in terms of domestic, emotional tangles: this is something feminist critics could usefully explore.

Problems of political interpretation

The political attitudes expressed in Galdós's novels are frequently contradictory, which is what makes them so interesting. Galdós himself was a lifelong professed liberal. In 1865 he had taken part in the student riots of St Daniel's Eve; in 1866 he witnessed the San Gil barracks uprising and the rebel sergeants being driven to their execution (a scene recreated at the start of *Angel Guerra*); and in September 1868 he cut short a family holiday to return to Madrid in time to see the revolutionary generals Serrano and Prim enter Madrid in triumph. In 1886 he was 'made' a liberal member of parliament by Sagasta, representing a district of Puerto Rico he never visited; during his ensuing four years in parliament, he did not make a single speech but was an assiduous attender. His late anticlerical play *Electra* (1901) was hailed as a political manifesto by the left-wing press and provoked riots (Electra lollipops, beer and cough sweets were sold as mementos). In 1907 he stood for parliament as Republican candidate for Madrid, and in 1910, by now going blind, accepted co-presidency (with Pablo Iglesias, founder and leader of the Spanish Socialist Party) of the Republican-Socialist Alliance; as part of that year's campaign for his re-election to parliament, he staged his anticlerical drama *Casandra*, again causing riots. His political activities led to the blocking by conservative prime ministers of his candidacy in 1882 for the Spanish Royal Academy (finally elected in 1889, he took up the offer only in 1897), and in 1911 for the Nobel Prize.

But this picture of solid liberal and republican sympathies is only part of the story. In 1886, while a member of parliament for Sagasta's Liberal Dynastic Party (in this case aptly named), he agreed to be a member of the official committee nominated to present the newborn heir to the throne, Alfonso XIII, to the nation (which at the time was technically a Regency, Alfonso XII having died prematurely in 1885, leaving his wife pregnant). Later in 1912, while titular head of the Republican-Socialist Alliance, he publicly met Alfonso XIII (who had acceeded to the throne on coming of age in 1902). The anticlerical political activity of his later years was undercut by a number of newspaper articles in the 1890s, insisting that the solution to what at the time was called the 'social question' lay not in politics but in religion (by which he did not, however, mean the established Church). This suggestion lies at the heart of his novels *Angel Guerra* (1890–1) and *Nazarín* (1895), but the irony with which the protagonists of both texts are treated makes it impossible to know whether Galdós is supporting or criticizing the idea. Indeed the irony of all Galdós's novels, and in particular his love of unreliable narrators, means that readers have to be wary of attributing the political views expressed in the text to their author (something critics have not always remembered). A classic example is *Fortunata and Jacinta,* where the unreliable bourgeois narrator repeatedly insists that Spain is not threatened by social unrest because of the 'happy confusion of classes' that is blending the whole of society into one big middle class: a claim that is patently contradicted by the plot of the novel, which is precisely about class conflict. The end of the novel will, however, propose a somewhat unconvincing reconciliation of classes, with the child born to the working-class Fortunata and the bourgeois Juanito Santa Cruz; many of Galdós's novels will follow this pattern of attempting to impose a reconciliation of extremes on to a plot that illustrates the impossibility of doing so. In the novels of the 1890s, Galdós abandoned this project of social reconciliation via a supposed bourgeois melting pot, and proposed a series of unlikely alliances between the aristocracy (represented by female characters) and the working class (represented by males). Nothing could have been further from the reality of acute social tensions and violence that characterized Spain in the 1890s. And yet there is a logic in the fact that, as class conflict increases, Galdós's novels progressively seek to defuse it. It is through their attempt to paper over class divisions that Galdós's novels acknowledge their intractable presence.

For if the post-1868 period marked the consolidation of bourgeois hegemony in Spain, it also saw the birth and growth of working-class movements. A delegate of the Russian anarchist Bakunin set up the Spanish section of the First Workers' International, founded in 1864 by Bakunin and Marx, in 1868. (Unlike the sections of the International established in other countries, this remained dominated by anarchism; the working-class movement in Spain was unusual in attracting large numbers of rural recruits.) Marx's son-in-law Lafargue founded the first Marxist group in Spain in 1871, which in 1879, under the leadership of Pablo Iglesias, became the Spanish Socialist Party. The Socialists had particularly strong support among printing workers, who were able to make their presence felt on the newspaper and publishing industries, and hence on intellectuals whose alarm was evident. The press gave huge coverage to the establishment of the International in Spain, which, in the wake of the 1871 Paris Commune, was banned by Sagasta's Liberal government after a long parliamentary debate (Sagasta would lift the ban on re-election to power in 1881). In the 1880s and 1890s, the Ateneo (the centre of Madrid intellectual life) saw a string of debates on the 'social question' (the title of an important article by Galdós, quoted by Goldman in this volume), and the first May Day demonstration of 1890 (which also prompted an article from Galdós, again quoted by Goldman) was met with near hysteria, further May Day demonstrations being banned until 1903. The 1870s had seen several political assassinations (that of the chief architect of the 1868 Revolution, General Prim, in 1870; the attempt on Alfonso XII's life, dramatized in Galdós's *La desheredada*, in 1878). The 1890s saw an escalation of anarchist terrorist attacks. In 1893 two bombs were thrown in Barcelona: one at General Martínez Campos, responsible for repressing rural violence under the First Republic and the Restoration, and another (spectacularly) in the Lyceum Theatre. In 1896 a bomb attack on a Barcelona Corpus Christi procession killed six and maimed 40, leading to a wave of arrests, torture, executions and deportations; in retaliation for these, Cánovas del Castillo – who had largely been responsible for the stability of the Restoration period – was assassinated by an Italian anarchist in 1897. Workers' strikes, agrarian riots, political murders, arrests, executions and deportations were in effect endemic to the whole period from the 1860s to the end of the century (and beyond, but that is another story).

The major intellectual advocates of social reform from the 1870s through to the 1890s were the Krausists, who – like many of Galdós's narrators and protagonists – promoted the reconciliation of social extremes, arguing that the problem was not just economic and political but moral, religious and educational. Galdós's fictional depiction of the 'social question' cannot be viewed as a simple reflection of class unrest at the time; rather, both Galdós's and the Krausists' insistence on non-political, reconciliatory solutions should be seen as part of a common ideological project for avoiding recognition of real political conflicts. In keeping with Foucault's view (to which I shall return) that the literary text does not mirror an existing political situation but is itself a political discourse that constructs a model of power relations, I would argue that the political function of Galdós's novels is not so much descriptive as prescriptive.[4]

Women – in life and fiction

This point holds true also for the presentation of women in Galdós's work. His own relationships with women were many: having avoided marriage, he is known to have had numerous affairs with women of all classes, one of whom – Lorenza Cobián, a woman of peasant origin, who in 1906 committed suicide – bore him a daughter María in 1891 (Galdós did not allow María into his house until he was dying, but made her the beneficiary of his will). Of particular interest is his affair in 1889–90 with the novelist Emilia Pardo Bazán, a militant feminist and leading protagonist of Spanish intellectual life, who would become Spain's first female university lecturer. Even without this liaison, Galdós would of necessity have been aware of the issue of women's emancipation for, after the 'social question', the most debated topic in Spain in the last three decades of the nineteenth century was the 'woman question'. Additionally, Galdós's drama of the 1890s and early 1900s would be influenced by Ibsen's treatment of the subject.

The contribution here of the Krausists – who championed women's education, in the 1870s founding training colleges for women teachers, telegraphists and commercial workers – was decisive. Their insistence on the reconciliation of opposites encouraged them to see woman as the complement to man: different because she is defined as what man is not. Their stress on education had the merit of pointing out that women are not born but made (many of Galdós's novels show a similar interest in how women are shaped by an educational process); but the Krausists goal was to make woman, who may not necessarily be born 'different', into man's 'other half'. It has been noted that the main reason the Krausists supported giving women a better education was to woo them away from the obscurantist influence of the Church, a point made by Galdós's history lecturer Fernando de Castro, who was active in setting up Sunday Schools and an Artistic and Literary Athenaeum for women after the 1868 Revolution, and in founding the Association for Women's Education in 1870.[5] This issue is dramatized in Galdós's *La familia de León Roch*, whose intellectual male protagonist singularly fails to change his wife's traditional 'nature'.

Galdós's novels show an ambivalence towards women in that on the one hand they stress the ways in which women are moulded by society (the result being a 'clipping of their wings'), but on the other hand they construct women as an image of society's natural (and unchanging) foundations: a supreme example is the working-class (and therefore pre-social) Fortunata, who represents fidelity and natural law. This ultimately biological view of women has its advantages, however, in that it allows Galdós to refer to women's sexuality (and its control) with a frankness that surprises readers used to the English realist novel. If Fortunata is shown to be governed by active sexual drives, it is because she is working-class; but even the angelic bourgeois wife Jacinta is shown in bed with her husband, albeit in a sexual relationship that threatens to become that of mother and child. Galdós's female characters represent emotion and intuition (what in *Fortunata and Jacinta* he calls 'the dialectic of the heart'), and as such are placed alongside children, whose psychology also fascinates him; but at the same time they represent primal energies that compensate for their over-civilized menfolk's 'emasculation' (only working-class males are depicted by Galdós as energetic). It is Galdós's female characters who mostly speak and act; his male characters are curiously given the traditional female attributes of physical debility, illness, and even (in the case of Maxi in *Fortunata and Jacinta*) hysteria. To see this as a sign of Galdós's support for women's emancipation would, I think, be a mistake: the point seems to be that something has gone wrong in this world where men are mostly tamed by women, to the point of illness. And it would certainly be a mistake to see Galdós's depiction of gender roles as a reflection of Spanish society of the time: rather, it represents a projection of anxieties about relations between the sexes. Or perhaps a better way of putting it would be to say that Galdós's novels, like the contemporary debates on the 'woman question', construct woman – precisely because of her strengths – as a problem.

The response to the European novel

Galdós's writing is not only a mediation of the social conflicts and contradictions of Restoration Spain, but also a response to literary trends in other European countries. On his first trip to Paris in 1867 he bought Balzac's *Eugénie Grandet*, and on his return visit the following year acquired all the remaining volumes of his work. The discovery of Balzac was followed rapidly by that of Dickens, and in 1868 the paper *La Nación* serialized Galdós's translation (from the French) of *Pickwick Papers*. His library catalogue lists 20 Dickens novels. His unusual two-year gap in productivity before writing *La desheredada* (1881) – from 1876 to 1879 he had published two to four novels a year – coincided with the discovery of Zola, six of whose novels he bought (in French) in 1878; 1880 saw the first Spanish translations of Zola's work (*L'Assommoir, Nana, Une Page d'amour*). In the winter of 1881–2 the Madrid Ateneo held a debate on **naturalism**; and in 1882–3 Emilia Pardo Bazán published a series of articles on the movement – *La cuestión palpitante* (The Burning Issue) – in the paper *La Epoca*, triggering a polemic that divided Spanish critics on largely political lines. The hold of religion in Spain, on believers and free-thinkers alike, was demonstrated by the fact that even those who, like Pardo Bazán and Alas, defended naturalism felt unable to subscribe to its determinist premises. Galdós did not take part in the controversy but, although his work cannot be called determinist, he is of all contemporary Spanish writers the one who, after 1881, pays most attention to material detail – notably money and food. In 1904 Galdós told the younger writer Baroja that he had (at an unspecified date) visited Zola in Paris, and examined the files of documentation he used to compose his novels.[6] Another coincidence with Zola is Galdós's interest in medicine; one of his closest friends was the pediatrician and medical reformer Tolosa Latour, who allowed him to examine interesting patients and advised him on medical details for his novels. Like Zola, Galdós had a particular interest in neurosis. His novels (the influence of the *Quixote* is also paramount here) are full of characters suffering from mental derangement, delusion or hallucination (in the case of the child Luisito in *Miau* coupled with epilepsy). The description of hysteria given in *Nazarín* shows Galdós to have been familiar with clinical writings on the subject. As in Zola's case, Galdós's interest in neurosis would lead him from belief in the supremacy of the physical to an increasing interest in the psychic. His later work, from *Fortunata and Jacinta* inclusive, contains some extraordinary hallucinations and dreams; in the 1890s this would develop into a fascination with paranormal states of perception bordering on the miraculous (Buñuel's film version of *Nazarín* misses a wonderful opportunity here).

Galdós's evolution away from the predominantly materialist position of his novels published between 1881 and 1886 (the date of Part 1 of *Fortunata and Jacinta*) owes much to the influence of the Russian novel, introduced into Spain by – yet again – Pardo Bazán: a copy of her 1887 Ateneo lectures *La revolución y la novela en Rusia* (Revolution and the Novel in Russia, largely cribbed from De Vogüé's *Le Roman russe* of 1886) is in Galdós's library. Galdós owned a copy of the first French translation (1884) of Tolstoy's *War and peace,* and several other works by him and Turgenev, all in French. His novel *Angel Guerra* is known to have been based on the marginal jottings he wrote in his copy of Tolstoy's *What I Believe* (in French *Ma religion)*; it has been suggested that *Realidad* is influenced by *Anna Karenina*. *Nazarín,* the story of a latter-day Christ figure, is reminiscent of the parable 'The grand inquisitor' in *The Brothers Karamazov,* in which Christ returns to sixteenth-century Spain; Galdós mentions Dostoyevsky several times in his journalism, though in the sequel novel *Halma* he makes his character Nazarín deny that his ideas are based on a reading of the Russian novel. Under the influence of Tolstoy's religious idealism, Galdós's later novels portray a series of saint figures, who in several cases leave the city to return to nature, calling into question the ideological premises of bourgeois society (including those of institutionalized religion); except that, unlike Tolstoy, Galdós undercuts his heroes with a Cervantine irony that makes it impossible for the reader to know how to interpret them. It is through Cervantes's ironic eyes that Galdós dramatizes the criminological theories of Lombroso (popularized in Spain by the ever active Pardo Bazán, in a series of 1894 newspaper articles *La nueva cuestión palpitante* [The New Burning Issue]), presenting his saints as simultaneously men of genius, anarchist individualists, criminals and madmen: in a word, freaks ('fenómenos'). Galdós's later novels in effect constitute a gallery of freaks, from the monstrously deformed child in *Angel Guerra* to the dwarf in *Nazarín* (here Buñuel's film version would rise to the occasion).

The critical tradition

Galdós's Cervantine heritage and exploration of the psychology of obsession and delusion were favourite topics with critics in the 1960s, when Spanish studies first expanded as a subject in the English-speaking world (the specialist journal *Anales Galdosianos* was founded in 1966); but they have latterly fallen out of favour. The article by Gillespie included here represents such early criticism at its best. Readers might like to pick up this interrupted critical thread in the light of later theories of intertextuality and the current vogue for psychoanalytic criticism. The majority of articles on Galdós in the 1960s came from Britain and betray Leavis's moralistic emphasis. The equivalent of Leavis in British Hispanism was A. A. Parker, whose '*Nazarín*, or the Passion of Our Lord Jesus Christ according to Galdós' (1967) was reluctantly excluded from this volume for lack of space. Despite his stress on Galdós's debt to Cervantes, Parker takes the novel's biblical references so seriously that he fails to notice the irony undercutting their supposed Christian message. Failure to appreciate Galdós's duplicitous humour makes much of the Leavisite criticism of the 1960s somewhat simplistic and dull. I have deliberately not included any of the well-intentioned essays from the 1960s, and early 1970s, that discuss the ethics of Galdós's characters as if they were real people who could, or should, have acted otherwise. This emphasis led to intense, and futile, debates about the 'proper' moral interpretation of the text in question – for example, Ramsden's (1971) polemic with Parker (1969) and Scanlon and Jones (1971) on 'The question of responsibility in *Miau*'.

Lack of attention to the text as fictional construct also characterizes the otherwise useful research into Galdós's biographical, bibliographical and historical sources done in the late 1960s and 1970s, which tends to assume that Galdós's novels constitute a straightforward reproduction of pre-existing material: a throwback to the 'life and works' type of criticism exemplified by the veteran Spanish critic Casalduero's classic but now outdated *Vida y obra de Galdós*.[7] Goldman's piece in this volume falls into this category, but also stands as a reminder to structuralist or post-structuralist enthusiasts that the text cannot be understood without knowledge of the world outside it (whether this world consists of historical events or other texts). Some of the most useful work of this period revealed real-life prototypes for Galdós's characters (see Braun, 1970; Lambert, 1973; Smith, 1975), or explored the debt of Galdós's later work to the Russian novel (Colin, 1967, 1970). The documentary emphasis on proving sources seems to have prevented critics from exploring the more tenuous relations between Galdós's work and that of his French and English fellow-novelists: a huge opportunity awaits comparatists here.

The late 1960s and early 1970s also saw the beginnings of what would become a steady flow of Marxist criticism on Galdós's work. In the case of American academics such as Sinnigen (see Chapter 9 on *Fortunata and Jacinta*), this may have been a response to the political radicalism of the time; but in the case of critics of Spanish origin it was rather a sign of the prestige of Marxism for the anti-Franco intellectual opposition, and for Republicans in exile such as Blanco Aguinaga, the outstanding and most productive Marxist critic of Galdós. The contribution of exiled Republican academics to Galdós scholarship is notable: Casalduero's previously mentioned classic was first published in Argentina, and its author spent most of his life teaching in France, Germany, Britain and the United States; Montesinos's massive study (1968–73), sadly interrupted by his death, was written in the United States; as was the sensitive work of Ricardo Gullón.[8] Even when – as is the case with Casalduero, Montesinos and Gullón – such critics do not adopt a Marxist approach, it is probably true to say that their sympathies with the realist novel have much to do with the high standing in Spanish exile circles of Lukács's work. (Both Blanco Aguinaga and Gullón have in fact produced a second generation of Galdós scholars, Alda Blanco and Germán Gullón, neither of whose work is unfortunately available in English.) The piece by Blanco Aguinaga I have included here is his most recent, reflecting the increasing sophistication of Marxist criticism as it moves away from a view of the text as direct expression of historical circumstance towards a more complex view of it as structural mediator of historical alternatives. Galdós studies have not yet gone beyond this to explore Foucault's suggestion that the text does not so much describe as prescribe historical possibilities: this seems to me a particularly fertile approach that readers might like to investigate, particularly given Galdós's sharing of Foucault's interest in medical and criminological discourse.

In the course of the 1970s, Galdós criticism followed the general move away from representationalism. With the exception of Engler's lucid account of narrative technique (1977), structuralist analyses have not prospered. But the New Critical tradition still strong in Anglo-American universities, which anticipated structuralism in its attention to the text's internal workings, in this period produced some excellent studies of the ironic aspects of Galdós's writing, which undermine any mimetic pretence. Bly's article included here is a good example of this new stress on Galdós's *trompe l'oeil* perspectives: theories of the baroque could usefully be applied to this aspect of his work, as they have been to the Latin American novel. Further studies of Galdós's use of irony were omitted from this volume with reluctance: particularly Cardwell's 1972 essay, which shows how even the apparently simplistic Manicheism of *Doña Perfecta* is ironically undermined; and Kronik's wide-ranging discussion of the grotesque in Galdós's writing (1978). There is room for more work in this area, particularly in relation to Galdós's use of carnival motifs (which no one has yet seriously related to Bakhtin's theories), and his humour (most studies of his ironic techniques paint a picture of a somewhat academic craftsman; it is time critics pointed out that his novels are great fun). In particular, his comic use of language is begging for linguistic analysis. Fallacious belief in the linguistic transparency of the realist novel has encouraged critics to be blind to Galdós's anything-but-transparent verbal wit. The earliest article included here (Gilman, 1961) is almost unique in its attention to Galdós's language, though Urey's recent semiotic studies have gone some way towards correcting this omission.

Urey's masterly Barthesian analyses of Galdós's texts (1982, 1985, Chapter 12 of this volume on the *Torquemada* novels, plus her many pieces on the *National episodes*) have dealt a definitive death blow to the notion that Galdós's novels have a mimetic function. Urey shows how the self-consciousness of Galdós's language turns the text into a commentary on its own production. Here her work joins hands with what has, since the late 1970s, become a veritable industry: namely, discussion of the metafictional dimensions of Galdós's work. Such discussion, following logically from earlier work on Galdós's debt to Cervantes and ironic narrative techniques, has produced a body of criticism of unparalled brilliance (see Kronik, Chapter 11 and Valis, Chapter 14; Kronik, 1981, 1982; Valis, 1984; Tsuchiya, 1988, 1989a, 1989b, 1990). For that very reason, future critics should perhaps look to new pastures. The sheer volume of discussion on the self-reflexive aspects of Galdós's work is in danger of creating a critical cul-de-sac, whereby the text appears to refer only – and endlessly – to itself. Scholars have perhaps now gone too far in reacting against the realist fallacy of earlier studies; what is needed is some way of relating the self-reflexive aspects of Galdós's work to the historical context in which they were produced. The appeal to Foucault's theories suggested earlier might be a way out of this solipsism. Another might be to appeal to Derrida, whose deconstruction of binary oppositions is echoed by Urey (Chapter 12; see also Castillo, 1985), but without reference to the breakdown of opposing categories which Blanco Aguinaga (Chapter 13) and Galdós himself (Chapter 2) see as the dominant feature of Restoration Spain.

A third alternative, which has already proved its potential, is that of feminist criticism (see Jagoe, in press, plus Chapter 15; Aldaraca, 1983; Charnon-Deutsch, 1985, 1990). The strength of feminist criticism is its awareness of the process of representation by which images of women (indeed, women themselves) are constructed; and its interdisciplinarity as it deconstructs the ways in which women have been represented in the multiple discourses (history, philosophy, psychoanalysis, science, in addition to the arts) that gender our view of the world and its inhabitants. This stress on representation, not as mimesis but as ideological project, puts feminist criticism in a particularly good position to relate textual manoeuvres to historical reality. Feminist studies of Galdós's texts, still few in number, have produced some startlingly new readings that uncover previously unnoticed contradictions. All of them adhere to the Anglo-American strand of feminist criticism, with its historical emphasis. What is conspicuously lacking is any attempt to subject Galdós's novels to the Freudian subtleties of French feminist criticism; indeed there is a dearth of psychoanalytic discussion of Galdós's works of any kind. This is especially odd since, quite apart from early studies of his treatment of psychology, several critics have pointed to the importance of mother–son relationships (literal and figurative) in his novels. Feminist critics might find a way of marrying psychoanalysis and historicism by examining the ways in which Galdós converts social tensions into family dramas.

How to use this book

The inclusion in this anthology of five contemporary articles (three by Galdós himself; one each by his fellow novelists Alas and Pardo Bazán) is intended to help readers relate Galdós's writing to contemporary discourse on the novel. Some of Galdós's own comments, and those of Pardo Bazán, allow scope for feminist criticism. The ten modern critical studies that follow are meant to give an overview of the major strands of Galdós criticism from the early 1960s to the present day; at the same time I have tried to strike a balance between general studies and pieces devoted to a single text, and have aimed at as wide a coverage as possible of Galdós's 28 contemporary novels. The need to square these aims, together with lack of space, required some painful decisions, and omission in many cases corresponds simply to the need not to over-represent any one critical tendency or novel. The only novel covered by more than one essay is *Fortunata and Jacinta*, Galdós's major work, cheaply available in translation, and also the one on which nearly all critics have written their best piece (an excellent anthology of criticism on this text alone exists in Spanish).[9]

The critical readings are arranged in order of their publication, to give an idea of the historical evolution of Galdós criticism. For readers more interested in the development of Galdós's work, I would suggest the following alternative sequence: first, the general chapters (Gillespie, Goldman, Blanco Aguinaga); and then the articles on specific novels in order of the latter's publication (Jagoe, Kronik, Bly, Gilman, Sinnigen, Valis, Urey).

All the articles included, contemporary or modern, are preceded within the chapter in which they appear by headnotes pointing the reader in specific directions and giving contextual information; where necessary, I have also appended editor's notes to the selected articles, clarifying allusions that may not be explicit to the English-speaking public. The chronological table that follows this introduction situates Galdós's biography and major novels in relation to historical events and the work of other European novelists. At the end of the book, following the Glossary of key terms and names, the Bibliography provides a list of Galdós's complete works, to give an idea of his incredible productivity; a list of his novels available in English (translations that are both out of print and not widely held in libraries are not included); and a reasonably full, though by no means comprehensive, list of critical works in English, which serves the double purpose of encouraging readers to read on, and of allowing me to mention those studies that could not be included in this volume.

I am indebted to Seán Hand for his guidance as General Editor, and to Longman for their efficiency in seeing this project to completion. Needless to say, any deficiencies this book may have are my own responsibility.

JO LABANYI

Notes

1. HAUSER, A., 1962, *The Social History of Art*, 4 vols, Routledge, London, vol. 4, pp. 2–4, 55–61.
2. GINZBURG, C., 1988, 'Clues: Morelli, Freud, and Sherlock Holmes' in Eco, U., Sebeok, T. A. (eds) *The Sign of Three: Dupin, Holmes, Pierce*, Indiana University Press, Bloomington, pp. 106–9.
3. 1989, Oxford University Press, Oxford.
4. See FOUCAULT, M., 1979, *Discipline and Punish: The Birth of the Prison*, Penguin, Harmondsworth; and 1981, *A History of Sexuality* (vol. 1, *An Introduction*), Penguin, Harmondsworth. NANCY ARMSTRONG's previously mentioned (note 3) *Desire and Domestic Fiction*, 1989, is a model application of Foucault's theories.
5. See SCANLON, G. M., 1986, *La polémica feminista en la España contemporánea (1868–1974)*, 2nd edn, Akal, Madrid, pp. 32–3.
6. See SHOEMAKER, W. H., 1980, *The Novelistic Art of Galdós*, vol. 1, Albatros/ Hispanófila, Valencia, pp. 171–2.

7. 1943, Losada, Buenos Aires.
8. MONTESINOS, J., 1968–73, *Galdós*, 3 vols, Castalia, Madrid; GULLÓN, R., 1960, *Galdós, novelista moderno*, Taurus, Madrid, and 1970, *Técnicas de Galdós*, Taurus, Madrid. None of these is available in English.
9. GULLÓN, G. (ed.), 1986, *Fortunata y Jacinta*, Taurus, Madrid.

Chronology

This brief table is limited to events and works that have direct or indirect relevance to Galdós's life and works.

	GALDÓS'S LIFE	GALDÓS'S MAJOR WORKS	SPANISH HISTORY	EUROPEAN NOVELS
1843	Born, Las Palmas (Canaries)			Balzac, *Illusions perdues*
1849–50				Dickens, *David Copperfield*
1850				Balzac dies
1856				Flaubert, *Madame Bovary*
1860				George Eliot, *The Mill on the Floss*
1860–1				Dickens, *Great Expectations*
1862	To Madrid to study law			Hugo, *Les Misérables*
1864				Tolstoy, *War and Peace*
1865	Starts to write for press		St Daniel's Eve riots	

	Galdós's life	Galdós's major works	Spanish history	European novels
1865–6				Dostoyevsky, *Crime and Punishment*
1866			San Gil barracks uprising	
1867	Visits Paris, discovers Balzac			
1868	2nd visit to France; buys rest of Balzac	Translates Dickens, *Pickwick Papers*	September Revolution overthrows Isabel II	
1870		First novel *La Fontana de Oro*	Amadeo of Savoy elected King; Prim assassinated; 3rd Carlist War starts	Dickens dies
1871				Zola starts *Rougon-Macquart* series
1871–2				George Eliot, *Middlemarch*
1873		Starts 1st series of *National episodes*	Amadeo abdicates; 1st Republic declared; cantonalist uprisings	Tolstoy, *Anna Karenina*
1874			Pavía's coup; 1st governments of Cánovas and Sagasta; Restoration of monarchy	Hardy, *Far From the Madding Crowd*; Valera, *Pepita Jiménez*

	Galdós's life	Galdós's major works	Spanish history	European novels
1875			Alfonso XII installed as King; Cánovas back in power; 3rd Carlist War ends	Eça de Queiroz, *O crime do Padre Amaro*
1876		*Doña Perfecta*	Krausist Institución Libre de Enseñanza founded	
1877				Zola, *L'Assommoir*
1878	Discovers Zola		Attempted assassination of Alfonso XII	
1879		Suspends *National episodes*	Spanish Socialist Party founded	
1880				1st Spanish translations of Zola; Dostoyevsky, *The Brothers Karamazov*
1881		*La desheredada*	Sagasta returns to power; start of 'peaceful rota' with Cánovas	
1882–3				Pardo Bazán, *La cuestión palpitante*
1883				Ibsen, *A Doll's House*

	Galdós's life	Galdós's major works	Spanish history	European novels
1884		*La de Bringas*		French translation of *War and Peace;* Pereda, *Sotileza*
1884–5				Alas, *La Regenta*
1885			Alfonso XII dies; Regency declared	Zola, *Germinal*
1886	Liberal member of parliament			Pardo Bazán, *Los pazos de Ulloa*
1886–7		*Fortunata y Jacinta*		
1887				Pardo Bazán, *La madre naturaleza;* gives lectures on Russian novel
1888		*Miau*		Eça de Queiroz, *Os Maias*
1889–90	Affair with Pardo Bazán			
1890				Ibsen, *Hedda Gabler*
1890–1		*Angel Guerra*		
1891	Daughter María born			Hardy, *Tess of the D'Urbervilles*
1892		1st play *Realidad*		

	Galdós's life	Galdós's major works	Spanish history	European novels
1893			Anarchist attacks in Barcelona	
1895		*Nazarín*		Fontane, *Effi Briest*; Pereda, *Peñas arriba*
1896			More anarchist attacks	
1897	Member of Spanish Royal Academy; sues his publisher	*Misericordia*	Cánovas assassinated	
1898		Starts 3rd series of *National episodes*	Spain loses Cuba, Puerto Rico and Philippines in war with US	Blasco Ibáñez, *La barraca*
1901		Play *Electra* causes riots		
1902			Alfonso XIII becomes King; end of last Sagasta Government	Blasco Ibáñez, *Cañas y barro*; Baroja, *Camino de perfección*
1907	Republican member of parliament; starts losing sight			
1910	Co-President of Republican-Socialist Alliance			

	Galdós's life	Galdós's major works	Spanish history	European novels
1912	Goes blind	Abandons 5th series of *National episodes*		
1914				Unamuno, *Niebla*
1915		Last novel *La razón de la sinrazón*		
1918		Last play		
1920	Dies			

Part One

Contemporary Documents

1 Some Observations on the Contemporary Novel in Spain*

Benito Pérez Galdós

Written in 1870, the year of publication of Galdós's first novel, this article is his earliest statement of literary priorities. Given that Galdós's novels prior to *Doña Perfecta* (1876) were, with the exception of *The Shadow*, historical, it is interesting that here he comes out in favour of the novel of contemporary life. Despite the hostility shown to French culture, the influence of Balzac, whose work he had first encountered in 1867, probably lies behind his stress on the importance of observation. Galdós's isolation of Cervantes as a model here is deceptive: what he will take from Cervantes is not observation but his fascination with obsession and ironic self-reflexivity. Galdós's mention of the vitality of popular fiction is worth noting, since much of his own work draws on popular melodrama. His laments about the lack of a reading public in Spain are echoed by contemporaries, and show a keen awareness of the role of the public, and of modes of production such as **serialization**, in shaping literary trends; much of his life was taken up with devising schemes for selling his novels. Most noticeable is Galdós's sensitivity to the changing shape of the Spanish class structure, and his interest in relations between the various classes. His rejection of regionalism for a novel of the urban middle classes and the world of commerce stands as a manifesto for his own future work. Feminist critics will note his awareness that the family is the key to bourgeois ideology, and that the domestic ideal is under threat from its internal contradictions.

* Originally the introduction to his review column 'Noticias literarias', 1870, *Revista de España* **15.57**: 162–93. Reproduced in Galdós, 1972, *Easayos de crítica literaria*, ed. L. Bonet, Península, Barcelona, pp. 115–32.

I

The great mistake made by most of our novelists is to have brought in extraneous elements dictated by fashion or convention, while completely neglecting those which present-day Spanish society offers them in such abundance. That is why we have no novel to speak of; the majority of those works which, claiming to be novels, feed the insatiable curiosity of an over-frivolous public are destined to enjoy a brief life thanks only to the superficial reading of a few thousand people, who turn to these books simply for momentary distraction or passing pleasure. There can surely be no country or period in history which has seen a more lamentable or less successful attempt to create a novel of its own than that of Spanish writers in recent years. [. . .]

People who like to find explanations for such things have claimed that we Spaniards have little capacity for observation and thus lack the main virtue needed to create the modern novel. [. . .] It is true enough that we Spaniards are incorrigible idealists, who prefer to imagine rather than observe. It is also plain that there is no one less practical in a whole range of activities than the Spaniard, even though in days gone by we managed to create such a stir in the world. Men of letters are by no means exempt from this particular disposition of our national character. However it is, I think, undeniable that this tendency is more an accidental product of the special conditions of our age than something innate and truly characteristic. If we examine the quality of observation in our earlier writers, we can see that Cervantes, the greatest genius our country has produced, was so richly endowed with it there can surely be no writer in ancient or modern times to match, let alone better, him. Turning to another branch of the arts, what was Velázquez if not the greatest of observers, the painter with the keenest eye and greatest skill in capturing nature? The capacity for observation does exist among us; it must be the terrible degeneration afflicting us nowadays that cloaks and stifles it. We need to look for the causes of the parlous state of our literature, the poverty of our novel, in the external conditions affecting us, in our social make-up, perhaps in the weakening of our national spirit, or in the continual crises that have assailed us without respite. The novel is a true son of peace: unlike heroic or jingoistic literature, it can prosper only in quiet times, and in our day and age there are few pens which are not thrown into some political battle or other. The only thing expected of the greatest talents of our day is that they produce magnificent diatribes.

We also have to take into account the lamentable state of literature as a profession. The dominant mood among our impoverished men of letters is one of dismal gloom. Asking them to produce serious, honest works of purely literary interest is like asking for the moon. They are far too busy rushing from one newspaper to the next to gain a livelihood, which mostly eludes them; the crowning reward for their labours, the goal of all their endeavours, is to see themselves installed in an office, that pantheon of Spanish glory. [. . .]

In the meantime, despite what people say, reading is popular and we Spaniards read all kinds of things: politics, literature, poetry, art, science, and above all fiction. But those readers, those Spaniards who like to buy a novel, who devour it from cover to cover and genuinely appreciate its craftsmanship, are catered for by a special market. For the demands of this particular public determine the kind of novel produced. They want something tailored to suit their tastes, they sample what is available and put in their orders made to measure; and the customer must needs be satisfied. This explains why, instead of a national novel based on observation, we are saddled with a conventional, bland variety churned out to order, a plague imported from France which has spread with the dizzying speed of all contagious diseases. The public said: 'I want pale, shifty villains, angelic dressmakers, harlots with haloes, fatally flawed duchesses, romantic hunchbacks, scenes of adultery, extremes of love and hate', and that is what it has been given. Satisfying its tastes was easy enough, for such contraptions are turned out with amazing ease by anyone who has read a couple of novels by Dumas and Soulié.[1] The writer does not take the trouble to write anything better, because he knows he will not be rewarded for it; and I think we need look no further for the reason why we have no novel in Spain today. The one literary genre which our unfortunate writers have cultivated with some success, and which manages to support a few small publishing firms, is this novel of sentiment and action. Reading this kind of literature has had a profound effect on the youth of today, shaping our upbringing and possibly marking us for life. [. . .]

II

This novel of sentiment and action aimed purely at the distraction and entertainment of a certain type of reader has achieved what it set out to achieve, namely to flood Spain with a disastrous plague in the form of the proliferation of printed matter that has made the modern publishing industry. Part works, a brilliant invention from an economic point of view, are the scourge of serious art. They represent the extension of journalism to all forms of literary expression, and confirm a current tendency to adopt in all things the English principle of making a little go a long way, which that nation is so good at applying universally. First and foremost, these part works substantially increase the opportunities for publicity. Split up in this fashion, a book enters every home page by page, and is accessible to those of even the most modest means. Yet it would not be fair to put all the blame on this system; that is not where the main problem lies. Because it is such an excellent distribution system, serialization has broadcast works of little worth; but it could just as easily disseminate things of merit, giving them a mass circulation with the speed and accessibility of newspapers. [. . .]

There have also been attempts here in Spain to create the upper-class salon novel, but this is a breed which adapts to new conditions with difficulty. In general these attempts have little value, being scarcely more than pale, botched imitations of the French genre of boudoir literature. The blame for this lies in the French way of life which our aristocrats have adopted, thereby losing all their own distinguishing features. [. . .] The aristocracy in Spain today takes no risks, makes no show of passion; it is no longer devoted to bullfighting, no longer a model of hypocrisy. It is a class perfectly at ease with the spirit of modernity, which helps rather than hinders the progress of civilization, co-existing quietly and peacefully in the midst of a civilization it neither dominates nor leads, content with its role, contributing to the collective life of the nation as far as its power and influence permit, mixing with the rest of us during the day before withdrawing at night into the sanctuary of its salons, which anyway are accessible nowadays to all manner of mortals. Moreover, lovers of the picturesque and idiosyncratic will find this aristocracy rather ordinary: the adoption of French rituals for all their ceremonies, the constant use of the French language and rules of etiquette, their love of, or rather mania for, elegant voyages, has completed this levelling process, making them akin to the nobility everywhere. All of this has made the salon novel, based essentially on notions of elegance and sport, an exotic, short-lived bloom in Spain. It is also true that the circle of our high society is very reduced in numbers; the rest of us have little interest in what those worthy people get up to in their enchanted retreats. [. . .] Being the most complex, the most varied of all the literary genres, the novel needs a wider canvas than that offered by a single class, especially one that is now so unremarkable. The novel becomes stifled in the perfumed air of the salon, needing the wide open spaces in which society as a whole breathes and moves.

The only kind of novel to have produced results in recent years is that of the popular classes, doubtless thanks to our picaresque tradition, whose characters and style are still engraved on our national mind. It is of course easier to portray the common people, as they are more colourful, their personality more sharply defined, their customs more idiosyncratic, their speech more able to give life and variety to the novelist's style. It is more difficult to depict the urban lower classes, because they have already suffered the influence of the middle classes, particularly in the big cities. The new elements which political reforms have introduced into society, the rapid divulgation of certain ideas to even the lowest classes, the ease with which a passive and vividly imaginative populace like ours assimilates certain customs, all make the task of portraying them harder and more complicated. We know little about the common people of today's Madrid: they are studied only superficially, and there can be no doubt anyone wanting to depict them faithfully and graphically would encounter all kinds of problems, and would need to undertake first-hand research of an extremely tiresome kind. It would be a mistake to think they are to be found in the works of Mesonero Romanos. [. . .] Everything nowadays is new, and the society Mesonero described today seems almost as remote as the fables of antiquity, or the gallery of rogues, social climbers, fools, constables, gamblers, impoverished squires and other members of the underworld immortalized by Quevedo.[2]

As far as descriptions of country life go, Fernán Caballero and Pereda have produced inimitable but minor works. The former has portrayed the worthy rural populace of Andalusia with immense style and simplicity. [. . .] Pereda is a highly skilful artist: his *Escenas montañesas* are tiny masterpieces destined for immortality. It is only a shame they are so localized and he cannot apply his talents to a broader canvas. The bucolic realism and strange poetry with which he endows his endearing yokels cannot completely satisfy the literary aspirations of today. They are too narrow, expressing only one aspect of our populace. [. . .]

III

It is the middle class, so neglected by our novelists, which is our model, our inexhaustible source. The social order nowadays is built on the middle class: through its initiative and intelligence it has taken on the sovereign role in all nations; it is there that nineteenth-century man is to be found, with all his virtues and vices, his noble, insatiable aspirations, his passion for reforms, his frantic activity. The modern novel of manners must be the expression of the good and evil at this class's centre, of the constant upheavals that give it form, of its efforts to attain goals and solve problems that concern us all, of its search for the causes and remedies to those ills threatening family life. To lend form to all these things must be the chief aspiration of contemporary literature.

There are those who claim that the middle class in Spain has not produced the necessary personalities or distinguishing features to sustain the production of this novel of manners. They say our current society lacks the vitality to serve as model for a great theatre like that of the seventeenth century, and is not sufficiently original to produce a literary age to match that of the modern English novel. This is not true. In addition to the artistic possibilities offered by the constants of the human heart and everyday events, today's society, epitomized by the middle classes, can also, as it appears to our modern eyes, offer striking examples of originality, style and form.

It is enough to take a close look at the world around us to appreciate this truth. The middle class is the one which determines political orientations. It is the class which administers, which debates, which provides the world's great innovators and libertines, its ambitious geniuses and pretentious fools. The middle class dominates the world of commerce, a major manifestation of modernity; it is the middle class which holds the key to economic interests, which have such a powerful hold on society today, and are responsible for so many dramas and such strange reversals of human relations. In public life, the determining characteristics of the middle class are extremely marked since it is at the centre of politics and trade; and these, although fundamental agents of progress, are responsible for two great social defects, namely unbridled ambition and positivism. At the same time, what a vast canvas this class offers on a domestic level, constantly preoccupied as it is with the organization of the family! What is most striking is the problem of religion, which causes such upheavals in families and creates disturbing contradictions since, while in some cases the collapse of beliefs loosens or breaks the moral and civil ties that bind the family, in others fanaticism and piety produce precisely the same effect. One can also observe with alarm the harm done by adultery, that vice which above all others disrupts the family unit, it being hard to know whether this problem is best remedied by a religious solution, an ethical one, or simply by civil reform. We know it is not for the novelist to intervene directly in such serious matters, but it is his mission to reflect this underlying confusion, this unending struggle of principles and events which goes to make up the marvellous drama that is contemporary life. [. . .]

Editor's notes

1. It is not clear whether this is a reference to Alexandre Dumas *père*, author of popular historical novels such as *The Three Musketeers* (1844) and *The Count of Monte Christo* (1846); or to Alexandre Dumas *fils*, whose sentimental romances included *The Lady of the Camelias* (1848). Melchior Frédéric Soulié was a popular writer of serialized fiction in the 1830s and 1840s, noted for his anticlericalism and sympathy for the lower classes.
2. Francisco Quevedo's prose works *El buscón* (1626) and *Los sueños* (1627) are known for their mordant social satire.

2 Present-day Society as Material for the Novel*

Benito Pérez Galdós

This text is Galdós's speech on being elected to membership of the Spanish Royal Academy in 1897, towards the end of his career. As in his 1870 article, he adopts a sociological approach to the novel, seeing it as the reflection of society and as a product of market forces. In this retrospective overview, Galdós expresses his disillusionment with the middle classes, on which he had pinned his hopes in 1870, and which he now sees as lacking direction and cohesion: here he coincides with the negative critique of Spanish society being made at the time by the younger writers of the **Generation of 1898** (including Unamuno and Baroja), and with the general European *fin de siècle* sense of decadence. The key word here is 'dissolution': Galdós's novels from the mid–1880s increasingly explore the threat posed by the blurring of distinctions of all kinds. In the 1890s, his novels move away from middle-class subjects, and build some curious alliances between the lower classes and the aristocracy. Galdós's suggestion that social confusion is a positive factor for the novelist is borne out by his own work, the best of which is characterized by its exploration of contradiction and ambiguity. Despite Galdós's praise of the English novel, the only English novelist he is known to have read thoroughly (originally in French translation) is Dickens.

[. . .] Although on the one hand my lack of critical ability and instinctive disinclination to learning render it impossible for me to address a purely

* 'La sociedad presente como materia novelable', pub. 1897, *Discurses leídos arte la Real Academia Española en la recepción pública del St. D. Benito Pérez Galdós, el domingo 7 de febrêro de 1897*, Est. Tipográfico de la Vinda e Hijos de Tello, Madrid. Reproduced in Galdós, 1972, *Ensayos de crítica literaria*, ed. L. Bonet, Península, Barcelona, pp. 173–82.

literary topic for you, on the other the inescapable weight of tradition and custom dictate that these pages should deal with the literary form which has been my preferred, indeed exclusive, activity ever since I succumbed to the temptation of writing for the public. What can I tell you about the novel without passing critical judgement on examples of this sovereign art from times past and present, on the geniuses who have cultivated it in Spain and abroad, on its development in our own day, and the immense favour this appealing genre enjoys in France and England, two nations which are at the forefront in this as in so many other fields of human knowledge? The Novel is the image of life, and the art of writing it consists in reproducing the variety of characters in humankind, their passions and weaknesses, everything about them that is great or small, their bodies and souls, everything spiritual and physical that constitutes us and surrounds us, as well as the language that is the mark of our origins, the dwelling places that are the sign of family life, even our clothing which supplies the final external touches of personality; and all of this without once forgetting that there must be a perfect equilibrium between the accuracy and the beauty of the reproduction. One can talk of the novel in two ways: either by studying the images offered by writers, which amounts to examining the body of novels which make up the literature of whatever nation we are concerned with; or one can study life itself, the source writers draw on for the fictions that instruct and delight us. 'Present Day Society as Material for the Novel' is the topic on which I propose to hazard some opinions here today. Instead of looking at books and considering their immediate authors, I prefer to consider the supreme author who engenders them and who, once this material has been transformed in our hands, receives them back as judge; the primary author of our artistic work, the public, humankind, whom I do not hesitate to call the common people, in the sense that there is a mass of individuals who share a common denominator of ideas and emotions; the common people, that is, the raw material and destination of all our artistic endeavours, because it is they who, as mankind, supply us with the passions, characters and language we need, later as our public calling us to account for the way we artistically arrange these ingredients to form their image: so that, if they start out as our model, they end up as our judge.

[. . .] If we consider how the state of the society in which we live affects the production of literary works, what most strikes us in the human mass of which we form part is the loosening of all unifying principles. The great and powerful forces that once worked towards social cohesion are in decline, and it is no easy matter to predict what new ones will take their place to help direct and govern the human family. We are convinced that such forces are bound to reappear, but the forecasts of Science and the prophecies of Poetry cannot or do not yet know how to lift the veil behind which the key to our destinies is concealed.

This lack of unifying principles goes so deep that even in political life, which by definition is made up of disciplined groups, the dissolution of those extended families formed by the urge to associate, by traditional affinities or by more or less persuasive ideals can clearly be seen. Moreover it seems there has also been a decline in fanaticism, which used to bind together huge masses of people, imposing a uniformity of feelings, behaviour and even physical appearance and thus creating generic types easily adopted by Art, which relied on them for many years. This fragmentation of political life is the most recent example of that fearsome call to 'Break ranks!' which is to be heard from one end of the social army to the other, like a cry of desperation before the rout. It could be said that society has reached a point at which it finds itself surrounded by high cliffs that block the way forward. Cracks are appearing in these harsh and fearful crags, opening up paths or escape routes which may lead us to open ground. But we tireless travellers were counting on some supernatural voice to tell us from on high: this is the way, this and no other. This supernatural voice has not yet made itself heard, and our men of learning are caught up in endless arguments as to which cleft or passageway could or should get us out of this boggy hole in which we are sinking and choking. [. . .]

We can also see in this bewildered multitude, which invents a thousand distractions to hide its gloom, the disintegration of those historic social classes which had retained their internal organization intact until almost our own day. The populace and the aristocracy are losing their traditional characteristics, the latter due to the dispersal of wealth, the former because of advances in education; there is only a little way to go before these two basic classes lose their distinguishing features entirely. The so-called middle class, which as yet does not have a well-defined existence, is still a shapeless mass of individuals who have come from either above or below; the product, one might say, of the falling apart of both extremes: of the plebeian family which is on the make, and the aristocratic family which is in decline. The deserters from both ends of the social spectrum have set themselves up in this intermediate zone characterized by education, officialdom, business (which is nothing more than enlightened greed), and political and civic life. This huge characterless mass, which is busy absorbing and dominating the whole of existence, subjecting it to an endless stream of regulations, legislating frantically on everything under the sun, including spiritual matters which ought to be the prerogative of the soul, will undoubtedly end up swallowing the splintered remains of the top and bottom classes, which are the fount of elemental emotions. When this happens, a ferment will grip the heart of this chaotic mass throwing up social formations beyond our present imaginings, vigorous groupings we are prevented from defining by the confusion and bewilderment in which we live.

From all that I have in my rambling and naturally clumsy way tried to express, we can see that, as far as Art is concerned, the distinguishing characteristics represented by those basic groups of the human family are now vanishing, losing their vitality and colour. Even human faces are not what they used to be, however absurd it may seem to say so. One no longer encounters those features which, like masks moulded by age-old custom, could represent the passions, follies, vices and virtues. What little the common people have retained that is typical and picturesque is losing its colour and fading; even in language we can see distinguishing peculiarities dying out, with the resulting standardization of ways of speaking and expressions. At the same time, urbanization is slowly undermining the particular features of different towns; and although in the countryside people and things still possess the distinguishing marks which betray their station, this too is diminishing with the continual traffic of the steamroller that is levelling all outstanding features, and will continue to do so till everything spiritual and material has been reduced to the desired equality in shape and size.

[. . .] Do not imagine all I have said leads me to the pessimistic conclusion that this social disintegration must mean days of anaemia and death for our narrative art. The disappearance of unifying principles in our society does entail the loss of those generic types society used to offer us ready made, as if already roughly hewn by art. But as generalized definitions of people and things weaken, so human characteristics stand out all the more clearly, and it is in them that the novelist must study life if he is to reap the harvest of a supreme, enduring Art. Intelligent critics will recognize that, when a society's ideas and feelings are manifest in well-defined categories, then characters are in danger of reaching Art already spoiled by being mannered or stereotyped. But as these categories crumble, the mask falls away and the true face appears. We may lose the different typical groupings but man is revealed to us all the more clearly, and Art draws its value from endowing its imaginary beings with human rather than social life. It is also widely accepted that it takes a greater effort of the imagination, and a more profound and difficult process of elaboration, to express life when dealing with this individual material, just as the representation in art of a naked figure is harder than that of one in clothes, however close-fitting they may be. As the difficulty increases so too does the value of Art's creations, which in times of strong social cohesion project a keen sense of social relevance but during the hazardous days of transition and evolution can and should take on a profoundly human quality.

At this point the ideas I have been expressing, without any dogmatic arrogance, lead me to a conclusion which may strike some as false and paradoxical, namely that this very lack of unifying principles encourages literature to flourish; a statement which would logically lead to the destruction of the myth of the so-called Golden Age in this and other literatures. That fact is that the history of literature in general does not allow us to state categorically that sublime poetry and its related arts blossom more vigorously at times of unity than at times of confusion. Indeed the opposite might prove to be the case if one were to look at the history of different nations, paying special attention to private documents rather than to established versions of History, which are often contrived and embellished. [. . .]

Armed with patience and sufficient books one can prove anything, and I would willingly set out to demonstrate what I have just suggested, did my reluctance to compare texts ancient and modern not outweigh my desire to do so. I shall therefore leave it to others to resolve this question, and simply conclude by saying that the state of our present-day society, with all its confusion and anxieties, has not been sterile for the novel in Spain, and that perhaps this very confusion and bewilderment have favoured the development of our noble art. We cannot say how far the current disintegration of society may go. We can, however, affirm that our narrative art has no reason to disappear because of the demise or transformation of outmoded forms of social organization. New forms may appear, even works of incredible power and beauty, heralding the ideals of the future or paying homage to those of the past, just as the *Quixote* is a farewell to the world of chivalry. Be that as it may, the human imagination flourishes in all environments, and it blossoms not only in splendid, triumphant porticoes but also in gloomy, desolate ruins.

3 Preface to 1913 Edition of *Misericordia**

Benito Pérez Galdós

This extract is one of the few texts where Galdós describes the first-hand documentation undertaken, in naturalist fashion, for his contemporary novels from 1881 onwards. (His historical *National episodes* also made use of extensive documentation.) Here he describes his research for *Fortunata and Jacinta* as well as *Misericordia*. His inquiries into working-class life clearly situate him as a member of a higher class, as we see from his recourse to a police escort, and his need to disguise himself as a municipal medical inspector when visiting brothels (laws requiring prostitutes to submit to medical inspection were introduced in the 1860s). His fascination with the Moorish beggar Almudena also betrays a taste for the exotic, and an anthropological interest in popular forms of speech. The comparison of the slums of Madrid to London's East End refers to Galdós's visits to England from 1883 onwards, during which he made a point of visiting the locations of Dickens's novels. Galdós also comments on his technique – borrowed from Balzac – of returning characters. In addition to the documentation described here, Galdós based the death of Mauricia la Dura in *Fortunata and Jacinta* on a viaticum he attended in a Madrid tenement, where he met the model for Doña Guillermina. Needless to say, Galdós does not refer in this preface to the 'research' conducted in the course of his affairs with working-class women, including – according to his biographer Berkowitz – the real-life version of Fortunata. (The younger writer Blasco Ibáñez recounts seducing a working-class woman who complained to him about the meanness of her 'Old Man'; on entering her bedroom he

* This preface was written for the edition of *Misericordia* (1897) pub. 1913, Nelson, Paris. Reproduced in Galdós, 1972, *Ensayos de crítica literaria*, ed. L. Bonet, Península, Barcelona, pp. 223–6.

found on the mantelpiece a photograph of Galdós, whom she acknowledged to be the 'Old Man' in question (recorded in R. Gómez de la Serna, 1961, *Retratos completos*, Aguilar, Madrid, p. 759).) An alternative view of Galdós's 'descents' (as he tellingly puts it) into working-class life is given by another younger writer Baroja, who accompanied him on one of his tours of the Rastro (flea market) while documenting *Misericordia* and was shocked by the lack of time and attention he gave his informants (reported in the same volume by Gómez de la Serna, p. 524).

[. . .] In *Misericordia* I set myself the task of descending to the lowest depths of Madrid society. I wanted to present and describe the most wretched people, the extremes of poverty, professional beggars, vice-ridden vagrants, absolute misery that is almost always painful, sometimes picaresque and at other times criminal and worthy of punishment. To achieve this, I had to spend months in observation and direct studies from life, visiting the hovels of the poor and the lawless in the crowded neighbourhoods of south Madrid. I went with a police escort to investigate the lodging houses in Calle de Mediodía Grande and Calle del Bastero. To gain entry to the disgusting places where the lowest followers of Bacchus and Venus celebrate their rites, I disguised myself as a doctor from the Public Health Department. To complete my study of the worst instances of human degradation I felt it necessary to call on the friendship of several administrators of those buildings known as tenements where the families of the lowest proletariat are herded together. There I got a good view of both honourable poverty and the most heart-rending examples of the suffering and deprivation that occur in our crowded capitals. Years earlier I had visited Whitechapel, the Minories and other districts near the River Thames in the East End of London. I am not sure whether the misery there or that of Madrid's slums is worse. Certainly, in Madrid the glorious sunshine at least makes everything look more cheerful.

'Mordejai', the Moor Almudena who plays such an important part in the action of *Misericordia*, was taken from real life thanks to a happy coincidence. A friend of mine, like me accustomed to strolling around the streets observing events and people, told me there was a ragged blindman begging on the steps of the Oratorio del Caballero de Gracia who seemed by his features and language to be a Moor. I went to see him, and was amazed at his uncouth barbarity as in his broken Spanish, constantly laced with the most horrendous oaths, he promised to tell me his romantic story in return for some modest aid. I took him with me through the streets of the centre of Madrid, stopping off in various taverns, where I invited him to replenish his exhausted body with offerings that were against the laws of his race. That was how I came by such an interesting character, whom the readers of *Misericordia* have found so true to life. All the truth comes from the picturesque Mordejai himself – I had little to add in my description of him. To study him and his kind more closely, I explored the dusty, desolate district of Las Injurias, near the gasworks. The most pitiable people live in its miserable shacks. From there, I ventured into the Cambroneras neighbourhood beside the River Manzanares, which is relatively agreeable and is home to the gypsies who with their donkeys create an entertaining spectacle, although the place is often dangerous for the visitor. My study of the slums of Madrid was completed with visits to Las Cambroneras, the Estación de las Pulgas, the Puente Segoviana, and the far bank of the Manzanares down to the Casa de Goya where the famous painter had his studio. I discovered a rich vein in picturesque characters and striking language.

The character of the philanthropic maid Señá Benina, the purest of evangelical types, I took from the copious documentation I had gathered to write the four volumes of *Fortunata and Jacinta*. From the same source are Doña Paca and her daughter, examples of a bourgeoisie that has seen better days, and the elegant down-and-out Frasquito Ponte, who whiles away his old age eating a sad portion of snails in the Boto tavern in Calle del Ave María. Some characters in this book came from earlier ones, *Our Friend Manso*, *Miau*, the *Torquemada* series and so on, and likewise others from *Misericordia* re-appeared in the volumes I wrote subsequently: I have always tried to create a complex, heterogeneous and varied world in order to give some idea of the complexity of society at a given moment in history.

I ought to say a few words concerning the French translation of *Misericordia*. Maurice Vixio, a Parisian gentleman occupying a high position in business and banking, who was an adviser to the central committee of the Spanish Northern Railway and had lived in Madrid earlier in his life, acquiring an excellent knowledge of our language, did me the honour of rendering the pages of this book into French. [. . .] Naturally he wrote to me often in the course of his work to consult me about the problems of vocabulary he was constantly coming up against, since in this book, as any reader will confirm, I make unstinting use of popular language dotted as it is with idioms, turns of phrase and ungrammatical expressions which are as striking as they are picturesque. I answered him as best I could, but was not always able to help, as I myself cannot explain the meaning of some of the expressions the people of Madrid are constantly coining and putting into circulation. [. . .]

4 Review of Part 1 of *La desheredada**

LEOPOLDO ALAS

Leopoldo Alas was the leading literary critic of Restoration Spain, and author of *La Regenta* (1884–5) which rivals Galdós's *Fortunata and Jacinta* as Spain's major contribution to nineteenth-century European fiction. *La desheredada* was the first work by Galdós to show the influence of Zola, and this review of Part 1 of the novel is one of the earliest discussions of naturalism in Spain. Alas would become a protagonist of the debate on naturalism in the Spanish press from 1882–3, where he gave his qualified support. Here he adopts a polemical tone, setting Galdós up as a spokesman for progressive ideas. Alas's understanding of naturalism seems somewhat vague (he admits he finds the term ill-defined), but he notes the importance of Galdós's unsentimental depiction of the working classes. The terms used by Alas to refer to the working classes ('pollution', 'plague', 'throwback to some African race', 'rubbish tip') show how shocking such material was for middle class readers; as with other writers of the time (including Galdós), what Alas finds most threatening in the working classes is their refusal to fit the tidy categories represented by bourgeois domesticity ('piled on top of each other'). Unlike most contemporary Spanish critics, Alas goes beyond moral issues to describe Galdós's novelistic techniques: his comments on the novel's use of dialogue and **free indirect style** (introduced into Spain by Galdós, and later developed by Alas himself in *La Regenta*) are acute.

[. . .] Insofar as every epoch needs a literature that is exclusively its own, progress can be seen as those shifts which help it adapt to the new ideas,

* Pub. 9 May 1881 in the national newspaper *El Imparcial*, before publication of Part 2 of the novel in July of the same year. Reprinted in Alas, 1972, *Teoría y crítica de la novela española*, ed. S. Beser, Laia, Barcelona, pp. 225–31.

customs, tastes and needs of the period; stagnation, ruin and poverty in literatures are produced by unthinking traditionalism, which appeals to an absurd aesthetic chauvinism, and in so doing closes the mind of a nation off to any influence from new currents or from more advanced countries. There is no progress in literature if each period simply cultivates what is appropriate to it; progress occurs when an age finds the ways of writing it has inherited inadequate, insufficient, unable to express all it considers essential.

It is in the novel, the literary genre most adapted to our age, that a determined man of genius can most help bring about change in a literature that is always in danger of falling into decay, which if reduced to the mechanical repetition of antiquated forms becomes a trivial game that cannot be taken seriously. Without allying himself to any particular school, without falling for the extravagances of fashion, without indiscriminately swallowing wholesale literary forms, theories, aesthetics, procedures or movements from outside Spain, Galdós calmly and coolly studies the progress of artistic life in that part of the civilized world which most understands these matters and sets the standard of intellectual activity for the rest of us.

There is a new tendency in literature today which, while still battling against schools rooted in the past and against those passionate but thoughtless friends who are always our worst enemies, is definitely gaining ground, due to the fact that it contains within it great possibilities for progress and important truths. This tendency is known, by a term rather more vague than one would wish, as naturalism, and it is bound to triumph one day, even if not in the absolute manner that its disciples would wish, since it will have to modify itself to some extent as it comes up against traditional obstacles. While it may be easy to curry fashion and declare oneself a devoted follower of naturalism, it is easier still to condemn the movement, to mock its doctrines and leaders [. . .]. Galdós has studied this question impartially and, without copying Zola's theoretical exaggerations and still less his practice, he has decided Spanish letters would benefit from following many of the procedures and proposals of the naturalist school, as much vilified as it is misunderstood and treated superficially. It requires so little effort to come out with four or five hackneyed aphorisms of aesthetic dogma which, *a priori*, and as if with the authority of the Vatican, condemn naturalism and all its works! But if we look at life now, and its changes in taste, at the inability of our art to fulfil the needs of our modern-day spirit, then we can come to accept this new movement, even if not all its extravagances; and without rejecting our glorious past, we can learn to appreciate that literature in our time, in order not to grow stale or become a childish game, has to look for new directions, to aim at something more than it has done up to now. [. . .]

Galdós's current tendency, although not yet fully developed, was already apparent in the *National episodes*. However in *Gloria, Doña Perfecta, Marianela* and *León Roch*, and especially in *Gloria* and *Marianela*, we can see our novelist following a different path, returning apparently to the philosophical, idealist novel and the creation of symbolic types, however true to life and natural they may seem, and with a plot that is aimed at proving a thesis. I am one of the foremost admirers of these novels by Galdós. *Gloria*, the most idealist as well as the most popular of them, seems to me a model of this kind of work; but one can admire beauty in one kind of art and prefer another: for example, to me *Les Misérables* is like a bible of the nineteenth century [. . .]; but I can accept that the novel of our times should take other directions.[1] That is why I think the change that Galdós shows in *La desheredada* is to be welcomed and praised. I have just read the first part of the novel and from this I can see that the author has used many of the doctrines and examples of the naturalist school to good effect in his own work.

One of the things which has provoked most laughter among many French critics, and subsequently among some Spanish reviewers (who know as much about naturalism as they do about the secret doctrines of Pythagoras) is the simplicity of the plot in naturalist novels. Lack of imagination! is their cry, not realizing that they thereby condemn not only the author of *Un Coeur simple* but, more seriously, the writer of *Eugénie Grandet*.[2] This simplicity, which some authors have taken to the extreme [. . .], is in fact classical and deserves applause rather than mockery when it implies not a lack of imagination but keen observation and a well-chosen plot, qualities which give a short work stripped of superficial complexities a strong sense of vitality. The first part of *La desheredada*, 252 dense pages, is a fresh example of this unjustly condemned simplicity. Its plot consists of no more than the following: Isidora Rufete, who believes she is the daughter of Virginia de Aransis, wants her claim recognized and with it the right to the properties owned by the Aransis estate. This is ample for the author to study in depth the havoc caused by a pride fuelled by poverty and over-active fantasies.

In the same way that *Un Coeur simple* is no more than the story of a spirit born for sacrifice and denial; that *Eugénie Grandet* is simply the story of a miser and his victim; *Madame Bovary* that of the lustful dreams of a woman lost in the French provinces; or *La Curée* no more than a picture of how a weak-willed woman born into bourgeois society is led astray and becomes a courtesan . . . so the first part of *La desheredada* is no more than the story of the pride felt by a poor, dreamy young woman who has to struggle to earn her daily bread but yearns for enchanted palaces; who thinks she was born to wear glamorous gowns, but who treads the muddy streets in worn-out shoes.[3] By setting the action of his novel among the life of our poor classes, Galdós has also followed the practice of the naturalist writers. It goes without saying that the poor people depicted in *La desheredada* are far removed from the fake, unbelievable poor as portrayed in the vulgar kind of novel which for so long was all the rage among a certain public. Nor does Galdós present us with the common people idealized as they are in the socialist novels of Eugène Sue and his followers, where the downtrodden classes (as they are called) are blown up to such fantastic proportions that sometimes their suffering becomes grotesque, or their virtues are transformed into hyperboles of praise, or their heroism into that of the heroes of legend, in the supposition that, for this suffering people to have right of redress, both their hardships and their good qualities have to be exaggerated.[4] The naturalist school has seen things differently, and Galdós has followed them in this faithfully and successfully. Just as for Zola the common people of the Second Empire, especially in Paris, cannot be the good-humoured, heroic, supremely virtuous band that figured in melodramas or bandit novels, so for Galdós the lower classes of our own capital are not the ones invented by Escrich and others.[5] For Galdós, as for Zola, the greatest misery of the common people, the proletariat, to give them their proper name, is their moral impoverishment, which means that the first task must be to save their souls.

To do this, the best way is to portray their current moral state: to show the wretchedness of the soul together with that of the body; alongside the ragged clothes, alongside the contaminated pigsties that pass for their homes, to show the debris of their vices, the pollution of that lust which breeds in the slums, like a plague rife wherever human beings are piled on top of each other in penury. In *La desheredada* Galdós, a keen observer who is extremely precise in the expression of what he observes, takes us to the miserable hovels of that part of society which for so long was thought to be unworthy of figuring in artistic works. One thing Galdós does not do in the strictly realistic portrait he offers us of these sad places, of these characters so worthy of study and compassion, is blot the pages of his book with unseemly language; apart from that, he risks everything, and for that deserves a thousand thanks. It is the first time that one of our good novelists has dealt with this poverty-stricken, fetid Madrid, prey to hunger and humiliation, which on the one hand is close to the barbaric and all its aberrations, and on the other seems to express the pestilential decadence of an exhausted race that once possessed a refined culture. In *La desheredada* this Madrid is sometimes portrayed as a throwback to some African race, full of terrible passions, but is also shown to be the rubbish tip that is a necessary part of our modern capitals. With great skill and accuracy, Galdós focusses on the area in which this degradation and squalor most offend, offer the saddest spectacle: that of childhood. Pecado, Zarapicos, Colilla and their street-urchin companions, cynical angels, already jail bait, are presented with eloquent realism; the scenes in which they appear, far from being simple-minded entertainment as some might imagine, give rise to the saddest reflections, to bitter reactions.

Another aspect closely studied and marvellously described in *La desheredada* is that of the poverty which attempts to conceal itself, whose deprivations are such that even compassion for others is lacking; a kind of wretchedness which at first sight is comical but on second thoughts is perhaps the worst of all, since to the deprivations of the body it adds those of continuously frustrated fancy. This kind of despair affects many classes, even those we call the well-off; the desire to seem more than we really are has bred an almost universal sickness in our society, and it is this which is the basic argument of *La desheredada*; but I cannot here deal with this global aspect of the novel, and will leave its consideration until the whole of the work has been published.

Galdós has always been a master in the art of dialogue; he has always known how to convey individual characters and their social position through their speech; but the even greater difficulties he faced in this book have served only to bring out the best in him. Take La Sanguijuelera, for example, or Pecado, or Miquis, or Relimpio: what a way to talk! If I were writing this article simply to sing Galdós's praises, this is where the music would reach a crescendo!

Another technique which Galdós here employs even more aptly and precisely than before is one which Flaubert and Zola have also used to good effect, namely that of substituting the reflections the author normally makes about his characters' situation for those made by the characters themselves, in their own style, but presented not as a monologue but as if the author were inside the characters and the novel were coming from inside their heads. The chapter in which Isidora lies awake is a model for this way of developing the novel's characters and action. The only piece which stands comparison with this interior revelation of a mind is what Zola has written along the same lines in *L'Assommoir* to show us Gervaise's inner workings.

That is all I have to say for now, although I have scarcely begun. It is not my purpose today to examine a novel of which we know only the first half; we must leave a final, complete judgement until we can appreciate the whole work. I have here merely wished to point out the trend towards naturalism (in the best sense of the term) in Galdós's latest work, a trend which I applaud since I consider that the theory of the naturalist writers, if properly applied, will win the battle of schools, and even more importantly the battle of artistic practice. Obviously Galdós has made this naturalism his own rather than writing a servile imitation and, as we shall see when the time comes to consider the novel more fully, it is clearly stamped with the personality of its author, who is perhaps the novelist with the best balance of qualities, the least affected, the most painstaking and careful of all those great writers who are currently working to transform, slowly but surely, the literature of our day.

Editor's notes

1. Hugo's novel of 1862 was immensely popular in Spain with a lower-class audience, and much imitated by writers of part works.
2. Works by Flaubert and Balzac respectively. Alas is an inveterate name dropper; to avoid confusing the modern reader, I have cut most of the references he makes to writers – Spanish and foreign – who today are little known.
3. *La Curée* was one of Zola's early Rougon-Macquart novels, published in 1872.
4. Like Hugo's *Les Misérables*, the socialistic melodramas of Eugène Sue – particularly *Les Mystères de Paris* and *Le Juif errant* – were immensely popular and much imitated in mid-nineteenth-century Spain.
5. Enrique Pérez Escrich wrote a number of best-selling serialized novels from the 1850s to the 1870s, including *La mujer adúltera* (The Adulterous Woman) of 1864.

5 Review of *Tristana**

Emilia Pardo Bazán

Emilia Pardo Bazán was Spain's leading woman novelist of the late nineteenth century. A champion of women's rights, she led an unconventional private life, including an affair with Galdós in 1889–90, shortly before this review was written. Recent feminist critics have not gone much beyond Pardo Bazán's lucid analysis of the novel's contradictory depiction of the position of woman. She rightly spots the feminist potential of the novel (largely excised from Buñuel's film version of the same name), but also rightly notices how Galdós 'amputates' this potential by arbitrarily cutting off Tristana's leg. Particularly perceptive is Pardo Bazán's observation that, by turning Tristana's quest for independence into a love story, Galdós fails to see what women's emancipation is about. The one point on which the modern reader is likely to disagree is her objection to the fact that the character of Don Lope evolves from Calderonian stereotype to an ambiguous complicity in Tristana's affair with another man: it could be argued that, by showing male tolerance to be a more effective weapon than tyranny, Galdós is making a particularly subtle point about the workings of patriarchal power.

In the midst of all the fuss caused by the first night of *Realidad*, *Tristana* dropped like a stone into a well, in a sepulchral silence.[1] It could almost be said that neither the title, plot nor style of Galdós's latest novel has been so much as mentioned in the press or literary conversations. Whilst I do not think *Tristana* is among the best of Galdós's novels, and might

* Pub. 1892 in *Nuevo Teatro Crítico* **2.17**: 77–90, the journal which Pardo Bazán wrote and edited singlehandedly from 1891–3. Reproduced in Bazán, 1981, *La mujer española*, ed. L. Schiavo, Editora Nacional, Madrid, pp. 135-42.

even be regarded as considerably inferior to other recent works, everything that this author and half a dozen other Spanish writers produce will always merit close attention. [. . .]

The theme of *Tristana* is slight, and it could be said there is scarcely any plot. One Don Juan López Garrido, a Don Juan in his dotage, all but consigned to an invalid home, takes on the guardianship of his friend Reluz's daughter, an orphan without protection in the world. He takes her to live with him and seduces her, clinging to his last conquest like ivy. Although Señorita de Reluz's ambiguous position forces her to live the life of a recluse, one day she happens to meet the young painter Horacio, and this marks the start of their idyll, which from shy, hesitant beginnings becomes passionate and fervent. The old rake, Tristana's domestic tyrant, soon sniffs what is in the wind and at first wishes to take drastic measures, which he subsequently abandons for a mixture of apparent tolerance and sly opposition, by which he hopes to disrupt their affair and set the couple against each other. All his tricks and ruses would have been in vain but for two fortuitous events: Horacio has to go away for a while, and Tristana contracts a horrible white tumour which leads to the amputation of her leg. With the lover away and the young woman mutilated, love dies a natural death; Horacio takes a wife, and one-legged Tristana, the unfortunate wreck of adversity, seeks refuge on the arid sands of the senile love offered by her ancient seducer, whom she finally marries for convenience, with no illusions, only weariness. 'And were they both happy? Perhaps . . .' the author writes as a corollary to the novel.

I should make it clear straightaway that I have nothing against the simplicity of this plot. A great many novels, among them the greatest I know in world literature, have an extraordinarily simple plot. In Spain, to say that a novel 'has hardly any plot' usually conceals a reproof, as though the work were already being dismissed as anodyne or innocent. I protest against this, and even more strongly against the attitude which I will not say my good friend Señor Altamira has been responsible for, but which he has adopted without reserve: the idea that affairs of the heart have no substance, or at least are not as interesting as social, political, philosophical, religious, scientific or economic subjects.[2] If we consider the matter carefully (and that is our duty), I would say that affairs of the heart are the most substantial of all. The key lies in the way they are treated, that is, in the author's skill, talent and sureness of touch. As far as plot is concerned, we must also be careful to distinguish between its internal and external workings, between what happens and its wider implications, between the text's surface and what lies underneath waiting to be prised out by the trained reader. [. . .]

That is why I affirm that *Tristana*, despite the simplicity of its plot, still has too much of one: its internal workings did not need Horacio, or

Horacio's absence, or the amputated leg, because the substance of *Tristana* is not really Don Lope's seduction of the girl, nor Horacio's falling in love with her, nor the break-up of their affair, nor the marriage at the end. [. . .] The substance of *Tristana,* which is new and remarkable but not fully developed, is the awakening of the consciousness of a woman who rebels against a society that condemns her to everlasting shame, and is incapable of offering her a respectable way of earning her living, of allowing her to escape her decrepit beau's clutches instead of regarding living with him as her only source of protection and support. If only this idea – which in *Tristana* is presented in a confused, embryonic way, in a kind of haze, as if the novelist did not clearly see the dramatic force it contained – had been worked out with the precision and vitality of the plot of *Our Friend Manso* and the characters of *Fortunata and Jacinta,* then *Tristana* could perhaps lay claim to being Galdós's best novel.

Unfortunately, the story of Señorita de Reluz lacks the kind of unity, vigour and self-assurance that come with clarity of vision and the wish to convey it in words. This is particularly true in the second half of the novel, which quite clearly tails off and is inferior to the first part, as it hastens towards the final episode of the operation and its decisive consequences for Tristana's future. I must confess that the novel's opening chapters had built up great expectations. The initial situation is sketched quickly and boldly as from the hand of a master, a few brushstrokes in the style of Velázquez sufficing to flesh out the colourful, true-to-life figure of our fine gentleman, who 'deserved either to be killed or to be called Don Lope'. Equally touching and expressive is the figure of his victim, the Señorita de Reluz, the 'paper doll' who 'in the opinion of all the neighbours was neither Don Lope's daughter, niece, wife nor anything else; she was nothing and yet was everything, since she belonged to him like a tobacco pouch, a piece of furniture or clothing . . . and she seemed so resigned to being a tobacco pouch, a tobacco pouch forever!'. In this illicit union between the ageing beau and the beautiful young woman – the true drama – the internal struggle should arise at the precise moment Tristana becomes aware of the indignity of her situation, to escape from which she throws herself into an unequal battle that for this very reason borders on the sublime. The second chapter of *Tristana,* and from there until the episode of her falling in love with Horacio, are a constant source of hope: we are given glimpses of a strong, outstanding novel of the highest quality, a remarkable psychological case study. Tristana is already twenty-one years old, at an age when she is beginning to be aware of longings for independence 'with thoughts that overwhelmed her mind regarding the extraordinary social situation in which she was living' (I suppose Galdós describes it as 'extraordinary' not because it is so infrequent but because it is such an affront to reason). There is something sacred about this crisis of Tristana's soul, as she shakes off her lack of self-awareness and doll-like passivity, her incapacity to think for herself, having until then always taken other people's thoughts for her own, and suddenly blossoms like a vigorous plant, filling out with ideas, tight buds at first, then splendid, branching blooms, as she starts to feel curious and eager for something beyond and above her reach, and as the rag doll takes on the flesh and blood of a real woman and comes to feel abhorrence and repugnance at the wretched life she is leading in Don Lope Garrido's clutches.

All alone, cut off from the outside world, with no friends to talk to or any hope of relief, Tristana confides her new hopes – to whom? – to her maid Saturna. What splendid exchanges take place between the romantic young woman and the doughty servant! Saturna, with all the down-to-earth practicality of her artful kind warns Tristana of the risks she is running. 'Do you know, miss, what they call women who venture to stick their heads out? Well, they're called free women, not without reason . . . The tiniest dose of respectability means a double dose of slavery. If we women had professions and careers like those male scoundrels, things would be fine and dandy. But take my word for it, those of us in skirts have only three careers to choose from: getting married, which is a career and a half, the theatre . . . I mean being an actress, which is a fine way to live . . . or else . . .' And the young lady replies: 'I know, I know it's hard to be free . . . and honourable. How is a woman with no income to live? If only we could become doctors, lawyers, even chemists or clerks, let alone ministers or senators, then we might have a chance . . . But sewing, always sewing . . . Just think how many stitches it takes to keep a house . . . Oh, if only I had the stuff of a nun, I'd be queuing up to enter a convent right now! But I can't contemplate shutting myself away for life. I want to live, to see people, to find out the whys and wherefores of our being put on this earth. I want to live, to be free . . .'

This dialogue, to my mind, gives us a glimpse of what the main issue of *Tristana* should have been. Titillated with preludes like this, readers think they are going to witness a transcendental drama; that they are about to follow the liberating, redemptive struggle of an individual soul, a soul representing millions crushed by the same dreadful weight, consciously or unknowingly . . . but it is not to be. Just as we think the struggle is about to begin, Horacio appears, and with him a banal love story; Tristana surrenders to passion with a relish I will not deny is entirely natural, but which has nothing to do with the novel sketched in the opening pages of the book. The fight for independence becomes relegated to a corner, and all but disappears. Nor is there room for another kind of struggle, the struggle for free choice in love. At the outset Don Lope seems a slave to points of honour, a beau straight out of Calderón, a portrait perfectly suited to his time-worn manly beauty, like a figure out of Velázquez's *Surrender of Breda*, which serves admirably to point up the contrast with his ward in revolt. Little by little his character changes into that of a modern psychological hero in the French style, as in a novel by Paul Bourget,[3] a temporizing, sceptical man who puts up with what he cannot avoid, sure in the knowledge that time and circumstance will return his prey to him and content to be *le plus heureux des trois*. He lets the torrent of love between Tristana and Horacio run its course, and Señorita de Reluz does not have to fight to achieve, if not complete rehabilitation, at least the kind of dignity which comes with sincere feelings and disinterested, profound emotions. With the result that the author, after misleading us over the character and role of Tristana, does the same again with Don Lope; we thought (and it was not our fault, we had good reason to do so) that Galdós was going to show us the terrible conflict between traditional man and the new ideal, the clash between armour plating and locomotive, whereas all we are given is an old man who is both condescending and stubborn, an out and out rake; a young girl dazzled by a somewhat vulgar man; and a story without resonance that is triggered by a chance event, a physical accident, the equivalent of a tile falling from a roof or a carriage turning over. I do not of course question the verisimilitude of the story, even less doubt that with these elements, or with still less substantial ones, Galdós can entertain, interest, move, stimulate thought and emotion in his readers, for I think him capable of making a novel out of a piece of flint or a tuft of grass. All I mean by my criticisms (and I do not deny that they are criticisms) is that *Tristana* promised something more; that Galdós offered us a glimpse of a wide new horizon, then drew the curtain on it. [. . .]

Editor's notes

1. *Tristana* was published in January 1892; Galdós's first play *Realidad*, based on his novel of 1889, had its first night on 15 March of the same year.
2. Rafael Altamira was a young Spanish critic and writer who had, against mass male opposition, supported Pardo Bazán's candidacy to membership of the Spanish Royal Academy in 1891.
3. Paul Bourget's novel *The Disciple* (1889) was noted for its break with the deterministic theories of Zola.

Part Two

Critical Readings

6 The Spoken Word and *Fortunata and Jacinta**

STEPHEN GILMAN

Gilman is rare among Galdós scholars in his attention to linguistic matters; anyone who has tried translating Galdós's work will, like Gilman, appreciate the brilliance of his manipulation of register and cliché. (If, as has been said, fondness for cliché is a key characteristic of postmodernism, this is another aspect of Galdós's work that is surprisingly modern.) Gilman is writing at a time (1961) when Galdós's reputation was at a low ebb (the Franco regime disliked the anticlericalism of his early and late work, but promoted his historical novels for patriotic reasons, thus alienating the opposition too). His article gives a useful summary of previous attitudes to Galdós's work. Gilman's basically representational approach to Galdós's use of language (viewed as the reproduction of existing speech patterns) is typical of criticism of the 1960s; however he stresses the uses to which Galdós puts his material, and is particularly sensitive to his exploitation of ambivalence. Gilman's interest in the fictional representation of speech raises issues about the relation of orality to literacy in the realist novel: readers of Walter J. Ong's *Orality and Literacy* (1982, Methuen, London) might want to explore this area. In his suggestion that the novel represents the social advancement of its working-class heroine in terms of her increasing linguistic competence, Gilman anticipates the insights of recent theoretical work on the relationship of women to language. Gilman's book on Galdós (1981) remains one of the major works in English.

When Valle-Inclán (*Luces de bohemia*, p. 4) called Pérez Galdós 'don Benito el Garbancero' ('Don Benito trader in chick-peas') he wanted to express,

---

* Reprinted from 'La palabra hablada y *Fortunata y Jacinta*', 1961, *Nueva Revista de Filología Hispánica* **3–4**: 542–60. Translated for this volume by Nick Caistor, 1991.

implicitly at least, criticism of his style both as man and as writer.[1] Valle-Inclán was referring to literary decorum, and had in mind the basic vulgarity which he and other members of his generation found so intolerable in Galdós's novels. At about the same time Ortega y Gasset made a different kind of criticism: Galdós, like Dickens, Sorolla and other nineteenth-century artists, had in fact no style whatsoever. Like theirs, Galdós's only virtues came from having 'character', in other words, having a meaningful and real content in their work. If to Ortega y Gasset the artists of his own generation were 'dehumanized', which meant for him that they were 'highly stylized', Galdós was typical of all those who had strayed from the 'highway of art', that is, from the path of style.[2] It is not my intention here to try to reconcile these two opinions (essentially Ortega and Valle are saying the same thing, from a different angle) but to remind devotees of Galdós that one of the most powerful factors preventing him from being judged as one of Spain's and the world's great writers is precisely his style. For decades, Galdós's choice of words and his way of combining them were seen as careless, vulgar, unartistic. And, as we have just seen, it was not only the academicians and traditionalists – the supporters of Valera or Pereda – who thought so, but also men of the finest literary and linguistic sensibility that Spain has produced. This is a fact which needs to be faced and understood, rather than denied or dismissed.[3]

In recent years there has been a revaluation of Galdós, though one can hardly call it a resurgence. What it amounts to is a series of sudden discoveries by individual readers – Madariaga, Amado Alonso, Federico de Onís, Casalduero, María Zambrano and many more – of Galdós's profound human importance and the artistic complexity of his great novels. One after the other, as they have realized the importance of what Galdós has to say for our time, these critics have tended to see themselves as pioneers and expressed their amazement at this new world suddenly opening up before them. This explains their tendency to leap impatiently over the stylistic barriers that blocked access for others.[4] As far as I am aware, only Joaquín Gimeno Casalduero has paused at the stylistic level to study what can be seen – and heard – there, and to reflect on it.[5]

In his article 'El tópico en la obra de Galdós' ('Clichés in Galdós's work'), Gimeno subtly analyses the use of oral clichés as an important source of linguistic raw material in Galdós's novels. He has tried to establish, on the one hand, whether or not this is a kind of oral realism – a simple transcription – and, on the other, that it helps show the radical emptiness of social and political life in Spain at the end of the nineteenth century.[6] Taken either from parliamentary oratory (for which Galdós had a particular loathing), from the pseudo-intellectual terms used in the press (usually mistranslations from French or English), or from common speech,[7] these set formulas are a favourite with the inhabitants of Galdós's world – and also serve to define them. They offer a comforting but fragile refuge for national consciousness: 'Galdós observes how nineteenth-century society is completely taken up with these clichés: they enable it to feel, think and speak' (Gimeno, 1956, p. 45). There is nothing odd then that the members of the next generation, with their sensibility for style and their concern to renew and breathe life into the Spanish language, should have been disconcerted by Galdós's novels.

The mere reproduction of the clichés of his day does not constitute a style. What did Galdós do with this raw material? Gimeno offers two answers, which complement each other: 1) most of the clichés are a vehicle for irony, as in the great tradition of the novel;[8] but at the same time, 2) certain social classes (specifically, the 'non-leisured') offer formulas 'that are meaty, full of life and wit', and Galdós uses them to enliven his style. I am not convinced by these sociological conclusions. After all, the members of the 'productive entrepreneurial bourgeoisie' – who, in Gimeno's view, are those most likely to renew the language[9] – can, in certain circumstances, use either kind of cliché. For example, Doña Lupe's language (in *Fortunata and Jacinta*) is a mixture of dead phrases – 'in the fullest sense of the word', etc. – with lively popular metaphors.[10] Despite this, it is impossible to deny the duality of type and attitude as demonstrated by Gimeno. Linguistic inertia and linguistic vitality, ironic undercutting and humorous acceptance are all fundamental to Galdós's transcription of the clichés of his day. Whenever Torquemada begins a sentence with the turn of phrase: 'Starting from the assumption that', or when Tía Roma says to him: 'Don Francisco, you're off your rocker [literally '~chocolate cup']', our immediate experience of the text confirms Gimeno's conclusions. His article ably demonstrates the scope of Galdós's stylistic concerns.

That spectrum contains the whole range of Galdós's almost unbelievable idiomatic wealth, greater perhaps than that of Lope.[11] Ricardo Gullón quotes the splendid comment of Unamuno (whose ambivalent attitude towards Galdós has yet to be studied): 'Galdós's language – his supreme art – flows smoothly, solid, vast, dense, uninterrupted by waterfalls or obstacles, with no whirlpools, no stagnant backwaters [. . .]' (*Contra esto y aquello*, vol. 1, p. 357). What kind of waters constitute this epic flow? Doña Emilia Pardo Bazán, in a review of *Angel Guerra*, describes them as follows: 'In Galdós's books lies a treasure, a lexical flood of turns of phrase, words, current clichés, common or snobbish expressions, the oratory of the street, parliamentary or political jargon, all that is ephemeral or ingrained in our language.'[12] In other words, every novel by Galdós is a *summa*[13] of nineteenth-century Spanish, a *summa* which not only registers all there is to be registered, but which also revitalizes the language, since it inserts this treasure into the temporal order of things. For, as Gullón suggests (1957, Introduction to *Miau*, Ediciones de la Universidad de Puerto Rico/Revista de Occidente, Madrid, p. 237), Unamuno's river image is probably unconsciously derived from the expression 'current language': 'Galdós's language is current, simple; a language steeped in the inflexions, tone and echoes of the spoken word; as we read it we feel we are listening to it, hearing it with the accent and even volume it would have were it spoken by someone standing next to us.' Galdós, then, was a master in the use of the Spanish language as it is spoken. Moreover, he was a master in the use of a language full of resonances, which means he was a master stylist. We should not be surprised if his words are not literary, artificial or consciously picturesque; if they are simply (but what more could we want) the words spoken in the Madrid of his day, the words and phrases of a 'trader in chick peas', with all the good and bad which that entails. This, after all, has always been the great Spanish stylistic tradition, from its epic origins to the *Libro de buen amor*, from the *Celestina* to our own day.[14]

This implies that Galdós's use of clichés should be understood in the light of the oral quality of his style. It is not enough to catalogue, compare and classify the abundance of set phrases that fill his novels. This is because spoken words are even more resistant than written ones to being taken out of context. They are words spoken by one person to another, always in a given situation and party to it. To evaluate them correctly, we have to check when and where they were spoken, by whom and to whom. They travel directly from mouth to ear and, though we cannot see them fly, they have wings. In spite of their origins in vulgar speech, their tradition extends beyond Spain to Homer. Or perhaps it would be more apt to say that, in Galdós's nineteenth-century Madrid, Homer's 'winged words' become 'winged clichés', as winged and accurate as their Greek forbears, despite their total lack of heroic singularity. For this reason, we should look at each clichéd expression Galdós uses in the context of the novel, chapter and paragraph where it occurs.

This is my only disagreement with the opinions expressed in Gimeno's revealing article. When, in *Fortunata and Jacinta*, Doña Isabel Cordero goes for a walk with her seven single daughters, pretty but unendowed (one of them being of course Jacinta) and uses a term from her husband's business to describe the operation: 'showing off her wares', we have to take into account that naturalistic reproduction, ironic humour and creative linguistic renovation are all present in a single stylistic unit. To think that spoken language, that is, language with a human context and purpose, can express one single attitude, value or meaning is to be blind to reality. What is normal in spoken language is multivalence and ambiguity, the co-existence of meanings which may fuse but do not mix, which are complex but not contradictory. It is not a case, therefore, of two kinds of cliché: one hackneyed, the other creative. To read Galdós as he should be read, we have to realize that each and every clichéd expression, however worn it may be from common usage, can take on a new lease of life in certain circumstances. His linguistic prostitutes, like his human ones, always have the path of redemption open to them.[15] In almost every phrase of almost every novel, we find 'wit' and 'hollowness' side by side; only in extreme cases do they operate in such a way that one excludes the other. Such is Galdós's genius with spoken style.

To grasp the possibilities and limitations of this style, let us look first at what happens in a purely oral context. If we read *Fortunata and Jacinta*, the *summa summarum* of Galdós's work, we find a huge, complicated tapestry of oral situations, one which provides the context for Pardo Bazán's observations and more besides. The book is a seemingly boundless oral history, which records an infinite number of conversations in an equally infinite number of places. Moreover, these conversations are for the most part many-sided, taking place in cafés, social gatherings, private homes or shops. Much has been said about Galdós's social dissection of Madrid café life, the 'natural environment' of Juan Pablo Rubín;[16] but this constitutes just one semi-institutionalized oral situation within Galdós's limitless repertoire of 'Turkish customs', as he calls them. At the bottom of the social scale, we find the 'hour's chat that [Segundo Izquierdo] regularly engaged in at the butcher's' (p. 533); to list all similar situations would be a never-ending task.[17] Then there are 'specialist' meetings, in which we are treated to the exclusive vocabulary of, for example, unemployed civil servants, card-players or pharmacist's assistants. Elsewhere – the vast majority of cases – we meet common, everyday Spanish, of the kind used in ordinary conversation, the Spanish of the 'amateur'. But whether it is specialized or everyday Spanish, this plethora of regular, semi-institutionalized oral situations is basic to the art of *Fortunata and Jacinta*.

Taken as a whole, the language of the novel is that of table talk, the 'peña' (bar) and the 'tertulia' (social gathering). It is a semi-public, social language, situated midway between oratory and the verbal intimacies of private conversation. While concerned with the remarks and discussions of human groups, it almost always serves to show the aspirations of the individuals who use it (Maxi or Fortunata, for example), and their desires for betterment. Whether humorous or stale, violent or sententious, the tone rises and falls according to the different speakers (who between them comprise a whole city) and the infinite network of relations between them. Clichés are always in evidence, but not for their own sake or solely for the purpose of Galdós's ironic manipulation. On the contrary, each hackneyed phrase or expression illustrates the social lexis of the highly segmented oral world that characterizes Galdós's Madrid.[18] These clichés – meaning words and phrases that, apart from their constant repetition, take on stereotyped meanings and nuances – typify the language of these different groups. Galdós uses them to create – or perhaps one should say invoke – the vast canvas of oral situations that operate in the novel in the same manner, and to the same effect, as the books of chivalry in *Don Quixote*.

I should like to dwell on this at first sight fanciful idea that the café atmosphere in *Fortunata and Jacinta* plays the same role that the *Amadís de Gaula* plays in Cervantes's novel.[19] Galdós's efforts to reproduce spoken language, to capture it in mid-flight, as it functions in its natural environment, give rise to his incredible repertoire of clichés. But, as in the case of the (written) chivalric clichés used by Cervantes, they represent something more: they create by implication a whole environment, particular ways of thinking and particular kinds of human relationship. They can thus be used to point the contrast between external, universally accepted modes of interpretation and the internal authenticity of the self. As we shall see in *Fortunata and Jacinta*, the gap between social language and the singular realities of isolated individuals are the source of constant thematic conflicts. Here we have an oral version of that standard theme of the nineteenth-century novel: society versus the self. I am not saying that Fortunata cares what people say about her (though in a sense I suppose she does find herself in an English-style scandal novel); it is rather a matter of how she can get to know and understand herself through the clichéd language offered her by society (and by her various lovers). This, basically, is what Galdós meant when he wrote: 'Style is a lie. Truth looks on in silence' (*Tormento*, *Obras completas*, vol. 5, p. 1488). But whereas in *Tormento* Galdós was still concerned with the quixotic confrontation between literature and life (Amparo's 'truth' versus the novels of the 'stylist' Don José Ido), by the time of *Fortunata and Jacinta* he has discovered in contextualized spoken language, in the stereotyped talk of the café and *soirée*, a legitimate way of renewing Cervantes's theme in his own century. Fortunata lives – Galdós stresses this time and time again – in a society that is still basically and predominantly oral.[20]

This view of Galdós's use of language does not of course exclude its use for intimate exchanges, or prevent each character from having his own particular style.[21] The most elementary manifestation of the latter are the verbal 'labels' that are repeated over and over again (though less insistently than in Dickens): the comically absurd use that Torquemada makes of the word 'materialism', Doña Lupe's emphatic 'in the fullest sense of the word', or Aurora Samaniego's strange habit of inserting 'for example' in the middle of a sentence.[22] More important, however, is Galdós's ability to lend a personal stamp to the speech of each of his characters. The inhabitants of *Fortunata and Jacinta,* living as they do in an oral world, are in a very concrete sense creatures of style; each one of them is a complex construction with his or her own range of stylistic possibilities. Doña Guillermina Pacheco's words are always razor-sharp, getting straight to the heart of the matter and to the heart of her interlocutor. Nicolás Rubín reveals his pompous nature by his use of repetition and the second person plural form beloved of incorrigible sermonizers. These two styles, one so keen, the other so flat, mirror their respective religious vocations and could not be more different. However, the most striking of these countless styles of falsification (what Fielding would term affectation) is perhaps that of Torquemada. His language is a masterpiece of verbal caricature. We can almost hear his unctuousness, his singsong intonation, the underlying hard-heartedness, the betrayal of hidden intent by external form. Here, above all, 'style is a lie'.[23]

But, in my view, Galdós is most successful when he places his stylistic creations in unusual situations, situations which are revealed and produced by means of changes in the particular character's speech mannerisms. One example of this is the decisive meeting between Doña Guillermina and Fortunata. The 'saint' has been unable to prevent Jacinta hiding in the bedroom to overhear the conversation. And the effects of this as far as speech is concerned are fatal: 'What was truly strange was that Guillermina, normally so in command of her language, was also on tenterthooks that day, and did not know how to proceed.' She begins in her usual manner: 'Let's be sincere and speak frankly to each other'; but after a few sentences, when Fortunata comes out with her 'rogue idea' ('a wife without children is no wife at all'), her only refuge is futile, fragmentary moral censure: 'My God . . . be quiet, will you . . . I've never heard such a thing . . . What an idea! What a nerve! There's no hope for your salvation' (pp. 404–5). So, as Galdós dissects their encounter, he also uses speech to illustrate an essential aspect of the intrigue. It is clearly implied that, had Doña Guillermina not lost her command of language, she would have been able to talk Fortunata out of her decision to have a child by Juanito. Another less dramatic but perhaps more typical example is the change in Doña Lupe's language whenever she is in Doña Guillermina's company. The effect on Doña Lupe of her meeting with the 'saint' is marvellously expressed in the grotesque social formulas of her farewell: 'My heartfelt friend, duty calls me to my humble home' (p. 381). Doña Lupe's language, normally so precise, here both understates ('humble home') and overstates ('duty') because she is trying to win Doña Guillermina's stylistic and social complicity. This combination (which Doña Guillermina sees through straightaway)[24] points up a subtle comedy of human confrontation, despite its hackneyed nature.

There are two central characters whose spoken behaviour differs from that of the rest. One of them is Estupiñá, the familiar spirit of this world of words:

> Estupiñá had a chronic hereditary vice, against which all his other spiritual reserves were powerless, a vice all the more oppressive for seeming so innocuous. It was not drink, nor love, nor gaming, nor luxury; it was conversation' (p. 35).

A virtual incarnation of Galdós's style, Estupiñá never changes, always dispensing his 'blarney' wherever he can find someone willing to listen. Estupiñá, who figures mainly at the beginning and end of the book (the apartment off the Plaza Mayor where Fortunata meets Juanito, and where she returns to die, is underneath that of Estupiñá), provides a thematic frame to the whole novel, reminding us each time he re-appears of its oral nature. Whatever the situation, we know what he is going to do. He will talk, for his life depends on language. In this sense – and it is strange that Galdós seems to have no particular interest in reproducing his language – Estupiñá is the most Dickensian character in the novel. Among all the other 'rounded' characters, as E. M. Forster would call them, he is the only 'flat' one. His life spans the nineteenth century and, like the nation he represents, his reaction to historical experience is overwhelmingly oral.[25]

The other character who differs from the rest is Fortunata herself. What characterizes her language is the fact that she seems to talk in a new, unexpected way each time we meet her. To some extent she is the antithesis of Estupiñá (with whom she forms, in this respect, a binary opposition), because the quantity and quality of her speech change continuously. Fortunata exists in a state of constant linguistic metamorphosis. A great deal of the attraction she exerts on other characters stems precisely from this: her lack of formation, the difficulty of classifying her, which, in the novel that bears her name, means a lack of stylistic formation and classification. At the start of the book, Fortunata almost seems unable to speak. Her first conversation with Juanito is extremely rudimentary: two short phrases and an 'All right, coooming!' shrieked in such a highpitched tone it sounds more like a birdcall than a human sound. Throughout the rest of Part 1, though we only hear of her at second hand,[26] her presence continues to make itself felt albeit with minimal oral self-expression. Subsequently the novel seems almost to turn into a Shavian *bildungsroman*, in which the heroine gradually learns how to speak. Maxi enjoys teaching Fortunata new words and correcting her pronunciation, and, although she sometimes seems to be a less gifted student than Sancho Panza, it is obvious she is learning something. It would be wrong, however, to see the novel this way. It is Fortunata's lovers who think she is mute. During the days she spends in the reformatory of Las Micaelas, she shows herself able to speak in a sustained and highly intelligent manner. The passage about her 'white idea' is a noteworthy example of her ability to think coherently and express herself effectively. Throughout the novel we encounter this same oscillation between apparent linguistic inhibition and an astonishing facility for self-expression. We never know how Fortunata is going to speak next, precisely because she is someone who lives so intensely. It is not that she lives her passion, rationality and self-awareness more dramatically than the other characters, but she does so more fully, with a total human authenticity. This is the only advantage she has over the other characters and, true to the novel's conception, this advantage manifests itself in the way she speaks, in her words. Fortunata says what needs to be said and what she feels. This manner of speaking can at times seem elementary, at others inspired. Fortunata is an oral genius like Estupiñá but, whereas he operates on the social and historical level, her domain is the personal one of human experience.

To recap briefly, I would say that when we examine any phrase or sample of Galdós's style, we should ask ourselves first and foremost: 'Where?' and 'Who?'. This is a style necessarily made up from individuals who talk in particular places and situations: the endless dialogues in the novel make this obvious. But if for some reason a character cannot speak, or if Galdós prefers not to let them speak, their words still infiltrate the narrative through the countless varieties of reported speech it incorporates. It is impossible here to deal adequately with the question of reported speech and narrative point of view. But we cannot understand the oral structure of *Fortunata and Jacinta* as a whole if we neglect to mention one aspect closely bound up with reported speech: Galdós's continual interest in the limits or boundaries of spoken language. As with many other novelists, Galdós constantly moves between the direct reproduction of speech and third person narration, taking in reported speech on the way.[27] But in *Fortunata and Jacinta*, where spoken language acquires thematic importance, there seems to be a special awareness of those zones or situations where the act of speech begins or ends. We have just seen how Fortunata swings between two extremes: oral poverty and abundance. In general the author's style can be said to do the same. In a series of exercises and experiments, his style constantly tests its own limits.

What are the boundaries of speech, and where are they located? One possible and obvious answer is that its boundaries lie in noise.[28] Some of the most intense acoustic experiences are constructed precisely in this way. A character has a tremendous desire to listen or speak, but finds him or herself prevented from doing so by noise – a noise which is often the animated hum of a café or the rumbling of carriages in the street, but which may also include interruptions normally considered as pleasurable, such as birdsong or music. So, as Maxi feeds Doña Desdémona's canaries: 'when they all began to chirp and sing at once, it was impossible for the people in their midst to hear themselves speak. Doña Desdémona resorted to sign language' (p. 492). In a world whose theme is the spoken word, music – whether produced by birds or people – is heard as noise.[29] A few pages further on, Maxi tries to hear a conversation Aurora Samaniego is engaged in, to confirm his suspicions that she is having an affair with Juanito: 'Maxi, pretending to have all his five senses concentrated on the piece Olimpia was playing, did not lose a single syllable [. . .]. Luckily the subject came up when the girl's hands were busy with the *andante cantabile molto* for, had it done so during the *allegro agitato*, God himself would not have caught a word [. . .]' (pp. 496–7). In the last of these situations, there is no irony whatsoever. On her deathbed, Fortunata tries feebly to follow a conversation. Its meaning escapes her, not only because of her delirium but also because 'the birds' chirping [. . .] flooded that gloomy spot, not to mention Juan Evaristo's screaming for his bottle' (p. 536).[30]

Galdós is, then, interested not only in those situations where speech and listening are possible and even predictable (social gatherings, conversations, encounters) but also in those where they are impossible or, at least, seriously impaired. Each of these occurrences is the necessary complement of the other. The reader's sense of the primary importance of Galdós's oral art, the impression of being taken to a world defined by orality, is increased by the deterioration of language and speech when it reaches limit situations.

Other frontiers of spoken language explored by Galdós derive, not from the particular situation, but from the ignorance, inexperience or incapacity of the particular speaker. As far as decorum is concerned, the most primitive and vulgar speaker is without doubt José Izquierdo.[31] The low level of his verbal environment is precisely one of the factors that attracted the two young gentlemen, Juanito and Jacinto Villalonga, to make their first foray into Madrid's slums. Juanito is not ashamed to parade his mastery of the expressions he has picked up there, showing them off on his honeymoon in a kind of tasteless counterpoint to the childish language he normally employs in his relationship with his bride. But (as he explains to Jacinta), physical combined with linguistic disgust led him finally to abandon Fortunata and her family:

> I can still hear those fine words of theirs: 'Rotten bastard, snake-in-the-grass, pickpocket, louse . . .!' That kind of life was impossible. I said no. I was so fed up I couldn't take it any more. I even hated Pitusa [Fortunata], just as I hated their foul language (p. 61).

Mauricia la Dura's language is almost as foul, though she has a capacity for eloquence and imagination totally lacking in José Izquierdo. At the opposite end of the spectrum is the Calderonian rhetoric employed by poor Ido in his fits of jealousy (pp. 91–2), or the disturbing and highly rational speeches Maxi delivers when he becomes a 'sane madman'.[32] It seems to me significant that Galdós does not take decorum to its usual limits of refinement and vulgarity. Instead, he shifts the axis a few degrees so that his new poles are ignorance and madness. In other words, his idea of decorum – like that of Cervantes – is more individual and experiential than social.

This interest in the limits of language explains Galdós's curious fascination with the origins of speech, that is, with the way children talk.[33] *Fortunata and Jacinta* offers an extensive range of infantile speech, from Pituso's obscenities (pp. 133–4) to Feijoo's final, senile babbling. See, for example, the cloying imitation of childish speech that the newlyweds indulge in, Fortunata's enchanting conversation with her doves (p. 60) and later with her own baby, or even the anguished words that Jacinta directs at the symbolic man–child in her obviously Freudian dream (p. 87). Even Maxi, in his fits of madness, adds his quota:

> His laugh terrified the two ladies; and of late no one could understand a word of the many that streamed from his mouth, imperfectly pronounced like those of an infant just starting to talk (p. 471).

Although not quite at this limit, the language of children proper also receives attention. Galdós carefully registers Papitos's intonation, as well as that of the urchins Jacinta meets on her 'visit to the fourth estate':

> They differed little in their clothing, and even less in their language, which was harsh, with slovenly inflections. 'Watcha . . . look at 'im . . . I'll smash yer face in . . . get it?' (pp. 99–100).[34]

Babies' first words and the traditional, stereotyped speech of young children represent a temporal, experiential boundary that seems to have fascinated Galdós as much as boundaries of decorum.

Apart from age, social level and physical circumstance, the feelings that the speaker has at a particular moment can also impose a definitive limit on discourse. In certain states of excitement or intense passion, communication becomes impossible or is seriously affected. Maxi above all, despite his frequent loquacity, is prey to complete mutism in the throes of emotion. When Fortunata finally offers him all her love (if he will kill Juanito and Aurora):

> Maxi, dazed and dumb, stared at her; finally his eyes grew moist . . . He was starting to melt. He wanted to speak but could not. His voice came out as though he were choking (p. 525).[35]

Otherwise, if the speaker does not lose his speech entirely due to overpowering emotion, then the sounds he or she emits can change into those of animals. Time and time again, when a character is carried away, the initial 'says' becomes 'roars', 'bellows', 'grunts' or 'bleats'. One step further, and speech itself is abandoned and replaced by 'lowing', 'bleating', 'howling' or even 'grunting [. . .] like a pig talking to itself' (p. 506). Galdós was greatly influenced by Zola, especially between the years 1880–5, when he was starting to write his second series of contemporary novels. It would thus seem logical to interpret these cries, grunts and howls as a sign of his prolonged interest in the author of *La Bête humaine*. The fact is that, in Galdós, this metamorphosis of speech has nothing to do with heredity or environment. In almost every case, it is the result of momentary incursions beyond the boundaries of verbal consciousness.[36] In this sense, the function of animal noises is not really to scandalize the reader, as may be the case in Zola, but rather to define, delimit and point up by contrast those truly human areas of consciousness – a consciousness identified with discourse – which constitute the novelist's prime object of concern.[37]

The last frontier of language is death. Casalduero (1951, *Vida y obra de Galdós*, Gredos, Madrid, p. 109) has spoken of the recurring funereal emblems that the deaths occurring in the novel weave into its overall fabric. But, if *Fortunata and Jacinta* is among other things a nineteenth-century Dance of Death, we should not forget that, in every case, death is presented not as a dialogue but as the decisive interruption of all discourse. Mauricia's final oaths appear to emerge from 'the mouth of some deep pitcher, as if they came from far off' (p. 393);[38] while Moreno Isla, whom death surprises in the course of one of his rambling interior monologues, feels a huge wave flood his throat, 'choking him' (p. 461). Fortunata's death is especially striking for the anguish she feels at not being able to speak. After forgiving Juanito in sign language,[39] 'her agitated breathing indicated her efforts to overcome the physical barriers stopping her speaking'. Doña Guillermina comforts her:

> 'There's no need for you to speak . . . all you have to do is nod your head. Do you forgive Aurora? . . .' The dying woman moved her head in a way that could have been affirmative, but hesitantly, as though she only partly agreed, not with all her soul.
>
> 'Again, more clearly.'
>
> Fortunata nodded more firmly, and her eyes grew moist.
>
> 'That's more like it.'

> And then something akin to poetic inspiration or religious ecstasy spread across the face of the unhappy Señora de Rubín. She miraculously overcame her exhaustion, and found the energy and words to say: 'I too . . . don't you know . . . am an angel . . .'; she added something more, but her words had become unintelligible again . . . (pp. 540–1).

After this, Fortunata twice manages to repeat 'I'm an angel', then her voice fades away forever. 'Had she said something? Yes, but Nones could not catch it.' The link between one consciousness and another has snapped; the bridge of words collapses; and, as when Hamlet dies, the rest is silence. This is the natural and necessary end of that monumental oral construction called *Fortunata and Jacinta*, a title which by its very dualism of names seems designed to 'let words loose' (p. 37) in dialogue.[40] But even if the human voice must come to an end, that does not mean it is defeated. The fragments of speech which immediately precede that crossing of the boundary of death are the most intense in the entire book. They validate and give definitive meaning to the whole oral scenario.

If we look back, we can see that the artistic mastery Galdós shows in presenting the spoken word is one of the great differences between his work and the *documents humains* of the naturalist writers. The naturalists transcribe dialogues and oral clichés as part of a written whole; they do not use them creatively. For the naturalists, it is typical for a character to betray his fundamental lack of consciousness through his limited capacity for meaningful speech. Whereas Galdós, situated in the oral tradition of the *Lazarillo*[41] and the *Celestina* (in *Don Quixote* there is a more complex relation between the written and spoken word), focusses his intention on his characters' consciousness. Each one of them speaks, and in doing so comes to know himself. Each one of them listens, and in doing so comes to know others. Américo Castro has characterized the squire in the *Lazarillo* in the following terms, contrasting his portrait with those of the *Decameron*'s two-dimensional characters: 'Beneath the surface of the "gentleman" – seen as a generic, abstract, social category – we are made aware of one man's consciousness struggling with the difficulties that arise from being such a "gentleman"'.[42] We could say exactly the same of the beings that inhabit the world of *Fortunata and Jacinta*. They do not interest Galdós as victims of heredity or history. They interest him in so far as their language puts us in touch with their consciousness 'struggling with the difficulties that arise from being' what they are. This is how Galdós achieves that synthetic 'realism' in whose favour Doña Emilia Pardo Bazán argued. He uses the possibilities of the nineteenth century to renew the oral art of the past, and in so doing finds a way of combining 'classical realism' with the technical innovations of naturalism.[43]

At this point we might return to the fundamental objections that have been made against Galdós, looking at them from a different angle. Might not language, and in particular clichéd language, be a sign of fatalism, as inexorable as the determinism of Zola and the positivists? Are Galdós's characters not just as irrevocably reduced to the level of 'traders in chick peas'[44] by their speech as Galdós himself has so unjustly been accused of being? My reply is as before, but even more emphatic. Words, however clichéd, are not rigid, inflexible moulds of thought. They are always capable of redefinition and renewal in the appropriate circumstances and in the mouth and mind of the appropriate speaker. A decisive example in *Fortunata and Jacinta* is the word 'rasgo' ('grand gesture') which at the start of the novel appears with all the hollowness, conventionalism and slipperiness of its origins in the press and theatre, but towards the end of the book takes on a sublime quality. It is probably no coincidence that the first person to use the word is Juanito Santa Cruz, who at the novel's outset finds himself caught up in a minor historical event provoked by the aggressive use Castelar made of the term 'rasgo' in *La Democracia*.[45] When later in the book Juanito is trying to restore his reputation with Jacinta (who has just learnt of his renewed affair with Fortunata) and is attempting to portray his actions in a favourable light, he says to himself 'What I need right now is to come up with a grand gesture' (p. 313). We can clearly hear the melodramatic triviality, the journalistic overtones, the cheapening of a noble action, which seem inherent in the word. Juanito's cynicism is echoed later in Feijoo's sarcasm when he repeatedly warns Fortunata against her tendency to 'grand gestures'.[46] Just as Castelar has used the word as a weapon against the false generosity of the 'people's queen', so Feijoo uses it to belittle and ridicule Fortunata's noble (or at least impractical) impulsiveness. But at the end of the novel, when Fortunata entrusts her son to Jacinta, Doña Guillermina sees her action as a 'felicitous Christian grand gesture', suddenly filling the word with meaning. The cliché, like the heroine, is saved at the very moment the novel reaches its oral climax. The naturalist determinism of character by mode of speech has been transcended, and with it the tone of ironic detachment. A grand master of style thus succeeds in redeeming the language of his day.

It is important to note that the inspiration for Fortunata's 'grand gesture' came to her just when she 'was deprived of speech' (p. 537). As we have seen, the novel's oral structure is based on the continual confrontation of the spoken word not so much with silence as with 'non-language', with that region where speech is powerless or impossible. This explains the constant exploration of the boundaries of the spoken word; the oral definition of characters who, when they are most authentically themselves, go beyond language to the world of dreams and visions. And yet Fortunata's mute inspiration is something more than a final repetition of the structural scheme of the whole novel. It shows something that hardly needs to be made explicit for any close reader: that this oral structure is organically related to an oral theme. Being a novel deeply rooted in the tradition of Cervantes, the theme of *Fortunata and Jacinta* is bound to be that of individuals who are struggling to know themselves within social and stylistic contexts that are alien to them.[47] But each and every novel must develop this theme in its own way and, in the case of *Fortunata and Jacinta*, that alien context is above all the spoken word, language as cliché. That is why it is profoundly appropriate that, in the silence of her encounter with death ('when she was deprived of speech'), Fortunata comes to a full realization of herself, is most authentically herself. It is also appropriate that, once this definitive integrity of being has been achieved, it then filters into the oral context of her life in the novel and redeems it.

Notes

1. *Editor's note*: The playwright and novelist Valle-Inclán is known for his break with literary realism, moving with his best known play *Luces de bohemia* (1920) from an earlier symbolist and decadent mode to an avant-garde experimentalism influenced by expressionism and futurism: hence his derrogatory dismissal of Galdós.

2. Ortega y Gasset, *The Dehumanizaton of Art* (*Obras completas*, vol. 3, p. 368): 'Realism [. . .] by inviting the artist to passively follow the shape of things, is also inviting him to have no style. That is why someone who admires Zurbarán will say of his paintings, since he has nothing else to say, that they have "character", just as Lucas or Sorolla, Dickens or Galdós have "character" and not style.'

   Editor's note: *The Dehumanization of Art* (1925) rejected realism as a style appropriate for the uneducated, instead proposing an artistic avant-gardism suited to the tastes of an educated elite. Ortega's elitist defence of the avant-garde would make many left-wing Spanish writers of the 1930s and the Franco period turn back to realism.

   Zurbarán, a contemporary of Velázquez, is best known for his paintings of saints. The early nineteenth-century artist Eugenio Lucas painted a Goyesque series of popular scenes (the Prado Museum has an excellent collection). Joaquín Sorolla was Spain's major Impressionist painter (see the collection held in the Sorolla Museum, Madrid). Ortega's suggestion that these three painters lack style shows a remarkable lack of artistic sensitivity.

3. Galdós himself seemed to agree with this, especially in his frequent criticism of what Doña Emilia Pardo Bazán called 'officially approved, elegant, pure style', especially style in oratory. When describing his own art (for example, in the prologue to the Nelson edition of *Misericordia* [*Editor's note*: reproduced in Chapter 3]) he insists on his interest in the naturalistic reproduction of

characters and settings. But, even taking this into account, we can see that both Galdós and his critics have a limited, ambiguous definition of style: for them style is 'stylization'.

4. Although these individual discoveries are now leading to a more general acceptance, in 1956 Torrente Ballester could still observe, in his incredible *Panorama de la literatura española contemporánea*, that Galdós 'is not a great writer either, though he is not so bad as is commonly said'.

5. First in his thesis on *Galdós and Naturalism* (1955, Universidad de Murcia), then in the quoted article, which he published in the virtually unobtainable *Boletín informativo del Seminario de Derecho Político de la Universidad de Salamanca* (January–April 1956). *Editor's note*: The Joaquín Gimeno Casalduero mentioned here is not to be confused with the doyen of Galdós scholars, Joaquín Casalduero, author of *Vida y obra de Galdós* (1943, Losada, Buenos Aires).

6. In his thesis, Gimeno quotes these revealing observations by M. Baquero Goyanes (his doctoral supervisor): 'it could be said that the naturalist novel feeds off clichéd themes, abounds in clichéd ideas and expresses itself using clichéd formulas [. . .] we could see naturalism as a movement revaluing clichés, as well as – paradoxically – declichéing existence' (1955, *La novela naturalista española: Emilia Pardo Bazán*, Universidad de Murcia, Murcia).

7. Other sources proposed by Joaquín Gimeno are official documents, sermons and religious books. A reading of *Fortunata and Jacinta* seems to show that the language of childhood is also a fertile source. In this sense it is a shame that commercial advertising was so undeveloped in Galdós's day.

8. To some extent Galdós's novels go further than the satire of 'affectation' that Fielding proposes. Rather than being a superficial, comic perversion of acceptable style, clichéd language touches the roots of historical existence. That does not prevent the ironic treatment of clichés being ever-present. J. PÉREZ VIDAL (1952, *Galdós en Canarias*, El Museo Canario, Las Palmas) observes that in his student work Galdós often criticized the stylistic clichés he was forced to learn. What I am trying to suggest is that Galdós's use of clichéd language goes beyond traditional novelistic irony (that of a Fielding or Dickens).

9. Gimeno states that this theory is taken from an article by E. TIERNO GALVÁN (1952, 'El tópico, fenómeno sociológico', *Revista de Estudios Políticos* **45**: 111–31).

10. So, in her first talk with Maxi, she begins by saying: 'We've got to have an *exhaustive* talk', and ends: 'Calm down: that's you all over, when you're not apathy on two legs, you're pure gunpowder . . . at least, you are now; before to move one foot you had to ask the other's permission' (p. 181). Quotations are from the *Obras completas*, vol. 5., Aguilar, Madrid.

11. *Editor's note*: Lope de Vega, prolific sixteenth-century playwright and poet, known (among other things) for his use of popular language and verse.

12. 1891, *Nuevo Teatro Crítico* **8**: 57–68 (quoted in Gimeno's thesis).

13. On the novel as *summa*, see the penetrating study of *War and peace* by Thibaudet in his *Réflexions sur le roman* (1938, Paris).

14. In his admirable *Gustave Flaubert* (1935, Gallimard, Paris), ALBERT THIBAUDET studies the way in which Flaubert renewed the style of the novel by incorporating the expressive possibilities of popular speech (for example the

use of the imperfect tense, which conveys both life and feeling). For his own style, Flaubert carefully chose those aspects of spoken French which he judged could enrich and enliven the narration. He used clichés (which he of course detested) only for the speech of people like Homais or Bouvard and Pécuchet. What a gap there is between this scrupulous discrimination and the way Galdós takes advantage of all the aspects of the spoken language around him! Whereas Flaubert condemns clichés to an oral limbo, Galdós, as we shall see, fully accepts their contribution to the complicated orchestration of oral styles.

Editor's note: The early fourteenth-century *Libro de buen amor* by Juan Ruiz and the *Celestina* by Fernando de Rojas (1499) are classics of early Spanish literature, whose bawdiness has largely been responsible for the prevalent (but misleading) notion of the 'essentially popular' nature of Spanish literature.

15. To quote one example: the phrase that Don León Pintado solemnly declaims to his audience in the reformatory for fallen women: 'As ever, he thundered against freethinkers, whom he called the "apostles of error" at least fifteen hundred times' (p. 251). This musty phrase will later produce unsuspected fruit: when Mauricia is expelled from the convent, and the child sweeps are laughing at the drunken woman, 'she stood defying them arrogantly, raised her arm and pronounced them "apostles of error!"' (p. 260). At the end of this article we shall have occasion to see a fundamental and deeply serious example of this kind of metamorphosis.

16. We should not see this portrait of café life as simply satirical or critical. After all, Cervantes himself was a great reader of books of chivalry. In the following passage there is more than a touch of genuine emotion: 'What did those men talk about for so many hours? Spaniards are the most talkative people on the face of the earth, and when they have nothing else to talk about, they talk about themselves [. . .]. In our cafés, people talk about everything encompassed by human speech from the time of Babel, when God first created opinions. In cafés everything can be heard, from gross vulgarities to ingenious, well-founded ideas. This is because cafés are frequented not only by wastrels and loud mouths, but also by polite, educated people. You will find gatherings of soldiers or engineers, though those of employees and students are the commonest, while strangers from the provinces fill any gaps left by the latter. In a café, you can hear the most ridiculous and the most sublime things. There are some who have learnt all they know of philosophy at a café table, from which it follows that there must be others at those same tables who give agreeable lectures on philosophical systems [. . .]' (p. 297).

17. Other notable examples are the 'after-dinner conversations' of the Santa Cruz family, the social evenings at the Samaniegos's house, the 'endless conversations in the Arnaiz store', and José Izquierdo's 'carousings'.

18. The oral structure of the novel is based on the separation of the speakers into watertight compartments (according to social acquaintances, professions, class, etc.) and also on the linguistic unity of the world of Madrid as a whole. The language of cliché is that vital sap which runs through the entire novel, flowing through every organ and particle to such an extent that the reader becomes aware of the existence of a kind of *de facto* unanimism. To put it another way, the main speaker in *Fortunata and Jacinta* is Madrid, in perpetual dialogue with itself.

19. *Editor's note*: Cervantes's *Don Quixote* sets out to debunk the romances of chivalry – *Amadís de Gaula* (1492) is Spain's major contribution to the genre –

but in many ways recreates their structure. The *Amadís* is one of the few romances of chivalry which the priest in *Don Quixote* spares from his censor's bonfire.

20. Naturally I would not deny that the main difference between this oral society and that of epic poetry is the fundamental existence and importance of the printed word. Often the fossilization of language in clichés, such as 'seen through the prism of' and others listed by Gimeno, seems to me the result of the lack of mobility words suffer when printed in the press, in pamphlets and official documents, which are read and then copied by speakers. This is a very different process from the creation of stereotyped phrases and proverbial sayings in a completely oral society.

21. Galdós sometimes makes fun of the style used in intimacy, precisely because it thinks of itself as completely private and unique. The most striking example of this is the childish language that Juanito and Jacinta use when they are first married.

22. This is probably a Gallicism that Galdós's keen ear has picked up somewhere: 'Just look: a man, for example, who could have brought happiness to any honest girl . . .' (p. 443). Aurora has lived in France, and has introduced French fashions into the Madrid textile and clothing industry which forms the commercial basis of the novel. It is characteristic of Galdós's habit of understatement (which he shares with Rojas [*Editor's note*: author of the *Celestina*]) that he lets these words speak for themselves, without explaining the reason for their use.

23. For an example of this brilliant use of oral caricature, see Torquemada's incredible speech on p. 195. Moreno Isla, Ballester, and even Juan Pablo Rubín (in *Fortunata and Jacinta*) are further wonderful examples of characterization through speech.

24. Her reply says all: '"Yes, yes," Guillermina replied, "duty always comes first. Goodbye."'

25. The visual counterpart to Estupiñá is Izquierdo, who compensates for his scant speaking ability with his heroic presence, which makes him a model for the kind of historical painting so in vogue at that time. They are a couple created by Galdós's sense of irony, and highly representative of his art as a novelist.

26. Through the memory and voice of Juanito during the honeymoon confessions. Of course, the picture Juanito paints of her is very limited when compared to the Fortunata we get to know so well later in the book. When Villalonga meets her in the street, the first question that occurs to him is 'I wonder how she speaks now?' (p. 152).

27. See the observations Denah Lida makes concerning *Misericordia*: 1961, 'De Almudena y su lenguaje', *Nueva Revista de Filología Hispánica* **3–4**: 307–8.

28. Noise appears to play in this novel a role very similar to that of physical distance and obstacles in the *Celestina*. These are also present in *Fortunata and Jacinta* of course; but as the novel is so obviously a three-dimensional world, these pointers and emphases are less remarkable than in Fernando de Rojas's book, which 'inaugurates' the use of dialogue in Spanish literature. But Galdós thought it worthwhile to use noise in his novel, precisely because of its oral rivalry with human discourse.

29. Another case occurs in a dream in which Fortunata has bumped into Juanito:

'Fortunata is trembling, and he takes hold of her hand to ask how she is feeling. As the barrel organ is still playing and the drovers are shouting curses, both of them have to raise their voices to be heard' (p. 410). Something similar also occurs when Jacinta, before she has an equally Freudian dream, is lulled to sleep by a passage from Wagner: 'in which the orchestra made a high-pitched whine similar to the sound with which mosquitoes regale us on summer nights' (pp. 86–7). There is an abundance of interruptions caused by other kinds of noise.

30. It is worth noting here the obvious return to the beginning of the novel. Our first meeting with Fortunata is full of symbolic allusions to birds. The next step in the exegesis of *Fortunata and Jacinta* could well be a study of its network of symbolism.

31. See, for example, his almost unintelligible speeches on pp. 109–10. Mauricia, whose language is socially at the bottom of the scale, is often eloquent by comparison to Izquierdo.

32. Typical passages are to be found in the chapter 'The reason of unreason'.

33. Curiously, in the whole novel there are no examples of Spanish spoken by foreigners (the drunken Englishman in the inn at Seville hardly says more than a couple of words. Almudena had not yet attracted the novelist's auditory attention. Neverthess, the description Galdós gives of his meeting with the real-life Almudena and of the immediate fascination he felt with his way of speaking (prologue to the Nelson edition of *Misericordia* [*Editor's note*: see Chapter 3, this volume]) is highly revealing for anyone interested in Galdós's oral art. See Lida, D. 1961, cited above.

34. Another well-developed example is the dialogue between Bárbarita and her little friends, in Chapter 2 of Part 1. This is Galdós's first foray in the novel into the world of orality.

35. A list of all these cases of momentary inability to speak would be extremely lengthy.

36. Even Jacinta, with her 'dove's anger' (after hearing Fortunata's 'rogue idea'), 'could not speak . . ., felt she was choking. She had almost to spit out the words in order to say with intermittent vehemence [. . .]' (p. 407). Izquierdo on the other hand, so limited by nature, sometimes has the ability to reel off whole paragraphs.

37. This also accounts for Galdós's interest in, and use of, dreams. Often more visual than oral, dreams represent other areas of the mind, and so complement Galdós's central area of interest.

38. Doña Lupe describes her last words thus: 'Then we saw her move her lips and push out her tongue as if she wanted to moisten them . . . Her voice sounded as if it were coming up from the basement through a pipe. I thought she was saying "more, more" . . . other people who were there claim that what she said was "at last". As if to say: "At last I can see heaven and the angels". Rubbish; what she said was "more", meaning "more sherry"' (p. 393).

39. As in the *Celestina*, the *Poema del Cid* and other works based on the spoken word, gestures are extremely important for Galdós, who describes them in detail. A study of this aspect of his work would be extremely interesting. *Editor's note*: The *Poem of the Cid* is Spain's major epic poem, now generally

ascribed to the early thirteenth century. Critics have debated the extent to which it is based on a popular oral tradition.

40. The two popular idioms referring to speech most often used in the novel are 'soltar la palabra' ('let words loose') and 'pegar la hebra' ('knit words together'). Each describes a basic mode of speech. Words can be 'let loose' (like an arrow) at the listener, or can be 'stitched' into the more or less pleasurable fabric of a conversation.

41. *Editor's note*: The anonymous *Lazarillo de Tormes* (1554), the first Spanish picaresque novel, consists of a string of burlesque stories drawn from a popular tradition of oral narrative.

42. Introduction to Hesse E. W. and Williams H. F. (eds), 1948, *Lazarillo de Tormes*, Madison, Wisconsin, p. xiii.

43. I am here referring to the the precepts set out in Emilia PARDO BAZÁN's *La cuestión palpitante* (1883, Imprenta General, Madrid).

44. In his historical novel *La de los tristes destinos* (*Obras completas*, vol. 3, p. 641), Galdós applies the adjective 'agarbanzado' ('vulgar', literally 'reduced to the level of a trader in chickpeas') to Isabel II in her later years.

45. In his historical novel *Prim* (*Obras completas*, vol. 3, p. 565), Galdós refers to Castelar's article 'El rasgo', in which he attacked Isabel II's supposed generosity and in so doing triggered the student riots of St Daniel's Eve (1865), in which Juanito gets caught up.
    Editor's note: The republican politician Emilio Castelar, an admirer of Galdós's *National episodes*, was renowned as a parliamentary orator. As one of the short-lived presidents of the First Spanish Republic of 1873–4, he proved a failure. He was also the author of six historical novels and various historical studies.

46. For example: 'So forget about your grand gestures, if you don't want to be booed, because nowadays you only see cheap tricks like that in second-rate plays' (p. 327). For other cases, see pp. 338, 343 and 475.

47. There are of course many ways of expressing this idea. I prefer mine to Eoff's formula, 'Art is life, and life is process', if only because it attempts to show the meaning Cervantes gave to this 'process'.

7 Reality and Fiction in the Novels of Galdós*

GERALD GILLESPIE

Gillespie's article is representative of the dominant interest in the 1960s in Galdós's treatment of psychology. Such criticism often fell into the realist fallacy of discussing chararacters as if they were real people; Gillespie mostly avoids this, stressing Galdós's debt to Cervantes, particularly in his fascination with forms of obsession. Incomprehensibly, Galdós's exploration of delusion and dreams, and his intertextual dialogue with the *Quixote*, have since the 1960s received little critical attention (apart from recent metafictional studies, which implicitly – and sometimes explicitly – draw parallels with Cervantes's work); time seems ripe for a revival, particularly since psychoanalytic criticism makes it possible to analyse the psychological aspects of Galdós's texts without falling into the realist fallacy. Gillespie's Cervantine focus allows him to highlight Galdós's use of irony: this would (rightly) become a favourite topic of Galdós criticism in the 1970s. This article is particularly useful for the way it situates Galdós's work in the context of the French, Russian and German realist novel (again, more cross-cultural work of this kind could be done today); and for its coverage of a wide range of novels by Galdós, including many not otherwise represented in this anthology. The attention of readers relying on English translations is drawn to the perceptive comments on *Miau* (1963, Penguin, Harmondsworth) and *Nazarín* (1992, Oxford University Press, Oxford). This piece provides a good introduction for those coming to Galdós's work for the first time.

* Reprinted from 1966, *Anales Galdosianos* **1**: 11–31.

> 'Don't worry, Father, when we get there they'll let you off on grounds of insanity. Two thirds of the prisoners who pass through our hands escape punishment because they're mad, if it's punishment they deserve. Even supposing you were a saint, they wouldn't let you go for that, they'd only do it because you're mad; nowadays they're all for the reason of unreason, they reckon it's madness that makes the exceptionally wise wise and the exceptionally stupid stupid, that makes people stand out whether by excess or default' (vol. 5, 1814).[1]

These words, which the guards speak in piety to comfort their broken prisoner, the priest Nazarín, serve as a fitting epigraph. For no discussion of Benito Pérez Galdós's mature realism is, of course, complete without reference to the impact of Cervantine wisdom upon it. The question of truth and illusion has been standard in the European novel since *Don Quixote*, which became the revered model for English 'humor' and German 'romantic irony'. Cervantes's haunting suggestion that, in addition to the opposites reason and unreason, there was a paradoxical 'reason of unreason' also undermined any neat distinction between reality and fiction – perhaps in spite of his own intention of separating them. Through the interaction of Quixote and Sancho, through the treatment of literature as a subject, even the very same mock romance in process of being created, and through the mingling of aspects of the creative personality, was born the 'reality of fiction'. Nineteenth-century naturalism applied the by then considerable body of psychological theory in its examination of humankind's mental life and tried to effect a clear scientific definition which classified all impulses of the brain as sound or unsound. Two major theses were held, both connected with the 'facts' of evolution: the physiological or deterministic, and the developmental or organic. Because of its older realism in the picaresque genre, Spain could not be as impressed by the inroads of naturalism. The nation was more receptive to a developmental view (Hegel, Wundt, *et al.*) which salvaged its Christian faith. As Sherman H. Eoff has shown, Galdós absorbed the fundamental tenets of the post-romantic organic concept of man.[2] But it was through the Cervantine tendency to transcend his own subject, that Galdós achieved genuine universality and renewed the mission of the Spanish novel.[3] From his more clinical case histories (*La desheredada*) to his depictions of sublime self-deceiving (*Angel Guerra*), Galdós tirelessly ascended from the wry irony of naturalistic truth to indulgent meditation, progressing along a pathway analogous to that of his great predecessor from Part 1 to Part 2 of the *Quixote*.

It is appropriate to affirm this pattern before we focus too exclusively on late works imbued with the spirit of primitive Christianity (*Nazarín*,

Misericordia) on the lofty plane of Dostoyevsky's *Idiot*. Otherwise we will fail to take seriously the ending of symbolic works like *La loca de la casa*, which asserts that the 'good' cannot live without 'evil' (vol. 5. p. 1721). 'Mad' Victoria is actually not simply a pious fool, but rather in the Cervantine tradition of the 'sane madman'. She wins her struggle with her beloved 'monster', but out of it grows mutual reconciliation; brute strength of nature in her *nouveau riche* husband and spiritual grace in her womanhood, with its aristocratic pride, achieve a synthesis. If the story of their marriage is a metaphor for mankind's development, it is only more obviously so than Angel Guerra's quest to commune with his beloved, the mystic Leré. When Victoria decides to save her family and offers herself to Cruz, she is virtually a martyr challenging the world for recognition; her imperious demands are answered in kind; and the dramatic contest of wills forms our fable set in reality. While Victoria gives up becoming a nun, Guerra moves in the opposite direction toward fulfillment, drifting from his early activity as a radical and from original love to a religious vocation that keeps him close to the woman he believes is a true saint. Guerra's 'foolishness' ends in a disillusionment without rancor, when 'the blow of reality' both clarifies his mind and brings him to death (vol. 5, p. 1573). Simultaneously, he confesses his own self-deception, understands that he has only been sublimating his nature, and declares 'that the only kind of approximation that truly satisfies me in the full reality of my being is not the mystical but the human one, blessed by the sacrament' (p. 1573). No rejection occurs except the banishment of illusion; led by his Beatrice, Laura and Dulcinea in Leré, Guerra's soul has climbed to heights of noble acceptance.

Guerra penetrates to the 'reality of his being' in a process of growth toward self-discovery, not toward bitter disappointment. If we compare Galdós's treatment of the 'real' and the 'illusory' with that of Balzac and Stendhal, what distinguishes the Spaniard's realism is its Cervantine consciousness. In *Le Rouge et le noir*, for instance, the fundamental contest is between the power of the individual heart and the tyranny of an already debunked world. The established order, wearing many masks of splendor, is a very traditional realm of hypocrisy. Hollow secular and religious glory continually threatens to debase the 'happy few', those noble souls who live from the knowledge of their own existence in enmity to everything shallow and corrupt. Sorel literally mortifies himself in order to progress through the several spheres of society to high position; his deepest experience of bliss occurs, correspondingly, in prison under sentence of death. In extremity, he at last lives with sincerity. His execution represents the martyrdom of the heart, and Madame de Renal's beatific passing confirms the unassailable validity and absolute commitment of love. Balzac still renders isolated tributes to an élite of romantic individualists in his *Comédie humaine*, as, for example, in the case of Madame de Beauséant. But, generally, his more sensitive figures go rapidly up or down in the harsh, money-dominated society which he depicts. All destinies proceed over the crossroads of finance, and those who do not capitulate fall by the wayside. Balzac reinterprets many 'virtues' as maladies, tragic but pathological, and unfortunately on a par with many 'vices' in a purely abstract, 'scientific' sense. All drives and ideals which do not further worldly success rank as obsession. When Balzac's fuller characters like Rastignac 'awake', their sardonic consciousness of the incompatibility of noble aspirations and survival under the laws of nature still generates considerable pathos. Galdós does deliberately create similar tensions, but never externalizes the problem to the same extent. For Galdós 'fiction' and 'reality' are not dichotomous, but interacting, aspects of human existence.

That Galdós fuses the nineteenth-century theory of man as a creature in evolution and another heritage from the romantics, an elaborate psychology, is clear throughout his works. What provides cohesion is not, however, any particular doctrine that sunders fact and fancy. Rather, the Cervantine interplay of various 'fictions' and 'realities' – the character's, his world's, the reader's, the author's – binds together a complex realism. Returning to our epigraph, we note that even the guards are aware of some puzzling relationship between saint and madman, but certain only of the fact that folly is everywhere causing things to happen. Yet how carefully they phrase this, clinging to their realism which is a comforting surface order – with loopholes. The real trouble for Nazarín comes when he tells the judge what actually went on, because he cannot keep it to himself. Naturally, the judge thinks he is crazy, since the truth, which is much simpler, may not be accepted without certain 'revisions' of reality. The confrontation with established reality includes, of course, paradoxical inversions, as when villagers (Part 3, Chapter 3) claim that Nazarín worked a miracle on a child, whereas he claims only that he prayed to God; Nazarín actually believes in scientific medicine, after the exhaustion of whose remedies one then turns in humble supplication to the Almighty. Galdós's fascination for scientific discoveries is alive still, in spite of his attempt to portray a mystic sympathetically. For example, he follows the naturalistic vogue by equating neurosis and unfulfilled desire in Nazarín's disciple Beatriz; as soon as she has met someone who can polarize her in another direction, her symptoms become pleasant and she has visions of angels instead of devils. Galdós nevertheless shows no commitment to Nazarín's or his questioners' opinions, when he is handed from the mayor to a judge in Madrid. The parallels to Christ are presented typologically, without a breath of dogma; and yet, Galdós introduces himself into the novel as an eye-witness in order to give all the objections to the reporter's accusations, on a rather materialistic level, against Nazarín as anti-social, escapist, parasitical, and so forth (Part, 1 Chapter 5).

Galdós's objectivity is subtle and gratifying in comparison with the usual partisan writings of the nineteenth century. Indeed, it is through this objectivity that he can suddenly overwhelm us with the intensity of 'prophetic' statement – a term to which we shall again refer. Nazarín's dream, closing the novel, both expresses his piteous state and removes him from the terrestrial limitations it has imposed. In his own mind, Nazarín reverently is celebrating mass and, when he takes the Host in his hands, he hears Jesus speak to him:

> 'My son, you are still alive. You are in my holy hospital, suffering on my behalf. Your companions, the two fallen women and the thief who follow your teachings, are in jail. You cannot celebrate the holy office, I cannot be with you in flesh and blood, this mass is the deluded figment of your imagination. Take a rest, you have earned it' (vol. 5, p. 1814).

The divine voice asks him not to be discontent and promises that he has 'much more' to do, whereby the author, of course, prepares us for Nazarín's career in *Halma*. The intimacy of this message avoids any question of veracity – a feat which we can compare only with Ivan's vision of the devil in Dostoyevsky's *Brothers Karamazov*. By allowing Nazarín to hear in his own thoughts, from the highest authority, that his experience is hallucination, Galdós demonstrates convincingly both the priest's sincerity and his probable recovery. This is a moment of crisis that is transcended by profound growth – a mysterious 'disillusionment' which occurs through dream in the brain of a visionary, a prime example of the reality of fiction on the highest level of storytelling. Objectively considered as a 'message' of his own mind reaching the plane of consciousness, the poignantly subjective dream by Nazarín conveys truth. The priest's genuine holiness is deepened and enhanced when his mind integrates his experiences of outside 'reality'. The validity of his mission is guaranteed by pious acceptance of his natural state.

The general tone of Galdós's novels is so literal that whenever the fantastic is introduced, it produces a very special effect on us. Galdós completely deglamorizes stereotyped romantic situations such as the life of prostitutes. In *Nazarín*, for instance, he introduces the ugliness of one downtrodden woman by having her nicknamed 'Camella' ('she-camel') from 'Camelia', for her tall, bony frame (Chapter 2). This rather sympathetic humor may strike us as cruel or sublime, according to our conception of Galdós's role as narrator, in a work like *Miau*, whose title derives from the insulting sobriquet with which the Villaamil women have been dubbed. Sáinz de Robles ably argues that 'generally, the satirical and the ironic are not creative' (vol. 4, p. liv); in defending Galdós against the charge of impassiveness and cold isolation, he explains the author's non-cohabitation 'neither for the good or ill of his creations' (p. xxxii) as transcendental humor, in analogy to God's role. While one cannot quarrel with this interpretation, it still avoids a puzzling and intriguing aspect of Galdós's artistry in particular cases. How should we accept the strange interplay of stark realism, vision, and nightmare in a book like *Miau*, through which even the title runs as a motif of the ludicrous, as a whimsical apprehension of harsh truth? No warm humor of late Dickensian variety can explain away the commingling of the grotesque and sentimental, as in the 'oracular' utterances of little Luis – a sweet boy, who tells his grandfather to commit suicide. A contemporary European phenomenon may be reflected in this novel: the upsurge of a phase of late realism which we can well term 'sentimental naturalism'. As the strictures imposed by doctrinaire determinism loosened and writers had already grown aware of the new spheres which the novel could explore, their interest in the mental life of the masses increased. Psychology was brought to bear on the condition of the lower classes of society, with the result that hitherto stereotyped figures could be analysed spiritually. An example would be Gerhard Hauptmann's play *Hänneles Himmelfahrt*, which contrasts the wretched death of the abused girl in a barren poorhouse with her childish dreams of apotheosis. The dream episodes, fading in and out of reality, integrate materials from Hanna's environment and experiences, including her juvenile crush on a sympathetic teacher, who is transformed into a heavenly redeemer.

Galdós was in many respects in advance of this wave, as we shall indicate below. Likewise, because of his Cervantine heritage, he was independently in the vanguard of a closely associated movement: psychologistic impressionism and symbolism. Let us examine these two related sorts of realism, which have in common a considerably developed psychology, now expanded to all reaches of society. The fundamental naturalistic trait of the novel *Miau* is its depiction of several generations in one family with related, and presumably, inherited mental illness. Luis's visions of God, so filled with pitiable rationalizations about the course of his own and his family's life, are brought on by epileptic fits. His own mother, now dead, had gone beserk and tried to kill him before the time of the novel. His dignified grandfather, driven to his wits' end by the women in his household and constant, debasing rejection by the bureaucratic machine for which he formerly worked, chooses release. The boy's aunt shows the same weakness for his reprobate father, a sexual adventurer, and conceives a similar compensatory hatred for her poor nephew. The night she almost murders him in his troubled slumbers is a ghostly scene, in which the reality of her action is scarcely distinguishable from nightmare, for with terrifyingly irrational logic, she slips back into normal behavior. Our realization that daytime and the waking state are only a patina over horror lifts this story from the ordinary level of naturalism toward symbolic drama, but not quite all the way. The meaningful center of motivation is never shifted fully to external agencies, such as the complex of offices which old Villaamil clings to desperately. There is no monstrous symbol to which people are subordinate that compares with the mine in Zola's *Germinal*. Rather the pathological symptoms are identified with psychic pressures in a kind of chronicle that represents with continuity the adjustment or failure of a living strand of humanity in the larger fabric of Madrid. Thomas Mann's *Buddenbrooks* exploits this kind of realism more extensively. We might distinguish Galdós by noting that he tends to favor a more horizontal examination of society in a collection of cases in several novels, as does Balzac. Mann follows the fraying life-line through several periods of history, encompassing thereby also many features of the development of European bourgeois civilization.

The symbolic implications of settings and moments are perhaps clearer in the earlier novel of naturalistic bent, Galdós's *La desheredada*. In the chapter 'Church interlude', idle, deluded Isidora finds herself staring at a dark, unknown man because she has felt his insistent gaze. Galdós relates:

> While Isidora was making these and other observations, she noticed that some of the elegant female members of the congregation were being intently eyed by the young dandies, and that in their turn the former were eying the latter with feigned casualness, so that she began to think that, if all those glances shot at each other were to trace a line in the air, the church interior would look like a huge spider's web. Wretched Humanity! (vol. 4, p. 1071).

The social theme of the secret religion of the magdalenes would be ordinary in itself, were it not for the sinister evocation that springs from the woman's own brain of the very web in which she will perish. This fleeting prefiguration is less a naturalistic statement than an 'impression'. The author's outcry sharpens our sense of danger, but also makes us aware of the sickly thought processes of the protagonist, briefly coming to the surface. There are many similar moments in which external appearance and internal pattern merge in an impression that is revelatory, as, for example, when Isidora masquerades as a Carmen type at festival time in the chapter 'Cytherean gypsy', foreshadowing her descent into low life. The metamorphoses of the public squares of Madrid occur so subtly that we may not at first notice how unfixed, how lacking in hard classical edges they are. When Miquis and Isidora first contemplate the swirling spectacle of society in ostentatious motion, she is rapt in contemplation of its patches of color, whereas Miquis vainly unmasks the phenomena for her, a 'believer' in the aristocratic system headed by the queen. But, after Isidora has failed to convince the marquise, her imagined grandmother, of her noble identity, she equates the external scene upon the banishment of the royal household with her own 'transition'. Her switch to a dishonorable but effective party is associated with power to topple established authority, i.e. the marquise.

Galdós's imposing talents as an impressionist transform the novel from a harsh analysis of human ills into a great book with depth and breadth. The chapters entitled 'Beethoven' and 'More Beethoven' are, of course, a deliberate *tour de force*, two moods in analogy to major and minor key. They surely rank alongside Mann's depiction of little Hanno Buddenbrooks evoking through the piano the music of his own languishing soul and Tolstoy's 'Kreutzer Sonata'. And the sheer beauty of these passages painting the marquise's anguish furnish, by aesthetic proof, as it were, all the knowledge we require to grasp what true nobility of spirit is. Among the number of chapters on Isidora's sleeplessness through mental disturbance, 'Insomnia number fifty something' should be singled out for its brilliant treatment of interior monologue – again an impressionistic technique. Galdós skilfully weaves together, in a compressed simulation of hours of reverie, the train of thoughts stimulated or deflected by minute occurrences. Acutely perceptive, Isidora hears the bells, scratching, and so forth, details which elicit the whole range of her consciousness and reveal to us the roots of mania under the surface. Although Galdós has not yet gone as far as Joyce in creating a stream of consciousness by (artistically contrived) totally free association, he ought to be recognized for his rather astonishing proximity to Arthur Schnitzler, the master of psychological impressionism and first great exponent of the associative technique (*Leutnant Gustl*, etc.).

The rather obvious analogy to Flaubert's *Madame Bovary* would be exaggerated, if one took no account of the greater variety of techniques in Galdós's novel. To be sure, Galdós too pursues ironically the romantic type who lives 'studied farces or chapters from novels' (vol. 4, p. 1050) and seeks to 'find correspondences between her moral state and Nature' (p. 1051); who through this sickly pride would be 'bad . . . if you like; but never vulgar!' since 'it's better to dream than to see' (p. 1116). But since the naturalistic analysis is set in a framework, the Quixote tradition, a more specific irony reigns over Galdós's story. The region of La Mancha remains throughout the author's works a Spanish hinterland which is the breeding ground for deluded souls and extravagant idealists. A census of the Madrid of Galdosian novels would show a rather extraordinary migration of these types to the capital. To underscore his thematic adaptation of Cervantes, Galdós divides Isidora's history into two parts, the first of which ends with the humorously mad letter from her uncle the canon, Quijano-Quijada, on his deathbed. It is filled with superficial, vain advice, a shallow conception of things religious, opinions on side issues that rankle Spanish pride, such as French cooking, and unconsciously ironic literary reminiscences, such as his assertion, 'I have great faith in the force of blood' (vol. 4, p. 1056). Galdós accomplishes much with this reiteration of the context of his narration. He summarizes the illness, points to its roots in the influence of environment, refers to the naturalistic thesis of inherited characteristics, and establishes a parallel for Isidora's case, her foreseeable finish, while temporarily raising our spirits with a comic piece.

The literary context is supremely important, for we note that – unlike Don Quixote – the canon dies *sans* disillusionment. Thus the scientific realism of Galdós's times, which his careful documentation through Isidora's father at the madhouse, her criminal brother, her macrocephalic son, and touched uncle reflects, also makes sense in 'classical' Spanish terms. For her history is not a copy but an inversion of the knight-errant's idealism. Isidora's obsession does not ennoble anything nor lend enchantment to our world. That point is made as an opening statement with consummate irony, when Galdós depicts the delicate beauty of nature which the inmates of the insane asylum ignore in their frenzied self-occupation, in the 'End of another novel'. Isidora's typical statement – 'How ugly this is!' (p. 1051) – reveals this 'certain hostility towards Nature'. She demeans the ordinary inn which Quixote would have transformed into an enchanted castle (p. 986). She wastes a chance to marry a good man, Juan Bou, and the sound advice of Miquis, who generously elaborates the serious implications of the gap between illusion and reality for her. She finally dies when her illusion is destroyed, but in vileness contrasting with the sober dignity and salvation of Quixote. In a corroborative inversion, her loyal Sancho, the meek gallant Don José de Relimpio, perishes of a broken heart. Galdós uses the Cervantine tradition to show us what a non-poetic obsession is. Not divine madmen, but wretched creatures lacking any true inspiration, fill the asylum and the prison.

La desheredada is a carefully constructed book which conveys through the rigor of its formal repetitions a sense of tragic dissolution under the pressure of given forces. For, unmistakably, Galdós emphasizes the analogies between collective mankind in his city and the above institutions. In the chapter 'Christmas', the symbolic season of rebirth, man's activities offer ironic counterpointing to the meaning of the holiday. 'Madrid is like an asylum on the loose. Its inhabitants are prey to a fever that has three distinct symptoms: the delirium of gluttony, the feverishness of the lottery, the tetanus of gratuities' (p. 1037). Galdós's vision of the frenetic upsurge of 'pleasures' is more than clinical; the gross appetites, passions, and manias are presented with moral asperity as in the medieval fool tradition. Folly has broken out in an entire population, giving rebirth to thousands of lesser and greater tragedies. Isidora is busy at this sacred turning of the year first getting her brother from jail, and second acting the role of a story-book heroine at the marquise's palace ('Anagnorisis'). Miquis, who in this novel demonstrates lively wit and intellectual control over life, explains to Isidora:

> The whole of life is a prison, it's just that in some places there are iron bars, in others not. Some people are locked in cells, others are locked inside the azure walls of the firmament (p. 1123).

Galdós is scrupulous and unrelenting in this more severe mood, even while joking. The motif of the carnival and its masks, the motif of collective folly, the motif of the world as prison and hospital (favorites of the Spanish Golden Age) support a fundamental proposition that man must, of necessity, pass through darkness in his progress toward a higher state:

> [. . .] error also has its laws and, [. . .] in the forward march of the universe, every dark urge strives for satisfaction and obtains it, producing overall harmony and that *ciaroscuro* which constitutes Humanity's main attraction, and the fun of life (p. 1145).

On the one hand, the above words spoken by the author evoke the grand outline of seventeenth-century theodicy, the tension of a drama in which our lives are roles and over which hovers a benign Creator, enacting and beholding what to us is largely confusion. On the other hand, it suggests a *process* toward some higher synthesis; even man's 'dark urge' (as in Goethe's *Faust*) contributes to the evolution of this *ciaroscuro*. The organic view, which was predominantly a product of late eighteenth-century German thought, dovetailed neatly with the Christian conception of a world theatre – an affinity which the romantics thoroughly exploited.[4] The distinctive romantic ingredient added to this literary marriage was, then, a developmental view of psychic processes.[5] We shall discuss Galdosian traits which are analogous further below. For now, let it suffice to point out the considerable literary consciousness behind the tiniest details in *La desheredada*. This book, in a positive sense only, is contrived. If, for example, we take too seriously the above quoted reflection, we are missing one of the principal joys in reading the story – an aesthetic delight in form. For the same sentiment appears originally in the mouth of the amanuensis at the insane asylum: 'Let us all console ourselves with the thought that the great harmony of the world consists in carrying out the sovereign will' (p. 986), and so on. Unknown to us, Isidora, the listener, will disintegrate too. Unknown to her, the philosophizing secretary is about to blow up in a psychic explosion; he is subject to cyclic fits connected with his pondering of the imponderables. With choice self-irony, Galdós as author cites another 'writer-philosopher' inside of his own novel. Such self-quotation in altered circumstances is a technique for which perhaps Thomas Mann is best known (e.g. *Tonio Kröger*); it pertains to the overall 'scientific' objectivity which discovers purely abstract patterns behind vital phenomena. But in the case of Galdós, it derives also from the Cervantine irony of being now involuted in one's own fictions, now hovering over them.

Galdós's reworking of Cervantine themes raises questions about man's reality and freedom long before Unamuno. The novel *Our Friend Manso* is appropriately, like *Tonio Kröger*, an autobiographical relation by an intelligent, sensitive self-observer. Manso, a professor of philosophy, like Mann's artist, possesses full competence to speak for the mind painfully aware of its own laws in separation from life, nasty life, of which, however trite and shallow it may be, the intellectual is jealous. Indeed, so bitter is Manso as narrator that he begins by declaring, 'I do not exist', and tells his story from the 'other world' with sardonic disillusionment; looking back and down from the clouds in his last words, he sees reality as a puppet play:

> Happy the state, happy these regions from which I can watch Irene, my brother, Peña, Doña Javiera, Calígula, Lica, and all the other puppets with the same disdain with which the mature man looks at the toys that amused him when he was a boy! (vol. 4, p. 1283).

Since Manso is one of the most lovable characters created by Galdós, we cannot comfortably ignore his quirks – or the abstraction of reality as a grotesque fiction. Manso's ability to so envision life is bound up with his destiny to suffer deep anguish. His alienation finally passes the mark of 'neurotic failure' in life and enters a new realm, the problematic metaphysics of modern forlornness. Even in his 'real' or fictionally real supernatural state, Manos remains forever alienated. The scope of Galdós includes both the estrangement of an Isidora from sane living and the alienation of disabused intellect from the ridiculousness of life. Manso does not blindly degrade nature; however, he cannot help perceiving that there is something 'unreal' about reality, its factual lack of 'verisimilitude'. An important question which Galdosian criticism must ask is whether the author conceives of such understanding as Manso commands as a kind of 'liberation'. When Isidora loses her dream, she falls apart too. Manso begins in disillusionment, but does this set him free?

Late figures like Nazarín attain spiritual freedom, yet lack the visible signs of any cerebral dissection of human existence in search of its key. Rather they appear to share something of the instinctive impulse which asserts, against all logic or illogic, life itself. We have noted this reconciliation with existence in the dream through which Jesus tells Nazarín of his insanity. Dreams in Galdós are the first manifestation of psychic forces which, flowing from the darkness of human nature, shape character in the dynamic process so ably expounded by Eoff. Galdós seems to agree – probably by general intellectual osmosis – with the post-romantic formulation of human mentality as an organism, whose evident layers interact with hidden layers in a continuum of growth or 'unfolding' (*Entwicklung*, development). The hidden nucleus of the mind never is dormant, even though it is impossible to witness its activity, and we only learn about its operations when, on the surface of consciousness, thoughts happen. Manso is quite aware of the pressures of the mind – in fact, he is a nascent 'psychoanalyst' at moments, and his probing is connected with his doubts and malaise about the 'fiction of reality'; for example:

> The world of dreams is not wholly arbitrary and vain, and if we were to patiently analyse the cerebral phenomena that cause dreams, we should perhaps discover a hidden logic. Once awake, I began to examine the relation that might exist between reality and the battery of impressions I received. If dreams are what happen when our intellect and sense organs take a rest, how is it that I thought and saw? But how silly of me! There I was calmly lying in bed, interpreting dreams like a Pharaoh, when it was already nine o'clock, and I had to go to class, and then [. . .] (p. 1219).

An estimate of the measure in which Galdós reproduces dreams with the stamp of authenticity, as we understand it in the light of modern science, or 'contrives' them for romanesque effects is not to the purpose of this essay.[6] More important here is the consistency of his use of dreams and reflections about dreaming with his art.

Galdós's novels belong to the dawning period of 'analysis', in which art becomes self-conscious to the point of ambiguous self-denial and fastens on 'absurdity' for both its aesthetics and metaphysics. But his faith in the integral 'occurrence' – whether human personality or work of art – still prevails. This confidence in the *creative action* whose model is nature, knits together the amazing variety of his own productions. Doubtless the observable 'reason of unreason' in the instinctual pathway of evolution intrigues Galdós as much as anything negative or pathological. The novel *Tormento* offers us a vibrant example in the earlier Galdós of a positive utterance of inner needs. Amparo, a mere underling in a petty bourgeois household, has emerged from a grisly affair with a priest by the end of the story; she has an opportunity to marry an older man, Agustín, who has made money and seems to crave placid respectability. A deep need to confess overwhelms her, and she experiences the agony of growth in telling him about her life, at the price of rejection. But Agustín is strong enough to develop reciprocally in this confrontation. He rebels against the pretenses of society, religion, the inauthentic 'what will the neighbours think?' which is not his own voice. To be sure, his heart is not entirely free of prideful lie; however, under the dominant 'rules' of life then in force in Spain, his decision to accept Amparo in a common-law marriage, though disgraced, and rescue her by going away to France is a human triumph. The seemingly anarchic impulses of nature deny the 'fiction' of our world and proclaim healthy 'reality':

> Strike out along the broad path of your instinct, and put yourself in the hands of the free, glorious God of circumstance. Put no trust in the conventional majesty of principles, but kneel before the shining altar of facts . . . If this is error, then so be it (vol. 4, p. 1556).

The complexity of Galdosian art prohibits any simply tragic dualism from usurping the larger Reality, which encompasses both the historical milieu and the myriad intrahistorical dramas within it. The success of Agustín is not canceled out by the failure of Isidora; nor do Manso's own discoveries about himself and his world negate its independent validity. There is no easy formula for a Reality that is not classically fixed, but in flux – very like a Story. Hence Galdós's maturest vision offers us not statuesque, representative 'truths' wrapped in the mask of a personality as *persona*, but organically 'happening' personalities who appear to be polarized around basic drives and ideas. His Cervantine framework proves to be exactly that: a matrix of storytelling, through which we learn something also about the nature of a 'story'. This can be demonstrated by a comparison of *La familia de León Roch*, a novel which marks a turning point in Galdós's own development, and his acknowledged masterpiece *Fortunata and Jacinta*. Superficially, they have in common obvious elements of a very traditional plot arrangement. Disregarding the considerable differences, we might name the type after Goethe's famous novel, *Die Wahlverwandtschaften*, whose title is borrowed from older chemical theory of the 'elective affinities' of primary substances. Since only the plot type is of concern, we may oversimplify and define it as an exposition of natural laws which operate when 'molecules' (i.e., couples) encounter and, through inner forces or needs, break apart and their 'atoms' (i.e., individuals) either form new molecules, or separate. To the compassionate 'scientific' eye, such an encounter in the turbulent 'solution' of society has 'tragic' implications, because it may set loose events which gainsay established morality.

The significant point is the recognition of 'atoms' which need to 'elect' other atoms for reason of inner nature and can be subsumed in a molecule, or synthesis, whose bond varies in strength according to that fateful involvement in the flow of existence known as fate. Galdós, however, only makes a half-hearted try at a configuration of lives in an aesthetic pattern in *La familia de León Roch*. He appears to initiate the lines of an 'hour glass' when he allows the childhood friends Pepa and León to diverge. León, the idealist, is drawn to María Egipcíaca, one side of whose life is dominated by religious fanaticism. Pepa drifts to the cynic Cimarra. The first couple are both deluded as to their total needs and motives; the second couple are both more truthful, Pepa in a vital way, Cimarra as a decadent. Emotionally, we hope for a repolarization of León and Pepa, who do again come together but do not quite meet, because of the separation forced on them by her family for its own selfish reasons. Galdós does not seek symmetry, however, and any formal design is secondary to the dynamics of the tragedy. The forces are internal – mainly in the self-deceivers María and León. León is less interesting, for Galdós obviously wishes to make him, as the noble champion of liberal idealism, virtually invulnerable to criticism from bigoted quarters. María's case is more dramatic, because she is split between her suppressed sensual drives and religious obsessions; she is, as León aptly puts it in anger and disappointment, not his dream of 'a Christian wife' but 'a hypocritical odalisque' (vol. 4, p. 799). In Part 1, María falls under the malign influence of her brother, who would dominate her in a 'spiritual' marriage of twin souls. This polarization to the sickly mystic effectively splits her from León and, changing her baits of mortification for a stunning outfit, she sets out to win him back. Her failure entails devastating consequences for her; she pines away, appearing to the innocent eyes of Pepa's daughter to be a 'dead doll' (p. 887).

The death of Luis Gonzaga, ending the first third of the novel, generates new events – the passing of León into Pepa's orbit, and the wrongheaded isolation of María. The near death of Monina draws together her mother and León, who worships this image of Pepa. María's dying, which is a major section of Part 3, leaves León, at least in his own mind, morally isolated and bereft. For when Cimarra intervenes to enforce a pact of mutual separation of those left in a triangle, León's principles prevent him from escaping with Pepa into an illicit union outside society. The novel opens and closes with letters, by María and Fúcar, which exude the hypocrisy of a blind and greedy aristocracy that holds sway over Spanish mores. We may think of the novel as three unwieldy acts, conflict, climax of doomed happiness, and dénouement, with distinct raisings and lowerings of the curtain. But these external parallelisms do not grip us with the same intensity as Galdós's revelations, mostly through his characters' dreams, of the course of the *hidden* drama in the depths of their souls. For example, though largely prevailing in her stubborn campaign against her own husband, María's suppressed anxieties bubble to the surface (Part 1, Chapter 15):

> What a dream! Just imagine [. . .], I dreamt you had died and that from the bottom of a dark pit you were staring up at me, staring, and you had such a face [. . .]! Then it passed [. . .] You were alive; in love with someone else [. . .] I don't want you to love anyone else (p. 799).

This 'message' occurs right after León's angry charge that she is 'a hypocritical odalisque'. María's suppressed desire is manifested in her nightmare of the viper nesting in her (Part 2, Chapter 13). The conflict in her soul is brilliantly exposed through her vision of hell, which integrates scenes from a visit to the Krupp works in Germany (Part 3, Chapter 1). Despite her need to see León punished in fires of damnation, she cries out to save him (p. 899).

These various disclosures of psychic happenings are not just planted like flags on certain high points in the terrain of the book. In María's case, for instance, the seeds of all future mental development are present in Part 1. Even the possibility of her own love-death is prefigured in the sudden reversal of the above quoted dream:

> What a dreadful vision! Now I see myself dead, looking up at you from the bottom of that deep, dark pit [. . .] You were embracing another woman, kissing her [. . .] What, is it day already? (p. 801).

Galdós's considerable reliance on, and talent for, dream sequences doubtless indicates that he is not the kind of writer in love with plot. His moments of dreaming, such as the outstanding chapter 'Combatting the angel' (Part 1, Chapter 21), do not really interrupt the book but give it a 'substitute' for the missing drama of outward facts. The briefer announcement of dreams reminds us off and on that this hidden drama is continuously at work under the surface. To state that Galdós does not manipulate outward facts in a dramatic configuration implies no criticism, for the ghostly 'reality' of León's struggle with his 'adversary', just after contemplating the splendor of the night heavens, lifts this book above successful artificiality to the poetic plane. Galdós here approaches the realm of the great masters of prose who have time for fantasy and prophecy, because they also have the ability for it. Our standard of comparison, to which Galdós may not measure up, must nonetheless be Mann and Dostoyevsky: Hans Castorp's watching of the constellations

(*Der Zauberberg*) and Dimitri's visionary ride through a lugubrious, wasted steppeland (*Brothers Karamazov*).

Fortunata and Jacinta has been extensively treated elsewhere, and is mentioned now only to corroborate that Galdós is more concerned about characterization than plot.[7] His interest in the individual lives occupies him so thoroughly that he 'allows' their story to develop out of the given materials of their existence, and often devotes great attention to 'secondary' figures. If some critics object that Galdós is diffuse, rambling, lacking in style, they mean precisely that he is not out to offer us neat narrative shapes. The book *Fortunata and Jacinta*, for example, is really a tetralogy of unwieldy acts. Fortunata is actually off-stage throughout Part 1, except for a single glimpse. Then Part 2 recapitulates the earlier beginning (Chapter 1 'Juanito Santa Cruz') by introducing the male half (Chapter 1 'Maximiliano Rubín') of a new 'molecule' and its particular chemical history. But Parts 3 and 4 no longer pursue the very ready possibilities of 'pattern', and are concerned, rather, with the psychological unfolding of the principals. As Eoff has shown, both of the women 'grow' in the measure that each approaches the nature of the other and their characters interact in the depths of the mind and heart; so much so that, with the consciously symbolic exchange of the child, we may be tempted to interpret their essence as some sort of allegory in motion. True, plot too demands a certain interdependence of protagonist and external history, parallels between individual reality and visible happenings in his world, a degree of subordination to the unity of the work. But the requirement of 'unity' never curtails the validity of Galdós's treatment, because he does not need to set events in relief according to their *causality* by means of plot.

Causality is buried in the seeds of character; it unfolds within the circumstances of the story, which thus appears to be a relation according to simple time sequence, close to the most primitive mode of story telling dominated by a 'voice'. This recognizable tone, no matter how faint it may be at moments, runs through every utterance about what is 'happening' and keeps us captive, waiting for the next detail. Of course, in switching back and forth among locales – or minds – Galdós actually operates on the simpler level of plot as well, in the sense that we must suspend our knowledge about some things while proceeding with others, must ponder, relate, anticipate. Yet, as Eoff emphasizes, Galdós never falls back on 'static' character to bring about confrontations. This Galdosian preference for *life* rather than *style* (in its limited sense) is the core of his artistry, and criticism has rightly concentrated upon his convincing portraits with their palpable substance. But this judgment is only a partial explanation for the fact that Galdosian novels have ample proportions, without having the titanic sense of space and history which, for instance, Tolstoy's *War and Peace* commands. And the matter of

Galdós's expansiveness is not resolved by pointing to his borrowing of the Balzac 'panoramic' technique for the purpose of achieving vast scope. The totality of Galdós's creations exhibits a nation and society, of course, but the particular works after the *National episodes* usually dilate upon the 'ordinary' in various corners of Madrid. The romantic writers had discovered that one could write about a single room because it contained a 'story', then that one could examine a building whose inhabitants offered a microcosm, finally that the city was a universe with its own laws. Galdós moves about mainly in interior spaces, secondarily over streets and squares. The royal palace in *La de Bringas*, a symbolic city within the city, is a visible complex not far removed from Mann's sanatorium in the *Zauberberg*. But even the latter gives way to the spaciousness of the enveloping landscape of the mountains in many an excursion.

Except for dream passages, Galdós's novels are cut off by their own kind of realism from the universals of Heaven and Hell, lack the vastness of God's arena, and reach few epiphanies as transcendent as those in the great Russian works of the nineteenth century. The Spaniard may occasionally suggest the shadows of 'myth' in the complementary questing of two beings like Fortunata and Jacinta for intangible wholeness in their femininity, but he generally bypasses the enormous for the local and limited sphere. Yet Galdós is exciting, because we sense that he is performing an amazing anatomy, baring the skein of 'reality', without reference to any pre-existing Galenic chart. He gives us the simulated experience of being observers, simultaneously, on the informed, scientific level and on the more obtuse, involved level. The Galdosian method of characterization is also a distinct statement about reality.

Our world is not peopled by 'round' characters alone. Indeed, most individuals of the human race are in our vision quite limited to a few exaggerated traits and features. We cannot see anything but their 'flatness' until we learn about their inner life – and even then, we remain to one another and to ourselves largely hidden. From chapter to chapter and novel to novel, Galdós bridges the way as do our own minds. After fleetingly perceiving, we may discover more profoundly. Fortunata, for example, appears briefly in Part 1 in a stark encounter with Juanito. The attractive woman is sucking a raw egg on the doorstep of her aunt's poultry shop. She possesses all the qualities of an artistically achieved 'flat' character, because she radiates meaning and implications like an intense apparition. In the back of our minds, we keep waiting impatiently to discover the secrets under the surface vanished from direct view. A similar moment is when María Egipcíaca receives a sudden visit in *La familia de León Roch* from the mysteriously 'ignored' figure called Doña Perfecta. The blood of those who have already read the novel by that name freezes, for they at once sense the *meaning* of an entire human existence approach; that destiny is fully attested elsewhere in the annals of reality. The complexity of life converges in a *symbol*, and that is what Galdós's 'flat' characters make us feel upon first encounter as well. The ability to expand into three and four dimensions his own stereotypes, or to see his formerly 'round' figures as accessory shadows on the fringe of a tale, permits Galdós to use the so-called panoramic technique without the introduction of burdensome doctrines to govern or explain their behavior. Naturally, the author sheds his polemical commentary step by step during his career, and not all at once; however, we may point to his achievement as a definite trend after 1880, with the 'contemporary series'.[8]

Galdós's ability to convince us that we experience not shaped art, but life shaping itself, is, of course, the power to conjure illusion – which brings up several subjects for later discussion: his turning to pure dialogue, and his very modern examination of the *relativity* of 'reality'. The linkages between clusters of personalities do give us the feeling of experiencing mankind at large in social context. But Galdós does more than depict customs or exposit naturalistic tenets; he is not the secretary listening to Spain's unvarnished dictation, or to any 'spirit' which determines and directs our lives. Because his figures develop organically, the creative process is always flowing from the particular to the universal, and institutions are composite products of lives interacting. The energies emanate from within his individuals, and not from any 'world spirit' that impinges on humanity; the world is co-existence and nothing more. The *rhythm* of the psyche informs the individual in reaction to its bodily, social, and intellectual environments. Galdós doubtless conceives his obligation as a realist not merely to record the external, historical 'facts', but to listen to the pulse of the secret generator, the flow into consciousness of creative and harmful desires. Because he does not believe in a determinant physical environment, we should not conclude that his interest is solely the 'complex of social and moral ideas'. Galdós does not penetrate into the intrahistorical flux just for 'confessional' glimpses; he is out to capture the symphonic simultaneity of humankind.

Individual lives are allowed to sound, fade, interact, now dominate in variations upon themselves, cede to other passages in the music. This musical analogy touches again on the fundamental contrast between pictorial and psychological realism, between 'classically' fixed patterns and organic rhythms. In this regard, Galdós's collection of novels should not be associated with Balzac's *La Comédie humaine*, but with Proust's continuum held together by the musical threads of interior existence. Let us not exaggerate the relationship. Galdós is not conscious, as are Proust and Mann, of the literary leitmotif principle based on Wagner's operas.

The connection is rather through the artistic affinity of Galdós's developmental characterization and the late nineteenth-century trend toward impressionism – the capturing of moments in their peculiar subtlety which depended on subjective, as well as objective, 'reality'. Imitation of nature cedes to the orchestration of vital continuity. Galdós must have felt the pull of this creative urge to achieve what Wagner called 'total art' – a favorite romantic term. The romantics had already postulated at the start of the nineteenth century the possibility that the *novel* might become the vehicle for 'universality'; also, that every work of art is merely a 'fragment'. Considering this typical paradox, we can understand that Galdós's period had several choices for the direction it would take in developing romanesque form. The novel did not need to be a sealed unity, in order to avoid being chaotic; it did not have to present a microcosm, in order to reflect an established macrocosm.

Cervantes directly, and not the romantics, taught Galdós about subjectivity. His tendency to shift the 'point of view' is evident in his earlier novels. Now he catches the secret revery fading from a character's mind, now he describes persons from without in a context of history, now he projects three-dimensional figures in a scene, with stage directions and dialogue, now he meditates, withholds comment, merely smiles. It is a river fed from many sources. That is why Galdós's interesting experiments in form are not actually complete departures from his predominant method. It may be that the urge to espouse a thesis induces him to move toward pure drama. Dramatization helps tighten form into clear configurations, principle contending with principle. But it also flattens out Galdós's characters, since their being is concentrated into the explicit words, gestures, motions, the mainly surface phenomena of events subordinated to 'plot'. Unless mixed in as scenes in the body of a narration, dialogue tends to make figures more opaque and symbolic. What makes Galdós's best creations great art is the third dimension of the mind. A serious objection may be raised that Galdós infrequently treats persons of intellect, or blunts their consequence by making them ineffectual in the management of their lives (e.g., León, Manso). The charge is justified, with the reservation that the author does, nevertheless, demonstrate the possibility of human success on *all* levels of intelligence. Both a Dr Centeno and a Benina can redeem life from the powers of decay and despair. Naturalism was in many regards a bad influence on Galdós, keeping his attention too often on human weakness and vice. But since great artists are our only witnesses to reality, except for the chronicle of outward happenings which historians record, we are obliged to accept the Galdosian vision of a 'disappointing' era. Artists are not good or bad according to the quality of the parade which passes before their eyes, but according to the sharpness of their eyesight. Hopefully, the time is past when chauvinists or hispanophobes will fasten on Galdós personally as 'hero' or 'villain' for his contribution.

Galdós does not belong to Spain any more than Mann does to Germany or Tolstoy to Russia. Galdós belongs to a great tradition whose standards were established by Cervantes. As an artist, dealing with reality through fiction, he is – in a different context from Nazarín's – 'an Arab from La Mancha' (vol. 5, p. 1729), a Benengeli and indulgent critic of him, a strange mixture of different layers of consciousness. Galdós's modernity is seen in his matching of two novels about the same subject. *La incógnita* is his only fully epistolary work, and tells its story through the exchange between two friends. Manolo writes to Equis about the strange events which are the talk of Madrid and with which he has intimate connection, yet the lowest level of understanding. Even in observing himself, Manolo can but dimly see through the opacity of the living persons whose relationship – a love triangle – he explains only obliquely to Equis. Equis and the reader must probe and construct hypotheses through the agency of the distant viewer on the spot, and through his reports of the numerous theories current in Madrid. *Realidad (novela en cinco jornadas)* [Reality (a novel in five acts)] brings the principals and Manolo on stage; now we witness directly the dramatic action whose surface was reported. Much of the play consists of internal monologues with many analogies to O'Neill's technique in *Strange Interlude*, except that Galdós's figures, especially Federico, often ponder the enigma of their relationships and the problematic aspects of 'deception'. Augusta, his lover, seems impelled to recreate ordinary life as a higher, exciting 'reality': 'I long for all that's strange, all that fools dismiss as being fiction, because they think novels are stranger than reality' (vol. 5, p. 851). Orozco, her husband, is attempting to discover 'ultimate reality by and within himself', elevating himself through spiritual discipline and abstractly observing his own reactions, with increasing alienation from the world he pretends to serve.[9] If we follow the detective work of Manolo as a figure inside of the drama and accept his conclusions about the participants, it is only to find out he is wrong.

Introspection dominates the being of these uncommon personages in quest of reality – and certainty. But in their world truth is not fixed; it changes with their groping, and in a sense, they are producing it as they move along the pathways of the psyche, rather than 'discovering' it. No one character possesses it, nor by implication do we have more than a partial view as audience to the spectacle of our own existence. Galdós seems to foreshadow the modern theatre's theme of inexorable loneliness within the walls of one's own mind: 'There is no spiritual empathy' (p. 924). Only the symbolic perceptions and occurrences such as Orozco's vision of the suicide's image, have convincing intensity; and yet, these we understand to be not supernatural, but psychological epiphanies. They too are not final guides. For all the differences in possible philosophic intent, the writing of two works, one about the other, foreshadows the twentieth-century 'novel of a novel' – as done, for instance, by Mann for *Doctor Faustus* or by Gide within *Les Faux-monnayeurs*. Galdós does not revive the old romantic technique of purposeful ironic disruption of the simple 'illusion' of fiction by constant commentary upon the work of art itself. Nevertheless, his separation of the same story into two generic presentations forces upon us the task of reflecting about such an 'illusion' and relating it to the human condition. Federico puzzles over the fact that 'fictions' of the mind have their own strange validity: 'I experience the reality of what took place [a talk with '~the shade of Orozco'] inside myself; but is this internal phenomenon what we commonly call reality?' (p. 899).

These paired 'novel' and 'dialogue novel' offer us many insights into Galdós's artistry, for in one respect they are an analysis, i.e., a 'taking apart', of his realism. On the one hand, there is the *historical* method. In *La incógnita*, a 'witness' interprets and records somewhat as would a Jamesian obtuse narrator. Characters are introduced, described according to visible traits, and their known statements about one another, as well as reportable observations of other parties concerning them, are given. Our task is to assess all this information for what it may be worth; we too become 'historians'. On the other hand, there is the *psychological* method. By a direct intrusion into the intrahistorical mind processes, we learn what it is ordinarily impossible to know. In this regard, *Realidad* is 'unreal'; it goes so far beyond the limited asides and glimpses of dreams in older drama that it is part of the symbolic 'realism' of a new age in art, when distinctions between hard fact and meaningful fantasy dissolve. These distinctions are only a further subject for profound meditation, but no longer divide the realms of our experience into that which is 'false' versus that which is 'true'. In dialogue passages set within his novels, Galdós does not use this fuller revelation of psychic truths but simply portrays an action which we must look at from the outside. In *La desheredada*, for example, or in *Miau*, he is only affording us a close-up experience of actual scenes, tiny documentaries still part of outer, historical reality. Just as dramatization of stories can suddenly force us to change our perspective, so now in *Realidad* omniscient peering into the hearts of *dramatis personae* jolts us from any complacent projections into the artistic illusion's mere surface. Basically, the Galdosian method of narration comprises several points of view; the author's 'reality' is multidimensional, in keeping with his Cervantine heritage.

Our theme has been limited to one aspect of Galdós, his ability to move back and forth with multiple vantage points. This was not a kind of intellectualism that could enfeeble the Spanish novel of the nineteenth century, which was in the rut of simply describing habits and customs, and only rarely motives.[10] While one may admire the aesthetic accomplishment of a writer like James in maintaining a unified point of view and perfect plot, that order of mastery is at a price too. Jamesian characters are usually so subordinated to the beautiful pattern of his books that their lives are held in check; lives are nasty, uncooperative, always threatening to go off on their own with the 'reason of unreason' that impels them, and must be 'domesticated' to conform to his pattern. Galdós is quite aware of himself as a creator, with his own way of doing things. The subject matter of which he wants to speak – life in Spain – seems paramount to him; the subject itself suggests the shape of a plan.

> I know that my style does not appear as such to many who are trying to achieve . . . something else. They think it's easy to do what I do. I can understand them, and I recognize that they go to great efforts. But it would be ingenuous of me to get involved in such designs when I have *so many stories to tell*. For me, style begins with the plan . . . You will appreciate that, in defining style so broadly, I can afford not to worry too much about what for you is essential and almost taken for granted . . . In general, it is not errors of style which I regret, but over hasty planning.[11]

Galdós does not eschew practising any tricks of the trade, but they are secondary. Considering him as one of that breed of writers of mammoth appetite, the hearty digestion which absorbs life without too many qualms or finickiness, we must, however, also ask whether Galdós is merely robust or indeed has a sensitive palate.

We may apply his own standard here to the theme of man's many-layered world of dream and waking, illusion and reality. For purposes of illustration, one example must suffice of the growth of his artistry. In the chapter 'The thaw' in *León Roch*, María is traveling in great perturbation of soul by coach to reclaim her husband. The moment is masterfully portrayed. Her anxiety that is nigh to blindness, the internal ruminations as she rehearses and worries over her encounter to come are put in compact relief in this paragraph:

> She paid no attention to the accidents of the terrain or anything she could see. For her, the coach was traveling through a dark, empty region. But, as happens when our thoughts are filled with a particular kind of idea to the exclusion of all else, María, unable to see the obvious, noteworthy objects on her journey, picked out instead a few tiny, insignificant details. She saw a dead bird by the wayside, and noticed that an inn sign was missing an 'a'; she did not register the passing of a tram, but noted that the driver was one-eyed. Although

> this may seem absurd, it was the most natural thing in the world (vol. 4, p. 880).

This passage already reveals the greatness of a maturing novelist. The veracity of his pinpointing of salient details, the successful impression of vague psychological time, while a large measure of external time must be flowing by, and the irrational suggestiveness of the 'things' of a peculiar reality which her mind isolates all combine convincingly. There is also the virtually 'surrealistic' quality of her journey that makes it into a 'sign', like appearances of the balloon-man as a 'herald' in Flaubert's *Madame Bovary*. Yet Galdós is so taken with his own achieved 'truth' and the theory behind it that he cannot refrain from interpreting for us. Or perhaps he is eager that we not miss the point, because it is important.

In Chapter 30 of *Miau*, Galdós portrays a similar traumatic moment when Abelarda, meeting Víctor in church for what she thought was an amorous tryst, is fathoming the scoundrel's smooth speech – and needing to look at the statue of the saint by his name with the question 'whether it was true or a dream' (vol. 5, p. 669). Víctor has cruelly toyed with her and now is breaking their relationship. Abandoned, in a state of shock, Abelarda kneels at the altar unable to pray.

> The figure of Christ, many times larger than that of his mother, towered on the wall, touching the roof of the chapel with his crown of thorns, and stretching out his arms incredibly wide. Beneath him was an assembly of candles, symbols of the Passion, wax ex-voto offerings, a collecting-box with a filthy-edged hole and dirty, rusted padlock; the altar cloth was covered in dribbles of wax; it was set on a ledge painted with streaks to look like jasper. Señorita de Villaamil stared at all this, not taking in the whole but fixing on the tiniest details, her eyes darting here and there like a needle that pricks the surface but does not penetrate it, while her soul pressed against the vinegared sponge, soaking up the bitterness (pp. 669–70).

The dream-like reality of her emotional crisis simply *happens*. The outer 'facts' and the inner pressure interact. Instead of explaining what is occurring and why, Galdós demonstrates it with immediacy. And the fundamental human experience of desolation flows naturally into the symbolism of the environment itself. The author still intervenes to a certain extent, by speaking about her 'soul', but since we have already submitted with Abelarda to the moment, this statement only lifts us gently onto a slightly higher plane, from the intensity of inner truth to a conscious paradigm.

Not many hours later, Abelarda conceives a strange antipathy toward her nephew Luisito, whom she has hitherto treated affectionately, and it develops steadily into an urge to murder him. Here Galdós slips back into 'scientific' explanation, because he may fear that the reader will balk at the next events. He links her insane desire with the already violent hatred for her own father, 'an anti-natural hatred; doubtless the fruit of one of those epileptic emanations that subvert the soul's primary feelings' (p. 671). But such naturalistic asides do not very much upset us, for they are less frequent and more and more offset by the penetrating veracity of what he narrates. The scene in the bedroom which aunt and nephew share is uncanny, a plunge into the grotesque region of human mentality from which tragedy springs, and yet a sublime moment of insight into the affinity of 'dream' and 'reality'. Little Luisito cries out in his sleep:

> I can see his black legs stained with blood; I can see his knees, covered in black bruises, auntie . . . I'm scared . . . Come, please come! (p. 671).

Even while his aunt is on the verge of killing him, Luis's thoughts turn to the 'other God', a dignified grandfathergod who does not frighten him like the image in the chapel. Galdós weaves together the motifs of divine immolation and human agony. Thus Luis's nightmare assumes a quality of truth, becomes as it were oracular. The ominous linking of the two figures, the victim Son-of-Man and the Father, is later confirmed when grandfather Villaamil kills himself. Luisito translates the vibrations of other minds into his own distorted dreams; however, these specters have validity in analogy to the evident symbolism of our world, notably the 'mythic' pattern in Christian belief.

Not patterns of plot, but patterns of reality come forward in Galdós's novels. They are clearest in a novel like *La de Bringas*, with its odd beginning – a thorough description of a picture made of bits and pieces of hair. This frivolous composition progresses parallel to the Galdosian relation of events in the life of a government employee's family up to the revolution; a space of months, during which we explore the ever more ramshackle 'inner city' of the palace, until the evanescent reality there established is swept away, like the hair-picture. It is a fitting 'cenotaph' (vol. 4, p. 1562) for the period coming to an end, and in it we sense Galdós's powers of whimsical irony over our transitory show. Likewise, the fevers and vomiting fits of the little Bringas girl are not just arbitrary local 'color', but hint at a pattern in the larger world – which we first understand fully when the nation has its fever and casts out its tokens of indigestion (including Bringas, hair-artist). Rosalía de Bringas is also cast out, economically, or rather, must expel any unrealistic moral principles: 'Time was pressing; the situation allowed no delay' (p. 1645). Galdós could have ended his novel here and earned the reputation of constructing a neat plot shape. But he cannot resist continuing with several confrontations which Rosalía now has to experience. The meeting with Refugio really forms a short story in itself. But Galdós does not believe that a pat fiction can be superimposed on reality; fiction ultimately subserves realism. And he knows, as he often enough says in his chapter headings, that where one story ends another begins. All these stories together first suggest the story of humankind, for the telling of which great patience and lofty irony are required.

Notes

1. All quotations will be cited by volume and page numbers from the Aguilar edition edited by Federico Carlos Sáinz de Robles (1942, Galdós, *Obras completas*, Aguilar, Madrid).
2. *The Novels of Pérez Galdós: The Concept of Life as Dynamic Process* (1954, Washington University Press, Saint Louis), the best book overall, takes up at length, for example, possible Hegelian influences (pp. 147 ff); but its argument that Galdós 'integrates environmental influence with personality development' (p. 34) and is 'aware of the unevenness of psychological growth' (p. 59) can stand on its own merits; Eoff carefully shows that 'at no time, however, does Galdós use a particular case to generalize upon the inability of the human species to rise above its surroundings' (p. 38), though he must be 'regarded as a historian of society in movement' (p. 111).
3. Without very much interpretation of his materials, J. Chalmers Herman (1955, *'Don Quijote' and the Novels of Pérez Galdós*, Oklahoma State Press, Ada) has nevertheless compiled an impressive catalogue of quotations, allusions, themes and motifs from Cervantes.
4. Shakespeare and Calderón were the favorite dramatists of the German romantics, and as a result of their being well translated, they became standard poets in the German repertory – and still are. The romantics associated their own concept of creative freedom, i.e., 'romantic irony', with the complex illusory reality of the seventeenth-century theatre and its sense of transcendental irony. The romantics themselves never created great drama, however, but rather analysed it 'ironically' in virtuoso demonstrations of the (if necessary, irrational) 'spirit' controlling 'matter'. Thus plays like Tieck's *Der gestiefelte Kater* actually are forerunners of Pirandello and the art of 'absurdity', rather than continuations of the world-play of theodicy. The organic view, whose roots are in the late Renaissance (Böhme, Bruno, *et al.*), seemed to offer a parallel principle of freedom, in contrast to mechanistic views (French rationalism, English empiricism).
5. Many psychologists existed after the considerable impetus given by late Renaissance thinkers like Robert Burton in his *Anatomy of Melancholy* (1621). But the developmental theory received its stamp at the same time the German *Bildungsroman* originated, a novel of education that included psychic processes; e.g., Moritz's *Anton Reiser, ein psychologischer Roman* (1783–90), which followed a case history in analogy to natural growth, showing the interrelationship of early experience and later drives, psychosomatic factors, education, wish-

fulfillment and illusions, etc., in the biography of a superior personage. Romantic scientists like C. G. Carus then codified such knowledge in accordance with the theory of biological evolution of the race; the 'mind' of the individual grew organically during the history of its vessel, just as 'spirit' developed organically during the entire story of humanity from unconsciousness in the primitive animal state through various levels of fulfillment. The romantics made the evolution of spirit into a vitalism.

6. JOSEPH SCHRAIBMAN (1960, *Dreams in the Novels of Galdós*, Hispanic Institute, New York) catalogues the author's numerous instances of dream, revery, hallucination, vision, etc., according to storytelling functions, which are conceived of only as 'devices'; the study is more a handbook of references and statistics, than an interpretation.

7. ANTHONY ZAHAREAS (1965, 'The tragic sense in *Fortunata y Jacinta*', *Symposium*, **19**: 38–49) brings out the developmental interaction, 'the mystery of human life in its clash between the "inner" and "outer" forces', by which Galdós 'succeeds in destroying the formulas of human relationships given by some philosophers and many naturalists'; according to Galdós's presentation, 'the spiritual life of man can at times be deformed, but not easily rationalized', as 'man's position in the universe is first, to suffer, for it is a tragic position, and then, to understand' (p. 47).

8. This study is limited to what is described as 'the second phase' and 'apogee' by ROBERT RICARD ([n.d.] *L'Evolution spirituelle de Pérez Galdós*, Université de Paris, Paris, pp. 6–8). The upper boundary line is roughly *Misericordia*. The upsurge of fantasy in the late works such as *El caballero encantado* (1909) does not indicate a revolutionary change in Galdós, but only the assertion of already latent and dormant traits, first notable in *The Shadow* (1870). These traits will be touched on as they appear in *Our Friend Manso* and the dialogue novel *Realidad* within the 'high' period.

9. Eoff, S., 1954, p. 143.

10. For an examination of Galdós's historical position, consult BERKOWITZ H. C. 1948, *Pérez Galdós: Spanish Liberal Crusader*, University of Wisconsin Press, Madison. The tolerant humanity of Galdós's intellect so far as his stands on politics, moral issues, etc., are concerned is, of course, also an important contribution to Spanish literature, made through remarkable tenacity against the pressure of criticism, indeed an achievement of magnitude.

11. LUIS BELLO, 1928, 'Aniversario de Galdós: Diálogo antiguo', *El Sol* (4 January). Quoted in Angel del Río, 1953, *Estudios galdosianos*, Librería General, Zaragoza, p. 13, n. 4.

8 The Use of Distance in Galdós's *La de Bringas**

Peter A. Bly

This article develops the exploration of irony in Galdós's work in order to highlight his manipulation of distorted perpectives and his use of an unreliable narrator. In so doing, Bly moves towards a view of Galdós as a non-representational writer, who foregrounds the artificial nature of his text. Indeed, as Bly would show in a later book (1986), *La de Bringas* is all about how seeing is not believing. In many ways this short article marks a watershed in Galdós criticism, which in the late 1970s and 1980s would become increasingly concerned with the ways in which Galdós departs from, and effects a critique of, the mimetic tenets of realism. Particularly interesting is Bly's concluding parallel between Galdós and the early twentieth-century writer Valle-Inclán, who (as Gilman observes on pp. 57–8) regarded his avant-garde experimentalism, for which he coined the term *esperpento*, as a break with the 'pedestrian' realism of Galdós. As Bly perceptively notes, the use by both writers of techniques of distortion is remarkably similar. Bly's analysis could also be usefully related to Bakhtin's theory of carnival: a frequent motif in Galdós's work, including this novel. *La de Bringas* (translated by Gerald Brenan's wife Gamel Woolsey as *The Spendthrifts*, 1951, sadly long out of print) is perhaps Galdós's most perfectly constructed book and a classic novel of adultery.

In general, literary historians have not hesitated to describe Galdós's contemporary novels as accurately observed pictures of nineteenth-century Madrid.[1] M. Romera-Navarro remarks: 'they are the novels in which observation outweighs every other quality'.[2] J. García López uses similar language: 'the atmosphere of the capital is reflected with

* Reprinted from 1974, *Modern Language Review* **69**: 88–97.

admirable precision. Their author here proves that he is a keen observer of physical reality'.[3] However, a careful examination of the use of physical space and distance in *La de Bringas,* supposedly one of the most representative novels of this realist style, will show, I hope, that Galdós goes beyond a simple objective photograph of the material world. He is constantly breaking down what one would expect to be the normal spatial relationships between various points to produce a picture of disorder, confusion, and repulsion. He even disrupts the normal literary 'distance' between the novel and its reader. The conscious manipulation will appear inevitable, if he is to expose without ambiguity the true moral fibre of his characters.

It is not that Galdós does not accumulate accurate physical details. He does, as can be seen from his description of the servants' quarters in the Royal Palace in Chapter Four. Yet more important are the significance and arrangement which he sees in these details, and which he conveys to the reader through his choice of similes and explicit comment. The quarters are indeed a disordered collection of different structures and spaces, but Galdós's words go beyond an impartial relation of detail to express his deep feelings about the area: it is a chaotic jumble, where the normal perspectives of the physical world are broken down: 'that labyrinthine world, with its nooks and crannies, hidey-holes and surprises, an architectural whim and mockery of symmetry' (p. 1592). Galdós's images increase the impression of confusion and disorder, to the point of distortion and inversion. The locality is like a city with its own streets and districts, or a subterranean labyrinth, comparable to that of Hades, or of the Cretan Minotaur. The last image is clearly forged by his reference to the guard at the entrance as 'a Cerberus in a three-cornered hat' (p. 1591), and reinforced by his information that Pez ('Fish': an apt name in the context) is a reader of Jules Verne: 'Pez had picked up his ideas of geography in the books of Jules Verne; now he was putting them into practice' (p. 1593). The bureaucrat takes his bearings in the Palace 'with the geographical studiousness of a Jules Verne character' (p. 1592).[4] The reader is quite disconcerted as simultaneously Galdós had been building up an aerial perspective by stressing the high elevation of the quarters. Francisco Bringas has to climb one hundred and twenty-four steps from his office to the apartment on the second floor, a not inconsiderable ascent by any standards. And there is still another floor to the top of the building, where the lesser servants are housed. From the large window on this floor the buildings in the city below are seen as unnaturally diminutive objects: 'Felipe IV's horse looked to us like a toy; the Teatro Real a fairground stall' (p. 1593). The soaring flights of the Palace pigeons down to the ground and up again, and Galdós's expressive image: 'the upper edge of the Palace's cornice [looked like] a wide bridge over a precipice, along which anyone not suffering from vertigo could run with ease' (p. 1593), underline the already vivid picture of a lofty edifice. Which image does Galdós wish us to retain? Both, I think, for he wants to stress the unnaturalness of this building. From both within and without, it is a disconcerting, perplexing object for the observer defying the laws of optics and physics. It is difficult to resist the impression that Galdós intended us to see in these elevated apartments an eloquent symbol of the disordered minds and values of their inmates, removed from the realities of life.

Selecting the Bringas family as his particular example of these deranged inhabitants, he is at pains to indicate that their dwelling is representative of the outer macrocosm of the Palace, just as the Palace itself is a microcosm of the greater entity, Madrid. There are a reasonable number of rooms but Galdós emphasizes their unnaturally large size. Bringas cordons off a studio for his labours around the window of the *main cabinet office*, Paquito has similarly made a library around the large window of the other *cabinet office*. The pieces of furniture 'were lost in the huge room with its arched ceiling' (p. 1594) and the bedrooms have 'a cathedral-like capacity'. Even the alternation of bright light and gas-lit murkiness found in the corridor outside has its parallel here. Francisco's windows which look on to El Campo del Moro receive 'torrents of light and joy' whilst the bedrooms close to the corridor 'received light from the door and skylights covered with wire netting [. . .]. Through some of these skylights, the glow of gaslight came in even during the daytime' (p. 1594). The identification is strengthened by the family habit of applying the names of the Royal Apartments below to their own rooms. This tendency had been discernible in *Tormento* when Francisco, having just moved into the new house in the Costanilla de los Angeles, remarks to Rosalía: 'don't you feel you're looking at the Gasparini Room?' (p. 1478).[5] Having achieved the summit of his ambitions in the Crown Estate Office, Francisco's loyalty and affection for the Queen increases to the point of adoration (p. 1591). Hence it is not surprising that he should identify his dwelling with that of his sovereign. But Galdós's carefully sustained use of this technique throughout the novel creates the illusion at times that the events are indeed taking place in the Royal Apartments. The inference is that what is happening on the second floor is happening downstairs too. The Bringas household is symbolic of the whole Palace structure. Although it is situated on the second floor and on the west side, we are not given its precise location, the number on the front door is 'erased'; in fact one feels that the apartment could be placed anywhere in the Palace.

Galdós does shift his attention to the ground floor on occasions, but significantly he prefers to retain an elongated perspective; he remains at a unnatural distance from the scene he describes. The result is once more a distorted picture. For all the gossip about the Queen and her exile at the end we never meet her face to face. Only on Maundy Thursday do we catch a glimpse of her and her courtiers. At first it is from the staircase leading into the Chapel and behind a half-closed door: 'they were able to stand on the staircase to the chapel till they caught a glimpse, through half-open doors, of the patriarch's mitre, and two extinguished candles from the Holy Week candelabra, an altar covered in a maroon cloth, the odd cleric's bald head, and the occasional gentleman's chest weighed down with crosses and sashes; but that was all' (p. 1598). The participants lose their human identity, represented by an individual piece of clothing or part of the body which equates them with the religious objects described. The implication is that the courtiers have a hollow, superficial faith which consists of external ceremony. In the subsequent distribution of food to the beggars in the Hall of Columns, Galdós again choses to view the scene from a distance: the lofty perch of the skylights. To the spectators 'the flowers of the carpet, seen in the distance below, looked like miniatures' whilst the painted figures on the ceiling 'look monstrous, crudely painted' (p. 1598). The reduced exposure of the author's lens occasioned by the high position succeeds in highlighting the marionette movements of the courtiers, the disbelief of the recipients, and the ultimate futility of this act of charity when the food is cheaply bought up by merchants outside. The meaning of the picture seems explicit enough, but Galdós is anxious to add his own commentary: 'If no effort of the imagination will allow us to imagine Christ dressed in tails, in the same way no powers of reason could persuade us that this palace comedy has anything to do with the gospels' (p. 1599). And later he presents further details of the events through the distorting medium of Isabelita's nightmare; the courtiers have now lost all human identity:

> Through all the doors of the upper part of the Palace a variety of liveries appeared – red and blue cloths, gold and silver braid, countless three-cornered hats . . . As the delirium deepened, she saw the city gleaming in a thousand shiny colours. It was a city of dolls, without a doubt, but what dolls! . . . White wigs appeared on all sides, and no door opened on the second floor without revealing a pretty wax, cloth, or porcelain figure, all of them rushing along the corridors shouting: 'It's time . . .'. On the staircases, the braid going up collided with the braid going down . . . All the dolls were in a hurry.

La corte de los milagros of Valle-Inclán offers a strikingly similar picture of the same scene: 'Along the corridors and down the stairs sycophantic uniforms and cloaks rustled as they left that stage on which they had been glittering extras [. . .]. The white gloves stood out cruelly from the elegance of the uniforms, and all the hands were those of clowns'.[6]

Galdós is not so direct as the master of the *esperpento*; he hides beneath the convenience of a child's hallucination, but one cannot help feeling that Galdós held the same pessimistic view of the Isabelline régime: that they were a collection of puppets.[7] The detailed account of Isabelita's nightmare and the author's own comments reinforce beyond doubt the significance of the earlier picture of distortion permitted by the unusual perspective. Galdós is concerned that the reader should not misinterpret his technique.

The one event which affects the lives of all the characters, great and small, is, of course, the September Revolution of 1868, the details of whose development are so carefully recorded in the novel. Critics have rightly indicated that Galdós draws an important parallel between the political fall of the Monarchy and the moral fall of Rosalía.[8] Of more importance for this article is the observation that the author never presents this secondary plot directly to the reader's attention; it is always viewed from a distance. We are never allowed to visit the revolutionaries, nor are we informed directly of events by the author in his capacity as the omniscient historian or chronicler. All political news is filtered through distorting media. This is to a certain extent justifiable in that we are following the lives of two monarchists one of whom, Francisco, has an almost paranoiac fear of 'the so-called Revolution' (p. 1591) and thus one would not expect too much reference to such a calamitous possibility. Indeed Pez has to tone down the alarming news in his talks with Bringas (pp. 1606, 1631). When Francisco is eventually forced to accept the truth of the situation from the reports in the newspapers and the dispatches received in the office, he becomes almost insane, barricading the family in the apartment when he thinks the militia are attacking the Palace (p. 1681). The later disclosure by Cándida that the revolutionaries are far from being the bloodthirsty barbarians Francisco has imagined serves to ridicule and underline the latter's willing escape from reality, aptly symbolized by his reluctance to leave the upstairs flat. Cándida urges him, 'Come down and you'll see, you'll see' (p. 1681). And at the end of the novel he does leave his lofty perch, but one cannot help feeling that had he done so earlier, he might have saved some part of his sanity, for as it is, Francisco leaves the Palace a broken man, even more paranoiac and liable to self-deception. But this weakness of Francisco is clear from the other events of the novel. The historical sub-plot, conveniently muted until the closing pages, only serves to reinforce that impression, and whilst aesthetically pleasing, is not all that necessary. I think that there is a more important point to all this indirect reporting. Galdós does take care in presenting the details through the words of several characters: Pez (pp. 1637, 1653–4, 1682–3), Milagros (p. 1642), Cándida (p. 1621), Pez and Vargas (p. 1651) (further distorted through Isabelita's nightmare), Paquito (p. 1670), and Refugio

(p. 1676). Surely Galdós wants to convey an impression of mystery and foreboding in the mind of the reader, to make him share the expectations or fears of those who talk about the Revolution. These extreme feelings heighten the sense of absurdity of the ending when 'the so-called Revolution' is revealed directly (or almost, for we still see events at a distance, through the filter of Cándida's eyes) and in its true colours: the revolutionaries are seen as country bumpkins, more interested in shooting pigeons than people. The Revolutionary Junta and the later Provisional Government hardly differ from the *ancien régime* except in name. Patently, 'revolution' is a misnomer to describe Galdós's vision of the events of September and October 1868. More pertinent, it would seem, is Cándida's jocular comment: 'After all that, it's a joke' (p. 1681). Galdós seems to be saying that everything is devoid of serious value. And once more, his adroit positioning of events from the reader has allowed him to make this point most effectively.

Agnes Moncy's observation that 'Everything happens in the framework of the Royal Palace' is not wholly accurate.[9] For although the Palace is the principal location in the novel we do travel outside its walls: to the city of Madrid, for example, and one or two specific places inside and outside Spain. Moreover, the nature of these excursions is curious, and worthy of note. Our view of the streets of Madrid, for example, is obtained only when we follow the movements of Rosalía. For three-quarters of the novel, Rosalía retains a certain degree of shame and apprehension about her growing passion for clothes and is frightened that it will be discoveed by her husband. Her sorties seem to be hurried and secretive. Galdós very effectively conveys this impression by omitting any description of the street scene on her visits to the dress-shops (pp. 1603, 1605–6): one only sees her and Milagros in the shop. This is unusual, for Galdós in other novels is rather meticulous about supplying street names. This sudden and hasty transfer from one locale to another is repeated when Rosalía takes her children to the Royal Pavilion of the Retiro Park, accompanied by the hopeful Pez. The absence of topographical details becomes all the more pronounced and significant when one considers that the party has crossed the breadth of Madrid to reach the Retiro. An additional effect is that the reader's attention is focused on the scene, and is not distracted by what the author sees in the street. The Royal Pavilion, with its poor-quality architecture and statuary, seems an extension of the parent body on the west side of the city. Similarly, when Rosalía attends Milagros's *soirée* in the Calle de Atocha (p. 1610) or when she rushes to the church where her friend is sponsoring a ceremony (pp. 1616–17), details of the itinerary are scarce and vague, whilst the description of these respective locales and what takes place there seems inordinately long, even by Galdós's own standards. Perhaps his purpose is to demonstrate conclusively the pettiness and sordidness of that world which so bedazzles Rosalía.

In the last quarter of the book, Rosalía's apprehension about deceiving her husband disappears completely. Galdós very skilfully mirrors this change in the description of her travels in Madrid. We are now conscious of Madrid as an area of considerable size, a pattern of streets and squares, in which it takes time to travel between two points. Rosalía dallies looking at the window-displays of the various dress-shops (p. 1659) or gazing at prospective 'catches' in the Paseo del Prado (p. 1665). Her estrangement from her husband and the régime he supports in the Palace, which had been foreshadowed by her earlier sallies, now seems complete. Her home is now the streets of Madrid, the scene of the impending triumph of the Revolution. Fittingly, Rosalía looks forward to its arrival for the change of fortune it may bring her (p. 1679). For the first time in the novel, we have a rival locale to the Palace. Yet it does not seem to be much of an alternative: the confusion and vulgarity of the Palace compound is here reflected in the unbearable odours and litter of the streets and the swimming pools on the banks of the Manzanares (pp. 1658–60). By adjusting his shots of the city to the changing attitude of his main protagonist, Galdós skilfully succeeds in excluding any pleasant view of Madrid. (As the story begins towards the end of February 1868, he could easily have shown Madrid in its spring freshness.) Thus he is able to maintain the uniform tone of sordidness evident in the individual scenes throughout the novel.

The usual summer alternative to Madrid, San Sebastián and other northern resorts, is a frequent topic of conversation in the Bringas household. Yet we are not taken to the area, nor do we glimpse it through the imaginations of the characters: it remains a name which Pez and Milagros can only associate with shopping sorties into France and contraband merchandise smuggled by hilarious methods back across the border: some people 'dress up in all they've bought, and pack the clothes they were wearing in trunks', putting on (and in the summer heat) 'two winter coats, one on top of the other, six pairs of stockings, two skirts and four shawls' (p. 1654).

A similar note of absurdity is struck by Rosalía's account of the Bringas honeymoon spent in Navalcarnero (p. 1640). Again, we only see this village at a distance through the distorted reminiscences of a dissatisfied Rosalía. The same ridiculous actions witnessed inside the Palace are repeated in the country at large wherever these courtiers travel. The effective foreshortening of the physical distance between these geographical points creates the illusion that one is the physical extension of the other. In fact, for these courtiers of Isabel, whose lives are centred upon the Palace, the rest of Spain hardly exists, except as a playground on certain occasions.

There are a few minor references to points outside Spain which are likewise seen by the reader from the epicentre of the Palace. We do not follow Golfín on his summer vacation to Germany nor are we taken to Bordeaux to see Amparo and Agustín in their new home. Again, Galdós is interested in the distorting effects of an abnormal distance: these expatriates living abroad (Golfín has really spent most of his time abroad) show a certain obtuseness in their dealings with Francisco, Rosalía, and Refugio. This obtuseness is all the more surprising as in previous novels they had shown themselves to be aware of the hypocrisy of their relations. In *Marianela*, Teodoro Golfín had correctly seen the hollowness of the social charity of his sister-in-law, Sofía. In *Tormento*, Agustín and Amparo are aware of the weaknesses of Rosalía and Refugio. But in *La de Bringas* Teodoro is misled by the prosperous appearance of Rosalía and her children into believing that Francisco is rich. And the Caballeros, after only a few months' absence from Madrid, invite the Bringas family to Arcachon for the summer. Although the invitation is well-intentioned, they fail to consider that Rosalía will welcome it for very different reasons: 'The thought of a trip to France, of meeting the occasional Spanish family of one's acquaintance at the station in San Sebastián or St Jean de Luz and, after the initial greeting, announcing to them: '~I'm off to Arcachon', was like admitting some family connection with the Eternal Father' (p. 1660). Rosalía's social ambitions and subsequent frustation are only increased by this generous invitation from the Caballeros. Amparo shows a further lack of judgement when she tries to establish Refugio in the drapery business (p. 1635) by sending her the latest fashions from Paris. The venture is a complete fiasco, as Amparo should have realized from her knowledge of her sister's character and the reckless habits of the female clientele. Refugio herself says almost as much: 'I'm no good at this. I don't know what my sister was thinking of when she imagined I could become a businesswoman' (p. 1672). Galdós does comment on Golfín's short-sightedness (ironical in view of his ability as an oculist): 'This Golfín was rather innocent in the ways of the world and, as he had spent most of his life abroad, was ignorant of our customs and that peculiarity of Madrid life which elsewhere would be called its "mysteries", but which here is a mystery to no one' (p. 1647). Galdós seems to be saying that Golfín needs to spend all his time in Madrid close to events if his interpretation of them is to be correct. Amparo and Agustín chose to move away to a safe distance, but such a removal can only harm their proved ability to perceive the true nature of things which occur in Madrid. The long distance which separates the Palace epicentre from surrounding points is mutually harmful to the respective visions of reality. Neither observer nor observed is able to see the other in the correct perspective. We have been chiefly concerned in this article with Galdós's use of physical distance within his fictional world. It now remains for us to see how he distorts the traditional literary 'distance' between the reader and the book.

From his earliest novels Galdós had shown that he could not be the impartially objective recorder that the Realists had aimed to be. In *Marianela* and in *La desheredada* he had interrupted his narrative to censure respectively Positivism (pp. 714–15) and the primitive conditions of mental asylums (p. 987). He had already demonstrated in *Our Friend Manso* that interest in experimenting with different narrative techniques which is so prominent in such later novels as *Lo prohibido, La incógnita,* and *Realidad*. Given this tendency to experiment, perhaps one should not attach any significance to the narrator's role in *La de Bringas*. But I think that Galdós has given careful attention to this matter. Firstly, the author has a double existence as narrator and actor, but not in any autobiographical manner. We assume that Galdós is the narrator, as we are never informed to the contrary; yet we cannot really believe that he took part in the activities described. So we assume that it is Galdós speaking through the voice of a literary persona who can conveniently step into the action when he wants. But we can never be sure as Galdós is silent on his identity. If Galdós had limited his *alter ego* to the introductory visit to the Palace with Pez, there would have been no reason for the reader's bewilderment. As in *Nazarín*, the device could be justified as a convenient method of describing a very strange setting. The narrator's brief appearances when he sees Pez and Rosalía leave the Retiro (p. 1613), and gives an eye-witness account of Tula's soporific *soirée* (pp. 1636–7) would merely continue this strictly functional role. However, his emergence in the concluding pages as an important functionary of the Revolutionary Government, appointed to take charge of the Palace administration, and his involvement with Rosalía (pp. 1682–3), forces one to reconsider his role. Certainly this technique is not used to achieve complete objectivity, for there are many scenes which he could not possibly have witnessed as a third party. Why then does the narrator deliberately focus attention upon himself? The view expressed by Ricardo Gullón: 'The fusion of the novelist with the material of the novels deliberately blurs the frontiers between life and the novel and, paradoxically, puts the author and his fictional creations in a freer position' is only half the truth.[10] On closer examination, we find that the reason for his visit to Bringas, arranged by Pez in return for past favours, is to have a possible court action by the Crown withdrawn by the responsible authority, Francisco. The possibility had arisen because a Crown official in Riofrío, presumably a small country village, had noticed 'grave irregularities in the allocation' (p. 1595) of plots of land and forest which the author had been able to secure. From the beginning, then, we are aware of a narrator who is not at all scrupulous in his own matters, and quite willing to forget moral principles to get what he wants. There is a strong implication in his relationship with Pez that this manoeuvre has been employed before. Although he is shown as a member of the monarchist circle of Doña Tula, his appointment by the Revolutionary Junta at the end raises doubts as to his real political allegiance. He seems as ambiguous and materialistic as Pez. His interviews with Rosalía at the end seem to have led to more than the narrator is willing to disclose. She looks at him 'with looks that blazed' (p. 1683) and later 'made further attempts to renew her calamitous intimacy' (p. 1683). It seems clear to the reader that the author has fallen a willing victim to her physical charms and had supported the indigent family for a time. A minor detail, curiously recorded at the beginning of the book, would seem to corroborate this and also show that Galdós had his dénouement in mind from the inception of his work: 'I gave him [Don Francisco] two Bayonne capons and a dozen bottles of my own wine on 4 October, his saint's day, and this courtesy still did not seem to me adequate compensation for the favour he had done me' (p. 1595). Why did he wait such a long time after the visit, which presumably would be some time in the spring, before Easter, to show his gratitude? Admittedly, Francisco's birthday was not until October and that would have been a convenient occasion to offer some fresh wine after the harvest. But it surely would not have been the best in his cellar. In view of the precise attention accorded the chronology of events in the novel, the fact that such a detail comes out of logical order has significance, which is only fully comprehended at the end, when 'we were in the full throes of revolution' (p. 1683). Any payments to Rosalía for favours received could now be disguised as a long-overdue sign of gratitude to Francisco. Consequently, the author's strong, high-minded denial of any further relations with Rosalía needs to be accepted with a pinch of salt: 'I did not feel it incumbent on me to be [the provider for the out-of-work family] against all the prescriptions of morality and domestic economy' (p. 1683). The narrator is only another actor in the farce of 1868, with the same faults and foibles that he is so ready to ridicule in others. The reader is disturbed and becomes wary of accepting the narrator's account of his own activities. Does this mistrust extend to the narrator's version of other people's lives? I think not. Galdós deliberately raises doubt about the reliability of the narrator at the end to ensure that the reader will not by lulled into a complacent attitude, once he puts down the book. Having laughed at the distorted images spread through the book, he is not to be excluded from the game at the end. He too must be made to doubt and question, if not his image, his own reading of the story. And what more effective way than to undermine the authority of the narrator, the reader's necessary guide to the events of the story? The treatment of the narrator's role in *La de Bringas* is certainly more complex than in many of the novels cited above, but more important, it succeeds in encasing the outside of the novel with the same layer of confusion which surrounds the inner parts. A novel about confusion, *La de Bringas* itself is meant to confuse the unwary reader. The opening words of the novel 'It was . . ., how shall I put it?' (p. 1587) aptly express this desired reaction.

This aim is also evident in another use of a literary 'distance': that between this novel and its predecessors, by which I mean those novels prior to the two of the trilogy of which *La de Bringas* is the conclusion: *El doctor Centeno* and *Tormento*. Galdós forges the connexion by his oft-noted practice of reintroducing characters presented in earlier works, in imitation of Balzac in *La Comédie humaine*. The surprising aspect of this motif in *La de Bringas* is that Galdós reintroduces an unusually large number of known faces, or names, especially amongst the peripheral characters: Pez, Milagros (and their respective families), Cándida, Alejandro Sánchez Botín, Gloria and cousins, Cimarra, Rafael del Horro, Torquemada, Torres, Teodoro Golfín, Moreno Rubio, Cucúrbitas, the Marqués de Fúcar, Joaquín Onésimo, Trujillo, Don Buenaventura de Lantigua, Mompous, Máximo Manso, Pilar San Salomó, Serafinita Lantigua, and León Roch. One is even reminded of the second series of the *National episodes* by the portrait of Don Juan de Pipaón, an ancestor of Rosalía, which hangs opposite the entrance to Bringas's apartment (p. 1594). Francisco himself recalls his famous historical namesake whose heroic exploits had been chronicled in *Los apostólicos*. The number of reappearances seems abnormally high, if not a record, for a single novel. One can only conclude that the author must have had a deliberate intention. The reader is not reminded of one but several novels by these characters who may have reappeared in one or more of them: *Marianela, Gloria, La familia de León Roch, La desheredada,* and *Our Friend Manso*. He has to pause awhile in order to establish the correct relationships between *La de Bringas* and these predecessors. The task is rendered more difficult by the fact that the latter describe events which occurred *after* those in *La de Bringas*, but yet they were published *before*. Galdós's own comments, particularly about Cándida's ultimate decline and ruin (pp. 1594, 1619, 1624) recorded in *Our Friend Manso*, and that of Milagros (p. 1601) in *La familia de León Roch*, only serve to maintain the reader's confusion; he is told to think of a future condition of which he is already aware. The distances between past, present and future seem rather blurred, more so when those characters from *Tormento* and *El doctor Centeno* remind us of events and episodes which occurred in these two novels and which refer to the past. José Montesinos was particularly perturbed by certain incongruencies of details observable when *La de Bringas* was compared to its predecessors. He could only conclude that Galdós was filling up space: 'he had no need to repeat himself, and repeat himself clumsily, just to fill up space and pad things out'.[11] In view of the findings presented in this article which would substantiate N.

G. Round's assertion that 'very few things in the construction of *La de Bringas* have been left to chance', I think that Galdós had a specific purpose when he chose to recall both directly and indirectly earlier novels.[12] He certainly wanted to point out how poeple's lives interrelated in a bizarre manner in society, but he also wanted his regular reader to pause and think about the meaning of *La de Bringas*. And again, what better way to disconcert him than by making some old friends appear in an unusual light?

In a recent analysis of Valle-Inclán's *esperpento* style, Ricardo Gullón makes some interesting comments which could be well applied to Galdós's method in *La de Bringas*: 'Visual distance is a decisive factor in the process of turning reality into an *esperpento*. From afar the individual is diminished and dehumanized. This, in turn, lets him be observed ironically, so that the onlooker does not participate in the movements and gestures which seem ridiculous or even senseless. The onlooker can not participate in what he sees because he is incapable of distinguishing or discerning'.[13] For, throughout Galdós's novel, we have seen how the author subtly disrupts the normal physical distances between buildings and places, either shortening or elongating them, pushing them out of their normal perspective with the aim of focusing special attention on the people who live in these places or the events which occur there. The resultant close-up pictures are dehumanized, distorted: people seem like marionettes, events and material objects repulsive and vulgar. Like Valle-Inclán, Galdós uses the disruption of normal perspectives to expose the real truth about this period in Spanish history. The artist has to use a special, deformed technique to capture accurately a special, deformed society. Normal perspectives and visions do not suffice. To ensure that his reader does not lose the importance of his special technique, Galdós disrupts those traditional literary distances which join the reader to the book: the narrator is to a certain extent unreliable, and the book itself seems to fit awkwardly into the chronological sequence of the series hitherto published, as if it were 'odd man out'. Indeed, *La de Bringas* is an exception amongst Galdós's novels, for it is surprising to note that the reader hardly sympathizes with any of the characters. Refugio, to a certain extent, but she is a minor character, and hardly a tragic victim of society's ways. As Gullón remarks, 'the onlooker can not participate in what he sees because he is incapable of distinguishing or discerning'. The distance between the reader and the novel is so distorted that he cannot identify with any character. And that is Galdós's intention. But unlike Valle-Inclán, he does not impose his deformation with every word. He allows the reader to think for a while that he is in a normal world, but only to undermine this impression further on. In *La de Bringas*, we can appreciate the distance that separates the normal from the grotesque. But, indeed, we are very close to that world of total absurdity so bitterly represented in Valle's *esperpento* writings.

Notes

1. All page references from *La de Bringas* and other novels by Galdós are to Galdós, 1969, *Obras completas*, ed. F. C. Sainz de Robles, 7th edn. Aguilar, Madrid, vol. 4.
2. 1928, *Historia de la literatura española*, Heath, Boston, p. 579.
3. 1964, *Historia de la literatura española*, Editorial, Vicens, Vives, Barcelona, p. 518.
4. Galdós extracts the full irony of these details. For all his submarine expertise, Pez has to acknowledge defeat by this particular ocean of the Palace, unable to reach the west side where Bringas's rooms are: 'Oh! I give up, I need a pilot' (p. 1593). Pez himself continues these marine connotations when he likens the Palace to a tossing ship (p. 1593), not an inappropriate image in the context but even less so when one recalls the traditional image of the Ship of State. In the early months of 1868, the Spanish Ship of State, as represented by the régime of Isabel II, was indeed floundering and soon to sink.
5. *Editor's note*: The novels *El doctor Centeno* (1883), *Tormento* (1884) and *La de Bringas* (1884) form a trilogy.
6. VALLE-INCLÁN, R. DEL, 1927, *Opera omnia*, Riradeneyra, Madrid, vol. 21 pp. 28–9.
7. Significantly, in *El doctor Centeno* he again uses children to convey his vision of the Royal Palace as a box of puppets: Felipe and Juanito pass by, on their way to deliver a message, and the very imaginative Juanito remarks: 'Everything here is on a spring. Just think: you press one button, and up pops a table fully laid; you press another and out jumps the altar with the priest saying mass for the Queen' (pp. 1353–4). Earlier the author had brought to our attention the massive size and mystery of the Palace: 'its dark mysterious bulk, all those closed balconies, sturdy pillars, enormous walls, like a sculpted mountain simultaneously expressing majesty, grandeur and sorrow' (p. 1353).
8. See GULLÓN R., 1967, *La de Bringas*, Prentice-Hall, Englewood Cliffs, New Jersey, pp. 12–14. Also SHOEMAKER, W. H., 1959, 'Galdós's classical scene in *La de Bringas*', *Hispanic Review* **27**: 423–34 (p. 423).
9. MONCY, A., 1965, 'Enigmas de Galdós', *Insula* **2**: 1–12 (p. 12).
10. GULLÓN, 1967, p. 18.
11. MONTESINOS, J., 1970, *Galdós*, 2 vols, Castalia, Madrid, vol. 2, p. 127.
12. ROUND, N. G., 1971, 'Rosalía Bringas' Children', *Anales Galdosianos* **6**: 43–50 (p. 53).
13. GULLÓN, R., 1968, 'Reality of the *esperpento*', in *Valle-Inclán: Centennial Studies*, University of Texas Press, Austin, pp. 123–37 (pp. 135–6).

9 Individual, Class and Society in *Fortunata and Jacinta**

John H. Sinnigen

The realist novel has, since Lukács's *Studies in European Realism*, been a happy hunting ground for Marxist critics, whose view of the text as the product of social and economic forces largely coincides with the sociological attitude to literature prevalent in the nineteenth century. Galdós's work is no exception. Sinnigen's essay is one of the most successful Marxist analyses of a Galdós novel, largely because it sees the text as mediator rather than reflector of historical contradictions. By concentrating on the ways in which *Fortunata and Jacinta* both constructs and deconstructs the ideological project of Restoration Spain, Sinnigen opens up unacknowledged textual contradictions: deconstructionist critics could take his insights further. In particular, Sinnigen's thesis that the unreliable male bourgeois narrator is in the course of the novel 'educated' by his female working-class protagonist anticipates later feminist criticism (see Jagoe, in press). This notion of a narrator battling to impose control on a text that ends up controlling him produces a reading that is almost Pirandellian (compare Kronik on *Our Friend Manso*, Chapter 11). Later metafictional studies of Galdós treat the text as an autonomous entity abstracted from its historical context; future critics might look to Sinnigen's essay as the model of a kind of metafictional analysis that avoids the problems of ahistoricism.

It was in 1886 that Galdós completed the first part of *Fortunata and Jacinta*, and although this novel deals primarily with the revolutionary years of 1868–1874, it is clearly concerned not just with that period and its movement from revolution to reaction but also with the contradictions of

* Reprinted from Robert J. Weber (ed.), 1974, *Galdós Studies*, vol. 2, Támesis Books, London, pp. 49–68.

Restoration society and of bourgeois society in general. As Raymond Carr has suggested, the Restoration tried to incorporate peacefully all dissident forces in a futile effort to avoid social revolution.[1] In this study I shall examine – with particular reference to the unresolved class conflict – the portrayal in *Fortunata and Jacinta* of the hypocrisy of that attempt.

In his discussion of the political regime forged by Antonio Cánovas del Castillo, Carr tells us:

> The Restoration monarchy was the most stable political structure erected by nineteenth-century Spanish liberalism, but its stability was based on a diminishing asset – the *ansia del vivir*, that desire for a peaceful life after anarchy which became, once more in 1939, a powerful force in Spanish politics. [. . .] As long as the moral atmosphere was dominated by the fear of a relapse into political chaos and social revolution, the institutions of constitutional monarchy remained inviolable for all but Republicans and Carlists. [. . .] The Restoration would have neither conquerors nor conquered: it would be the most merciful and tolerant restoration in history (p. 347).

Aside from the *ansia del vivir*, the early years of the Restoration were also supported by what Jaime Vicens Vives has called the 'gold fever', a boom based primarily on a tremendous influx of foreign capital (especially during the years 1875–1881). This boom lasted about ten years and ended with the crisis of 1886, a crisis which was a foreshadowing of what lay ahead in 1892 and, finally, in the disaster of 1898.[2] The juncture of 1886 is, then, crucial in that in this year the instability of the Restoration 'tranquility' became obvious. Social criticism and the search for new values go hand in hand throughout Galdós's work. Structurally these themes are frequently presented in terms of the opposition of an outsider, a representative of new, positive values, to a stagnant, retrograde society. For example, in *Doña Perfecta* Pepe Rey opposes science and an open mind to the closed, traditional society of Orbajosa. In *Tormento*, Agustín Caballero opposes the industriousness and frankness he had developed in America to the indolence and deceitfulness represented by the Bringas family. And in *Misericordia* the evangelical figure of Benina stands in opposition to the crass materialism of such characters as Carlos Moreno Trujillo and Juliana. In all of these novels the resolution – or lack of resolution – of this opposition is determined by the transformation – or lack of transformation – in society which results from this clash.

This outsider-society opposition is also the basis of the structure of *Fortunata and Jacinta*. Here the outsider, Fortunata, the 'working-class woman', stands in contraposition to the vast array of bourgeois and petty bourgeois characters who try to control her. Fortunata is regarded by members of the middle class as an object which they can manipulate to fulfill their particular egotistical ends. Juanito Santa Cruz sees her as a love object who can provide him with some variety whenever he tires of the regularity of middle-class life. And the members of the Rubín family and Guilermina Pacheco regard her as a kind of *tabula rasa* on whom they can impress a new being molded according to their wills. Yet, precisely while being handled as an object, Fortunata acts as agent, for she refuses to be either just a love object or a *tabula rasa*. While these members of the middle classes think they are playing with her, she is effecting significant changes in their way of life. Fortunata is such a strong agent that she even affects the structure of the novel by changing the role played by the narrator and by breaking up the separation of classes portrayed in the first two parts. Thus throughout Parts 3 and 4 the narrative focus moves about the worlds of the middle classes and the working class as Fortunata captures the attention of various characters. So this poor 'daughter of the people' who is regarded by the members of the middle classes as an object to be manipulated according to their will, turns out to be the most powerful agent of this novel. And through this strength she resolves her alienation from bourgeois society, not by accepting the conventions of that society but rather by overcoming the power through which those conventions had subdued her.

I. The bourgeoisie[3]

Part 1 of *Fortunata and Jacinta* is concerned primarily with describing the condition of the established Spanish bourgeoisie in the Madrid of the early 1870s, as seen through the story of the Santa Cruz family. This society is one in which the narrator is quite comfortable; he is acquainted with all the Santa Cruz family and many of their friends, and he repeats the philosophical commonplaces of this class. So, when he examines how the family attained its current position, he is presenting the history of a class whose ideology and attitudes he shares.

This presentation, however, is not always sympathetic, for the narrator recognizes that the bourgeoisie has separated itself from its popular base during its period of ascendancy. Therefore he is critical of the way in which the modern age – manifest in changing styles and ideas – has been introduced in Spain. His account of the change in the status of the 'mantón de Manila' (embroidered shawl) is particularly revealing. This once democratic garment ('both aristocratic and popular at the same time' [p. 20]) has begun to lose its appeal among the women of the aristocracy and the middle classes 'and only the common people, with admirable instinct, still wear it' (p. 21).[4] Along with the embroidered shawl, the working class has also become the only class which continues to display the once universally popular bright colors.[5] This attitude within the upper and middle classes demonstrates their desire to imitate the 'European sobriety' which had accompanied the bourgeois revolution in other countries: 'We are under the influence of northern Europe, and those accursed northern parts force upon us all the greys they borrow from their smoke-filled skies' (p. 29), and 'Crêpe has been in decline since 1840, not only due to the afore-mentioned rise of European sobriety, which has swept over Spain, but also to economic causes which we cannot escape' (p. 29). This last sentence suggests that Spain had been unprepared for the bourgeois revolution which swept across Europe in the nineteenth century. So the narrator criticizes the upper and middle classes for imitating their European counterparts without considering the consequences to the national character. He further notes that this national character, as represented in the bright colors and the embroidered shawl, is retained solely by the populace.[6]

This commercial imitation was accompanied by imitation in the realm of ideas. Thus the principle of 'progress' is an important thematic element throughout Part 1. It, along with its corollary, 'changing times', governs Baldomero Santa Cruz's attitude toward the education of his son: 'What reason was there for him [Baldomero II], who had been so strictly brought up by Don Baldomero I, to be so soft on his son? Why, the effects of the evolution in education, which went hand in hand with political evolution! . . . "Where would the world be without progress?" Santa Cruz thought, and with the idea came a desire to leave the boy free to follow his instincts' (p. 27). The idea of progress dominates all of Baldomero's attitudes, whether the subject be economics, politics (he is a 'progressive'), or the upbringing of his son. In this way he and his kind pay homage to the bourgeois revolution.

A product of this devotion to the ideal of progress is the creation of a new caste, the bourgeois 'señoritos' (young gentlemen), here represented by Juanito Santa Cruz.[7] Because of his father's and grandfather's success, Juanito is able to enjoy the leisure which previously had been the exclusive privilege of the aristocracy. Juanito has never had to work, has been provided with any money he might need, has been encouraged to travel, and, generally, has been free to conduct himself as he has pleased. The portrayal of this 'señorito' is not, however, entirely favorable. When they meet for the first time, the narrator describes Juanito as 'very good-looking and likeable, one of those men whose looks win people over before they are bewitched by their behavior, one of those who win more friends in an hour's conversation than others do by actively courting favor. His articulate way of speaking and the wit of his opinions gave the impression he knew more than he actually did, and on his lips paradoxes sounded better than truths. He dressed so elegantly and was so well-mannered it was easy to forgive him for talking too much' (p. 15). Here the narrator's ironic comments undercut the impression the young Santa Cruz gives of being a potentially great man and show him to fit the stereotype of the 'señorito' whose apparent profundity gives way to a vacuous reality.

Through his capricious political attitudes and his infidelity in love Juanito proves himself to be the epitome of inconstancy, and the narrator suggests that his inconstancy parallels that of Spanish society: 'Towards the end of '74, the Dauphin had entered a period of calm such as always followed on his excesses. In truth, there was little virtue in it, he was simply tired of vice; it was not a genuine, proper respect for order, but a surfeit of revolution. It could be said of him what Don Baldomero had said of the country as a whole: that it swung like a pendulum between liberty and peace' (p. 311). In this instance there is even a temporal correlation between Juan's 'surfeit of revolution' and his 'restoration' to Jacinta and the 'surfeit of revolution' of the Spanish bourgeoisie and the Restoration of the Bourbon dynasty.

This correlation between Juanito Santa Cruz and Spanish society is further demonstrated in their mutual preoccupation with appearances. For example, Juanito is attracted to Fortunata each time she reappears in a different role: 'Appearances, wretched appearances . . . were to blame. That unhappy, abandoned, penniless and possibly unwashed young woman had only had to transform herself into a clean, elegant, seductive adventuress, and the disdain felt by that man of his times, who placed etiquette on a pedestal, likewise changed into a burning desire to witness at first hand that fascinating transformation, so typical of our silken age' (p. 155). Likewise the Spanish bourgeoisie, which had echoed in 1869 the 'Never!' of Juan Prim, was ready in 1874 to embrace that dynasty which it had banished only a few years before. Through the parallel drawn between Juanito and Spanish bourgeois society we can see that these changes of government are inspired by a lack of conviction and not by any virtue or 'genuine, proper respect for order'. The values of the 'señorito' which are based on appearances and not reality are the values of this society.

The dichotomy between form and substance is obvious in the language of the inhabitants of this bourgeois world. For example, political debate is characterized by the heated argument between Casa-Muñoz and Aparisi: 'They outdid each other in trying to find the most elegant phrases: if the Marquis went to town with "constituting", "ad hoc", "sui generis" and other Latin terms, the other would rack his brains to come up with such choice examples as the "concatenation of ideas"' (p. 81). The substance is removed from political debate as it turns into a contest of rhetoric. Furthermore, as we might expect, Juanito Santa Cruz is a model of glibness. This characteristic is especially obvious when he finds it necessary to convince Jacinta that he has not *really* been unfaithful: 'What he wanted was to come out of it well, [. . .] presenting his wrongdoings as merits, distorting the whole story till what had started off as black and shameful . . . ended up looking white and noble. He did not have to over-exert his ingenuity to succeed, because his was a mind well-suited to such devious tricks' (pp. 313–14). Juanito is not only attracted by forms, but he is also a master of them. By his skillful manipulation of language he could appear to know more than he really did, and as we see here, he can turn the ugly truth into a polished lie. Juanito, then, uses language to hide rather than to express reality.

Yet, in spite of the narrator's recognition of the flaws of this society, he affirms strongly its innately positive nature:

> It is curious to see how this age of ours, so unfortunate in other respects, presents us with a happy confusion of all social classes or, to use a better phrase, their harmony and reconciliation . . . This confusion is a good thing: thanks to it we are not afraid of being infected by social strife, for we already have in our blood a mild, inoffensive form of socialism. Imperceptibly, helped by bureaucracy, poverty and the academic education received by every Spaniard, all the classes have become mixed and their members cross from one to another, weaving a dense web that binds and strengthens the nation. Birth means nothing to us, and all that is said about pedigree is mere talk. There are no social differences other than the essential ones based on good or bad education, stupidity or discretion, or spiritual inequalities as eternal as the qualities of spirit itself. The one other positive class distinction, that of money, is governed by economic principles which are as solid as the laws of physics; to try to change it would be like trying to drain the sea (pp. 65–6).

That this statement is only partially true is evident even in Part 1 where we are still limited to the point of view of the bourgeoisie. Certainly Fortunata and the crowds of children who are part of the fourth estate have never even dreamed of 'the academic education received by every Spaniard', and their difference from the members of the upper and middle classes is immediately obvious from their different ways of dressing and talking. Moreover, we see later on at a dinner at the home of the Santa Cruz a group of people which is supposedly a 'perfect sample of all the social classes' (p. 138), at which the two representatives of the lowest social position are Pepe Samaniego who is in exactly the same position where Baldomero I was when he began building his commercial empire, and Estupiñá who is nothing more than a glorified servant of the Santa Cruz and Arnaiz families.[8] There is, however, some truth in this lofty statement, and that truth is based on the transformation of the estates of the feudal world into the classes of modern society. Consequently members of the wealthy bourgeoisie were able to intermarry with members of the declining aristocracy, thereby blurring the line separating these two classes. Also correct is the affirmation that money is a (and in fact the most important) 'positive class distinction' since bourgeois society is historically unique in that within it social relations have a purely economic articulation. Thus in spite of the occasional 'success' of a Pepe Samaniego or an Estupiñá, the populace remains apart from the middle classes precisely because it cannot obtain capital. Nevertheless, although the growing importance of money and the lessening importance of birth in determining social rank is an accepted fact, to describe this change as 'a happy confusion of all social classes' is a gross distortion of that fact. For by maintaining that the laws of capitalism are 'as solid as the laws of physics', the narrator is merely echoing the opinions of bourgeois economists who cannot conceive of their system being superseded by another. In this rather long theoretical statement, then, the narrator expresses that view of society which is typical of the apologists of the bourgeoisie (and of dominant classes in general) according to which the status quo represents a state of concord, and therefore any talk of class conflict must necessarily be irrational and unjustified.[9]

Many of the narrator's other theoretical comments also reflect common bourgeois attitudes. For example, chapter IV, which is entitled 'The *Dauphin*'s perdition and salvation', is concerned with the period in Juanito's life when he immersed himself temporarily in the life of the common people. This temporary immersion is, of course, the 'perdition', and the 'salvation' is his return to the norms of bourgeois life. To an extent, then, the narrator shares the patronizing bourgeois attitude toward the common people. This attitude is manifest in Juanito's feeling that 'The education of a man of our times is incomplete if he does not come into contact with all kinds of people, if he does not get a glimpse of all possible situations in life, if he does not take the pulse of all the passions. It's all a form of study and education . . .' (p. 48), and it is further emphasized in his treatment of Fortunata. For Juanito, Fortunata and the entire working class exist merely as a plaything to amuse him whenever he wishes to be so amused. He regards them purely as objects, and he never stops to consider their humanity. This patronizing attitude is also manifest in Guillermina Pacheco's treatment of the working class. She is 'charitable' towards the poor but only within the limits of bourgeois ethics.[10] Thus she condemns Fortunata but excuses Juanito, and she handles the affair of Izquierdo and the false Pituso as though this child were merely another commodity. Like Juanito Santa Cruz, Guillermina sees the populace as an object which she can use to fulfill her egotistical needs without ever recognizing these people's humanity.

Both Juanito and Guillermina classify Fortunata according to the same commonplace philosophical concept. When Fortunata declares that she will always be working class, Juanito responds: '"That's right, the common people . . ." Juan observed with a touch of pedantry, "in other words: the basic ingredients of Humanity, its raw material, for when civilization loses touch with elemental emotions, primary ideas, then it has to look for them in the unhewn block, the quarry of the common people' (p. 278). The narrator undercuts Juanito's sincerity by noting that this observation was made with 'a touch of pedantry'. And his statement that 'when civilization loses touch with elemental emotions [. . .] it has to look for them in the unhewn block [. . .] of the common people' is merely a rationalization of his whimsical sexual appetite. Again he creates a linguistic mask to hide the true nature of reality. Finally, he reveals again in this statement his condescending attitude toward Fortunata and the working class. They exist merely as an object ('unhewn block') for the bourgeoisie ('civilization') to exploit whenever it 'needs' to do so. So Juanito's 'touch of pedantry' allows him to justify his despicable treatment of Fortunata to himself and to his class.

When Guillermina confronts Fortunata's 'idea', she observes, 'You [Fortunata] have no moral sense; you can never have principles because you're prior to civilization; you're a savage who belongs entirely to a primitive stage of development' (p. 407). Here Guillermina repeats a philosophical commonplace similar to the one pronounced by Juanito, and she too shows again her patronizing attitude toward the working class which is 'prior to civilization' while Guillermina, of course, lives in that advanced, progressive society characterized by the reconciliation of all classes![11] Here, in spite of his previous criticism of Juanito, the narrator restates his adherence to the dominant bourgeois thought by reiterating and expanding Guillermina's statement: 'in societies such as ours, the common people preserve all the primary ideas and emotions in their crude entirety, just as a quarry contains marble, the raw material from which form is created. The common people possess these great truths in the form of an unhewn block, and civilization turns to them as the petty truths that sustain it become exhausted' (p. 407). In this statement the narrator conceptualizes what he had suggested in his discussion of changing fashions; as the bourgeoisie rose as a class, it left behind in the common people certain styles and 'truths' which were essential to the existence of society. Now that, through its control of the national wealth, the bourgeoisie has established its separation from the populace, it must from time to time return to this 'unhewn block' to rediscover the 'great truths' it has left behind. This patronizingly benign attitude toward the common people is a further way of denying class conflict; if the 'civilized' bourgeoisie is so willing to admit – and even admire – the virtues of the lower classes, then why should these 'primitive' folk complain? And since in their poverty they are the retainer of the 'great truths', why should they aspire to anything else?

Throughout the novel – though particularly in part I – the attitudes of the bourgeoisie are expressed clearly by such characters as Baldomero, Juanito, and Guillermina, and are further reflected in the observations made by the narrator. In his portrayal of the rise of the bourgeoisie and its current status the narrator has presented a comprehensive bourgeois consciousness; even his criticisms of the status quo have been only vague commentaries which in no way threaten the interests of the ruling class. And these criticisms have been counterbalanced by an affirmation of the eternal nature of the underlying laws of capitalism and by the repeated denial of the existence of a basis for class conflict. Only as Fortunata emerges to become the dominant figure of the novel is the inadequacy of this stance fully revealed.

II. The petty bourgeoisie

In part 2 the novelistic center shifts to the petty bourgeois world of the Rubín family. The narrator is not so at home here as he was with the Santa Cruz. He has not known these people personally, and he is not too familiar with the history of this family. Therefore he cannot assert – although he doubts it – whether or not the name Rubín is Jewish, and he cannot verify the truth or falsity of the gossip about the infidelities of Maximiliana Llorente, the mother of the three Rubín brothers. This lack of history contrasts with the detailed account of the rise of the house of Santa Cruz, and it reflects the secondary social importance of the petty bourgeoisie as seen from the narrator's point of view.

The children of this class do not have the leisure to complete two university courses, as Juanito Santa Cruz was able to do. Rather, they must worry about practical economics, something which is never of concern to Juanito. Therefore Nicolás Rubín becomes a priest and Maximiliano a druggist. Lacking a university education, they do not mouth the commonplace philosophical sayings which came out of the university. So within this world there are no theoretical statements about the common people or the reconciliation of the classes, for these are not matters of immediate interest to the members of this class.

Since the petty bourgeoisie mediates the separation of the working class and the bourgeoisie, members of this class engage in daily interaction with the other two classes. For example, Doña Lupe employs Mauricia la Dura to peddle confiscated goods, and Maxi and Juan Pablo Rubín find themselves in café conversation with José Izquierdo and José Ido. On the other hand, petty bourgeois usurers, like Doña Lupe and Torquemada, gain a degree of control over certain 'señoritos' by keeping them in their debt, and Doña Lupe desires to be able to mix with the bourgeois ladies.

From this intermediate position, the Rubín family can consider Fortunata in a way very different from that in which the Santa Cruz saw her. Whereas Juanito Santa Cruz family scorned Fortunata because of her inferior social position and was attracted primarily by her beauty, the Rubín family are mainly concerned with the state of her virtue and are attracted not only by her beauty but also by other qualities such as her thriftiness and sincerity.

In spite of their somewhat sympathetic attitude toward Fortunata, the Rubín family, in different degrees, still regard her as an object through which they hope to satisfy egotistical impulses. Maximiliano falls deeply in love with Fortunata, but his love is inspired by his desire to redeem her, to make her 'respectable': 'his insane enthusiasm drove him to undertake the social and moral salvation of his idol, and to devote all his clamouring mental energies to this glorious task' (p. 173). Maxi becomes so caught up in his 'plan of regeneration' (p. 174) that he loses sight of the real Fortunata. Doña Lupe is attracted to Fortunata by a desire to reform her: 'Her passion for domestication was awakened by the sight of this magnificent beast asking for a skilful hand to tame her' (p. 224). Doña Lupe vacillates ('It's impossible, she's too much of a woman for someone who's not enough of a man' [p. 225]), but in the end her 'passion for domestication' wins. Finally, Nicolás Rubín sees in Fortunata an opportunity for him to show off the efficacy of his priestly talents: '"Here's an opportunity for me to shine," he thought. "If I pull this one off, it'll be the most glorious Christian triumph a priest could ever boast of"' (p. 214). Fortunata provides Nicolás with an opportunity to improve his professional position and prestige. For all three of these characters, Fortunata becomes merely a means to an end, and her humanity ceases to be of importance; in spite of their appreciation of certain of Fortunata's human qualities they see her as an 'unhewn block' which they will model to suit their taste.

Their method of educating her is based on bourgeois convention. Doña Lupe and Maxi are continually correcting the popular idioms in Fortunata's speech, and Nicolás instructs her according to 'routine formulas or stale aphorisms from books written by saints cast in his own mold' (p. 216). Her instruction by the Micaelas is merely a continuation of Nicolás's formulaic approach. Thus the Micaelas, like her other educators, did not deal with Fortunata's personality: 'The truth was that, in everything concerning the vast realm of the passions, the nuns scarcely employed their educatory capacity – either because they knew nothing of that realm, or because they were frightened of approaching its frontiers' (p. 248). Fortunata is educated by convention and formula, and her educators expect this instruction to lead her to adapt herself to the established pattern of middle-class living. They are destined to fail because they treat Fortunata as an object and disregard the very human passion which is crucial to her existence.

III. The working class

Unlike the middle class, the working class does not have any one part of this novel which is essentially all its own. Rather, the role of the most important representative of this class, Fortunata, is dependent upon her relations with members of the middle classes. In fact, since the narrator shares the perspective of the bourgeoisie, we can see that her story never would have been told had she not been found by Juanito Santa Cruz; the narrator asserts that 'if Juanito Santa Cruz had not paid that visit [during which he met Fortunata] this story would not have been written. Another one would have, because wherever man goes, he takes his novel with him; but it would not have been this one' (p. 40). If Juanito had not made that visit and therefore not found Fortunata her story would probably never have been told, for that hypothetical 'other' story would surely still have been Juanito's, that is, another account of the life of the bourgeoisie. Moreover, since Juanito is the only narrator of his first affair with Fortunata, our initial responses to her are based on his egotistical bourgeois point of view.

Aside from the background information which Juanito provides about her, Fortunata too fills in a few details about her past. The narrator, however, has made no effort to investigate this part of Fortunata's life. This lack of 'history' shows that Fortunata's past is of little interest to the narrator because it would merely reveal a lack of variation in the role played by the common people. Thus, like Fortunata's mother, her aunt is an egg-seller, and, if she had not fallen into the hands of Juanito Santa Cruz, her own fate would have been similar. Unlike the middle classes, the lot of the working class was not improved during the nineteenth century, and so it produced none of the interesting details which the narrator found in the stories of the bourgeoisie and petty bourgeoisie.[12] Whereas the histories of the Santa Cruz and Rubín families represented the rise which their respective classes experienced during the period of bourgeois ascendancy, the lack of history in Fortunata's case represents the constancy – in terms of its place on the social ladder – of the experience of the working class during that same period.

In Part 2 Fortunata emerges from this sparse background, and she asserts her presence in such a way that she remains the center of attention for most of the rest of the novel. She reappears for the first time since that brief moment in Part 1 when Maximiliano's friend, Olmedo, introduces the young Rubín to this 'delectable morsel' (p. 164). Maxi immediately falls in love with her and begins formulating his plans for reforming her. At first Fortunata thinks Maxi's declaration is merely another deceit, but eventually his sincerity convinces her that he is quite serious. At this point she begins to vacillate between accepting Maxi's offer because she desires to achieve a respectable position in life and rejecting it because he is physically repulsive to her. This vacillation between her desire for respectability and her physical impulse persists and becomes the basis of Fortunata's behavior throughout the novel. When the former desire dominates, Fortunata consents to marry Maxi, but then as soon as she confronts Juanito again, her physical impulse erases all desire for respectability. Later in the novel she again accepts the dominance of this desire when Feijoo arranges for her reconciliation with Maxi, but this solution also fails, although, as we shall see, for different reasons.

This battle between her desire for respectability and her physical impulse is reflected in Fortunata's attitude toward Jacinta. She admires Jacinta in many ways, and she goes so far as to posit her rival as a model of moral perfection. So, despite Fortunata's resentment of Jacinta's 'theft' of Juanito, she feels a strong motivation to become exactly like her: 'I detest her, but I like looking at her, which means I'd like to look like her, be like her, and I'd change all my natural being to make myself just like she is' (p. 336). Here the vacillation which Fortunata felt regarding her impending marriage to Maxi takes a different form. The physical impulse within her which finds Maxi repulsive also produces a feeling of resentment towards Jacinta while her desire for respectability which leads her to marry Maxi also makes her admire Jacinta.

After the two rivals meet, Fortunata feels a 'strong desire to be not just equal but superior to the other woman' (p. 386). This desire then turns into a reassertion of her physical impulse, this time in the form of scorn for Jacinta's sterility. She tells Guillermina. 'Even though I like her [Jacinta], and would like to be like her in some ways, in others I wouldn't, because she may be as saintly as you say, but she's beneath me in one thing: *she's had no children,* and when it comes to having children I don't stoop to her, I lift my head, ma'am . . . That's my idea, it's an idea I've had' (p. 405). Here for the first time Fortunata's 'idea' emerges, replacing her previous wish to be 'just like' Jacinta. Never again does she repeat this first wish which sprang out of her initial impression of Jacinta. Although she still wants to be like Jacinta in some ways, in 'others' – namely the ability to have children – she now recognizes her superiority to her rival. The previous contradiction of admiring Jacinta while still hating her is redefined as the opposition of a tempered admiration to a sense of disdain. Fortunata still admires and desires Jacinta's respectability while on the other hand feeling that her rival is 'beneath her' because of her sterility.

We see, then, that as Fortunata struggles with her contradictory feelings she is continually developing an awareness of her situation. Her efforts to deal with the presence of Jacinta inspire a sense of class consciousness in her: 'If we were all like you [Jacinta], living with respectable people, happily married to the man we love, with all our needs satisfied, we'd be just the same as you. Yes, ma'am; I'd be what you are if I were in your place . . . There's no special merit in it, after all . . . If you think there is, try changing places with me, put yourself in the position I've been in since *he* deceived me, and then we'd see what perfections the little angel would come up with' (p. 376). Fortunata expresses here and in other places her awareness of the privileges Jacinta enjoys as a member of the bourgeoisie. And she recognizes that differences in social position have distorted the equation which otherwise would have existed between her own essential respectability and that of Jacinta.

She also despairs at being treated like a plaything by her middle-class companions:

> Things always turn out wrong for me . . . God never listens. Look how he sets all the odds against me . . . Why couldn't the man I loved have been some poor bricklayer? No, he had to be a rich young gentleman, so he could deceive me and not be able to marry me . . . Then the natural thing would have been for me to hate him; but no, just my bad luck, I love him even more . . . The natural thing after that would have been for him to leave me alone, so I could forget all about it; but no, sir, my bad luck again; he tries to track me down and lays a snare for me . . . Then the natural thing would be for no decent man to want to marry me; but no, sir, up turns Maxi and . . . there he is pushing me into marriage and, before I've had a chance to think about it, I'm before the altar . . . (p. 276).

This recognition of her condition of objectness goes along with a preoccupation about whether or not she will ever be able to break the bonds of this condition: 'She wondered whether she would ever have guts, initiative . . . whether one day she would do what came from deep inside herself' (p. 275). We can see, then, that Fortunata has a good understanding of the nature of her condition. She has been handled as a plaything by Juanito Santa Cruz, for whom she is little more than a love object, and by Maxi, Doña Lupe, Nicolás, and even Guillermina, all of whom see her as an object to be transformed by their redemptive powers. None of these characters understands the strength of Fortunata that comes 'from deep inside herself', the strength that is inspired by her sincerity and her constant love for Juanito Santa Cruz.

She, too, remains unaware of this strength until her 'idea' impels her to 'have guts', and then she decides to renew her affair with Juanito even if she has to search him out to do it: 'If he doesn't come looking for me, I'll go in search of him . . . I've got this idea of mine, no one can take it away from me' (p. 411). So, in their third affair, unlike the preceding ones, Fortunata is not merely letting herself be used by Juanito. Rather she is looking for something more than just her lover's company. She is seeking the fulfillment of her 'idea'.

When Juanito questions her about this 'idea', she refuses to explain it to him because she knows he will not understand:

> 'So what is this idea of yours? What kind of idea?'
>
> 'I won't tell you . . . It's my idea: if I told you, you'd think it barbaric. You wouldn't understand . . . But do you think I'm not capable of having original ideas like you?'
>
> 'What you have, my black eyes, is all the charm in the world,' he said, kissing her romantically.
>
> 'Well then . . . if you want the charm, you'll have to take the idea too . . . And if my idea works out . . . That's all I'm going to tell you' (p. 414).

Juanito cannot comprehend Fortunata's having an 'idea'. For him she can have 'all the charm in the world', that is, the primitive substance contained in the common people, but she cannot have an 'idea', for that would violate his conception of her as a primitive, passive being. Fortunata, on the other hand, shows that she has come to a new realization of her situation when she affirms that 'if you want the charm, you'll have to take the idea too'. Unlike the passive role she played in the previous two affairs, here she will take the initiative necessary to fulfil her plan.

The full meaning of this 'idea' does not become manifest until Fortunata again gives birth to a son of Juanito's. The birth of this heir to the house of Santa Cruz, the incarnation of Fortunata's 'idea', represents the fulfillment of her wish to be not just equal but superior to Jacinta ('I don't mind comparisons now. What a difference there is between her [Jacinta] and me! . . . ' [p. 504]) and establishes unequivocally her legitimacy by the 'true bonds [. . .] of blood' (p. 504). Therefore Fortunata does not appeal to Juanito for recognition and assistance, for she knows from past experience that he is untrustworthy. Instead she demands recognition from Don Baldomero and Doña Bárbara of their 'one and only grandson' (p. 505).

Here Fortunata is dealing with the opposition between substance and form. According to form, in this instance the convention of marriage, Jacinta is Juanito's legitimate wife and Fortunata is nothing but a prostitute, and according to that convention Fortunata could never challenge Jacinta's position. Yet Fortunata could never accept the 'reality' of the conventional viewpoint. She felt that she had a genuine claim to Juanito since he had loved her before he had loved his wife, he had promised to marry her, and she had had his child. She eventually realizes that within the context of conventional legitimacy she can never contest Jacinta's claim since bourgeois society would never admit a challenge to one of its conventions from a 'daughter of the people'. Fortunata's response to this predicament is the formulation and fulfillment of her 'idea' through which she establishes her position as an irreplaceable member of the Santa Cruz family. And this 'idea' is based on an affirmation of substance and a rejection of form. Fortunata dismisses the institution of marriage as practised by the bourgeoisie as 'so much smoke', as an institution which becomes impotent when confronted by 'the natural' (p. 483). She has understood that to bourgeois society she is nothing but a plaything, so to resolve her dilemma she has looked away from that society to the strength which she has 'deep inside herself'.

The contrast that exists between Fortunata's inner self and bourgeois convention is accentuated during the presentation of the events surrounding her death. She experiences a fatal hemorrhage during which she comes to understand that she will die. At the same time she is also inspired with a new 'idea', the plan to leave her child to Jacinta, and she feels that this 'idea' will provide her eternal salvation ('It's the key to the gates of heaven' [p. 536]). Since she believes that she has had direct contact with an angel from above, she denies any need for sacraments ('With my idea I've no need of sacraments; because it was a voice from above' [p. 537]). Guillermina, however, disagrees. As the spokesman for conventional religion, she insists on having these sacraments performed. When Fortunata tells her, 'I too . . . didn't you know . . . am an angel', Guillermina replies, 'An angel? . . . Sure . . . you will be if you cleanse your soul', and she demands that Fortunata confess and reject her 'fiendish idea . . . that marriage, without children, is null and void . . . and that you, having had children, are the true wife' (p. 540). From its inception, this 'idea', because of its unconventional nature, has escaped Guillermina's comprehension. Now, as Fortunata is fulfilling her sacrifice for the Santa Cruz family, Guillermina is still insisting on convention. Fortunata has sacrificed her life so that there could be an heir to the house of Santa Cruz, but Guillermina cannot comprehend this *substantial* action because it has not been accomplished according to established form.

Through the fulfillment of her 'idea', Fortunata achieves the reconciliation of the opposing sentiments which have been the foundation of her behavior. She no longer envies Jacinta nor does she despise her. Rather, now that she had provided the Santa Cruz with an heir, she feels a sense of companionship with her rival of old. Therefore, when she attacks Aurora (Juanito's current mistress), she does so in Jacinta's name as well as in her own, maintaining that 'both of us have been wronged' (p. 517). And she feels that her final sacrifice qualifies her, too, to be an 'angel' like Jacinta: 'I'm an angel . . . as well as her . . . a heavenly angel' (p. 541). In her effort to imitate Jacinta, Fortunata was forced to look into herself to discover how she too could achieve an 'angelical' status, and through the result, her 'idea', she achieved the reconciliation of her desire for respectability and her physical impulse; her respectability, in the form of the recognition of her son as the 'one and only family heir', is established precisely through the force of her physical impulse, her constant desire for Juanito Santa Cruz.[13]

This sense of companionship is shared by Jacinta:

> She [Jacinta] could not take her mind off the person who had . . . ceased to exist that morning, and she was amazed to find in her heart feelings beyond mere pity for that unfortunate woman, something that perhaps involved a sense of comradeship, a bond forged by mutual suffering. She remembered that the dead woman had been her bitterest enemy; but the final stages of their enmity and that incredible act of bequeathing Pituso to her brought with them a kind of reconciliation beyond her rational comprehension. Straddling death, one of them in this world of the visible, the other in the world of the invisible, it was as if the two women were looking at each other, trying and wanting to embrace' (pp. 542–3).

Although Guillermina is unwilling to admit Fortunata's 'angelical' status, Jacinta cedes it to her by recognizing her as an equal. And this experience leads Jacinta to a new level of awareness. When Juanito tries to make up with her by employing his always successful glibness, she rejects him firmly; 'Do as you like. You're as free as the wind. Your deceptions don't touch me', and the narrator adds, 'This was not mere words, and the trials of real life showed the Dauphin that this time she meant it' (p. 543). Jacinta rejects Juanito once and for all, thus putting an end to 'the continuance of that suffering [which] had destroyed Jacinta's respect for her husband' (p. 543). Jacinta's experience of Fortunata has led to this qualitative change; her continual suffering now turns into disdain.

As the novel ends, the structure of the relations among the central characters is rearranged. In Part 1 everything had been centered round Juanito Santa Cruz. As noted before, *Fortunata and Jacinta* began as Juanito's novel, and his presence had mediated the roles of his wife and his lover; with him as mediator, they had been enemies. At the end, however, Juanito is 'disowned' – rejected by his wife and rebuked by his mother – and the companionship of the former rivals is now mediated by Fortunata's son:

> Jacinta was devoted to him [the child] body and soul . . . When she was alone with him, the good woman passed the time by constructing imaginary castles in her daring thoughts, with flimsy towers and domes still less substantial, being built of thought alone. The features of the son of the house were hers and not the other woman's. So powerful was her imagination that the would-be mother even started to intoxicate herself with the fanciful memory of having carried that bonny baby in her womb, and to shudder at the thought of the pains she had suffered to bring him into the world. These games of her idle fancy were followed by reflections on the state of mismanagement of this world's affairs. She too had an idea about the bonds sanctioned by law, and broke them in thought, performing the impossible feat of turning the clock back, of altering and exchanging people's qualities, endowing this person with that person's heart, or this other person with someone else's head, all in all making such extravagant corrections to the world's overall fabric that God himself would have laughed had he known, as would his vicar in skirts Guillermina Pacheco' (p. 544).

This passage demonstrates the profound effect that Fortunata has had on Jacinta, for here Jacinta too begins questioning the propriety of established circumstances. When the narrator comments, 'She too had an idea,' it is clear that the person on the other side of that 'too' is Fortunata. And the imaginary process of changing around faces and hearts which Jacinta undergoes was experienced frequently by Fortunata, who repeatedly wished Juanito were a 'poor bricklayer', and who constantly rebelled against 'those wretched governing circumstances' (p. 413). The roles of the two rivals are now reversed as Jacinta begins to imitate Fortunata; as Fortunata used to dream about being Juanito's wife, Jacinta now imagines that she has had his baby. In this way, then, Fortunata's sacrifice has given the Santa Cruz not only a new life, but also a new sense of awareness since Jacinta now begins to question the conventions of bourgeois society which she had always observed so meticulously. And although she manages to erase Fortunata's image from the face of Juan Evaristo, her imitation of her one-time rival indicates that she cannot erase the substance of the contribution made by Fortunata.

Fortunata and Jacinta also began as the novel of the bourgeoisie, with the narrator as well as the principal characters serving as the articulators of the point of view of this class. Thus we were told about a society which had achieved a benevolent 'confusion of [. . .] classes'. Even at the moment of the first expression of Fortunata's 'idea', we were led by that patronizingly benign attitude which saw the common people as a primitive 'unhewn block'. In Part 4, however, this type of formulation of bourgeois attitudes is absent. We see, for example, a new 'confusion of [. . .] classes' at Fortunata's house in the Cava when, because of her son, such people as Guillermina, Jacinta, Bárbara, and Maximiliano come to visit this humble establishment. This 'confusion' is created not by Don Baldomero's 'patriarchal beneficence' but by Fortunata's 'idea'. Thus Fortunata demonstrates the new power she has attained, for she now commands the full attention of those who once disdained her. The 'daughter of the people' who was seen as nothing more than an object lacking all the qualities of 'civilized' society, has now forced members of that society to come to her and recognize her as the most powerful agent of the novel. But the narrator makes no comment about this occurrence. In his silence he seems to be respecting Fortunata's dictum that 'When nature speaks, men have to hold their peace'. Fortunata has overcome the barriers which society has placed in her way, and this achievement is reflected in the elimination of those commonplace pronouncements which had 'defined' all aspects of the novel according to the interests of the bourgeoisie; now the facts will talk, and worthless rhetoric will be disposed of. Not only has Fortunata transformed the lives of the other characters, she has altered the structure of the novel.

We can see, then, the extent of the impact produced by the fulfillment of Fortunata's 'idea'. That impact is so profound precisely because, through her 'idea', Fortunata demonstrates a capability to act as agent that her middle class companions had denied her. She is unwilling to be merely Juanito's love object, something he can take or leave as he chooses. So she shows that she is something more than an 'animal', and even more than 'the unhewn block of the common people, where those emotions have to be sought that civilization has lost by over-refining them' (p. 279). This commonplace attitude, espoused by Juanito Santa Cruz, Guillermina Pacheco, and the narrator, is shown by the action of this novel to be only a half truth. Fortunata proves herself to be more than just an 'unhewn block', for she does not allow herself to be molded according to the whims of her bourgeois companions. Instead she achieves self-fulfillment through a negation of bourgeois conventions.

This novel has also shown that the working class is more than just an 'unhewn block' in that it is composed of many different individuals with their own independent personalities. There is, for example, a great difference between the personalities of José Izquierdo and José Ido, Severiana and Segunda, and Mauricia and Fortunata. Their outstanding similarities are their poverty and their alienation from the middle classes. To regard all of these people as a collective, totally primitive block is wrong. Therefore, the statements about the common people as an 'unhewn block' or 'raw material' are right only in so far as they recognize this class as the retainer of the vitality of human existence which the middle classes are losing through their ever increasing preoccupation with things. For they are wrong in so far as they separate the common people from the rest of 'civilization'. As we see clearly in the case of Fortunata, the working class is not content with its alienated condition. Rather, the desire to achieve respectability and so be accepted by the rest of society competes with its physical impulse. But, unfortunately for society, the patronizing attitude of the middle classes towards the common people which, by denying its subjectivity, in essence is denying the humanity of this class, makes the fulfillment of this desire for respectability quite difficult. So a monumental figure like Fortunata must break those barriers from below, thereby providing the middle classes with a new awareness of the inadequacy of its conventions.[14]

Through her influence on Jacinta, Fortunata gives bourgeois society a new consciousness. Previously Jacinta had accepted Juanito's glib rationalization that 'Our ideas ought to be inspired by the ideas of the majority, since they form the moral climate in which we live. Of course I know we should aim for perfection, but not if this means upsetting the harmony of the world . . . which is . . . a grand machine composed of imperfections, wonderfully balanced and combined' (p. 147). Now, however, she rebels against 'the state of mismanagement of this world's affairs'. Jacinta finally recognizes that the platitudinous positivism preached by Juanito merely supports the position of those who benefit from it, and so she recognizes the necessity of challenging the status quo.

In spite of the drastic changes effected by Fortunata, *Fortunata and Jacinta* is clearly not a revolutionary novel nor is the class conflict its only focus. For one thing, as such critics as Sherman Eoff and Stephen Gilman have pointed out, it is an intensely psychological novel.[15] Moreover, an argument can be made for reversing the relation that I have established between the *natural-social* opposition and the class conflict. And, most importantly, Fortunata brings redemption rather than revolution to the middle classes.[16] For, although one degenerate element (the 'señorito', Juanito) has been 'disowned', and Jacinta has been given a new awareness and a new motivation, the foundations of bourgeois society have not been overthrown. Thus, despite the dialectical development of her rebellion, Fortunata is still tied to religious vocabulary at her death, and her son is to be reared in bourgeois surroundings, however regenerated they might be. This choice of redemption rather than revolution demonstrates the petty bourgeois nature of Galdós's consciousness. For even though he was able to see and portray the immense contradictions (which a purely bourgeois, ruling class, consciousness would deny) in the smooth façade that Restoration society tried to present, he did not (as would proletarian consciousness) see the historical task of the proletariat as being the revolutionary transformation of society. Therefore, in spite of the great strength and independence which Fortunata achieves, she is unable to break definitively with the bonds which tie her to her 'betters', and consequently she ends up making a sacrifice for a 'healthier' continuation of bourgeois society.

The end of the novel is then necessarily ambiguous. To an extent it is 'optimistic'. The union between the 'señorito' and the 'daughter of the people' has produced an offspring which, unlike so many others, will be reared by the bourgeoisie because Fortunata has willed it that way; this child is not to become another forgotten member of the 'unhewn block'. And the working class has provided the bourgeoisie not only with a new life but also with a new sense of awareness which *should* lead to a less conventional, more vital society in the future. Yet this 'optimism' is guarded. After the narrator describes Jacinta's rebuke of the *Dauphin*, he turns immediately to examine her dedication to the *little Dauphin*. This is the first time the baby is referred to by this name, and it suggests that Jacinta may never realize her 'idea' and that, in spite of her new sense of awareness, the child may be raised to be a 'señorito' just like his father.

This hint of 'pessimism' is carried out in the final moments of the novel. When Ballester takes Maxi to see Fortunata's grave, they see the funeral procession of Evaristo Feijoo enter the cemetery, and this occurrence recalls Feijoo's oft-repeated assertion that he did not want to die without leaving Fortunata 'in a proper, decorous situation' (p. 352). This situation which Feijoo conceived of as the restoration of Fortunata's married life with Maxi turns out to be her death. Moreover, Maximiliano's experience of Fortunata and especially of her death leads him, too, to a new sense of awareness. He admits that their marriage had been a mistake because 'We didn't take Nature into account' (p. 547). So Maxi, too, realizes that Fortunata was not merely the object he had conceived her to be. This recognition of his error leads him to desire a withdrawal from this world which had fooled him so badly, and so he requests to go to a monastery. But, convinced of her nephew's insanity, Doña Lupe has him taken to an asylum, Leganés. Maxi, however, is not deceived: 'Do these fools think they can deceive me? This is Leganés. I accept it, accept it and keep quiet, to show the complete submission of my will to whatever the world wishes to do with my body. They cannot shut my thoughts behind walls. I live among the stars. They can put the man they call Maximiliano Rubín in a palace or a dung heap. It's all the same' (p. 548). Only through this escape from the reality of everyday life can Maxi come to solutions for all his problems, since his logic, which functions very well when it is not interrupted by emotions, in incapable of coping with the person of Fortunata. This ending suggests, then, that the only true 'proper, decorous situation' is death and that absolute solutions can be found only in the realm of Pure Thought. Therefore the resolution offered by Fortunata's 'idea' of the differences between the working class and the bourgeoisie can only be a potential solution to the problems of society, for those who must carry out this resolution continue, unlike Feijoo and Maxi, to live in the world of material reality where it does make a difference if one is in a palace or a dung heap and where idealist solutions cannot be realized.

Notes

1. Carr, R., 1966, *Spain: 1808–1939*, Oxford University Press, Oxford.
2. 'In 1876 an intercyclical crisis occurred [. . .] . Internationally this crisis meant a change for the worse, but in Spain it signalled the beginning of the most brilliant period of the nineteenth century: the decade from 1876 to 1886, on whose golden crest the Restoration was built. We shall refer to the period as that of 'the gold fever', since that was the term used in Catalonia at the time' (Vicens Vives, J., 1967, *Manual de la historia económica de España*, Editorial Vicens Vives, Barcelona, p. 674).
3. I will differentiate between the bourgeoisie and the petty bourgeoisie, but for convenience's sake I will at times group these two classes together under the term 'middle classes'.
4. All reference to *Fortunata and Jacinta* will be to volume 5 of the Sainz de Robles edition of the *Obras completas* (1950, Aguilar, Madrid).
5. 'Foreigners were disappointed at the drab European clothes that were ousting picturesque national costumes' (Kiernan, E. V. G., 1966, *The Revolution of 1854 in Spanish History*, Oxford University Press, Oxford p. 18).
6. This examination of changes in dress and customs suggests a type of romantic nostalgia for 'the good old days' before the advent of 'European seriousness'. In a discussion apropos of the Romantic experience, Ernst Fischer (1962, *The Necessity of Art: a Marxist Approach*, trans. A. Bostock, Penguin, Harmondsworth, p. 54) comments, 'The writer's and artist's "I", isolated and turned back upon itself, struggling for existence by selling itself in the market-place, yet challenging the bourgeois world as a "genius", dreamed of a lost unity and yearned for a collective imaginatively projected either into the past or into the future'.
7. 'The true power of the new class, its true liberation from a lineageless origin in the "tiers état" could very well be symbolized [. . .] in the rearing of a non-productive son, a "señorito" (only half in jest called *Dauphin*) who would compete with his aristocratic counterparts in uselessness and in his love of leisure and women of the working class' (Blanco Aguinaga, C., 1968, 'On the birth of Fortunata', *Anales Galdosianos* **3**: 15).
8. And in fact, thanks to Moreno Isla's assistance, Pepe Samaniego later becomes the proprietor of a clothing store.

9. This relation between progress and social harmony is an important tenet of Krausist thought. In his *El krausismo español* (1956, Fondo de Cultura Económica, Mexico City), Juan López Morillas observes, 'The progress of human social integration can be traced from the family, the primary level of association which in essence contains all the others, to the groupings of States or ecumenical religions; this progress does not exclude momentary relapses, but its general trend clearly illustrates man's instinctive or rational belief that living means "living in a positive, harmonious relation" with one's fellow human beings. Strictly speaking, this is the only meaning which Krausist philosophy attaches to "progress"' (pp. 80–1).

10. J. L. Brooks (1961, 'The character of Doña Guillermina Pacheco in Galdós' novel *Fortunata y Jacinta*', *Bulletin of Hispanic Studies* **38**: 86–94) says of her, 'Like so many other characters of her class in the novels, she is hampered in her efforts to be truly charitable by the unbreakable bonds which bind her to her background and by her oversimplification of religious doctrines' (p. 94). And Ricardo Gullón (1968, 'Estructura y diseño en *Fortunata y Jacinta*', *Papeles de Son Armadans* **48**: 223–316) observes that Guillermina 'is a bourgeois saint: she calls for charity for the poor, not justice; she wants to relieve their situation. She believes as much in middle class values as she does in Christian ones; and perhaps the former seem to her a convenient corrective to the latter, for these, if they were to be accepted as laid down in the Gospels, would hardly be compatible with the social organization she finds herself so comfortably part of. Her morality is that of the ruling middle classes: the poor are different, from another class' (p. 250).

11. This attitude has its base in the Krausist philosophy of history, according to which the history of Man is divided into three stages. López Morillas describes the first stage as follows: 'The first stage thus corresponds to that of the infancy of human societies. Primitive man is a rudimentary being who finds himself in a world in which he has not yet been able to define himself as an individual [. . .]. The vision that primitive man has of things is too confused for him to impose himself on them or use them as the basis of his own freedom of action. The embryonic state of his mind also makes him unable to achieve differentiation' (p. 42). According to these 'sophisticated' members of the bourgeoisie, Fortunata, although living in the nineteenth century, has not passed beyond this initial stage of human development.

12. Blanco Aguinaga observes, 'Fortunata simply belongs to the "fourth estate" and, like everybody else in it, she is socially speaking an orphan. This is the *basic* reason why, in opposing Juanito to Fortunata (*and* Jacinta to Fortunata), genealogy is contrasted with the lack of genealogy, and the birth of the hero to the sudden *appearance* [. . .] of the "heroine", as if from nowhere' (p. 18). Limited by his bourgeois consciousness, the narrator would not be interested in those changes – for example urbanization and increasing poverty – which the lower classes had undergone.

13. Sherman Eoff (1949, 'The treatment of the individual personality in *Fortunata y Jacinta*', *Hispanic Review* **17**: 269–89) also understands Fortunata's development in terms of dialectical process. He sees Fortunata as embarked on a quest for self-respect, but on a quest which is essentially psychological since 'The social themes [. . .] are strictly incidental' (p. 282).

On the other hand, I see the dialectical process of Fortunata's development within the context of critical realism.

Following Eoff's lead, ANTHONY ZAHAREAS (1965, 'The tragic sense in *Fortunata y Jacinta*', *Symposium* **19**: 38–49) also attempts to apply dialectics to *Fortunata and Jacinta*. He talks, for example, of the negation of certain personality traits by others. But he denies the possibility of the reconciliation of opposites: 'Thus the incapacity to synthesize vital realities projects, conceptually, the vulnerability of the human condition' (p. 46), whereas I would maintain that through the fulfillment of her 'idea' Fortunata does achieve the reconciliation of her contradictory sentiments. For it is precisely through this reconciliaton that she transcends the limits which society seeks to impose upon her.

14. In his discussion of the contemporary novels, ANTONIO REGALADO (1966, '*Benito Pérez Galdós y la novela histórica española*', Insula, Madrid) observes, 'In social and intellectual sectors, protests and calls to action are making themselves heard [. . .] These clouds on the horizon do not weaken Galdós in his resolve to write about the manners of the middle class, protected by Cánovas's stability and order, which he had openly and firmly supported. The criticism of the society of his day in his contemporary novels is not an attack on the Restoration' (p. 191), and 'Galdós's entire work is geared towards defending the *status quo* of the Restoration, and directed against the two main threats to its stability: political revolution and the forms of social change represented by the aspirations of the fourth estate, as expressed in socialist and anarchist ideology' (p. 193). True, Galdós did not portray accurately the revolutionary proletariat in these novels, and he did lend his support to Restoration politics by joining Sagasta's ranks. But I do not think that these aspects of his 'life and works' provide sufficient support for criticism like the above, nor do Regalado's brief analyses of the contemporary novels convince me that such criticism is valid.

In a discussion of nineteenth-century European realism, GEORG LUKÁCS (1950, *Studies in European Realism*, trans. E. Bone. Hillway, London) follows the lead of Engels in praising Balzac in spite of his monarchism and even though 'showing the revolutionary working-class was quite beyond the range of Balzac's vision' (pp. 45, 46). And although Lukács admires Zola the man for his staunch defense of democratic principles, he argues against Zolaesque naturalism. At least within the context of Lukács's Marxism, a writer's political views and actions do not necessarily affect the value of his artistic production. In agreement with Lukács, I would argue that Galdós's participation in Restoration politics does not mean that his novels supported the regime. To the contrary, especially in *Fortunata and Jacinta* he presents a picture of a middle class society which for historical reasons is decaying; having attained its position of dominance, the middle classes are satisfied and therefore want to deny the possibility of any further revolution. Furthermore, Fortunata, although no revolutionary, is both an individual and a representative of the working class, and her experience is firmly rooted in the problem of class cleavage. I cannot, therefore, agree with Regalado when he maintains that 'Galdós's criticisms [. . .] are those which any society makes of itself' (p. 191), for I see, especially in *Fortunata and Jacinta* (which, curiously, Regalado ignores), a critical realism based on the movement of historical currents.

15. Particularly Eoff, *art. cit.*, and Gilman, 1970, 'The consciousness of Fortunata', *Anales Galdosianos* **5**: 55–65.
16. For this and many other helpful observations I am indebted to Robert Russell of Dartmouth College.

10 Galdós and the Nineteenth-Century Novel: The Need for an Interdisciplinary Approach*

Peter B. Goldman

This piece represents the documentary strand of Galdós criticism which, in the 1970s in particular, sought to explain his work in the light of extra-fictional evidence (here Galdós's journalistic writings). Goldman is perhaps too ready to assume that the novels are straightforward reflections of Galdós's opinions as expressed in his journalism (leaving aside the question of whether journalism truly represents its author's opinions; it is a pity Goldman does not tell us what journals Galdós was writing for, and what their political bias was). His article would also have benefited from some theoretical discussion of the generic relations between journalism and fiction in the nineteenth century. Nevertheless this piece provides an essential compendium of Galdós's journalistic writing on various social issues. Galdós's hostility to state control, consistent with his liberal sympathies, is illustrated in his fiction: the novels of the 1880s show the institutions of the State to be the source of Spain's economic and moral problems; the protagonists of the novels of the 1890s reject all forms of institutionalism and explore individual solutions to social ills. Particularly interesting is the information given here on Galdós's interest in criminology: this is a subject to which Foucault's insights could profitably be applied. As Goldman rightly points out, for Galdós the figure of the criminal was indissolubly linked with that of the saint (and that of the anarchist and madman): a moral paradox explored in embryonic form in *Fortunata and Jacinta*, and foregrounded in the disturbing later novels *La incógnita*, *Realidad*, *Angel Guerra*, *Nazarín* and *Misericordia*, which deserve to be better known. Goldman's plea for an interdisciplinary approach to Galdós studies (which would hopefully go beyond the literary and journalistic disciplines

* Reprinted from 1975, *Anales Galdosianos* **10**: 5–18.

represented here) has been largely ignored; in this age of cultural studies it seems especially opportune.

The extremely lengthy notes to the original article have been reduced owing to limitations of space.

In recent years, several scholars have pointed out that few students of Galdós's novels make use of his non-fictional prose despite the fact that he worked with both forms simultaneously, and often borrowed material from his articles for incorporation into a novel.[1] Even fewer investigators have moved in the direction of studying Galdós and his contemporaries in their social and historical contexts.[2] Yet such an approach is particularly necessary in Galdós studies, since every line of his writing exhibits a remarkable sensitivity to Spanish national politics and to the issues of his day. Indeed, most Galdós scholars would agree that he utilizes contemporaneous historical and social realities as a framework for his novels. Such an assumption carries with it, implicitly, the recognition of a socio-historic dimension inherent in Galdós's literary aesthetic.[3] It further raises the fundamental question of his vision of reality, the particular view he entertains of the world around him and about which he is constantly writing. Therefore his aesthetic must be considered from three angles: first, what was the social reality in which Galdós lived and wrote;[4] second, how did he *perceive* that reality (what was important to him, what inconsequential); and third, what were the alterations which that reality and his view of it underwent as they were absorbed by Galdós, transformed by his imagination, and incorporated into his works? If we accept this tripartite approach to Galdós's novels and to their critical elucidation, we must also accept the need for complementing historically and sociologically the admirable work done thus far in Galdós criticism. Such a complementary approach would begin not only by defining Galdós's socio-historical context; it would also entail a study of how he considered that reality in his non-fiction, independently of an examination of the novels.[5]Recent efforts to place Galdós in his historical context have demonstrated the necessity of this tripartite methodology. For example, in 1965 Antonio Regalado García published a work which attempted to determine the ideological content of Galdós's novels in general and of the *National episodes* in particular.[6] He suggested that far from being progressive and liberal, Galdós was in fact quite conservative, and furthermore that his entire *corpus* was oriented in favor of the *status quo*. It has been shown elsewhere that Regalado's assumptions were basically flawed by his own misunderstandings both of the dynamics of Spanish history, and of Galdós's personal ideologies as manifested in his non-fiction.[7] Such an unbalanced critique was, of necessity, bound to fail when applied to Galdós's fiction. Clara Lida, an historian, made a similar attempt in 1968.[8] Working in the opposite direction, her analysis suffered from not having explored with any precision Galdós's personal view of reality as shown in his newspaper and magazine articles. Moving directly from Spanish history to its novelization without first examining the peculiarities of Galdós's historical perspective, Lida could only conclude that Galdós was tolerantly liberal and supported the regimes of Sagasta and Cánovas.

1. The Restoration: politics versus social justice

Now it is not our intention to recapture Galdós for Liberalism, nor to facilely bestow upon him a specific political orientation. We ought to attempt, however, to contribute to a clearer understanding of his ideas, and thereby move closer to an accurate comprehension of his novels. The fact is that Galdós's world and his vision of it are far more complex than has generally been assumed. An examination of his newspaper and magazine articles clearly shows this. During the years 1885–1898 Galdós began to discern the failure of the constitutional system in Spain. Of the breakdown in the political fabric he had this, for example, to say:

> As far as home politics are concerned, the legacy of '87 also has its dark side. There are problems which will not be solved in the new year nor for many years to come. For example 'caciquismo' [the rigging of elections in the rural areas by local political bosses or 'caciques'] is a national disease so entrenched it is harder to remedy than earthquakes, floods or cholera.[9]

Nor was he slow in placing the blame, which he laid squarely on the rulers of the country. A year earlier he observed ('Política menuda' ['Political small talk'], 19 December 1885: *PE*–1, 103–110):

> Cánovas was not worried about elections, because Romero [Robledo] could give him a nice, new majority pulled from the ballot box God knows how . . . Cánovas had allowed his lieutenant to get up to all kinds of dirty tricks, and cock a snook at the administration to serve the interests of half a dozen of his cronies . . . There are two kinds of politics: that of the country at large, which long-sufferingly toils away in the background, perhaps erring on the passive side; and that of gentlemen like these, which makes lots of noise but is completely contrived and ruled by personal intrigue (pp. 106–7, 109).

Never before had Spain enjoyed so many legal freedoms,[10] yet legal rights had not brought with them social justice, as Galdós noted in 1887 ('Política de verano' ['Summer Politics'], 29 July: *PE*–1, pp. 319–28):

> People think they have won freedom; but since this has not improved their conditions of existence, and since the so-called disinherited classes have seen that the panacea of freedom is something of an illusion, the masses are now unmoved by all political questions (323)[11]

Only socio-economic problems, and not political ones, now interested the masses. For some time Galdós was aware that whereas a revolution based on purely political grounds would fail, 'if in Spain social revolution could find sectors of the population ready for it, it would not lack a slogan or banner ('Un rey póstumo' ['A posthumous King'], 22 May 1886).[12] Furthermore, parliamentary Liberalism seemed less and less efficient in dealing with the increasingly difficult circumstances of urbanization, industrialization and regionalism..[13] Enormous socio-economic inequities were the disastrous by-products of the growth of Spain's cities and the modernization of her industry. The poor were the ultimate victims, as one of Galdós's most memorable articles makes clear ('La cuestión social' ['The social question'], 17 February 1885, C–1, pp. 147–56):

> With 16,000 inhabitants [of Madrid] unemployed, the crisis was bound to take on serious dimensions; building work has come to a sudden halt, and thousands of bricklayers, carpenters, marble cutters, blacksmiths and plasterers are out of work. The factories, in the case of Madrid less important than the building industry, are also suffering from lack of work, and this has caused much distress among the popular classes [. . .]. There can be nothing so sad as the sight of these multitudes clamouring at the doors of charitable institutions seeking some pitiful relief; and when these multitudes are made up of healthy, strong, hard-working men, what are we to think of the way our society organizes its labour? The great social problem which looks set to be the major battle of the next century is already looming large in the dying days of this one, throwing out sparks that show how serious it is. In fact the more industry progresses, the more terrifying the prospect becomes; and intense competition, which brings prices tumbling down at an incredible rate, means that the success of certain workplaces is built on the ruin of others, causing economic disasters that always fall on the luckless wage-earners. In such catastrophes, capital stands a chance of saving itself, but the workman almost always goes under (pp. 147–9).

As far as Galdós was concerned, Liberal politics were becoming the politics of stagnation;[14] self-interest, not ideals, kept the *peaceful rota* functioning and made government the bastard child of *caciquismo*.[15] Liberalism had become sterile, and the Liberals and Galdós's own middle class were to blame:

> Everything has changed. The extinction of the race of tyrants has brought with it the end of the race of liberators. I use the word tyrant in its old sense, because tyranny still exists, but *now we are the tyrants, we who in days gone by were the victims and martyrs, the middle class, the bourgeoisie*, who fought against the clergy and the aristocracy [. . .] those who before were disinherited now occupy the position of privilege. The struggle is starting all over again, except that the names of the combattants have changed [. . .] ('El 1° de mayo' ['May day']: *PE*–2, pp. 268–9, italics added).[16]

If Galdós rejected the political ideologies of his time, he could not reject ideals. While he understood that socialism and anarchism were expressions of the ideal of social justice, even as early as 1872 Galdós could not accept the expedient of revolutionary violence against his own middle class.[17] Furthermore, he could not overcome the pessimism engendered by his obvious class biases,[18] and accept social and economic equality. He admitted as much in 1885, for example:

> Following a more or less serious disturbance, depending on the particular part of the country, things will return to normal and everything will go on in the same old way, with the capitalists doing the exploiting as always, and the workers still providing the labour and living from day to day. The State, meddling in areas that are not its concern, can only offer palliatives. There will never be a remedy for inequality, because it is in-built, irremediable and eternal.[19]

Galdós's inner conflict culminates on 12 July 1893, in an article appropriately titled 'Confusiones y paradojas' ('Confusions and paradoxes').[20] Beginning with a description of Spain's confused and unhappy spiritual landscape, he asks:

> Do you not detect an alarming anxiety in our poor humanity? Is it the result of disenchantment with religion, closely followed by disenchantment with philosophy? Is it political disillusion, accompanied by social disillusion? We began this century fighting for political freedoms. We won them but the nations are not happy, and their societies are neither solid nor stable (pp. 185–6).

Galdós follows these questions with a strong critique of the society of the nineteenth century and its ostensibly democratic ideals:

> We fought for freedoms, which were won at the cost of a thousand sacrifices. Are we happy? No. *With all the concessions we have gained, we still live as before, surrounded by injustice, inequality, monstrous insults to our moral sense.* Some innocents still think everything depends on what kind of government we have [. . .]. Both sides are blind and cannot see that it makes no difference what kind of government we get (p. 187, italics added).

Structural change without internal, spiritual change is fruitless. The life of the spirit is dying. There are no viable religious or philosophical ideals. Philosophy contradicts itself (p. 186); religion, it is true, can at least fall back on its immutable dogma 'which sets the mind at ease' (p. 186), but when all is said and done, it must be admitted that reason has killed faith: 'We look back on religion, and in it seek solace from the longing for truth that consumes us; but we can see that faith is lost, and our over-cultivated reason prevents it from germinating in our hearts. No sooner does it rear its head than reason stifles it' (p. 186).

Self-interest and personal gratification are the motive forces which predominate in social relations (p. 190). In an emotional tirade which smacks of a critique of materialism and positivism, Galdós suggests that the reason for this disintegration of society is to be found in the non-intuitive, deliberate and deliberately critical approach to life:

> The fact is that in art, as in everything, *an over-developed critical faculty* kills off inspiration [. . .]. There can be no doubt of this; in this century of ours now drawing to its close, the over-development of our critical faculty is the reason for the lack of artistic life and, let it also be said, for moral and political decline. Criticism has killed off everything. Now that everyone knows, or claims to know, what life, religion or art are, human thought is becoming sterile. We must therefore come to the sad conclusion that the diffusion of knowledge, the ever-greater extension of education, Universities, Atheneums [cultural societies], libraries, are in fact the cause of this evident sapping of human energy (pp. 193–4, italics added).

Consequently, while we inhibit greatness, we raise up the masses from ignorance to mediocrity: 'We are making giant strides towards the ascendancy of educated mediocrity' (p. 194). Is this 'average' preferable to a generally low social and cultural level 'in which isolated figures stand out in all their splendour' (p. 194)? Galdós seems to indicate that elitism and isolated greatness are more desirable, but he provides no solution:

> I end by appealing to my readers' indulgence for offering this purely personal opinion by way of conclusion to the paradox I have set out. *We should not take paradoxes lightly, for they usually contain truths* (p. 195, italics added).

This is tantamount to an aesthetic of ambiguity, a complex, ironic vision of an involuted world, fraught with paradox and cross-purposes. But that is not all. In 1885, as urban society began to expand and was increasingly beset by conflicts of all types for which there seemed to be no answer, Galdós looked upon the possibility of socialism with a jaundiced eye:

> Spiritualism perhaps comes closest to a solution, since it proclaims contempt for wealth and Christian resignation, and counteracts an inequality based on externals with the consolation of an eternal equality, that is, the noble levelling of human destinies in the sanctuary of our inner conscience (*PE*–2, pp. 273–4).[21]

Now this is not, as has been believed,[22] a retreat from social conflict through religion. It is, rather, an attempt to reconcile both points of view, as Galdós himself states exactly two years later in 1887:

> It is an inveterate bad habit in Spain to suppose that, whenever a clash of material interests arises, neither party is acting from disinterested motives. It runs in our character, and this misguided idea perhaps derives from *an unhealthy, unquestioning spiritualism deeply ingrained in us since time immemorial* [. . .]. But this habit, despite being the source of so many ills, is not just a matter of malice; it is usually an expression of naivety and ignorance, apart from the spiritualism I talked about before [. . .]. In Spain we suffer from a widespread, traditional hostility to work, especially here in the central part of the country which is basically agricultural and where people seem to cling to a kind of cult of poverty. *The idea that poverty and honesty go together is not easily dislodged from many people's minds* (*PE*–1, pp. 299–301, italics added).[23]

He continues, noting that the coastal areas of Spain are finally liberating themselves from this 'spiritualism', and are therefore – in contrast to the central area of the country – making cultural and socio-economic progress.[24] In designating Madrid the capital of Spain, Philip II 'condemned Spain for centuries to domination by that unhealthy spiritualism, and *decreed the supremacy of poverty*, elevating it not just into a virtue but into a reason of state' (p. 301, our italics). It is not a proven fact that poverty leads either to greatness of nations, or to the sanctity of the individual; eternal glory, Galdós notes, has nothing to do with self-enforced poverty. Spaniards must learn that the material progress of the country is *not* immoral, but is in fact a necessity. The opinion that all business and progress is sinful will lead to stagnation, he warns, and will similarly discourage government-supported endeavors: 'We would end up with an unbending pro-spiritual legislature, which might be all very nice and Christian, but would soon turn us into paupers' (p. 303).

Galdós is saying that if, on the one hand, personal abnegation and resignation are necessary in order to resolve the pressing problems of contemporary society, then, on the other hand, this must not be static, since there are no easy answers, politically or morally.[25] That is, one must still continue to strive for the amelioration, both material and spiritual, of man's existential predicament. One must, in other words, make use of any available but – in Galdós's terms – ethical and nonviolent means to survive and by doing so, improve the condition of one's existence. Nor is it legitimate to dissociate one's own survival from that of others. Furthermore, by 1895 Galdós can no longer find any validity in categories such as politics, religion, or classes. He comes to use the middle class world not merely as a subject, but also as a container, in which all manner of life and lives move and interact, as César Barja perceptively observed many years ago:

> The world portrayed in them [Galdós's novels] is that of what is called the middle class, which as someone has said is neither a middle nor properly speaking a class [. . .]. It can rise above the world of commerce to rub shoulders with the aristocracy [. . .]. It can remain at the level of wealth acquired through business [. . .]. Or it can extend downwards to the world described in *La desheredada*, that of the servant [. . .] and the beggar [. . .]. The whole of this spectrum is encompassed by the bourgeoisie, whether in the ascendancy and scaling the heights of the political and social system, or whether on the decline and consorting with the beggar's rags or the prostitute's cottons and silks. In its depiction of this confusion of classes, Galdós's fiction shows the nature of the society that has produced it, a shifting, motley world (pp. 349–50).[26]

As never before, Galdós came to see the society of his time as being invested with tremendous fluidity. More and more, the novels of the period reflect the social structure which he described in his speech to the Royal Academy:[27]

> [. . .] what most strikes us in the human mass of which we form part is the loosening of all unifying principles. The great and powerful forces that once worked towards social cohesion are in decline [. . .]. We can also see, in this bewildered multitude, which invents a thousand distractions to hide its gloom, the disintegration of those historic social classes which had retained their internal organization intact until almost our own day. The populace and the aristocracy are losing their traditional characteristics, the latter due to the dispersal of wealth, the former because of advances in education; there is only a little way to go before these two basic classes lose their distinguishing features entirely. The so-called middle class, which as yet does not have a well-defined existence, is still a shapeless mass of individuals who have come from either above or below; the product, one might say, of the falling apart of both extremes: of the plebeian family which is on the make, and the aristocratic family which is in decline (pp. 9, 11).

Galdós's concept of society is organic: its components are subsumed to the whole. For example, he makes no distinctions between the 'social question' and the 'religious question'. There is only one 'question', that of survival in its total sense: survival of the spirit as well as the body, survival of the individual as well as society.

If we understand this, then we see that capitalism and socialism were simply the two sides of the same coin for Galdós. This rejection of ideology certainly did not imply an evasion of social conflicts, which in fact weighed heavily on him as his important article 'La cuestión social' indicated. Similarly, as we read in 'Confusiones y paradojas', spiritual ills could not be solved within the polarity religion–rationalism. The achievement of harmony in life, that is, the survival of personal and collective humanity, therefore became one of Galdós's principal interests and served as the core of the novels, particularly after 1885 and before 1898. This fascination with the struggle for existence led Galdós naturally to the common people, the lower classes, particularly those of his own Madrid where life was constantly lived on the frontier between destruction and fulfillment, madness and excruciating but redemptive self-awareness.

2. The common people

The lot of the common people was indeed unenviable. The years of the Regency in Spain witnessed the beginnings of a social disintegration which enveloped the urban lower classes. This group, particularly in Madrid, existed under the most extreme conditions of poverty and spiritual and material neglect. No institutions except the charities gave them either protection or consolation, and there is reason to believe that even the charities failed in this regard. The masses existed not merely without the aid of, *but in spite of*, the government, the Church and the economic system which exploited them mercilessly. The lower classes of Madrid, what Galdós calls 'the people', were not only considered eminently expendable by their 'rulers'; they were in fact geographically, physically and spiritually marginal to all aspects of Madrid society. They were even marginal to the economic system, for they could always be replaced by a constant stream of jobless workers migrating into the city from the provinces.

On the other hand, with the rise of positivism and social theory in the last half of the nineteenth century, a new consciousness beset the upper classes. In Madrid, they came to realize that beyond their shops and salons, beyond the fringes of their tree-lined neighborhoods, behind the Royal Opera and the Price Circus, there existed another world with values and lifestyles wholly different from theirs, a world characterized by crime and disease and deprivation. Its monuments were not palace and theater, but tenement and tavern where the hungry could kill their appetite with a glass of adulterated spirits.

And so a new tension developed in Spanish society, generated by guilt and later, as socialism and anarchism entered Spain, exacerbated by fear. With this tension came a defensive drive to ameliorate the lot of the lower classes in a way compatible with the interests of the middle and upper classes (Aranguren has described this atmosphere admirably).[28] Galdós was certainly not ignorant of this new movement to *maintain* the *status quo* by introducing small, acceptable reforms. During the months preceding the First Republic, he had written about the nascent workers' movement in Spain; in these and subsequent articles he demonstrated an awareness of society's increasingly difficult plight and its often contradictory nature. And Galdós, because he loved Spain and Madrid, because he also loved to *write about* Spain and Madrid, began to write also about the new social consciousness and the new tensions. More importantly, his attention was attracted to the ultimate source of the social unrest (as he saw it), the suffering of the masses. And as we observed earlier, he was also drawn into considering the question of the masses' ultimate release from deprivation by Liberal and bourgeois panaceas.

Now it is not our contention that Galdós sat down and with conscious intent began to write about the grave problems threatening Spain. Rather, he wanted to write about Spain, and therefore was driven also to analyze her troubles.[29] Galdós grew progressively disillusioned with the Restoration and Liberalism, as he came to see that the rising middle class was just as content as the upper classes to ignore the problems of the country. And as he also grew aware of the increasingly difficult situation of the masses, the common people in whom he also placed his hope, Galdós began to experiment novelistically, re-creating social ambiguities and contradictions – as he saw them – in the world of his novels, searching that world for new and viable solutions. Because the common people was so central to Spain's problems, it also became central to many of Galdós's novels. And out of the common people, out of the whirl of its life with all its tensions, characterized by constant engagement in the battle for survival, the purest forms of victor and vanquished emerge as saint and criminal; the one purified by the experience of conflict, the other debased. Galdós's newspaper articles indicate that the author, during the years 1885–1898, found himself penetrating ever deeper into the social arena to find and study such individuals.[30] His interest in crimes and criminals reflects a growing awareness of the conflicts immanent in the wellspring of social and political forces. Criminals and saints, that is, individuals of complete personal abnegation (as shown below, both types in their pure forms are self-denying: the former, through total dedication to evil, is self-destructive; the latter, through total dedication to good, is self-sacrificing), take on for Galdós a super reality. They are opposite ends of the life spectrum as he visualized it. But each extreme, by having endured the conflict of life, is bound to the other and is made larger: the saint by his/her sacrifice, the criminal by his/her waste and destruction. Two women, Ernestina Manuel de Villena – not a member of the lower classes but certainly involved in the battle for survival – and Higinia Balaguer, both subjects of long essays by Galdós,[31] best personify these templates much as, for example, Pecado and Benina do in the fiction.

3. Saint and sinner

We may chart the sociological origins of such individuals without difficulty, since the dilemma faced by any member of the lower classes was of relatively 'simple' solution (although it was never even remotely gratifying). As the awareness of their exploitation deepened and they realized that they could depend neither on existing institutions nor on prevailing value systems, the masses were confronted with three alternatives. They could, first of all, withdraw among themselves and simply live out their lives as best they could. The *caciques* anticipated this passive response when they tightened their control of the electoral process in 1890 (a measure advocated by Cánovas in a speech that year in the Ateneo).[32] Most members of the lower classes did withdraw, thus submitting (or at least manifesting submission) to the value systems and morality of the rulers of society who were in fact responsible for their predicament.

The other two choices for members of the lower classes also entailed moral decision, but both were in defiance of the prevailing values of Liberalism and the middle class. For the members of the lower classes could also deny themselves, becoming thereby either saints (and possibly also madmen), or criminals. Each of these two types could choose by sheer power of will to destroy the duality within them that Gumersindo de Azcárate described as follows:

> There is within us a perpetual dialogue between two distinct persons [. . .]; one voice leads us to fall and sin; the other voice lifts us up and redeems us; the fact is, we all have within us Adam the Sinner and Christ the Redeemer.[33]

The sinner or criminal, by rebelling against society, suffers intolerable deprivation; for as one isolates oneself from the social world – psychically at the very least and often also physically – one alienates oneself from human contact. The true criminal rejects the validity of human relations, of contact between people on anything but the most basic material level. One negates the things of the spirit because one must act aggressively and destructively against other human beings. For one's own peace of mind and self-preservation, one must therefore carry positivism to its *reductio ad absurdum*.[34] The criminal is self-dedicated to evil and crime for their own sake, not merely to satisfy personal appetites but to frustrate those of others. Inherent in this is the desire to establish control over life, to make others suffer as much as oneself, not out of an obsessive drive for vengeance but for power over one's own and others' existence. The imagination of many nineteenth-century writers was captured by those of their contemporaries who achieved this deep level of self-affirmation through crime, a self-affirmation which paradoxically was, on the spiritual level, equivalent to self-denial. Such individuals come alive for us in fiction, for example, in the character of Vautrin or Pecado, who are of the same mold; one member of Galdós's society, Santiago Alcántara, described the mold with blunt eloquence:[35]

> [. . .] the spirit of evil, which rebels against God and is the enemy of mankind, has succeeded in implanting in some of its slaves a hatred, disinterested and *pure* in its own way, which confronts yet mimics the most devoted sense of charity (his italics).

Emerging from the same world of intense deprivation, the saint similarly breaks with the established order. However, this individual seeks fulfillment not in things, nor in control over others, but in human relationships. The saint, like the criminal, by rebelling against society and its value system is subjected to extreme hardship; in this case such mortification is material, not spiritual.[36] The criminal sees society as a deterrent from the freedom of material well-being; the saint sees the necessity of freedom from the material in order to enjoy spiritual well-being. The criminal is ultimately anti-human, the saint sacrifices him/herself for humanity. The criminal denies the validity of human relationships and therefore denies the self as a spiritual and feeling entity. The saint ignores but does not efface his or her physical existence, in order to affirm the intangible, the belief that people should not be defined in terms of their possessions or of their interactions with the physical environment, but in terms of their relationships to each other. And each pursues their goal with a single-mindedness reminiscent of the ascetics.

Saint and criminal were therefore extreme results, or better, by-products, of the life process, of living and dying among the lower classes. And Galdós, like many other writers, discovered that in dealing with these by-products of an oppressive, frustrating life in society, one could get at the life process itself: one could, in short, portray a society by delineating and defining the forces at work on certain of its members. The stumbling-block, however, putting aside purely literary (that is, technical) considerations, was that the author might be blind to certain forces and choose to ignore others. In that sense, an author portraying a society according to his or her peculiar vision was, in the process, defining personal biases. Such biases are part of the creative apparatus from which a writer's aesthetic is fashioned, and therefore relate closely to his or her fictional works.

It is for these same reasons that Galdós, like all writers, must be studied in the context out of which his works spring. A solid grasp of the life of end-of-century Madrid, independent of what Galdós himself describes in his fiction, is vital if we are to come to a deeper understanding of the man, his biases, and his aesthetic.

Notes

1. See for example GOLDMAN, P. B., 1969, 'Galdós and the politics of conciliation', *Anales Galdosianos* **4**: 73–87 (p. 83 n. 1) for a list of the major works in which Galdós's essays are examined. William H. Shoemaker and Leo J. Hoar, Jr., are the two scholars who have dedicated themselves to collecting and analyzing the non-fiction. Galdós specialists owe a debt of gratitude to these two indefatigable investigators, and also to José Schraibman who, through the years, has unearthed a good deal of the writer's correspondence. Professor Shoemaker has most recently edited and published *Los artículos de Galdós en 'La Nación' 1865–1866* (1972, Insula, Madrid) and *Las cartas desconocidas de Galdós en 'La Prensa' de Buenos Aires* (1973, Ediciones de Cultura Hispánica,

Madrid), both excellent contributions. Professor Hoar's recent full-length edition, *BPG y la Revista del Movimiento Intelectual de Europa, Madrid, 1865–1867* (1968, Insula, Madrid) has been followed by a series of articles, of which the latest 'More on the pre – [and post-] history of the *Episodios nacionales*: Galdós's article "El dos de mayo" (1874)' (1973, *Anales Galdosianos* **7**: 107–20) also discusses Galdós's use of his essay material for novels; Hoar's 'Politics and poetry: More proof of Galdós's work for *Las Cortes*' (1973, *Modern Language Notes* **88**: 378–97) is useful in this context, providing additionally some bibliographical information (pp. 385–6 and n. 21).

2. This is a trend which has lately begun to change. One of the most eloquent and well-reasoned arguments in favor of the extra-literary approach is that of RODOLFO CARDONA (1971, 'Nuevos enfoques críticos con referencia a la obra de Galdós', *Cuadernos Hispanoamericanos* **252–2**: 58–72). GEOFFREY RIBBANS (1970, 'Contemporary history in the structure and characterization of *Fortunata y Jacinta*', in Varey, J. E. (ed.) *Galdós Studies*, Támesis, London, pp. 90–113), and BRIAN J. DENDLE (1969, 'Galdós and the Death of Prim', *Anales Galdosianos* **4**: 63–71), are good examples of the productive possibilities inherent in an historical orientation. Other extra-literary methodologies and their possible value are also discussed by Professor Cardona, and additionally in Professor Varey's fine introduction (1970, 'Galdós in the light of recent criticism', in *Galdós Studies*, pp. 1–35). See also GOLDMAN P. B., 1971, 'Historical perspective and political bias: Comments on recent Galdós criticism', *Anales Galdosianos* **6**: 113–24, esp. p. 122 n. 14.

3. This was the point made by SHERMAN EOFF, who declared in 1966 ('Galdós in nineteenth-century perspective', *Anales Galdosianos* **1**: 3–9) that the student of Galdós must also become a student of nineteenth-century Spain. CARLOS BLANCO AGUINAGA likewise observed in 1968: 'We frankly think that it would be wiser to approach the problem of the absolute uniqueness of "novelistic" lives by attending rigorously not only to their "contrasting" relationships, but – among other things, and preferably as a starting point – by attending to the dialectical relationship existing between these lives and world reflected in the work of fiction [. . . and] to the social reality from which is born the reality of realistic fiction' ('On the birth of Fortunata', *Anales Galdosianos* **3**: 13–24 [22]).

4. The answers to this question have been difficult to determine. Professor Varey (1970, esp. p. 16) noted that not even the extraordinary histories of RAYMOND CARR and C. A. M. HENNESSY have enabled us to truly understand the 'sociological, economic and ideological' intricacies of Spain's Restoration society (1875–1923). Hennessy (1962, *The Federal Republic in Spain*, Oxford University Press, Oxford) deals of course only with the political machinations during the First Republic and the years immediately preceeding (1868–1874). Carr himself stated at the end of his monumental work *Spain, 1808–1939* (1966, Oxford University Press, Oxford, p. 712) that there has been almost nothing produced concerning the development of Spanish society in the nineteenth century since Angel Marvaud's famous studies written in the early part of the twentieth century. The topics of urbanization and industrialization have lately attracted historians, although the lower classes in Madrid prior to 1900 are not given much attention in their work. FERNANDA ROMEU (1970, *Las clases trabajadoras en España*, Taurus, Madrid) and MANUEL TUÑÓN DE LARA (1972, *El movimiento obrero en la historia de España*, Taurus, Madrid) are both fundamental for an understanding of the nineteenth and twentieth centuries. Bibliographical information on recent contributions may be found in LINZ J. J., 1972, 'Five centuries of Spanish history: Quantification and comparison', in

Lorwin, V. R. and Price, J. M. (eds), *The Dimensions of the Past: Materials, Problems and Opportunities for Quantitative Work in History*, Yale University Press, New Haven, pp. 177–261; and Tuñón de Lara M., 1973, 'Problemas actuales de la historiografía española', *Sistema* **1**: 31–50 and 1975, 'Expansión de los libros de historia', *Cuadernos para el Diálogo* **120**: 499–501.

5. In addition to the works cited in n. 1 above, see for example Galdós, B., 1957, *Madrid*, ed. J. Pérez Vidal, Aguado, Madrid.
6. 1966, *BPG y la novela histórica española, 1868–1912*, Insula, Madrid.
7. Goldman, P. B., 1971; see also Olson, P. R., 1970, 'Galdós and history', *Modern Language Notes* **85**: 274–9, and Carr, A. R., 1968, 'A new view of Galdós', *Anales Galdosianos* **3**: 185–9, for other critical comments concerning the reliability of Regalado's *literary* assumptions.
8. Lida, C. E., 1968, 'Galdós y los *Episodios nacionales*: Una historia del liberalismo español', *Anales Galdosianos* **3**: 61–77.
9. Unless otherwise indicated, all articles by Galdós cited in the text are found in Ghiraldo, A. (ed.) 1923–4, *Obras inéditas de BPG*, Renacimiento, Madrid. Volumes utilized are *Fisionomías sociales* (hereafter cited as *F*), which is the first volume in the series; vol 2 *Arte y crítica* (hereafter *AyC*); vols 3–4 *Política española* (hereafter *PE*–1 and *PE*–2 respectively); vols 6–7 *Cronicón* (hereafter *C*–1 and *C*–2 respectively. For the passage quoted, see pp. 294–5 of 'Año de reparación', 28 December 1886: *PE*–1, 293–8.
10. See for example 'Un rey póstumo', 22 May 1886: *PE*–1, pp. 135–46, esp. 140, 144–5.
11. In the same article he also states: 'Nowadays the divorce between politicians and the country is growing daily [. . .]. Not surprisingly, the [political] system is increasingly discredited, because it has no solid grass-roots support [. . .]. It is worth remarking how cynical people have become about political and philosophical problems. Only economic and social issues can still generate passion' (pp. 322–3).
12. *PE*–1, p. 145.
13. On the Catalan problem and regionalism, see for example 'El regionalismo', 14 August 1886: *PE*–1, pp. 185–93. On pp. 192–3, he concludes, 'We must needs recognize that everything the people of Barcelona say against centralization has some truth in it, because in Barcelona there are initiatives in almost every sphere, and in every case these are stifled by the interference of the metropolis. It is clearly absurd that in Barcelona a street cannot be made, a sewer dug, or a building put up without having to ask permission from some office in Madrid, where everything is made complicated and drawn out to eternity. As I said before, centralization is absurd in the case of Barcelona, and it is perhaps this bureaucratic tyranny which explains that industrious people's complaints'.
14. See for example 'El parlamentarista', May 1893: *F*, pp. 209–30, esp. 209–11; in 'Vida legislativa', 31 December 1887: *PE*–2, pp. 85–9, Galdós confesses, 'It is already admitted by all those of good faith that the current regulations for both chambers make legislation impossible' (p. 87).
15. For example 'Régimen representativo', 22 May 1884: *PE*–2, pp. 19–26; 'Procedimientos electorales', 30 April 1885: *PE*–2, pp. 33–8; 'El "Encasillado" y

sus consecuencias', 19 March 1886: *PE–2*, pp. 123–33. Galdós is nevertheless equivocal in his attitude towards *caciquismo* [*Editor's note*: the rigging of elections by local political bosses in the rural areas], at times in the same article suggesting that it is a necessary evil. But he certainly has no illusions about democratic government, or its non-existence in Spain.

16. The article runs from pp. 267–77; see also 'El regionalismo', pp. 185–6.
17. See for example GOLDMAN, P. B., 1969 and 1971. Carr and Olson in a more general fashion make some well thought out remarks concerning Galdós's sympathies.
18. See CARR *passim*.
19. 'El 1° de mayo', p. 273.
20. *AyC*, pp. 183–95.
21. 'El 1° de mayo'.
22. For example REGALADO, p. 252.
23. 'La moral y los negocios de Estado', 14 April 1887: *PE–1*, pp. 299–310.
24. '[. . .] the coastal regions, where mercantile ideas and the common sense learnt from ambitious initiatives are making headway, are finally freeing themselves from this spiritualism' (p. 301).
25. For example 'El 1° de mayo': 'the social question cannot easily be solved by any known means, whether political or moral' (*PE–2*, p. 273).
26. BARJA, C., 1964, *Libros y autores modernos*, 2nd edn, Las Américas, New York.
27. *Discursos leídos ante la Real Academia Española en la recepción pública del Sr. D. . . ., el domingo 7 de febrero de 1897, edición académica* (1897, Tello, Madrid). *Editor's note*: included in this volume, Chapter 2.
28. ARANGUREN, J. L. L., 1967, *Moral y sociedad: Introducción a la moral social española del siglo XIX*. Edicusa, Madrid.
29. This point is made with lucid precision by GULLÓN, R., 1968, 'Estrucutra y diseño en *Fortunata y Jacinta*', *Papeles de Son Armadans* **48**: 223–316, esp. 274–75.
30. The pages of *C–2* in particular are full of these considerations, as a rapid perusal of its table of contents reveals. See for example 'El crimen del cura Galeote', 21 April–9 October 1886: *C–2*, pp. 145–82.
31. 'Santos modernos', 15 February 1886: *C–2*, pp. 7–17; 'El crimen de la calle Fuencarral', 19 July 1888–30 May 1889: *C–2*, pp. 87–144. Obviously, Galdós is eminently skillful also in blending both the saintly and the sinful in the same individual. Mauricia la Dura is far more human than Guillermina Pacheco, who sometimes falls short herself, particularly in her lack of patience with fallen angels. R. GULLÓN's essay is eloquent concerning Guillermina's character and 'bourgeois saintliness' (1968, pp. 250–6, 310–2).
32. ANTONIO CÁNOVAS DEL CASTILLO, *Discurso pronunciado por el Excmo. Señor D. . . ., 10 de noviembre 1890, Ateneo de Madrid* (1890, Tello, Madrid). The law of universal male suffrage provided for the first 'democratic' elections in 1891 (women and males under twenty-five years of age were excluded from the polls). Prior to 1890, there had been so many restrictions on voting rights that the electorate was a mere 800,000 men (in 1891, 4,805,000 men voted), or less than 5% of the general population of the country. Even with the so-called

universal suffrage, the voters constituted only 27% of the general population (see CUADRADO, M. M., 1969, *Elecciones y partidos políticos de España [1868–1931]*, Taurus, Madrid, vol. 2, pp. 529–31). Nevertheless, Cánovas called for vigilant management of the polls by Spain's ruling classes because universal suffrage (the law of universal suffrage was promulgated on 26 June 1890) made socialism a 'tendency which, however threatening, was undeniably legal' (p. 31). It must be stated, however, that Cánovas's advocacy of electoral management was well-known and longstanding, pre-dating the Ateneo speech. His man for such work was Romero Robledo, about whom we have heard Galdós speak (see text above). The Ateneo speech calls for the continuation of such policies, but is more implicit than explicit in this regard. Because of the well-known preferences of Cánovas, tactful indirectness was sufficient.

33. 'La religión y las religiones', lecture, Sociedad *El Sitio* (Bilbao), reprinted 1909, *Boletín de la Institución Libre de Enseñanza* **33**: 339–52. The passage cited is from p. 345. *Editor's note*: Azcárate was a well-known Krausist and friend of Galdós.

34. In other words relationships, because they are not concrete, are meaningless. Excellent anthropological profiles of criminals may be found in the fascinating work *La mala vida de Madrid* by CONSTANCIO BERNALDO DE QUIRÓS and J. Mª. LLANAS AGUILANIEDO (1901, B. Rodríguez Serra, Madrid).

35. *La política católica en España* (1894, ANGEL B. VELASCO, Madrid, p. 6). Another contemporary, Benito Mariano Andrade, explores writers' interest in those who were losers in the social struggle for survival in his *La antropología criminal y la novela naturalista* (1896, Est. Tip. Sucesores de Rivadeneyra, Madrid). Obviously, positivism was one of the great stimuli for such literary exploration, since it suggested that aberrant behavior could be empirically related to specific physiological characteristics of the individual. Hence, if deviance was rooted in physical causes, one could alter behavior by isolating and neutralizing the physical defect itself. In literature, this meant the precise, indeed almost microscopic examination of the anti-social or deviant character in order to find its linkage with the specific physical problem. Galdós's greatness and achievement lie in the fact that he came to understand the limits of such examination.

36. Many of Galdós's contemporaries considered the anarchist terrorist to have some of these qualities. BERNALDO DE QUIRÓS, a fine criminal anthropologist and student of rural lower class unrest (see his important *El espartaquismo agrario andaluz* [1919, Reus, Madrid]), published a paper in which he affirmed that the terrorist was motivated by universal love, piety and abnegation. Paradoxically, the terrorist acted out of both egotism and sacrifice (1913, 'Psicología del crimen anarquista', *Archivos de psiquiatría, criminología y ciencias afines* [Buenos Aires] **12**: 122–6): 'The avengers of all those wounded by hunger and cold, and oppressed by suffering, commit their violent, bloody crimes in such desperate ways that to some they seem like indirect acts of suicide' (126).

11 *Our Friend Manso* and the Game of Fictive Autonomy*

John W. Kronik

This article illustrates the move, from the mid-1970s onwards, away from a representational approach towards discussion of the metafictional aspects of Galdós's novels; one could put together an excellent anthology consisting solely of such metafictional studies. In this volume I have limited myself to two: that by Valis (Chapter 14) and this pioneering piece, which remains an outstanding contribution. (Readers are also referred to Kronik's excellent 1982 metafictional study of *Fortunata and Jacinta*.) This article is particularly useful because it gives a brief run through Galdós's use of metafictional devices in other novels. The explicit self-reflexivity of *El amigo Manso* made the novel a favourite with Unamuno, who modelled his own Pirandellian experiment *Niebla* (1914) on it. As Kronik notes, the self-reflexivity of Galdós's work, which derives directly from Cervantes, makes him a curiously modern writer; it is not surprising that this aspect of his writing is the one that has most appealed to contemporary critics. The strength of Kronik's analysis is his emphasis on the double metafictional dimension of *El amigo Manso*: its narrator-protagonist's awareness of his fictional status, and his fashioning of the other characters into his own intellectual creations. Kronik is particularly perceptive on Galdós's manipulation of the ludic potential of the self-reflexive novel, while at the same time stressing the relation of the novel's metafictional commentary to its critique of a society based on rhetoric and deception.

The length of the original article has made it necessary to cut the penultimate section which, inasmuch as it deals with the moral implications of Manso's role as artistic creator, shows the continued influence of the Leavisite criticism of the 1960s.

Our Friend Manso is available in English: 1987, Columbia University Press, New York.

* Reprinted from 1977, *Anales Galdosianos* **12**: 71–94.

Allowing, as his more recent heirs have, that art is a game, Galdós in *Our Friend Manso* has chosen to play with the game that is art and invites his reader and critic to join him in that game.[1] The game in this case revolves about a protagonist who functions as a purportedly autonomous character, that is, one who is himself aware of his fictional status and by virtue of that awareness gains a degree of independence from his creator.[2] That independence is projected at the start when Manso, after revealing that he is the evocation of a conjurer-novelist who is a friend of his, recounts:

> This fellow came to see me a few days ago and told me about his work. When he said he had already written thirty volumes, I felt so sorry for him I could not but be touched by his ardent entreaties. He was smitten once again with the unseemly vice of writing, and wanted me to be his accomplice in adding yet another volume to the thirty other known offences. He told me [. . .] that as he knew I had in my possession an agreeable, easy subject, he wanted to buy it off me [. . .] . This did not seem such a bad deal, so I accepted (ch. 1, pp. 2–3).[3]

Our Friend Manso won little esteem from its contemporaries: a novel without plot or action, they called it; Clarín, to the best of our knowledge, failed to review it; and Unamuno pretended not to have understood it. Early critics paid little attention to the fact that Chapter 1 and Chapter 50 constitute a frame that establishes Máximo Manso in his own words as a lie, a fictive invention. These critics read the novel as an autobiographical account or as a disquisition on Krausism and late nineteenth-century educational theories.[4] Even Casalduero, in his predilection to classify, still labels *Our Friend Manso* as a naturalistic novel in which Galdós exposes society to objective, scientific observation.[5] Vast as Galdós's readership has been, Galdós has yet to find *his* readers. The more recent commentators have tended to recognize the importance of the play on autonomy in this direct antecedent of *Niebla*, but in limited contexts or as a subservient component of the novel. Peter G. Earle, though concerned with other matters, has expressed well Máximo's duality as a creation: '*Our Friend Manso* is the novel in which Galdós most clearly situates his protagonist in the position of the novelist himself. He is an autonomous spirit whose "human appearance" is borrowed.'[6] Robert H. Russell has pointed to Manso's awareness of himself as a writer of fiction and says cautiously: 'It is not entirely imprudent to suggest that *Our Friend Manso* is as much concerned with literature as it is with education'.[7] However, he prefers to hover above Galdós's game as a knowing non-participant, assumes that the unnamed character in the novel to whom Manso refers as his creator is Galdós, and, collating his reading of the novel with the author's career, limits his thesis to Galdós's discovery that the humanity of his fictional creations is deepened if his own ideological posture does not obtrude onto their reality. Gustavo Correa has understood and insisted more than any other critic that Galdós projects his artistic consciousness as a thematic strain into his own novels. By that token, Correa has captured *Our Friend Manso*'s dimension as a novel about novel writing.[8] Even so, rather than fixing on it as an end in itself, Correa treats the self-conscious aspect of Galdós's artistry as a feature of the novelist's construction of the illusion of reality. Many of the most perceptive readers of *Our Friend Manso* have, in fact, responded to the work's suggestive treatment of the nebulous frontiers between reality and fiction.[9]

Máximo's apparent autonomous nature also has led the critics into social and ontological considerations – for good reasons, to be sure. Máximo's dual existence as the product of his creator and as an independent entity willy-nilly invites examination of the grey area between fact and fiction, reality and illusion. The autonomous character metaphorically raises the question of the split that exists between man as a social being with social dependency on others and man as endowed with the power to form and determine himself. Manso articulates that issue in his pithy utterance: 'it is a rule that the world fashions us, rather than being a product of our making'. On another level, man's relation to God is suggested (the novel's second paragraph establishes the parallel), or more broadly, man's subjection to fate – the uncontrollability of human actions. A further form of subjection that man is seen to suffer is the power of his psyche. If Máximo Manso is not the puppet of his creator, he is, then, under the control of his 'mansedumbre' ('meekness' or 'tameness'): he may be a free character, but he is not free *of* his character. The self and the other are in pernicious contest. From the author's position, the autonomous character – Máximo in this case – can be seen as a projection of the author's subconscious. Yet another reading of the novel turns it, like *Niebla*, into an attack on reason. Máximo, as an intellectual, a philosopher, a teacher, has the power to autonomize himself through thought. So defined, he functions as both subject and object, as an eye on society and as matter for examination. His failure, his apparent ingestion into the bourgeois mode, represents from this standpoint the collapse of the cerebral way.

The presence of these important questions in *Our Friend Manso* over and above its documentation of a social transformation and its ironic representation of a theory of education is testimony to the novel's richness. Beyond that, whether or not Máximo is, in fact, a truly autonomous character is in itself a root problem for critics. If he is autonomous, who made him that way? Who gave him his name? How can be he autonomous and such a perfect little bourgeois? Doesn't the structure of illusion within an illusion simply amount to fabrication? The problem is worth discussing.

But whether or not Máximo is autonomous – namely, free by appearances – is secondary to the illusion that he is. Though proportionately in greater view, the human disposition of Máximo Manso is always subservient to his fictional substance. The readers who fail to perceive that fact have ignored or forgotten the first chapter and many details of the narration. They have accepted all too readily Manso's invitation, 'Look on me as having a human appearance' (ch. 1, p. 2), and disregarded with equal alacrity his admonition that he speaks without possession of a voice and writes though he has no hands. The narrative trick that makes Máximo appear transcendentally conscious of his fictionality and therefore not to be Galdós's creation makes the novel appear to be Máximo's creation. *Our Friend Manso* is therefore a metanovel – a novel that investigates the nature of the novel, art about art. The autonomous – or supposedly autonomous – character in *Our Friend Manso* raises not so much the question of Galdós's bold novelistic technique in this particular work (a major concern of the critics who have paused to comment on the device), but the whole broad problem of fiction, its birth, the relationship of its constitutive elements, its power, and its immortality.'[10] Galdós's novel strikes beyond its evident link with *Don Quixote* to display the artistic self-consciousness that is so very much a twentieth-century phenomenon.

Lest *Our Friend Manso* be taken as a momentary aberration, a measure of Galdós's whimsicality in 1882, it is well to recall that throughout his career he made manifest directly within his novels his preoccupation with the creative process. In the last chapter of *Fortunata and Jacinta*, in the funeral scene, one sentence stands out for its bizarre timbre in the context of a mimetic narrative:

> On the long journey from the Cava to the cemetery (one of those in the south), Segismundo told the good Ponce all he knew of Fortunata's story, which was quite a lot, nor did he omit the last and perhaps best scene; at this the famous judge of literary works declared that there was enough there for a drama or a novel, though it seemed to him that the artistic fabric would not be proper without the introduction of a few strands necessary for the conversion of life's vulgarity into esthetic material' (vol. 5, p. 544).[11]

This delicious morsel of artistic self-revelation is Galdós's commentary on his way as a novelist and on his belief that there is stuff for a novel in every one of us. The sentences that follow the one quoted are a midway compromise between Galdós's positions in 'Some observations on the contemporary novel in Spain' of 1870 and his 1897 entry speech to the Academy.

On a larger scale, in one of his earliest works, *The Shadow*, the creative process is literalized when Paris, an 'imaginary being', comes to life out of a painting. At the same time, as Harriet S. Turner has indicated, Galdós produces the illusion of Anselmo's fictional autonomy by allowing Anselmo to assert his independence in a series of confrontations between character and narrator-as-character.[12] The daydreams of Isidora in *La desheredada*, in which, influenced by her readings of romance, she constructs herself into a fictitious heroine, are a form of inner recreation. As well as a commentary on a specific type of narrative, they are a commentary on fiction in general, a complicated but not uncommon case (*Madame Bovary* and *La Regenta* are well-known examples) where fiction fosters fiction. Another instance of reflexivity is *Tormento*, which, from a certain perspective, is the creation of José Ido del Sagrario as outlined at the end of *El doctor Centeno*.[13] In *Lo prohibido*, José María Bueno de Guzmán undertakes a literary venture in the writing of his memoirs. The God-visions of Luisito in *Miau* constitute an interior duplication of the creative process, so much so that Luisito replaces Galdós as the all-knowing power that determines Villaamil's suicide. Manolo Infante's last letter in *La incógnita* posits that reality is incomplete without its fictionalization, where the soul of truth lies, and so *Realidad* is born. The latter also questions generic distinctions in literature and the authorship of the literary creation. The name that her mother bestows on Tristana is, as the narrator explains it, an act of literary recreation that imposes, from the mother's viewpoint, the harmony and nobility of art on 'our rough, vulgar realities' (vol. 5, p. 1546). Her protector, for his part, is converted into a theatrical figure by acquaintances who call him Don Lope de Sosa, while he, himself, has engaged in a similar fictional self-recreation: 'with the passage of time, I learnt that the birth certificate boasted the name Don Juan López Garrido, and that the resounding Don Lope was the gentleman's own invention, like a layer of make-up put on to embellish his personality' (vol. 5, p. 1541). *Nazarín*, thanks to its peculiar structure, is a statement on the act of writing. And in *Misericordia*, the whole puzzling episode of Don Romualdo can be explained only, but quite easily, as a manifestation of fiction's miraculous powers of creation.

All these instances reflect the concern on Galdós's part with the problem that Erich Kahler in his interesting little book, *The Disintegration of Form in the Arts* (1968, Braziller, New York), considers a mark of our times. He says: 'more recently the problem of how to render the bewildering complexity of our reality has become the very subject matter of certain works of art. [. . . This] means the presentation in a work of art of the artist's struggle with his task – a kind of artistic epistemology' (p. 6). The French 'new' novelist Alain Robbe-Grillet, avowed enemy of art that signifies anything external to art, expresses the same thought: 'What constitutes the novelist's strength is precisely that he invents, that he invents quite freely, without a model. The remarkable thing about modern fiction is that it asserts this characteristic quite deliberately, to such a degree that invention and imagination become, at the limit, the very subject of the book'.[14] *Our Friend Manso* is at the least a venerable example of what Wellek and Warren call the 'romantic-ironic' mode of narration.[15] More than that, it is Galdós's most expansive statement on the problematic nature of fiction.

Chapter 1, with Chapter 50 at its heels, is the structure that shapes the entire novel. In fact, the two chapters are the unit that comprises the novel in question here: the story of fiction. The outer novel serves to distance the interior novel from itself and from the reader, along lines that turn out to be as Brechtian as they are Cervantine. The interior novel, if framed, must occupy a space inside and lesser than the framed whole (that is, Chapters 1 through 50 span more pages than Chapters 2 through 49). At the same time, the interior novel is perceived by the reader as a contained image. But in its function, the frame of a novel is quite unlike a picture frame, which one might rather compare to the covers of a book. The physical frame of a picture is normally an adventitious, externally imposed element, which the modern painter regularly prefers to suppress, leaving the picture to be bound by its natural limits. The novel's frame is an intrinsic member of the imaginative construct and does not outline decoratively the image it contains nor simply circumscribe that image spatially; instead, it infuses the construct with meaning and delimits that meaning. It is a sign superimposed on another sign, which latter can no longer be perceived independently of its informing structure. In other words, the novel cannot be reduced to what the frame contains: a social portrait of late nineteenth-century Spain or the dialectic between thought and action. The story of Máximo Manso is bound by a structure that forces a wedge between the bourgeois reality of the inner novel and the reader's own bourgeois reality all the while as it passes sentence on bourgeois reality. The two-tiered structuring compels in the reader a critical awareness of what the novel is about and what the novel is.

Roman Jakobson in a celebrated essay isolated the six factors that constitute a speech event: addresser, addressee, message, context, code, and contact.[16] Reading a novel can be considered a speech event. The function that language, or here the novel, takes on at any moment, explains Jakobson, depends on which of these elements is emphasized. In the bulk of *Our Friend Manso* – in the interior novel – focus is on the message in its context, and so the novel's function is largely referential. The frame or outer novel shifts the attention of the addressee (reader) to the novel's code, and its function thus becomes self-referential, that is, metalingual or reflexive.[17]

'I do not exist' are the novel's opening words (ch. 1, p. 1). 'I am Máximo Manso' is the title of the second chapter. There are two ways to interpret this transition. It can be said that Máximo emerges from nothingness (ch. 1) to assume carnality and identity (ch. 2). The novelistic process, here laid bare, demands, first, imaginative invention and, secondly, shaping of the invented object. An idea is fashioned in a character. Máximo, portrayed as conscious of himself as a text, actually reads himself the way the reader reads him. In telling his own story, he creates himself – again as the reader creates him by reading him. This way of looking at the initial chapters and the book confirms fiction as its subject.

The other perspective sets a value on the subject of fiction. 'I do not exist' is a flagrant declaration of Máximo's fictionality. The words are immediately corroborated: 'I am [. . .] an artistic condensation [. . .]. I am a chimera, the dream of a dream, the shadow of a shadow, the hint of a possibility' (ch. 1, pp. 1–2). But paradoxically, the cry of 'I do not exist' can be uttered only by a being existentially aware of himself. 'I do not exist', which says 'I am a dream', means 'I exist'. It is as much an averment of existence – more so perhaps – as Augusto Pérez's climactic 'I am myself'.[18] When the second chapter proclaims, 'I am Máximo Manso', that then needs to be read as 'I do not exist'. More accurately, the statement says: 'I exist because I do not exist.' The passage from 'I do not exist' to 'I am Máximo Manso' is the affirmation of non-existence, that is, the apotheosis of fictionality. Manso's opening protest against any possible investiture 'with the unequivocal attributes of real existence' must be taken literally. Later the text is dotted with efforts to project onto the reader Máximo's intuition of his fictional otherness: 'I saw myself as something out of a nightmare, or as if I were someone else and were dreaming of that other in the tranquil peace of my bed' (ch. 19, p. 116). Midway into the novel, Manuel Peña characterizes Manso to his face with words that most analysts of *Our Friend Manso* feel constrained to quote:

> You don't live in this world, Master [. . .]. Your shadow strolls through Manso's drawing-room; but you yourself remain in the grandiose limbo of thought, where everything is pure ontology, where man is a disembodied being, with no blood or nerves, created by the mind rather than by History or Nature; a being who has no age, no country, no parents, no betrothed (ch. 20, p. 124).

The meaning of these words in the context of Manolo's thought/action, theories/deeds, ontology/life dichotomy is clear. They are, beyond that, the novel's most explicit internal link with its frame. What Manolo takes to be a character portrayal of his teacher is a description of his fictional essence that matches his self-appraisal. The play here is complex: Galdós's autonomized creation recreates his creator coincidentally with the latter's self-creation. What I am saying – what Galdós is saying – is that Máximo Manso exists *because* he is a fiction, just as Unamuno exists not because he wrote *Niebla* but because he is a character in *Niebla*. Máximo as a non-existent entity acquires an existence that he could not otherwise have. Living in the bourgeois social atmosphere of Restoration Spain, Máximo as a man, even as a thinking man, is part of it; but as a fictional character he transcends it. He exists in space and time in a way that Castelar's mother or Galdós's third brother – or Galdós himself – do not.

Once his fictive autonomy is certified, Máximo can say: 'Someone is evoking me and, by means of I know not what subtle arts, is covering me with bodily form and turning me into the imitation or mask of a living person' (ch. 1, p. 2). Máximo's friend who evokes him – suppose, if you wish, that his name is Pérez Galdós – does not, in fact, exist prior to the narrative as his capacity to 'evoke' Manso might imply. He exists only thanks to Manso, who creates him within the narrative. So, the character evokes the author, the creation creates his creator; and one may ask, as twentieth-century writers so often have: who creates whom, who owes his existence to whom in the fictional relationship? The answers are as ambiguous as the question is intriguing.

Manso, ever gentle and good, is everybody's friend. For his part, Galdós as narrator is often the friend of his 'creatures'. But never is the friendship so close as it is between 'friend' Manso and Galdós. Why? Because, like the best of friends, they are inseparable. If Manso cannot pinpoint the 'subtle arts' of his creation, it is because the miracle of artistic birth cannot be defined or described with precision. The creator/creation dichotomy, when carried beyond the obvious and subjected to analysis, becomes so blurred that no order of sequential precedence between its two factors seems possible. As a consequence, a character like Manso endowed with the illusion of autonomy assumes a duality whose two sides the reader might forcibly isolate from each other if he wishes but which operate conjointly at every moment in the book. It is not, as Gullón would have it (1970, p. 88), that part of Manso's narrative 'I' participates and part contemplates: all of him does both at the same time. He is poet and empiricist, *histor* and eye-witness wrapped into one.[19] That is why Manso can first talk of someone who conjures him (ch. 1: birth *as* a fiction) and then go on to speak calmly of his father and mother, to whom he owes his life and all that he is (ch. 2: birth *within* a fiction). Truly, an imagined entity should not be depending on a bowlful of chickpeas for his sustenance. It should be sufficient for a reader to read him. Yet, in that paradox lies the secret of fictional creation, which must live out this tension of being and not being autonomous. Of course, it is easy to envision the protests against such a reading: You can't have it both ways! You can't have Máximo creating a creator who has created him! But that is precisely the beauty of fiction, as Galdós fully realized. Its delectable ambiguity not only allows us to have it both ways, but forces these paradoxes upon us. Wordsworth's dictum 'The Child is the father of the Man' seems appropriate to the case. Naturally, we know that there is no such unfathered creature as an autonomous character in the world of fiction. A character who is a paradox, a game, an irony, a phantom, is, in the end, impossible. Therefore, the question as to whether or not Máximo Manso or Grau's puppets or Capek's robots or Pirandello's homeless half dozen or Don Quixote are truly autonomous is beside the point when we acknowledge its illusoriness. The significance of the issue lies in our capacity to apprehend simultaneously that illusion of their possible autonomy and our knowledge of their dependency. The questions that follow upon that illusion constitute an inquiry into the nature of fiction through the problematic relationship between author and character. To the extent that he is known to us as an invention of Galdós, Máximo Manso here serves that investigative aim. And as happens regularly when the question matters more than the answer, the investigation produces no findings. At the end, in successive paragraphs, Máximo appears to will his own death – 'Such was my desire for rest that I never got up again' – while yet dependent on his conjurer to effect it – 'That same perverse friend who had brought me into the world took me out of it' (ch. 50, pp. 307, 308).

Máximo's death fits this scheme. Some critics have expressed puzzlement or sought vain explanations for his death from natural causes at the age of 35. But how old is Máximo Manso; how old is he *now*? Is he 35 as stated in the novel and therefore 35 forever? Is he 94, the age of the novel at this writing? Or is he 129, the sum of the two? The point, of course, is that Manso does not die; his story merely comes to a close. To borrow Nimetz's felicitous turn of phrase: 'Although a mirage, Manso never quite disappears.'[20] Manso's death is not physical; it is, like his birth, a conjurer's act. A text cannot die. It can only reach its natural end, at which point, with one state of the creative act completed, it lies in a continued state of dormant existence until it is read, reread, recreated, reexperienced. Manso can presumably die in his role as creator, though not as a creation, a fact which actually assures him of survival on both counts: as creator, he lives through his creations, as Galdós through Manso, even if his earthly traces disappear and his creations – Manolo, Irene – also autonomize themselves; as creation, there is no way in which he can suffer mortality, for a 'self without flesh or blood' (ch. 1, p. 1) is pure spirit.

In the novel's opening paragraph, Manso designates himself as a myth. A myth exists eternally, and a mythical figure enjoys life and significance beyond that of the ordinary human being. Novel writing is myth creation. Thus, when Máximo dies, he does not simply vanish from the earthly scene. His death is a signal that the process of his mythification has been realized: his story has been told; he has been created. He is now ready to pass into eternity. How is it he can tell us about his own demise? As subject and object, as teller of his tale, as creator of himself, he stands both outside and inside the fiction. He is a fictional being who is witness to his own fictionalization. From Máximo's perch outside the process of which he is the protagonist, his consciousness – his fictional consciousness – can embrace both the beginning and the end of that process. Again like the reader, he can read the text that he is – the *whole* text.

Furthermore, Máximo's death is not a disappearance into memory. His death is a very part of his existence, of his *continuing* existence. With his death, Máximo does not pass from existence into non-existence, but from process into state. The act of writing has come to an end; but the text exists, waiting to be read. What Manso imagines Irene telling him near the end of his development, we can all say quite literally: 'I can read you, Manso; I can read you as if you were a book written in the clearest of languages' (ch. 48, p. 299). Máximo is recreated every time *Our Friend Manso* is read; he can be recreated at will. I, as a critic, am now replaying that process of recreation. The rest of us, when we die, cannot aspire to that degree of immortality. Gullón (1970, p. 83) recognizes, as do characters in the novel, that Máximo is different from the rest, that he appears not to participate in this life as they do. Gullón has done well to seize upon this distinctiveness of Máximo and to interpret it as the abyss which separates the man of action from the contemplative soul. There is no doubt that the text must be read in this fashion; but the text with the same words also alerts us to the distinction between a being of flesh and a fictitious creation. These two readings together allow us to superimpose onto Gullón's elucidation of the ending – Manso's happy escape into limbo from the regions of life's demands – the view that his 'death' is a manifestation of his superior cognitive powers and his open reassumption of them.[21] Newton (1973, p. 123) explains the close of the novel as a retreat into literariness on Manso's part after he was denied, because of his passive, analytical personality, entry into the world of action. If it is a retreat, it is a return to the fictional heights whence he had emerged. More accurately, perhaps, it is not a retreat, but an ascension. Certainly, though, literariness is the shape of Manso's immortality. His discovery of his uselessness and his subsequent secession from life constitute his existential self-realization as a fictitious character. Such is the implication – or one of them – when he complains: 'I wasn't myself, or at least I didn't seem to be myself. There were times when I seemed to be the disfigured shadow of one Mr Manso' (ch. 50, p. 306). Only at that final point has the process of self-creation been consummated. At that point it makes full sense that at the start Manso should have seen himself existing, as myths do, in infinite time and that – 'savouring my not being' (ch. 1, p. 2) – he should have taken pleasure, as readers of novels do, in the contemplation of an invention.

The examination of the nature of fiction and of the problem of fictive autonomy is accorded yet a deeper dimension in *Our Friend Manso* through a secondary structure that duplicates the primary one. Máximo's relationship with Manuel Peña and Irene is parallel to Máximo's relationship with his creator, for Máximo in turn becomes Manolo's and Irene's creator, and they, as soon as they are shaped, declare their independence of him.

As a first-person narrator, Manso is naturally the creator of all the characters in the book. Doña Javiera, for example, does not exist for us until Máximo writes: 'Now I'll tell you about my neighbour' (ch. 3, p. 13). The account he then presents of her appearance, speech habits, and personality traits is the process of novelistic creation. Lica, for her part, is ingenuous, delicate, and kind, as Manso sees (makes) her, and not the unpolished peasant girl that she is in the eyes of Madrid's high society. In the cases of Manolo and Irene, Manso's creative involvement is redoubled, because not only is he responsible for their presence in the novel, he is internally the catalyst for the particular shapes they assume. Manolo is his pupil, and Irene is his mental construct of an ideal.

The chapter that marks Manuel Peña's entry into the novel (ch. 4) is entitled 'Manolito Peña, my disciple'. Since Manuel's discipleship breached the contraints of a purely formal academic education and Manuel before and after his contacts with his mentor was not the same person, 'my disciple' can be read as 'my creation'. That stands as fact not only for the reader, but also for Manso, who, interestingly, defines that relationship in artistic terms. Initially he says: 'My delight was that of a sculptor being given a perfect piece of the finest marble to carve a statue' (ch 4, p. 22). Assessing the raw material, Manso quickly determines that the esthetic terrain would be the most propitious for forming Manolo's character, a decision he smugly qualifies as 'An excellent plan' (ch. 4, p. 23). Later, with his task behind him – on the occasion of Peña's successful debut as an orator – Manso returns to the same idea: 'I had dressed his natural talents in the robes of art' (ch. 28, p. 171).[22] Irene, too, in the chapter in which she is introduced (ch. 6), is presented as raw material, full of potential, that can be misshapen or admirably developed, according to the creative circumstances. She, too, is estheticized:

> The sadness expressed [. . .] by her pretty eyes, that sadness which at times seemed to me an esthetic effect produced by the light and colour

of her pupils, at others the product of those expressive gestures through which the mysteries of the moral world are revealed to us, was perhaps an example of one of those fundamental self-deceptions in which we live for a prolonged period, perhaps all our lives, without ever realizing' (ch. 6, p. 39).

Irene is projected not as a creature of flesh, but as a phenomenon of esthetic, linguistic expression. The statement also adduces that art, here in the shape of Irene, is the affirmation of life's mysteries and that art's deceit, its ambiguity, is inherent and sustains us. That power of art forges the supernatural oneness that exists between creator and creation. 'She accompanied me everywhere,' writes Manso of Irene in terms even more explicit than his expressions of solidarity with Manuel. 'It was as if her nature had been miraculously injected into mine. I felt her as part of me, our spirits one' (ch. 17, p. 104). The long conversation between Máximo and Irene in which the details of her relationship with Peña are revealed is for all intents and purposes Irene's confession, but it comes from the mouth of Manso. It is as if he were reciting a drama whose script he had composed. This retrospective account that abounds in evidence of Manso's omniscience prompts Irene to exclaim twice: '"You know . . . more than God . . ."'; '"You know everything . . . You seem to have powers of divination . . ."' (ch. 26, pp. 256, 258). The reader is not so surprised.

The creator's control over his creation however – whether that creation is a pupil, an ideal, or a fictional character – is tenuous. Through Manolo, the pupil (the idea) is portrayed as potentially willful and rebellious, and the teacher (the artist) must conquer and tame in order to shape. In the course of the educational process, Manso discovers that he needs to adjust to his pupil's innate gifts. He cannot squeeze polished writing out of oratorical talent, and he cannot fan speculative interests where pragmatic inclinations persist. Even the name by which Manolo is most frequently called, Peñita, is given him by someone else and in spite of Manso's distaste for it. Small incidents these, yet proof that the artistic raw material is refractory from the start and subject to the interference of third parties. In Irene's case, too, Manso constructs her in a given fashion, as a woman of the North, free of his society's enervating moral climate: 'Here you have the perfect woman, the practical woman, the rational woman, as opposed to the frivolous woman, the fickle woman' (ch. 13, p. 77). Yet Manso is prompted to wonder: 'Do I know her that well? No; each day I realize there's something in her that's hidden from my eyes' (ch. 16, p. 100); and he recognizes how easy it is to portray an individual's unchanging traits variably as defects or perfections. Moreover, he is confused by the tension between his powers of observation and artistic dictates. After Irene's attack of hysteria and fever, he asks: 'Do her weakness and suffering increase her beauty or almost totally destroy it? Do they make her all the more fascinating, as pictorial convention would have it, or has she lost all her poetry?' (ch. 40, p. 252).[23] Galdós, Manso, art, nature, society: whose is the guiding hand here? Manolo's (mis)use of his education to join the ranks of the petty bourgeoisie is an act of independence or of rebellion, depending on the vantage point; in any event, a destruction of the mold in which he had been cast. As for Irene, her revelation to Manso of her true nature is her profession of autonomy. There is no rebellion in her case: 'What a mistake!' (ch. 42, p. 266); Manso's ideal Irene simply crumbles as she assumes a form at variance with the one he had imagined for her.

Here is a man who lives by order and by reason's absolute law, who boasts of method in his every act and defines life as a solemn plan, yet cannot control his creations. Small wonder, then, that he is given to self-doubt. When, contrary to all his habits and at Manolo's insistence, he finds himself confronting some 'churros' and brandy in a 'buñolería' (establishment making and selling fritters) he muses: 'Who can say they are masters of themselves [. . .]?' (ch. 20, p. 119). It would appear that the individual has so little sway over his order (whether it is social, ontological, or fictional) that the order imposes itself on him even though he has created it. Several times in the novel's pages Manso confesses himself to be his creations' creation and inferior to them.[24] So formed by his pupil is he that for a moment he rebels against analysis and knowledge and exalts the man of action over his own ways. Of Irene he says: 'The schoolteacher [. . .] would teach me certain things', and he imagines her echoing: 'we schoolteachers know more than metaphysicians' (ch. 48, pp. 298, 300). When at the end he says: 'I've borne fruit and am now superfluous' (ch. 50, p. 307), he is signaling not only the realization of his own fictionality, but Irene's and Manolo's and his acceptance of their autonomous status.

Why does Máximo lose control over Manolo and Irene? In accordance with life's patterns, although they owe their existence to the thinker-teacher-writer-artist Máximo, they, not he, determine their actions as they embrace the society in which they dwell. In the light of fiction, once created, they too become texts that others read and recreate. Their ultimate identity depends on these readers' recreation of them. Art is as relative to the beholder as reality is, and since the creator's perspective is no more than the perspective of yet another beholder, the creation's flight from its creator's particular perception of it is built into the creative act. Perhaps it lies in the nature of art that the artist, unable to sense the texture of his creations and powerless to track their future, simply programs their autonomy.

Máximo Manso's eruption into the novel, his death, and his education/idealization of Manuel Peña and Irene are the three principal phases of Galdós's structuring of the theme of fictionality in *Our Friend Manso*. To complete the picture, one must mention that the book brims over with direct and oblique references to the literary art. On the one hand, the frequent touches which signal that a writer is writing expand the work's self-referential dimension as art, fiction, and novel. On the other hand, specific literary styles and practices come under mischievous scrutiny.

From the beginning Galdós pokes fun at the artistic process, but with the double irony that informs the whole novel. That is to say, the ironic tone that subverts the object presented in this light is itself subverted by the measure of seriousness with which it must be read. Consequently, when Manso writes: 'I am a fresh example of those human deceits that populate the world since time immemorial, mass produced and sold by those I call idle wastrels, who have no sense of filial duty, and whom the benevolent public calls artists, poets and suchlike' (ch. 1, pp. 1–2), derision and exaltation are indistinguishable. If he is disrespectful of his progenitor, he does not disown him, for he declares himself openly as an artist (ch. 14, p. 84); and playful as the self-revelation is, it is nonetheless a revelation. The mysteries of the nature of fiction are outlined in Chapter 40, aptly entitled 'Lies, lies'[25] – to wit, fiction. It begins with the sentence, 'I say this because my narration now involves such incredible things that no one is going to believe them' (ch. 40, p. 247), and goes on to establish the following series of paradoxical facts: 1) this is a narration, *my* narration (fiction); 2) fiction is unbelievable; 3) fiction is truth attractively garbed; 4) truth is unbelievable; 5) I, the creator, am confused by my creation. With fiction's complexity thus posited, the ensuing irony is less jolting: at the very moment when Máximo awakens from a dream to a recognition of the creative power of rational consciousness, he also becomes fully aware (chs 40 and 42) of his loss of power over his creations. The autonomy of events and characters from their creator and the chasm that exists between them, as well as the illusion of reality that this autonomizing process bestows on the fiction, are expressed in words that could not have been lost on Unamuno: 'Following on that implausible tale comes the biggest, most outlandish improbability of the whole day. This one is really hard to swallow. I'm sure none of my readers will be gullible enough to fall for it; but I'll tell it anyway, and protest the truth of its falsity with all my might' (ch. 40, p. 251).

Manso's narration also draws attention to itself as fiction through the device of contrasting its potential and its actual course. Immediately after confronting Manuel about the relationship with Irene, the narrator sets up a dichotomy between what the conventions of sentimental literature would demand under the circumstances and the strange truth of his reactions:

> At this point I cannot conceal a fact which at the time, and still today, seems to me strange, unbelievable, extraordinary. In describing how I

> ate, I should like to conform to what is normal and habitual in such cases, painting a picture of myself as lacking appetite, more inclined to pour out my heart than down a single chick-pea; but my love of truth compels me to relate that I had a hearty appetite, and ate every single day [. . .]. I know full well that this will contradict everything the most serious authors have said about love, not to mention those medical experts who have studied the parallel effects of bodily functions and emotional states; but be that as it may, I must tell it as it happened, and readers can draw their own conclusions (ch. 39, pp. 242–3).

The reader of these lines is forced into an open consideration of the literary art; he becomes ally to the narrator in passing judgment on conventions that run contrary to the realities of life; and he is prevented from sentimentalizing the action by having his attention thrust on the mechanism of the narration exactly as Manso's craving for food brakes his emotional response. When that response does arrive, it has been rendered as bookish as the books under attack.[26]

Accompanying *Our Friend Manso*'s perambulations through the mysteries of fiction and its relation to reality is a series of reflections on the ways of the novel. Again operating on the dual plane of paradox, Galdós can have Manso cry, 'Order, some order in the narrative!' (ch. 1, p. 2), at the same time as he unabashedly subverts narrative order and with the next breath jabs at readers' expectations of chronology, motivation, background, context, and sequence. It is suggested that the novel has its own order, a private, non-chronological order (for example, ch. 6, p. 40), so private, in fact, that the reader of *Our Friend Manso* is led to ruminate all at once the need for and the absurdity of novelistic order. Máximo divulges his method as he proceeds: 'Turning now to external matters, I can say that [. . .]'; 'I'm impatient to talk about my moral being' (ch. 1, pp. 5, 10); and the opening of Chapter 22 is a description of narrative progress through plot complication and of the narrator's alternatives as witness and participant. All the while that he does what is expected of a narrator, Máximo says with a twinkle, 'I'm doing this because that's what's expected in a narration.' Or he warns us when he departs from the expected. In either case he is telling us that this is a novel.

In its declared status as work of art and novel, *Our Friend Manso* is also, at moments, an expression of esthetic concern and a disquisition on style. The difficulties of creation and the inadequacy of words to express certain ideas and emotions are underscored: 'appreciating beauty and expressing it are very different matters' (ch. 4, p. 24; see also ch. 16). Manso as a writer is self-conscious: 'Ideas about beauty filled my mind and whirled around it' (ch. 3, p. 16), he says; and he complains bitterly about Manuel's stylistic insensitivity (ch. 7, p. 40). After learning of

Irene's clandestine friendship with Manuel, Máximo writes a paragraph of resounding reproaches in the best declamatory style, but he then represents that outburst as hypothetical and opts for simplicity, thereby slapping at the practices of others. When Manso's taste lapses or when he takes liberties with his own standards, then the text's self-consciousness turns his self-consciousness into self-parody, as in the following jocular displays: 'The fair Doña Javiera . . . [in Spanish: "Doña Javiera era . . ."] (I don't like the rhyme, but never mind) was a widow' (ch. 4, p. 21); 'That's what I told her; I was eloquent, with a touch of the refined and gallant' (ch. 34, p. 209); 'To employ a figure from the mystical register, still beautiful if worn after being manhandled by so many poets and theologians, let me say that an angel had visited me and consoled me in my sleep' (ch. 39, pp. 244–5).[27]

If *Our Friend Manso* is an examination and revelation of its generic self, it is natural that its parodic component should also be directed against the novel and the novel's medium, language. Throughout the work Galdós satirizes the commonplaces and the spent formulas of novel writing. The surprising shape he gave to *Our Friend Manso* – not his most deeply human novel but certainly his most brilliant tour de force – is his cry for originality and for renovation of the genre.[28] In its focus on its own raw material, this novel already demonstrates its literariness, and in its relentless attack on the rhetorical tradition, it subjects the word to destruction through the word. It annihilates the signifier that has suffered the loss of its signified (a social commentary via language) and thereby subverts the sign on which the novel is dependent (a literary commentary). On the rubble of the destruction he has perpetrated for readers of *Our Friend Manso* to contemplate, Galdós is to build a new type of novel that has been linguistically cleansed.

Galdós throughout his career unleashed his venom at the ingrained Spanish penchant for rhetorical expression and in particular at the nineteenth-century's oratorical tradition. In *Our Friend Manso* that posture surfaces in several ways. As the novel's only narrative voice, Manso bears the sanitizing responsibility, and he carries it out both by default and actively. He himself becomes the unwitting butt of Galdós's satire when he falls into pedantry and jejune rhetoric in his writing.[29] Conversely, it is he who descries the incompatibility between lucid ideas and rebellious language. 'There's nothing harder than to say little about something important', he says (ch. 24, p. 145), and in the preparation of his speech for the charity gala, he voices his awareness of three requirements: to style the speech in such a fashion as to achieve a harmonious structure; to make it clear, direct, and brief so that it will be readily grasped; and to banish from it the surface effects of dazzling oratory. His own guilt notwithstanding, he hammers away at those who neglect these ground rules. 'Above all, Spain is the classic land of oratory,' he says sarcastically (ch. 17, p. 105), and oratory sits enthroned where its damage is greatest: in the political arena. José María's entry into politics provides the opportunity for repeated attacks on the debasement of language, which Máximo sums up twittingly: 'Our Congress, known for its high oratory, also has its music-hall style' (ch. 15, p. 93). Ramón María Pez, the political orator, is subjected to the most merciless satire in this terrain,[30] and the effects of his emphatic phrases on Máximo are graphically portrayed: 'his hollow phrases [. . .] resounded in my mind like the sound of an empty eggshell falling to the ground and smashing' (ch. 12, p. 72). Manuel Peña's fustian speech in the theater is enough to assure his political and social future and catapults him into prominence, though even José María is impelled to comment: 'How highly prized are the arts of oratory and that peculiarly Spanish ability to utter fine words that mean nothing in practice!' (ch. 31, pp. 189–90). As pervasive as political oratory is, poetry has not escaped the damaging touch of rhetoric either. Galdós's frequent derision of poets, from *La Fontana de Oro* on, for the sins they have visited upon the Spanish language is well known. In *Our Friend Manso*, Francisco de Paula de la Costa y Sainz del Bardal, to whom Máximo refers as 'That fellow' (ch. 12, p. 71), is the poetaster who thrives on a doting and tasteless moneyed class. From his name to his beard to his health to his character to his address to his talents as a versifier, this 'ignorant young gentleman' is unrelentingly caricaturized. The pompousness of his self-esteem is comparable only to that of his odes.[31]

The reflexive nature of *Our Friend Manso* filters through this attention to the word to a consideration of literary styles. Manso knows that his brother's house is six minutes or 560 paces away from his, and he phrases his report about Doña Javiera thus: 'one day she came into my home (third floor on the right) unannounced'; 'as she was going into her house (first floor on the left) [. . .]' (ch. 3, pp. 14, 15). Along with the ridicule these details heap on Manso's exaggerated sense of precision, they also show Galdós laughing at his way as a novelist, at the realistic novel's insistence on exactitude in its descriptive technique. More frequently, however, it is the romantic style that the author of *Marianela* chooses to burlesque.[32] Time and again in his narration, Manso adopts romantic postures and language only to collapse them by exaggerating,[33] by announcing them as hypothetical,[34] or by revealing them for what they are. The flowery, metaphoric language that Manso uses to describe Irene's first contacts with Manolo is immediately reduced to parody when he interjects: 'You'll have to admit I'm being poetical' (ch. 41, p. 255).[35] The reader perhaps swept up momentarily by the attractiveness of the language is roughly returned to his circumstance as reader of a text and made to reflect on the options of artistic expression. The mock epic language used to describe Doña Cándida (ch. 4) and the derogatory assessment of the declamatory style of the contemporary theater (chs 14, 15) are further elements of this anti-rhetorical stand, while Máximo's death is the positive highpoint of that posture: a simple exit, with no gestures, no drama, no bombast. In all these instances, *Our Friend Manso* exposes itself as a fiction about fiction, and the text assumes the power to create and to destroy through the word, one in the process of the other.

[. . .]

The game of literary reflexivity in which Galdós luxuriates in *Our Friend Manso* is a component of the novel which any reading of the book must embrace. That the novel should undertake an appraisal of its own constitution is enough to dispel the charge of gratuitousness that might be hurled at this absorption in game playing. The metanovelistic undertaking, however, is judged as sterile by those convinced that its view onto itself excludes the world, that which really counts. In *Our Friend Manso*, though, the game is not gratuitous because the work's investigation of fictionality and the social-ideological planes are fully integrated. The reader's acquisition of consciousness of the problematics of fiction permits him to capture all the more readily the corresponding social structure that evolves in the context of this self-examination of fiction. Doña Cándida is an example. 'Full of pompous lies' conceived 'in her dream-filled mind', she lives a lie in her new house: the silverware is not silver, the champagne is cider, the table is missing a leg. But she believes in her own creation. 'She turned her sorry state of affairs into an absurd comedy' (ch. 5, p. 29). A fiction has overtaken the reality from which it sprang. Like Doña Cándida, the members of this bourgeois society are fictional beings not only in the sense that they are the inventions of Galdós, but in that they have created themselves into something they are not and function in a society structured on such fictions. In the same way that any novelistic creation is given life through language, José María's family's birth into a new social role is legitimized in its fictionality by the members' adoption of new linguistic signs (Lica > Manuela, Belica > Isabel, etc.). The purchase of titles of nobility is the crowning step in their creation of a fictional identity. Máximo himself, who is ostensibly – but only ostensibly – independent of his creator, is also only ostensibly independent of his society where the clock strikes eleven at the hour of five. But just as the failure of Nazarín's peculiar evangelism is a measure not simply of his ineptitude but of the spiritual sterility of nineteenth-century bourgeois society, so too is Manso's sense of uselessness and ultimate withdrawal an indictment of a society in which the gentle, the learned, and the morally pure have no place.

Any judgment of Manso's nature that leaves his circumstance untouched falsifies the relationship between the two. Still, as we have shown, through the device of fictive autonomy Galdós distances the reader of *Our Friend Manso* from Máximo and his bourgeois world. In doing so, he draws attention to the workings of the esthetic object that is at once his creation and his medium. He causes the reader to fasten not on the social signification alone, but on the novel as signifer. His endeavor, like any metalingual enterprise, is semiotic and epistemological at the same time: it ventures in the telling of the tale to unravel that tale's system of signs and to probe the nature of knowledge dressed as fiction. In this art that exposes itself, the child in us that is normally swept into the game of belief is suppressed. That level here is literally reserved for the child, as when Pepito María hides his face in terror at the sight of the devil on stage. We are pitched, rather, into a more sophisticated game for adults. In words that Ortega was to echo some forty-five years later, Manso exalts the child's ingenuous faith before the work of art over the analytical process: 'Nothing human could withstand so much analysis! It is a misfortune to experience the bitter pleasure of criticism, to be driven by one's mind to pluck the petals from the flower one so admires. How much better to be a child and gaze with wild astonishment at the imperfections of some crude toy [. . .]' (ch. 14, p. 85). In this by no means rough-hewn plaything, Galdós has us not live the novel but view it as object, constrains us to become aware of ourselves as readers/players, and even edges us into a critical analysis of our awareness. In composing a novel that takes its own creation as its theme, Galdós joins a host of twentieth-century writers of metanovels, Proust, Gide, and Beckett among them. He makes a Pirandello play look much less astonishing than it did at first blush. He connects with the modern cinema's penchant for reflexiveness: Fellini's *8½* and Bergman's *Persona* come to mind immediately. If these names seem to constitute odd company for the likes of Don Benito 'trader in chickpeas',[36] one must keep sight of the fact that there is a difference between Galdós and the others. The nineteenth century's ever-increasing isolation of the artist from its social currents has pushed the modern writer to take refuge in an artistic hermeticism. When Galdós creates a self-referential art and leads his readers to experience a specific novel as an examination of the novelistic genre, he does so without jettisoning the bourgeoisie. Like Máximo Manso, he is not estranged from, or even by, the practices and values of the bourgeois society to which he belongs. He too is critical subject and corruptible object of his petty circumstance. *Our Friend Manso* therefore functions both in the sphere of socio-political commentary and in the hermetic realm of esthetic introspection.

The radicality of Galdós's procedure in his time lies in the fact that, narrators' interventions notwithstanding, the realistic novel does its best to hide its identity as a novel, while Galdós in *Our Friend Manso* creates an illusionist art that signals the coming break with illusionism. 'You think *Our Friend Manso* is life?' he asks us, straight in the tradition of Cervantes. 'Don't deceive yourselves! This is a novel!' We must remain awake to the fact that when we read a novel we are engaging in a game. Children play games to fill their time, to learn and grow. So do adults. Reading novels is one of our games. We know the rules beforehand; we learned them long ago. To play *Our friend Manso* requires a few new rules, because it is a game that plays with the game that it plays. The critic's game is to discover that game and its rules.

Notes

1. An embryonic version of this study was read at the 28th Annual Kentucky Foreign Language Conference, April 24–6, 1975. I am grateful to Brian J. Dendle for the invitation that sparked this essay.
2. I use the term 'autonomous' not to refer to a character's extranovelistic credibility, as in FRANCISCO AYALA 1970–1, 'Los narradores de las novelas de *Torquemada*', *Cuadernos Hispanoamericanos* **250–2**: 375; rather I apply it more narrowly to the illusion of independence from authorial control by means of a character's confrontation with his fictionality. JOSEPH E. GILLET, 1956, 'The autonomous character in Spanish and European literature', *Hispanic Review* **24**: 179–90, who makes only passing reference to *Our Friend Manso* and detours around the illusory nature of the device, discusses autonomy in this light as an author's willing abdication of his power, with the result that characters exist as citizens of a double world of reality and literature. This duality infuses the concept with its problematic nature, of which I am fully aware and which I shall develop later in this essay.
3. References to *Our Friend Manso* are to the first edition (*El amigo Manso*, n.d. [1882], La Guirnalda, Madrid), by chapter and page. I have modernized the accentuation and, where necessary, the punctuation.
4. EMILIO G. GAMERO Y DE LAIGLESIA (1934, *Galdós y su obra*, vol. 2 *Las novelas*. Imprenta Ruiz, Madrid) discerned that Máximo Manso is both 'a real being' and 'the product of the novelist's fantasy' (p. 86) but, not knowing what to make of that, made nothing of it. WALTER T. PATTISON, given to positivistic sleuthing, rejects out of hand the denomination of Manso as an autonomous character (1967, 'El amigo Manso and el amigo Galdós', *Anales Galdosianos* **2**: 151, n. 2).
5. CASALDUERO J., 1970 *Vida y obra de Galdós (1843–1920)*, 3rd edn, Gredos, Madrid, p. 223.
6. 1970–1, 'La interdependencia de los personajes galdosianos', *Cuadernos Hispanoamericanos* **250–2**: 129.
7. 1963, '*El amigo Manso*: Galdós with a mirror', *Modern Language Notes* **78**: 167.
8. 1967, *Realidad, ficción y símbolo en las novelas de Pérez Galdós*, Instituto Caro y Cuervo, Bogotá, esp. pp. 100–7. A propos of Felipín Centeno he says that 'the author discovered in the characters of the novels themselves the possibility of feeling they were real beings but, at the same time, being aware they were fictional creations' (p. 79). Some of his introductory remarks, which he restates in his conclusion (p. 291), bear repeating here: 'We find ourselves confronted by a work of art which sets out to be a faithful representation of reality, but

which at the same time insists it is strictly a fictional world. [. . .] the fact of converting this artistic preoccupation into the substance of the novel itself is one of the strange means by which the novelist transforms reality into a fictional world. Galdós's art of the novel thus reveals an internal artistic dimension which is intrinsic to its own creation' (p. 11).

9. For example LEON LIVINGSTONE (1958, 'Interior duplication and the problem of form in the modern Spanish novel', *PMLA* **73**: 393–406) includes a brief discussion of *Our Friend Manso* in support of his postulation that this technique of interior duplication and character autonomy is a statement of a relativist metaphysic in which fiction and reality have no fixed outlines. MONROE Z. HAFTER's introductory remarks (1951, Ironic reprise in Galdós's novels, *PMLA* **76**: 233–9) might suggest that he is to take up the problem of internal repetitions of the fictional construct, but he deals, rather, with characters' reflection of each other. He extrapolates the self/other antinomy from complementary pairings either of characters or within characters and thereby dramatizes Galdós's subtle illumination of an elusive human reality. EAMONN RODGERS (1970–1, 'Realismo y mito en *El amigo Manso*', *Cuadernos Hispanoamericanos* **250–2**: 430–44), aware of the frame's presence throughout the novel, takes note of Manso's mythic dimension but remains tied to a defense of the label of realism. NANCY A. NEWTON (1973, '*El amigo Manso* and the relativity of reality', *Revista de Estudios Hispánicos* **7**: 113–25) cleverly weaves Manso's autonomy into her thematic considerations. She defines his trajectory from object-centredness to subject-centredness as 'a dynamic act of auto-creation' (p. 122) and takes note of the special textual kinship between Galdós and Manso as a 'deliberate rupturing of the fictional illusion which the nineteenth-century realist novelist normally makes every effort to maintain' (p. 115). RICARDO GULLÓN (1970, '*El amigo Manso*, nivola galdosiana', in *Técnicas de Galdós*, Taurus, Madrid, pp. 57–102) examines various aspects of the Galdós text but is more interested in enlacing it with *Niebla* and in defining its self-exposure as a metaphor of the life process than in extracting its metanovelistic components. He does remark on the first chapter's 'magical operations' (p. 77); he also registers Máximo as an archetype of fiction, 'a paper character, an invented being who does not gloss over but proclaims his nature as artifice' (p. 61). Gullón was among the first to give Manso his real due, but he did not choose to analyze the novel as a commentary on the creative act. Since the completion of my essay, ARNOLD M. PENUEL has published a brief note (1974, 'Some aesthetic implications of Galdós's *El amigo Manso*', *Anales Galdosianos* **9**: 145–8), which bears on Manso's autonomy and Galdós's concern for fiction.

10. One is tempted to agree with JOSÉ F. MONTESINOS's apparent hyperbole: 'never so clearly as in this ironic novel has the writer understood the meaning of his creative endeavour' (1969, *Galdós*, vol. 2. Castalia, Madrid, p. 29), but precisely because in the context of our discussion the statement – ironically – is not hyperbolic at all.

11. References to Galdós's novels other than *Our friend Manso* are taken from the *Obras completas* (1965, 4th edn., Aguilar, Madrid).

12. 1971, 'Rhetoric in *La sombra*: the author and his story', *Anales Galdosianos* **6**: 10–12. Turner confuses the categories of author and narrator, but her point is well taken.

13. CORREA, G. (1967, pp. 80–99) develops this idea in ch. 6 'La realidad como ficción'.

14. 1965, *For a New Novel*, Grove Press, New York, p. 32.

15. Wellek R. and Warren, A., 1956, *Theory of Literature*, 3rd edn, Harcourt Brace, New York, p. 223.

16. 1960, 'Linguistics and poetics', in Sebeok T. A. (ed.) *Style in Language*, MIT Press, Cambridge, Mass., pp. 350–77.

17. Some critics attempt to distinguish between 'reflexivity' as a work's reference to itself generically and 'self-reflexivity' as a work's reference to itself specifically. Since these two facets of artistic self-consciousness are barely distinguishable and one implies the other, I do not propose to mark such frontiers here.

18. *Editor's note*: Augusto Pérez is the protagonist of Unamuno's *Niebla*.

19. See Scholes, R. and Kellogg, R., 1966, *The Nature of Narrative*, Oxford University Press, New York, ch. 7.

20. Nimetz, M., 1968, *Humor in Galdós*, Yale University Press, New Haven, p. 98.

21. If Manso's death is seen as the affirmation of his fictionality rather than as the obliteration of his immanent existence, one quickly senses how false is the distinction traced by Robert Kirsner: 'He began his narration as a fictional being and ends it as a non-existent one' (1950, Sobre *El amigo Manso* de Galdós. *Cuadernos de Literatura* **8**: 192). Kirsner's effort to draw critical attention to a neglected novel merits applause. Robert Ricard (1961, 'Quelques aspects du thème de l'*évasion* dans les romans de Galdós', in *Galdós et ses romans*, Institut d'Etudes Hispaniques, Paris, pp. 63–71) is close to the truth in his conviction that Manso's death is not a flight, but a departure for good reason, the reason being that his work is done. Ricard's assessment falls short of being a fully satisfactory formula insofar as it accounts for Máximo's social but not his fictional status.

22. In their respective speeches in the theater, Manso and Peña emerge as the imperfect halves of a unit, for Manso's is all content and Peña's is all form. Paternal pride aside, how do we explain Manso's enthusiasm for the gestures, the flowery phrasing, the empty metaphors that lead him to ask twice 'what was he saying?' and that in others he had relentlessly condemned? Only his instinctive recognition of the symbiotic dependency between creator and creation can serve as an adequate explanation.

23. Manso reveals, as omniscient creator, that he knows how the story of Manolo and Irene is to end; but then he feels sorry for himself because his role in its denouement is not clear to him: 'Should I intervene in it, or should I make good my escape and leave the criminals to sort it out as best they could? . . . Poor Manso!' (ch. 41, p. 258). Whether he is pawn of the action or its guiding force or simply withdraws (dies) depends on whether he plays character and participant or creator or narrator.

24. In an intelligent article that does not touch on the question of Manso's fictionality (1962, 'Galdós's *El amigo Manso*: an experiment in didactic method', *Bulletin of Hispanic Studies* **39**: 16–30), G. R. Davies singles out the 'buñolería' scene as an example of Manso's distanced state from the political and social realities of life and his inferiority, in this respect, to his own pupil.

25. Galdós's quaint use of chapter titles in this novel is a game that requires separate attention.

26. Further such instances are a scene with Doña Cándida concerning Irene: 'Drama was in the air. I could sense the violence, what in the artificial world of the theatre they call the situation' (ch. 35, p. 217); and after José María's sheepish retreat from Irene's quarters: 'There had been no drama, which was to the good of all' (ch. 36, p. 227). In another work, such comments would inject a note of verisimilitude into the fiction (only *real* people go to the theater!). In this book, the statement is yet another reminder of its fictionality as well as a criticism of a certain sort of fiction. This procedure takes hold early in the novel: 'I beg my readers not to miss this chapter for anything, at any price, though I should warn them not to get excited at the use of that word Neighbour, thinking it means the start of a romance, or that I'm going to get involved in some emotional business. No. Balcony scenes are not part of my scenario, and what I'm relating is no more than one of life's little ironies' (ch. 3, p. 14). Of course, it is that and it is not. At other times, this technique of a truncated potential is replaced by a duality produced through parody. For example: '"Then . . . right here," I said, and as I was saying it I recalled how solemn actors are when they say such things on stage. / In the most natural way in the world, I adopted a melodramatic tone"' (ch. 30, p. 182). The solemn conjugation of verbs in the imperfect subjunctive that encloses this scene lends both the scene and language their deserved weight.
27. The use of dreams as a narrative device also finds its open justification in this novel. At one point Manso recounts a nightmare he had and concludes by ridiculing the stale device of the surprise-ending tale: 'I will end this hectic day by declaring with that false candour storytellers use after they have put us through the most unbelievable nonsense: At that point I woke up. It had all been a dream' (ch. 25, p. 151). But he reverses the satirical thrust when he sees in the dream he had an indecipherable logic that connects it to his wakeful state of the evening before. With further thought, Manso succeeds in relating the dream to events in reality and endowing it with an equal measure of truth. The result is, on the one hand, a justification on Galdós's part for the inclusion of dreams in his novels and, on the other, a moment's insight into his deep understanding of the function of the dream in the human psyche. Most significantly, the act of dreaming is posited as yet another creative process, a fictive construct built on reality.
28. Nimetz, M. (1968, p. 61) understands that Galdós has used Manso's narration to cast barbs at stagnant artistic modes and to suggest that art requires constant reinvigoration. Had he stood farther back from Manso's words, Nimetz would have seen that all of *Our Friend Manso* is in itself a rejection of antiquated artistic patterns.
29. A good example, capped with a delightfully ironic judgment, is the following: 'I am the apprentice who sharpens a tool, or services a part; but I am denied any active penetration, any fruitful audacity, any bold creative act, as are the other mortals of my time. I am one of a throng of teachers who do their duty working ceaselessly to teach others what they themselves have been taught; I persuasively bring together all that I see around me, solid theory and voluble fact, incontrovertible phenomena and daring hypotheses; going forward each day at the slow, steady pace of the mediocre; building my own knowledge from the sum of what others know, and trying finally to make sure the ideas I have acquired, the system so laboriously constructed, are not simply an empty factory producing no more than wind and vapours, but a solid edifice grounded in the reality of my life and built on the solid foundations of my

conscience. The preacher who does not practise what he preaches is no preacher but simply a talking pulpit' (ch. 2, p. 5). It is a favorite trick of Galdós's to undermine a series of resoundingly elevated exclamations with a playfully self-revealing final sentence. See, for example, the first paragraph of Chapter 8, entitled 'Woe is me!'.

30. For his portrait and a snippet of his prose, see Chapter 26.

31. One is reminded of Leopoldo Alas's several satirical incarnations of this literary type in his stories: Miguel Paleólogo Bustamente in 'Bustamente' (1881, *Pipá*. Fernando Fe, Madrid); Don Tristán de las Catacumbas, the protagonist of 'El poeta-buho' ['The owl-poet']; Don Ermeguncio de la Trascendencia in 'Don Ermeguncio o la vocación' ['Don Ermeguncio or a case of vocation']; Don Teopompo Filoteo de Belem in 'Versos de un loco' ['Verses of a madman'], whose calling card identifies him as an 'Esoteric, ultratelluric poet' (all in 1916 *Doctor Sutilis*. Renacimiento, Madrid).

32. NIMETZ, M. (1968, p. 14), like Casalduero before him, points out that Galdós frequently satirizes romanticism and romantic taste in the contemporary novels, but he does not mention *Our Friend Manso* in this connection. The subject of Galdós's romantic parodies in his later career has provided fuel for a minor polemic between PABLO CABAÑAS and EDWIN PLACE (1971, *Hispanic Review* **39**: 473–4). *Editor's note*: *Marianela*, referred to here, is Galdós's most romantic novel.

33. 'Oh, black gloom! / Ill-fated leaden veil, who cast you over me? Why do these thoughts of death steal slowly over my mind, like mist rising from the waters of a warming lake? And you, hours of the night, what wrong have I done you for you to make a martyr of me one after another, as you implacably prick my brain with the sharp needle of your minutes? And you, sleep, why did you gaze at me with the golden eyes of an owl that tickled my own, but refused to extinguish with your blessed breath the torch burning in my mind? But above all I should like to inveigh against you, slender arguments of a hair-splitting sophist's reasoning . . .' (ch. 29, pp. 177–8). The paragraph that follows is an apostrophe to the imagination.

34. 'Irene was silent. She sat beside me on the front seat, and the jolting of the carriage made her elbow rub against mine. If I were more inclined to play with words, I would say that this rubbing produced sparks, and that these sparks flew to my brain, where they produced ideological conflagrations, explosive illusions' (ch. 28, p. 175).

35. The following example piles self-revelation onto a passage whose extended structuring and grotesque metaphor already give it a parodic tone: 'I have no idea what happened inside me. The effusion of my hidden affection, expanding and seeking a way of escape like a gas that suddenly finds a thousand fissures, was held back by a fear of treacherous solitude and by that restraint which the situation seemed to me to call for; so that, whereas the most obvious rules of romanticism demanded that I should go down on bended knee and pronounce one of those passionate speeches which are so effective in the theatre, my bashfulness only allowed me to say, in the silliest fashion imaginable: / "Let's wait and see, let's wait and see . . ."' (ch. 34, p. 207).

36. *Editor's note*: Valle-Inclán disparagingly referred to 'don Benito el garbancero' ('Don Benito, trader in chick peas') in his play *Luces de bohemia* (1920). See note 1 to Gilman's article, Chapter 6 in this volume.

12 Identities and Differences in the *Torquemada* Novels of Galdós*

DIANE F. UREY

The author of two outstanding books on Galdós, one of which (1982) is on the contemporary novels, Urey is one of the few critics to have successfully applied a semiotic approach to Galdós's work (see also Tsuchiya, 1990). This Barthesian analysis of cultural codes shows a sophisticated understanding of the ways in which literary realism, rather than reflecting a pre-existing reality, constructs meaning through the structural play of similarities and differences. Urey's approach also shows the influence of deconstruction, with its emphasis on the breakdown of binary oppositions. Unlike deconstructionists, however, Urey does not read against the grain, but implies that Galdós is responsible for the infinite chains of irony in his work, where everything is liable to become its opposite. (One thinks here of Galdós's comment in his Royal Academy speech – see Chapter 2 – that the dissolution of categories in contemporary society offers the writer creative possibilities.) Particularly perceptive is Urey's attention to Galdós's use of puns: more work could be done on Galdós's brilliant and often duplicitous use of language. Urey also shows how essential metaphor is to Galdós's construction of a social reality in which meaning, like goods, is based on exchange. In its suggestion that nothing has a stable identity, Galdós's work is, again, remarkably modern. The *Torquemada* novels are available in English translation (1988, André Deutsch, London).

The four *Torquemada* novels of Galdós offer a detailed, complex, and elaborate array of customs, characters, scenes, and events.[1] Hence it seems almost natural to read the novels as a reflection of Spanish society and culture during the later nineteenth century, as many scholars have

* Reprinted from 1985, *Hispanic Review* **53**: 41–66.

done. The studies which treat the novels in this way do so from a variety of perspectives. It is common to view the novels as illustrations of and commentaries on the social and political changes taking place in Spain, such as the evolution of the middle class and rise of bourgeois progressivism.[2] Often these social and political developments are viewed as the result of the dynamic interaction of contrasting forces in society; the story of Francisco Torquemada, a petty usurer become aristocrat, seems to emphasize the oppositions between working class and aristocracy, liberalism and conservatism, or the old and the new. These studies, at least implicitly, oppose the self to society and the novel to reality.[3] Another critical viewpoint distinguishes the historical content of the novels from the fictional content and regards both aspects as determined by dialectical principles at the material or ideological level.[4] Yet another, seemingly different perspective on these novels studies their thematization of moral and religious questions. From this perspective, the story of Torquemada symbolizes the conflicts of materialism and spirituality or sin and grace.[5] These moral and social analyses as well as any other which focuses on the content of the *Torquemada* series make certain unavoidable assumptions regarding the nature and function of the literary and historical knowledge which the texts seem to offer. One of these assumptions concerns the definition and identity of the categories which organize history and literature as objects of analysis. This essay seeks to examine some of the categories which commonly appear in criticism of the *Torquemada* novels. It questions the possibility of establishing and maintaining dialectical oppositions or thematic ideals within the texts. It attempts to suggest how such categories or terms as working class and aristocracy, material and spiritual, or history and literature also admit or even demand other types of relationships among themselves and other processes determining their meanings or identities. These other relationships and processes often allow only meanings or identities for the terms which are unstable, insufficient, and ultimately indeterminate.

One aspect of the *Torquemada* series in which the instability and indeterminacy of such categories emerge is the connection between money, material possessions, and class position. The function of Torquemada's money is to acquire property or material goods, whose function in turn is to mark a particular social status. Thus he must purchase the Gravelinas palace in order to demonstrate his new aristocratic standing. The money itself has no value until it is spent on things which give it meaning by identifying it with a determined social status. As Geraldine Scanlon explains, the goal is not simply to be wealthy, but to appear wealthy as well.[6] The connections between money, property, and class establish a functional value for each of them in relation to the others. The question here is never whether any of these elements exist independently, but whether they have any value, meaning, or identity apart from each other. In several notable instances in the novels the incomplete realization of the connections between money, property, and class calls into question the identities of all of them.

At the beginning of *Torquemada en la cruz* Torquemada has money, but a low social status. The Aguilas are aristocrats, but have no money. The move to rectify these imbalances, to make the full instance of one element correspond to the full instance of the other, also leads to the destabilization of those identities. Both money and class acquire their value and meaning through the property which functionally joins them, but which necessarily diminishes their full value. That is, Torquemada must spend his money in order to establish his class standing, while the Aguilas must compromise their nobility in accepting his money. The ideal values which constitute money or class are not self-sufficient, but require material and non-ideal goods in order to maintain a value which is thus always imperfect.

Another example in the novels of related terms whose functional values are both defined and compromised through their interrelation appears in various 'parasitical' situations.[7] A parasitical relation seems to oppose a parasite to a host, but the moment this opposition is established it begins to disintegrate since the ideal elements – parasite and host – affect each other's status. Their separateness dissolves since the parasite – or leech – becomes a victim at the same time as the host becomes parasitical. The *Torquemada* novels chronicle, at first glance, the perfection of Torquemada's parasitical role. Torquemada, as we know from the final scenes of *Torquemada y San Pedro* and the first ones of *Torquemada en la hoguera*, is first labeled working class, feeding off the working class through petty usury. Then the 'leech of the poor' ('sanguijuela del pobre', *TC* II.viii, p. 203), engorged with this blood/money, is transformed (through the possessions he acquires) into petty bourgeois, and finally an aristocrat – the 'Marquis of San Eloy'. As the terms describing Torquemada change, so do those describing his victims: 'In the end, he did as everyone else: after sucking the blood of the poor, leaving them totally drained, he flew off to the dwellings of the rich' (*TC* I.xiii, p. 135). Torquemada is not alone in his parasitism and it affects Spain as a whole, not only individuals. Thus, Cruz seeks to make 'the vampire of the poor turned regular financier look as respectable and showy as any of those who suck the colourless blood of the State, or the blue blood of the rich' (*TP* II.iii, p. 337). From these passages we can see how an apparently contradictory relation between parasite and host is actually one in which the parasite takes on the attributes of his prey, thus merging with it. Torquemada preys on and simultaneously is working class, middle class, wealthy, the State.

Similarly the host becomes like the parasite. In other words, the host values the parasite because he seeks to exploit that very identity which exploits him. This valuation is expressed hyperbolically, since Torquemada's victims at times see him as a savior. Whereas the tenement dwellers of *Torquemada en la hoguera* saw him as the incarnation of Satan (*TH* iv, p. 34), in *Torquemada en la cruz*, 'ruined nobles entrusted their salvation to him, which was tantamount to handing themselves over bound hand and foot' (*TC* I.xiii, p. 134). In *Torquemada en el purgatorio*, Torquemada, now a senator and, as always, serving self-interest yet ostensibly the interest of others, arranges the railroad construction in León. The Senate acclaims him as 'the father of the poor, the pride of Bierzo and the savior of our Leonese homeland' (*TP* II.xi, p. 381). The connection between the Aguilas and Torquemada renders this indistinction of apparently separate identities most obvious, of course. Torquemada initially entered into a relation with the impoverished aristocrats because he inherited a debt of theirs from Doña Lupe. His parasitical role diminishes as Cruz proceeds to use his money to restore their noble position; she views him as a solution (*TC* II.ii, pp. 162–8), salvation (*TC* II.iv, pp. 176–7), and as Providence (*TC* II.ii and iv, pp. 162–8, 174–9). Thus Torquemada becomes host to the Aguilas; with his money they will acquire the possessions associated with their class. In the instances discussed here, the relationship between parasite and host is one of mutual exploitation which simultaneously diminishes each ideal value. The fact that religious allusions invade these references (salvation, savior, glory, father, etc.), not only lends irony to the situation, but incorporates the moral questions posed in the novels within this parasitical structure.[8] This devaluation of the identities of parasite and host – or if one wishes, of classes – is continuous in the *Torquemada* novels. Rafael del Aguila, Torquemada's blind brother-in-law, recounts how the former servants of the Aguilas enriched themselves on the plenty of the upper classes, and from petty theft: 'that scoundrel Lucas the waiter [. . .] now has a railway restaurant. He bought a house in Valladolid out of the cigars he stole from my father, and with the champagne he pilfered he had enough to set up a brewery' (*TC* II.ii, p. 222). The same excess which enriched and fed the working class while diminishing the 'old' aristocracy in the Aguilas's past, now does so to the 'new' aristocracy. Torquemada complains about the remodeling of his house, thinking of the 'accounts he had to settle with carpenters, bricklayers, joiners, and other *leeches of the rich*' (*TP* II.i, p. 323). Later, when Torquemada incarnates both wealth and position – through his property, speech, and titles – he claims that his numerous servants in the Gravelinas palace are eating him out of house and home and are 'Leeches of the State' (*TSP* I.ii, p. 473). His position has become synonymous with the State itself; the wealth and class he personifies is that of the

Government. Yet at the moment this relation seems established – as wealth seeks to unite with class – the relation begins to decay, since the property is simultaneously diminished by the parasites of Torquemada, the wealthy, and the State.

In the same way that Torquemada must spend his wealth to attain class, and the Aguilas must compromise their class to have wealth, so the property which is the representation of both wealth and class is forever diminishing. The servants consume more than they produce: 'the button boy [. . .] doesn't render services that match what he consumes' (*TP* I.ii, p. 260); 'This super-abundance of servants was what chiefly made Don Francisco's blood boil [. . .] because the amount they ate every day was enough to feed half the world' (*TSP* I.vii, p. 493). Torquemada compares this 'blood-boiling' situation to the poorly administered government: 'We need to remove the unnecessary cogs in the administrative machine [. . .]. But then this sister-in-law of mine, what does she do? Turn my house into a government ministry' (*TSP* I.vii, p. 493). These passages illustrate the continuous disintegration of the values which are based on property or food. Identities cannot be fixed since the elements which define them are constantly in movement. This is what occurs in the class structure. Torquemada seems to change from parasite to host as he changes from moneylender to leading light; yet he continues to sustain his parasitical role, as his business deals are merely more socially acceptable. The Aguilas, particularly Cruz, seem to convert from hosts to parasites as they cease to be prey to moneylenders and prey on Torquemada; yet they still are hosts to their numerous servants and acquaintances. This essay attempts to show how such continual movement of the terms which identify certain meanings or values prohibits the fixing of those values and thus their positioning as contradictions. Each value is already compromised by the one it seems to oppose.

A return to a pre-parasitic existence in which completely autonomous opposing values could be identified is not possible. Rafael complains of the 'ignominy' of Torquemada's 'wealth, amassed with the blood of the poor'. But Donoso replies: 'Some of them [senators for life and marquises] made their fortunes selling slaves, others draining squandered fortunes through the syphon of usury. You don't live in the real world' (*TC* II.ix, p. 206).[9] Unable to accept this reality, Rafael escapes from his house, thinking he is liberated from the disgrace which the association with Torquemada's money and impending marriage to his sister Fidela bring. Cruz has already begun 'the restoration of the house' (*TC* II.ix, p. 208); thus Rafael flees Torquemada's property – that which to him signifies the compromise of his class. His sally is brief, however, as one night's hunger overcomes him. It is beneath his dignity to ask for charity from the passersby who are 'dealers, merchants' (*TC* II.xi, p. 227), in other words tradesmen like Torquemada. Since bread does not come to him without words, as God gave the little birds food (*TC* II.xii, pp. 226–7), he must ask it of Bernardina, the family's former servant, to whose house he has fled (*TC* II.xiii, p. 228). Again, aristocracy is sustained by working class. The identity which Rafael seeks to restore/maintain never existed in its pure integrity, since it was always a function of the existence of others, a dependent relationship.[10]

The instability of identities which such dependence fosters appears in the treatment of charity in this scene. Rafael thinks:

> Poverty was in no way ignoble; asking for public charity if one had no other resources was just as noble as giving it. Anyone who begged in good faith, the penniless wretch who asked for money to avoid dying of hunger, was Christ's chosen heir, poor in this world, but rich with immortal wealth in the next (*TC* II.xi, p. 217).

Both the giver and receiver of charity – the rich and the poor – are equally noble, according to Rafael.[11] The instrument of charity – money or food – indifferently serves both roles. The irony of this passage in regard to Rafael is of course that he is neither truly needy, nor in a position to offer charity, but he claims for himself the nobility attributed to each role. The relationship of charity, like that of parasitism and class, is an indeterminate one. The categories which seem to be opposed are not consistently distinguished by their representations – money, food, or linguistic characterizations. The recipient of charity, in obtaining it, becomes less needy; the giver diminishes his ability to give. Likewise if they are equally noble, their linguistic (as well as moral and even social) representations are undifferentiated. This same devaluation of oppositions appears in the relationship of borrower and lender. The borrower absorbs some of the attributes of the lender (money) as the lender becomes more like the borrower (less money). Both identities are indifferently represented in language by the single verb 'prestar' (borrow/lend). If the representations – monetary, alimentary, linguistic – deemed to define opposing values or positions slide between those positions with ease, then neither is there a functional opposition between the positions nor are their identities fixed. It is easy for any reader of the *Torquemada* series to see the ramifications of this dissolution of functional oppositions in the cases of charity and usury.[12]

Rafael attempts to reject money and property and seek food uncompromised by either. What he seeks is self-identical value, and food at first seems to naturally designate substance, that which literally 'stands under' identity. Yet this too, in numerous ways, functions only as one element in unstable relations which inform the *Torquemada* novels; terms pertaining to food are an important means of disarticulating oppositions. Rafael learned that food necessarily depends on other elements; we see this dependency elsewhere as well. Cruz constantly gives dinner parties, and Torquemada constantly complains about the expense. Like palaces, carriages, or refined manners, dining is an important aspect in the cult of appearances. In return for feeding others one acquires honor, prestige, business and political associations, topical familiarity with art and science. All this in turn promotes one's wealth and class position. Torquemada values what he gains through this exchange, but would prefer not to pay for it. In other words, he wishes to find value or meaning in money and food without having to exchange it. Believing everyone should eat in his own house, he searches for a word that describes those who do not. Fidela calls them parasites. Torquemada then states: 'I profess the principle that/for starters ("profeso el principio de que") all and sundry should eat in their own homes' (*TP* I.vi, p. 281). But he cannot avoid the dependent relation between money, food, and social acceptability. Neither money nor food by themselves or ideally are sufficient to create the meaning which Torquemada seeks in them. They have no vital function apart from those which they serve to sustain.

One of Torquemada's servants notes: 'He's a man, you might say, of rough principles/who likes unrefined starters ("de principios bastos"), who would eat like a poor man if he had his own way. He eats like a rich man so people won't gossip' (*TSP* I.i, p. 469). This remark immediately follows the scene where we learned that the servants were breakfasting on 'Bread and some scraps of truffled tongue' and 'exquisite left-over cuts of cold meat'. Several interesting relationships appear in these passages. First, we see again how the servants are consuming their employer. Moreover they linguistically depreciate while they physically devour this rich food, neither having to exchange money for it, nor seeking the social status associated with it. Taken apart from the money and social position which determine its value, this fine food is meaningless. Likewise an onion means nothing alone, but much when it is associated with the working class, Torquemada, and money, as will be demonstrated below. Any time an element lacks function within a context of relationships with other elements it is devalued or disestablished. The irony of the servants' perspective compared to that of Torquemada is emblemized in the almost oxymoronic phrase 'some scraps of truffled tongue' and in the oscillating usage of the term 'principle/starters' ('principio').[13]

The dynamic relationship between elements such as money, property and food, and position never achieves any equilibrium. Torquemada's attempts to fix or preserve one state of exchange between those elements results in the disintegration of the relationships themselves. This is evident in the birth of his second son, Valentín, in his fatal illness, and in his death. We can see how, for instance, this disintegration functions as

Torquemada is afflicted with a mysterious stomach ailment. He suffers memory loss after eating; thus he cannot imagine his own identity. Finally he is unable to retain any food at all; he cannot support his physical identity. Torquemada sees no logic to this situation:

> I don't know what's got into my economy, it's like a madhouse. It's ungovernable, my organs do what they like without regard for the system or established facts. What in the name of the Holy Scriptures is wrong with this body for it to refuse to feed itself, and reject the wholesome food I offer it? Revolution or anarchy must be brewing inside me (*TSP* II.vii, p. 577).

This humorous passage is an interplay of economic, social, political, alimentary, and even religious allusions.[14] It does not refer to some imminent political revolution, some rising of the masses and a socialist utopia; it is rather total self-destruction: established facts are made to be undone. Torquemada embodies the dissolution of the relationships which Restoration society and politics sought to fix.[15] In the *madhouse* money, property, and position are meaningless. The appearance of this extended metaphor in the text links the economic and physical health of Torquemada to that of the State through terms which are indifferently applied to both. Torquemada finally dies of hunger: 'His skin was like brown paper, and gave off a mousy smell, a symptom commonly found in those who die of hunger' (*TSP* III.x, p. 646). He self-destructs. In his hybrid nature the parasite eats the host, each being bound up in the other.[16]

Torquemada's statement above contains religious allusions such as 'in the name of the Holy Scriptures' in the same suggestive way that can be observed throughout the novels, where his clichés and blasphemies incur multiple senses.[17] The term *levadura* ('brewing/fermenting', 'rising', 'leavening') insinuates alimentary, political, economic, and religious allusions too. Later, Gamborena, the priest who attempts to save Torquemada's soul, tells him that 'the possession of exorbitant wealth is against divine law and human justice, and is a dreadful burden for the spirit as well as a terrible ferment ("levadura") for the body' (*TSP* III.iv, p. 620). As Torquemada's illness worsens, he complains that he cannot attend to his business: 'What do you gain from the fact that I . . . can't get out to discharge ("evacuar") my business? . . . Here I am . . . staring at my stomach and my economy and my guts, in the name of the Holy Scriptures, to see if they'll process . . . God knows what' (*TSP* II.vii, p. 579). Here not only does eating become business and economy, so does defecation. *Evacuar* ('discharge/excrete'), like *principio, prestar, noble, sanguijuela, salvación*, etc., is another word whose multiple functions serve to render meaningless those very meanings it seeks to identify.

Evacuar in Torquemada's refined vocabulary means to do business; in his illness we cannot help but understand it as elimination of what he has consumed: rich food and property.

Torquemada thinks he is being poisoned so he flees his palace and goes to his old neighborhood where he eats and drinks heavily with friends from his pre-Aguila days.[18] He looks out the tavern window at the Puerta Cerrada and hallucinates:

> It's called Puerta Cerrada ['Closed Gate'] . . . it's my cross ['cruz'], no . . . she [Cruz, his sister-in-law] is . . . and Puerta Cerrada is the Cross I have to bear inside my body and can't get out of my system . . . the cross of the Devil, the gates of Heaven that refuse to open, the closed gates of Hell . . . Look at me . . . the state they've reduced me to . . . They've put this house in my body . . . What the hell, in the confounded name of the Holy Scriptures . . . in the sweet name of St Francis [Torquemada's patron saint, his first name being Francisco], do I have to do now to get it out of me? (*TSP* II.x, p. 597).

Finally he regurgitates all he has eaten: 'The floor of the room was too small for everything that poured out of that wretched body' (*TSP* II.x, p. 598). The identity of the cross ('cruz') and Puerta Cerrada ('Closed Gate') from Torquemada's past merges with the Cruz of his present. The one which he seeks but cannot recover and the one which he refuses but cannot escape join in the same indistinction which closes the gates of both heaven and hell to him. The only result of Torquemada's efforts is to separate even further his present from his past, his inside from his outside, and himself from the food which now lies spoiled and useless about his feet. Torquemada's regurgitation of his food marks the difference between himself and his past in the same way that his confession of his sins could mark out a difference between himself and his future. His future salvation depends on his confession and until he brings this forth and apart from himself he can claim no other identity.

One of the horrified witnesses to this scene says: 'Let him spew it all out ("desembaular")' (*TSP* II.xi, p. 598). Torquemada begins to recover his senses and struggles to remember how he came to be in this place. But, he exclaims, the 'concordancia' escapes him (*TSP* II.xi, p. 599). The 'concordance', this agreement, is a series of associations which joins and thus fuses his illness and the need to return home, the luxury and ornament of the residence, the Massaccio which is there and Cruz as well, and finally Gamborena who 'assures me of my soul's salvation, provided I make a clear and full confession of all the sins on the *Debit* side of my conscience . . . and if they want me to confess right now, I'll cough it all up ("desembuchar") . . . today seems to be the day for coughing things up' (*TSP* II.xi, pp. 599–600). The narrator remarks that 'his legs were like cotton wool, and his trunk ("caja") weighed on him like a packing case full of stones' (*TSP* II.xi, p. 601). The association of Torquemada with all the other elements of his physical and psychic condition is complete in this scene. The words *desembuchar* ('cough up', literally 'disgorge'), *desembaular* ('spew out', literally 'unpack'), *baúl* ('trunk' in the sense of packing case), and *caja* ('trunk' in the sense of bodily frame, also 'box' or 'case', and 'cash till') at once link regurgitation, confession, and money.[19] Torquemada, as *baúl* and *caja*, is the vessel of food, sins, and wealth, which he spews forth as vomit, in his confession to Gamborena, and in willing one third of his fortune to the Church. All that he has horded – food, sins, money, his physical, moral, and economic capital ('the soul . . . is . . . the supreme capital,' says Gamborena [*TSP* II.v, p. 565]) – is thrown up in a revolt against the attempt to fix the relationship between the done and the undone, the inside and the outside.[20] At the conclusion of this gruesome episode, Torquemada returns to his palace. His old friends are glad to be rid of him; he is not one of them. And when his servants heave Torquemada onto his own bed, 'the mattress bounced on the springs as though it wanted to eject him' (*TSP* II.xi, p. 601). Neither is he at home in his own house (palace or body); as a product of differences he cannot truly rest anywhere. Torquemada is synonymous with the food he eats; neither he nor it can find a permanent place of rest or a fixed identity.

This association of Torquemada himself with food occurs at numerous other crucial points in the novels. One of the terms which becomes interchangeable with Torquemada is fish, and with this association another series of functional relations involving him, money, and morality is established. Cruz sees Torquemada as a 'little fish' (*TC* II.iii, pp. 172–3) in her somnolescent musings before the marriage arrangements are official. She proposes to refine his oafish manners as she would clean a fish, 'scraping off all his scales'. Torquemada is likewise a fish to Gamborena, according to connections which become evident in *Torquemada y San Pedro*, where we learn the beginning and ending to the story begun 'in medias res' in *Torquemada en la hoguera* about the beggar to whom Torquemada gave his old cape. And we know why Torquemada calls the priest San Pedro (St Peter). In his youth, Torquemada was majordomo of the confraternity of which St Peter is the patron saint: 'Saint Peter is the patron saint of fishermen; but since in Madrid there are no men of the sea, we money-lenders got together to worship him because we too, in a sense, are fishers' (*TSP* II.vi, p. 568). Elements of fishing, money, and morality join together and become functionally interchangeable. Torquemada fishes for 'farthings' (*TSP* I.iii, p. 478); St Peter fishes for sinners. The beggar looked like the statue, and Gamborena looks like the beggar; the label 'San Pedro' passes from one to the other. St Peter and Gamborena are fishers of men (see the physical description of him, *TSP* I.iii, p. 475), as Cruz is of Torquemada, who is then 'fish'. The associations of fishermen and fish thus coincide in Torquemada; by extension, each of the other fishermen is capable of being a fish, and vice versa, according to an economy of substitutions which calls into question their fixed identification with one or another of these elements.[21]

This economy of substitution also questions the relation of language to things, as can be seen with a further example of the word 'fish'. Cruz's image of Torquemada as a 'little fish' in *Torquemada en la cruz* follows immediately upon a dinner table scene with all the Aguilas present. We have just learned that their extreme poverty has led Cruz and Fidela to deceive Rafael, letting him think they eat when indeed they have no food at all: 'So he would not realise he had been tricked, Fidela mimed the scraping of the fork, the noise of chewing, and all the other sounds that sustained the pretence that the two of them were eating' (*TC* II.ii, p. 166). The best and often the only food is reserved for the blind man. He asks them during that meal: 'What about you? What have you got to eat today?' They respond: 'Us? . . . Ah! Something delicious. We've brought a fish' (*TC* II.iii, p. 168). They then proceed to describe how they prepared it, in detail, and both sisters insist that the other eat the elegantly narrated fish. They draw straws and Cruz wins the nonexistent fish for dinner. She eats a fish that only exists in words. Where most words substitute for something which exists somewhere or somehow, Cruz's fish exists nowhere and therefore its entire value depends upon how it exists. From the perspective of Rafael, the fish exists; all words effectively attain their referents only in the imagination. The functional values established in the structure of language can always exist independently of the things valued. This scene marks the difference between the world of things and language. Here fish is both a food and a word, but it is only really a word for food – in short, a word alone.

Another scene involving Rafael serves to illustrate some of the associative relations which independently maintain linguistic meaning or value apart from the things meant or valued. He willingly eats a sirloin purchased with Torquemada's money, unaware of its source; he refuses 'a bit of truffled boar's head' saying, 'It smells of onion' (*TC* II.viii, p. 203); he has already called Torquemada 'your wild boar' when speaking to Fidela (*TC* II.viii, p. 202), and he despises his custom of eating raw onion. As so often occurs, one term from among related terms is sufficient to actualize the value of all of them. For Rafael, 'onion' is one element in a system which represents plebian behavior and habits, and ill-gotten gain. Onion, money, wild boar, and Torquemada himself are elements of this system: 'That wretched smell of onion won't go away . . . Even you've got it on your hands. It must have got on to you from something you had in your purse that slipped in the house somehow'

(*TC* II.viii, p. 204). Ultimately it is not even the onion but another element – its odor – which (naturally) substitutes for it, and which activates the series of relations perceived by Rafael.

Characters' different perceptions of each other illustrate the polyvalent identity of terms. Torquemada is working class to Rafael because he eats onions; he is a 'leading light' to the high society which eats at his table, and he is compromised in between to the servants who perceive that he 'would rather eat like a pauper', but 'eats like a rich man so they won't gossip'. The term 'Torquemada' takes on a different identity according to his evaluation in a system based on the differential value of rich and poor. No one evaluation of him is necessarily truer than another; the system admits all its possibilities at once. There are no natural or absolute identities.

Characters change their evaluations of themselves as well as of others. We can see how Torquemada's self-concept changes when he consumes wine, for instance. At the wedding feast he drinks heavily; glowing with pride as he shows his property to Cruz, he exclaims to her that she and Fidela 'might well say that God has come to visit you' (*TC* II.xi, p. 243). The apparently transforming qualities of wine lead, as in a Bacchanalian ecstasy, to an exalted sense of self in which the differential value of the human and divine diminishes, and with it the identities which it founds. In his visit to his old neighborhood he consumes 'pure unadulterated wine' (literally 'without a sacrament'; 'to baptize wine' in Spanish means to water it down) and 'veal chops . . . capable of . . . resuscitating the dead' (*TSP* II.ix, p. 589). The result, as we know, is simply a gross display of his human, corporeal weaknesses. For Torquemada, the wine and food have divine or at least miraculous value: the green beans 'tasted heavenly' (*TSP* II.ix, p. 589); they drink an old wine so excellent that it 'called God by his first name' (*TSP* II.ix, p 590); Torquemada feels 'today I'm rejuvenated' during the meal and exclaims 'I feel as if I'd never been ill nor ever will be again in the rest of my days' (*TSP* II.ix, p. 591). He considers himself most divinely endowed and sustained at the very moment when his mortal nature is most painfully evident. The new identity which he perceives cannot escape association with the old and in fact their difference always makes one implicit in the other.

Wine, food, and various other terms mark the difference between identities and enable their reciprocity. The most poignant depiction of an illusory change brought on by wine occurs after Torquemada receives the last rites. Feeling physically renewed he exclaims: 'Blessed be the *Supreme Being*, who granted me this recovery, or this resurrection if that's the word, for if this isn't a resurrection, God can come and see for himself!' (*TSP* III.vi, p. 629). For Torquemada, resurrection is indifferently material and spiritual at the same time. What he fails to appreciate is this necessary difference and reciprocity, and alternates in defining his identity through one term exclusively. He soon lapses back to his miserly, unrepentant behavior after his illness recurs. The entire third part of *Torquemada y San Pedro* is a fluctuation between Torquemada's illness and improvement, between his conformity with his death and his rebellion against divine will, and between his obsession with the national debt and his personal salvation. The terms 'conversion' and 'resurrection' mark and activate this fluctuation in these chapters. These terms mediate between the material and the spiritual, thus rendering them inseparable, just as wine mediates Torquemada's perceived human and divine identities. Torquemada's consumption of wine or use of the words 'conversion' and 'resurrection' appear to distinguish values – life/death, God/man, sickness/health, material/spiritual – but instead they render them indeterminate.

Another term which marks the difference and reciprocity of the material and the spiritual is redemption. Rafael realizes that the Aguilas used Torquemada to redeem themselves (*TP* II.vii, p. 358) and one of the orators at the banquet sees him as the man sent to redeem Humanity (*TP* III.vii, p. 433). Just like Cruz, they see his material redemption of themselves as analogous to Christ's spiritual redemption of mankind.[22] The application of these terms and others like them indifferently mark the seemingly distinct values of human and divine, material and spiritual, etc. At the same time redemption, resurrection, rejuvenation, resuscitation, and similar terms illustrate the relationship of repetition and difference. For example, when some of Torquemada's former debtors meet him again, risen in society:

> they found he was neither as grotesque nor as horrible as legend had suggested, and this verdict gave rise to heated debates about his authenticity. "No, he can't be the Torquemada from the slums in the south," some of them said. "Either this is someone else, or one has to believe in re-incarnation"' (*TP* II.iii, p. 337).

The question which exercises Torquemada's old acquaintances is unavoidable. Any repetition – like any substitution or mediation – requires a difference in the repeated element(s), even when that element seems identical. Nothing can be absolutely identical to itself and still admit repetition. Galdós exploits the difference which enables repetition. He marks it with terms which especially serve to signal the impossibility of repeating a self-same 'authentic' or unitary identity. There can be no reincarnation, redemption, resurrection of what was without some great or small difference. The so-called Restoration of the monarchy also illustrates the necessary relation between repetition and difference.[23]

The most outstanding example of this phenomenon is the second Valentín. Torquemada looks forward to the birth of his son as a reincarnation or rebirth of the first Valentín, the mathematical genius of *Torquemada en la hoguera*. Both Valentíns are Christ figures: Valentín I through numerous explicit and implicit comparisons; Valentín II since he is born on Christmas Day.[24] This new Valentín is also a monstrous distortion of the first. Just as Valentín stood as both parallel and parody to Christ, so does Valentín II stand in relation to Valentín I. The difference which enables the repetition of Valentín also destroys the similarity of the repeated elements. Rafael describes the result of this repetition: 'I firmly believed that this absurd, unnatural union of angel and beast would not produce issue, and now this hybrid dummy has appeared, this monster . . . What an emblem of the lineage of the Aguilas!' (*TP* III.iv, p. 416). The relationship between the two Valentíns also marks the relationships between the Aguila family and their past, the new aristocracy and the old, the Restoration and previous governments, Torquemada and the working class, and between this narrative and Spanish society. These repetitions, representations, restorations, or reincarnations always incur a difference which distorts or destroys the identity which they iterate. Moreover, as in the case of Gamborena and St Peter, Valentín names a series of reciprocal substitutions which overcome an apparently fundamental difference. Just as Gamborena is both fish and fisherman, so Valentín II, like the first (*TH* ii, p. 20), will be both Christ and Antichrist. Yet this reincarnation of the 'reborn Newton' (*TH* ii, p. 17) is a megacephalic idiot. Valentín is both aristocratic and plebian, angel and beast, representation and distortion.

The second Valentín's distortion or destruction of repetition finds a parallel in the politics of his age. His mouth is oversized ('with a letter box for a mouth' (*TSP* I.ix, p. 505)) and he is continually biting, rooting, and feeding (*TSP* I.vii and xiii). This voracious product of the new age, the new class, must have two wet nurses, 'four breasts' as Torquemada complains, to feed his overwhelming appetite, but most importantly to copy the practice of the royal nursery (*TP* II.xiv, pp. 396–7). The food he eats, the property he owns, designate Valentín's lofty social position, and since the comparisons – made chiefly by Cruz – of the family to royalty become more intense after his birth we cannot help but associate his deformations with those of the restored monarchy. Valentín, like the government, feeds off the milk of the common people, and senselessly depletes his wealth. As an infant he tosses Torquemada's coins on the floor (*TP* III.iii, p. 413) and after his father's death, will inherit one third of that fortune.

Just as the second Valentín destroys rather than repeats the identity of the first, so Cruz, having regained her aristocratic status, seeks to undo all that she had done – with Torquemada's money – by giving away her fortune to the Church. She encourages Torquemada to do the same, telling him that the money he gained from the disentailment of Church lands actually belongs to the Church (*TSP* III.iv, pp. 620–2). Her class position has been compromised by Torquemada's wealth, yet she would not have had her position without him. She has sought to restore, to repeat, to represent her past, but now attempts to refuse the difference introduced by the repetition. Blanco Aguinaga writes of this scene: 'But, in history, former power is never 'restituted'; what one gets is a process of 'metamorphosis', of things changing into their opposite.'[25] Yet Cruz is not opposite to her past, nor to Torquemada, merely different from both, but inseparable at the same time: their mutual compromise. She expels the medium of this compromise – money – just as Torquemada expels his food. This attempt to throw away or cast off what has been created, bought, eaten, is an attempt to undo what has been done, to reassert the self-identical over difference.

Rafael exposes the Aguilas's difference from the past to Cruz, as Sinnigen observes: 'although the apparent glories of the family are the same as before, they are the product of a completely different reality'.[26] Rafael had always rejected Cruz's plans and Torquemada's money, but finally he realizes that 'I am the one who's twisted and out of kilter' (*TP* III.v, p. 426). He rejects his sisters now, but he is a composite of all of them – of Torquemada's wealth and of the Aguilas's nobility. When he attempts to discard the difference he sees in himself he leaps from his balcony to his death, destroying all trace of material and mortal hierarchies, and perhaps of spiritual ones as well.

The changes in position or status of Torquemada, Rafael, Cruz, Valentín, and of all the other characters, events, and objects discussed thus far serve to illustrate the variety of relationships and processes which the multiple terms of the novel's language can incur. The comprehension or reading of all these characters, events, or objects relies on determining (at least provisionally) a coherent meaning or identity for them, at the same time as the relationships and processes which create them subvert and resist those determinations. In this respect the meaning or identity of any term in the text is always provisional. The resistance to the determination of coherent, self-identical meanings for these terms occurs in different ways in the *Torquemada* novels.

First, many of the characters or things in the novels are connected to others in relationships which involve complementary functions or a necessary dependence among them. In these relationships, the related terms mutually compromise their identities. The disestablishment or even the development of these relationships then causes the kind of disarticulation or devaluation of identity noted in the cases involving money, food or property, and social status. Second, a series of successive substitutions of terms admits an unlimited regress and indeterminate reciprocity which ultimately define the metaphoricity of metaphor itself, as in cases like that of the onion or fish. Third, the substitutions may deliberately emphasize this regress and reciprocity in an attempt to assert the spatial and temporal continuity of a term through repetition; but these repetitions themselves belie the necessary difference which all substitution must assume. Fourth, difference affects the identity or meaning of any term and insinuates its irreducible heterogeneity; this appears most obviously in the case of those characters, such as Francisco Torquemada himself, whose identity the novels never attempt to stabilize.

Any of the terms used to create a character, event, or thing in the *Torquemada* novels ultimately admits devaluation or simply polyvalency in its identity; the difference which distinguishes one term from another finally requires their difference from themselves, as in the case of either Valentín. The recognition of these kinds of indeterminate, unstable, and heterogeneous relationships or processes clearly does not favor the development of critical perspectives on the novels which take the terms of their language as definite objects of historical or literary knowledge. The vicissitudes in meaning or identity among the characters, customs, scenes, objects, and events which Galdós offers in the *Torquemada* novels demand consideration of the fundamental and problematic function of language as a means of representation. Any criticism which too quickly moves to attribute a definite meaning or identity to the terms of the novels will have to arbitrarily refuse an equally extensive range of alternatives. Galdós's masterful use of realist discourse in the *Torquemada* novels does not in any way obviate the need to question their representational functions; indeed his seemingly facile ability to create a world in words should always attract our critical attention in the first place to the words themselves.

Notes

1. *Las novelas de Torquemada. Torquemada en la hogeura* [=*TH*]. *Torquemada en la cruz* [=*TC*]. *Torquemada en el purgatorio* [=*TP*]. *Torquemada y San Pedro* [=*TSP*] (1967, Alianza, Madrid). All references are to this edition, cited by part and chapter, and incorporated parenthetically in the text.
2. See, for example, Hall, H. B., 1970, 'Torquemada: the man and his language', in *Galdós Studies*, ed. J. Varey, Tamésis, London, pp. 136–63: 'The *Torquemada* series, if not his greatest achievement, is the work most central to his concerns as a novelist, the most coherent expression, in almost pure linear form, of his vision of nineteenth-century man and society. Stated in the crudest terms, Torquemada is the capitalist class, his life the rise of that class and the transformation it effects in society' (pp. 136–7).
3. For example, Sinnigen, J. H., 1979, 'Literary and ideological projects in Galdós: The *Torquemada* series', *Ideologies and Literatures* **3.11**: 5–19: 'In the tradition of classical bourgeois realism, Galdós carried on these fictional experiments

through an examination of the opposition between society and the problematic individual. This opposition is worked out within a constellation of individual-typical characters which presents a social space homologous to the real world' (p. 6).

4. For example, BLANCO AGUINAGA, C., 1977, 'Historia, reflejo literario y estructura de la novela: El ejemplo de *Torquemada*', *Ideologies and Literatures* **1.2**: 23–39: 'It is not that Galdós's novel is a *reflection* of socio-historical reality in the common, non-Marxist sense of the word reflection; but, more precisely, that socio-historical reality *determines* the significant structures of the fiction' (p. 30).

5. For example, SCANLON, G. M., 1976, 'Torquemada: "Becerro de oro"', *Modern Language Notes* **91**: 264–76: 'The central motif of all four novels is the religious-materialistic dichotomy and it is my purpose to attempt to demonstrate how Galdós manipulates this motif in order to underline the inversion of moral values which he sees as one of the most characteristic features of the society of his day' (p. 265).

6. SCANLON, G. M., 1976, p. 268.

7. JOAQUÍN CASALDUERO (1961, *Vida y obra de Galdós*, Madrid) observes the pervasiveness of this relationship: 'In money transactions, Galdós sees only a parasitical activity' (p. 115).

8. Scanlon writes that these types of religious analogies show that 'the gross inversion of values implicit in such ludicrous comparisons' is found in both Torquemada and Cruz (1976, pp. 266–7). This is one means by which Cruz and Torquemada become interchangeable, since they define their values through the same terms.

9. See Blanco Aguinaga's discussion of this episode: 1977, p. 29.

10. Biblical parody abounds here, as elsewhere; compare Rafael's wish to have food come to him to Torquemada's comments during the banquet in his honor (which Scanlon calls 'a grotesque parody of the Sermon on the Mount' [1976, p. 271]: 'The bread is there [. . .]. But you have to go and get it; because it, the bread that is, can't come and get us' (*TP* III.viii, p. 439).

11. Yet of course there is an 'otherworldly' distinction between the rich man and the poor. This is the religious commonplace that Gamborena and Cruz use against Torquemada in *Torquemada y San Pedro*, as Tía Roma did in *Torquemada en la hoguera*. In other words, only through discarding, as opposed to obtaining, property will the sinner/rich man attain another value or identity – salvation or eternal life.

12. For a similar discussion based on the use of words such as 'count', 'interest' and 'figure', in *Torquemada en la hoguera*, see UREY, D. F., 1982, 'The texture of irony', in *Galdós and the Irony of Language*, Cambridge, ch. iv.

13. Compare the oscillation among alimentary, social, and rhetorical functions of the word 'principle'/'starters' ('principio') in this scene to Torquemada's drunken exclamation to Cruz after the wedding: 'I profess the principle that/ for starters there ain't going to be starters except on Thursdays and Sundays' (*TC* II.xi, p. 244). Hall notes how Torquemada uses this expression and others from his newly acquired vocabulary at times parodically (1970, pp. 152–3).

14. In discussing another scene (*TSP* III.vii, p. 637), Hall observes the connection

between business dealings and religious symbolism in Torquemada's 'applying the term "economy" to his own digestive apparatus' (1970, p. 163, n. 27).

15. THOMAS E. LEWIS discusses the 'empty space of a progressive middle-class politics' in *Fortunata and Jacinta* and illustrates how that novel 'replenishes in consciousness the absence of such a practice from the ideological problematic of the Restoration' (1981, '*Fortunata y Jacinta*: Galdós and the production of the literary referent', *Modern Language Notes* **96**: 316–39 [339]).

16. CASALDUERO, J., 1961, p. 119:'He dies of indigestion: the inability to digest food and gold.' Also, the 'mousy smell' reinforces the parasitical allusions.

17. See HALL, H. B., 1970, who traces the development of Torquemada's language, the play of cliché in the novels, etc. See also Chamberlin, V., 1961, 'The *muletilla*: an important facet of Galdós's characterization technique', *Hispanic Review* **24**: 296–309, and UREY, D. F., 1982, for a discussion of specifically Biblical parody.

18. Torquemada thinks he is returning to 'Nature' here (*TSP* II.viii, p. 584); as Casalduero notes, it is his appetite that is triggered, not his aesthetic sensibilities: 'contact with nature, food in the inn . . . they are identical, but their meaning is the exact opposite' (1961, p. 119).

19. Confession and disbursement are recognized figurative or familiar uses of these verbs; see *Diccionario de la lengua española* (1970, Madrid), s.v. 'desembuchar', 'desembaular'.

20. Fidela's illness and death are described in terms similar to those describing Torquemada's ailments. She has difficulty breathing, 'as though an iron corset were squeezing her rib cage ("caja"), and something like an internal halter were tightening round her wind pipe' (*TSP* I.xii, p. 523). This is like Torquemada's 'tightening of the pit of the stomach' (*TSP* I.iii, p. 478). After the wedding, too, Fidela was stricken with 'violent fits of vomiting' (*TC* II.xv, p. 241), her attempt to undo what had been done. The armour in the Gravelinas palace is associated with Torquemada through linguistic indicators also: the morning light illuminates it 'finally encasing ("encajar") the brave figures in their entirety' (*TSP* I.i, p. 465), which are 'weary of the immobility that dislocated ("desencajaba") their cardboard muscles' (*TSP* I.i, p. 466).

21. Scanlon writes of Gamborena: 'his worldly vanity, his ambition, his businesslike approach to religion and his respect for appearance make him a St Peter worthy of his age' (1976, p. 276).

22. See note 8 above.

23. See some other uses of restore or restoration: *TP* III.xi, pp. 458 and 460; *TSP* I.vi, pp. 489–92; *TC* II.ix, p. 208.

24. UREY, D. F., 1982, p. 105.

25. BLANCO AGUINAGA, C., 1977, pp. 37–8.

26. SINNIGEN, J., 1979, p. 9.

13 Silences and Changes of Direction: On the Historical Determination of Galdós's Fiction*

Carlos Blanco Aguinaga

This article, published in 1988, has been selected not only because it gives an acute overview of Galdós's work and its relation to contemporary history, but because it attempts to respond to the challenge to Marxist criticism posed by the current critical rejection of representationalism. Earlier historical studies of Galdós's novels (e.g. Ribbans, Bly, 1983) tended to catalogue the historical references and abstract an authorial point of view on the events and figures referred to. Blanco Aguinaga, author since the 1960s of a stream of Marxist studies of Galdós's work, is careful in this article to avoid the realist fallacy. He takes on board the work of more recent Marxist theorists such as Fredric Jameson (1980, *The Political Unconscious*, Cornell University Press, Ithaca, New York), who are concerned with the way history shapes not the overt content but the underlying structure of the text. This essay offers a subtle understanding of the way Galdós responds to historical possibilities. It also offers a large amount of information about the period, succinctly analysed. (Incidentally, Blanco Aguinaga's view of the Restoration as the marriage of antagonistic forces fits nicely with Urey's preceding piece on the blurring of oppositions in Galdós's work.) Galdós's historical fiction is briefly discussed, but the main focus is on his contemporary novels.

---

* Reprinted from 'Silencios y cambios de rumbo: Sobre la determinación histórica de las ficciones de Galdós', in Peter Bly (ed.), 1988, *Galdós y la historia*, Dovehouse Editions, Ottowa, pp. 187–206. Trans. Nick Caistor, 1991.

[For Joaquín Casalduero
In memory of Steve Gilman]

> 'Oh, how funny, Don Tito: it's plain that wherever you go you come across History!'[1]

What I have tried to show in my previous work on the contemporary novels is not 'the established fact that Galdós's material is always "historical"'; nor that History for Galdós has, as it must, a thematic, background, allegorical or symbolical value; even less that 'Galdós's novels are the reflection of socio-historical circumstance in the ordinary sense of the term "reflection"'. The specific point I have tried to make is that 'socio-historical circumstance determines the structures of meaning' in Galdós's fiction, 'the result being that the story is structured according to the dynamics of History' (or more precisely, according to the novelist's awareness of that History).[2] In the following pages I should like to ask how this determining process affected one of the longest breaks in Galdós's career, causing it but also offering him solutions in the form of what he would call his 'second or third period' (in fact, his third).

Even more than usual, I am indebted here to numerous articles on the multifaceted relationship of Galdós's novels to history, as I am also to the invaluable work of Casalduero and Montesinos, the brilliant study of our much missed Steve Gilman, the books of Hinterhaüser, Regalado García, Rodríguez Puértolas, Gogorza Fletcher, and the excellent recent volume by Peter Bly.[3] In picking up the threads of my own and others' work, I hope to develop my line of approach by applying it to an issue that is well studied and familiar. At the risk of restating the obvious I shall begin at the beginning, since my main concern is to apply arguments elaborated in my previous work to the well-worn question of the division of Galdós's writing into periods. Since we can always learn from our masters, I shall start with a quotation from Joaquín Casalduero:

> It did not take Galdós long to find his subject: Spanish society. He does not turn to history to escape from reality and the present; on the contrary, he seeks the roots of his own time in the recent past. He uses the past to understand the present, at the same time recognizing that the past is past, as opposed to present [. . .]. His concern is the nineteenth century but, having identified the characteristics of his age, he is not content to limit himself to the contemporary scene and travels back to the origins of modern Spain to discover how his own society came into being.
>
> Galdós first tries to locate the beginnings of contemporary Spain by siting them in the years of Constitutionalist triumph (1820–3), then

quickly corrects himself and pushes them back to the final years of the reign of Carlos IV.[4]

Casalduero is right, I think, particularly when in this lucid synthesis he suggests that for Galdós the past is both inseparable from the present and in opposition to it, and when he speaks of Galdós 'identifying' the characteristics of his own age: an age which constitutes a specific structure within Spanish history and, like all historical structures, obeys a particular 'formation' process. In other words, Galdós quickly understood that the Restoration, like every 'identifiable' historical 'moment', needs to be dealt with both synchronically and diachronically.

In fact, even though Galdós appears to have found 'his subject' at the early age of 24–25 (at the time of writing *La Fontana de Oro*), we cannot presume – and nor does Calsalduero – that Galdós already had everything worked out: hence the first 'rectification' which led him to 'locate the beginnings of contemporary Spain' not in the three years of Liberal triumph but in 'the final years of the reign of Carlos IV', as Casalduero notes. Neither Galdós's original objective nor this rectification should surprise us because, if Galdós is travelling back 'to the origins of modern Spain to discover how the society of his own day came into being', it is important to remember that in the period from 1867–8 to 1871 (when *El audaz* was published) the society of his own day was far from clearly defined. Although the September 1868 Revolution took place between *La Fontana de Oro* and *El audaz*, nobody knew what it would lead to; and although – after much hesitation – Amadeo finally accepted the throne in November 1870, Prim's assassination in December of the same year tragically underlines the precariousness of the situation. This instability explains not only Galdós's attempts to find antecedents in previous Liberal failures (*La Fontana de Oro, El audaz*) but also the fact that he abandoned the search altogether for a time, publishing the second of these first three novels *The Shadow* (1870), supposedly 'contemporary' but in fact one of the few examples of 'the fantastic' in the whole of Spanish literature. Given this, it is not surprising that, after *El audaz*, the young novelist should suspend his literary production for nearly a year and a half, an exceptional state of affairs for a writer who in thirty years only twice took more than a year off between novels.

As we know, in January–February 1873, following this first break in production, Galdós initiated his first series of *National episodes* with *Trafalgar*, completing it in February–March 1875 with *La batalla de los Arapiles*. During those two years, in which his fiction takes us from 1805 to 1812, Amadeo abdicates (11 February 1873), order is seriously threatened by the cantonalist uprisings (brutally suppressed in 1873), the Republic arrives 'from out of the blue' (as Galdós puts it) only to be cut short by General Pavía's takeover (3 January 1874), and the confusion is resolved, formally at least, by General Martínez Campos's coup in support of Alfonso XII (29 December 1874), followed by the latter's accession to the throne in January 1875. As if more proof were needed that things were not in order, the Third Carlist War, which begins in 1872–3, ends only in February 1876.

The immense amount of creative energy that must have gone into the writing of this first series of *National episodes* in the midst of all this turmoil clearly shows Galdós's confidence in his ability to handle at least one facet of his subject: his exploration of the 'roots of his own time'. He immediately followed this first series with a second, begun June–July 1875 and ended December 1879 with *Un faccioso más y algunos frailes menos*, taking the reader from 1812 to 1834. In addition, in the period 1876–1878 he also wrote the first four novels classified by him as 'contemporary': *Doña Perfecta* (1876), *Gloria* (1876–7), *Marianela* (1878) and *La familia de León Roch* (1878).

It seems logical to conclude that, after the hesitations of his first three novels, Galdós had now hit on what Casalduero sees as the meaning and shape of his life's work: on the one hand, the exploration of the origins of his own time; on the other, as though belatedly heeding the call he himself had made in 1870 for a modern novel of 'manners', the depiction of contemporary society, that is, the Restoration which had begun exactly a year before the writing of *Doña Perfecta*.[5] A diachronic approach counterbalanced by a synchronic approach; and the two kept rigorously apart.

The scheme is clear, coherent and rational; ruthlessly schematic. Yet, although these first four 'contemporary' novels are a great advance on *La Fontana de Oro* and *El audaz*, it is obvious that the novelist is not entirely happy with his scheme, as several critics have noted and as is made clear by a hiccup that is generally glossed over. For at this point (*La familia de León Roch*, 1878; the end of the second series of *National episodes*, 1879) we encounter the second and last break in Galdós's career of over thirty years. Galdós will not start writing *La desheredada* (January–July, 1881) until over two years after finishing *La familia de León Roch*, and it will be a full nineteen years before he returns to the *National episodes* (third series 1898–1900).

Leaving aside explanations such as probable exhaustion (twenty-four novels in six years take their toll, but this rate of production is typical of Galdós and never again – except in old age – will he stop writing for so long) and the arrival of his brother from Cuba,[6] the decision to drop the *National epidodes* for such a lengthy period can be explained if we take seriously the famous words, written in 1879, from the end of *Un faccioso más y algunos frailes menos*:

> Enough then.
>
> Here the narrator completes his task, conscious of having only imperfectly accomplished it but having at least concluded it at the

> proper moment. [. . .] The years following 1834 are too close to us, they touch us, jostle us, are familiar to us. The men of this time could almost be men of our own. They are years which cannot be dissected because something lives in them that hurts, that reacts if pricked with the scalpel (vol. 2, p. 317).

To which Galdós adds, 'here they [the *National episodes*] come to a definitive end'.

The fact is that the Third Carlist War, which ended in 1876, was too close to Galdós when he wrote these words. In 1879 the peace and stability hoped for from the Restoration were still felt to be shaky. It seems only natural therefore that Galdós, who at the time favoured change without extremism, should not have wanted to write about the First Carlist War, which he would have had to do to explore 'the roots of his own time'. We should, it seems, take his words seriously. But why the two-year gap between *La familia de León Roch* and *La desheredada*, both contemporary novels not requiring painful exploration of the past? I venture a second, alternative source of dissatisfaction.

The first two series of *National episodes* had allowed Galdós to explore thoroughly the key period from the end of the *Ancien Régime* up to the First Carlist War. His handy decision to separate the *National episodes* from the novels depicting society of his time ought to have allowed him to devote the latter to the exploration of contemporary manners, which – since his readers were necessarily familiar with their own age – would make mention of historical events, painful or otherwise, redundant. This familiarity would allow Galdós to concentrate on the individual characters' private worlds, which would inevitably reflect contemporary ideological concerns but would not require mention of events and dates which his readers could be expected to know. How else was Galdós to preserve his schematic division between the synchronic and the diachronic?

And yet, as we know, the novels of Galdós's 'second period' are only partially and inconsistently contemporary. For example, while references to 'armed bands' and the lack of any mention of the first third of the century lead us to suppose that the events described in *Doña Perfecta* take place at some point during the Third Carlist War, that is between 1872 and 1876 (and thus basically at the time of the novel's writing), the events of *Marianela*, written in 1878, take place in the 1860s.[7] And yet the historical 'markers' we are given problematize the siting of *Doña Perfecta* in the period 1872–6, for there is not a single reference to the First Republic or to the start of the Restoration; it is equally incomprehensible that *Marianela* should make no reference to the various 'squalls' that preceded the 'Glorious Revolution' of 1868. This reference to/avoidance of the troubled events of 1865–75 justifies the description of these novels as 'abstract', an adjective used by Casalduero who had other aspects of their uncertain 'contemporaneity' in mind.

But it seems to me that, if we examine these four novels – not for nothing described as 'thesis' novels – in the light of Galdós's famous words in *Los apostólicos*, written in 1879 three years after *Doña Perfecta* and one year after *La familia de León Roch*, other issues are raised. The narrator of *Los apostólicos* writes as follows:

> That formidable middle class which today is the dominant power responsible for everything that is done or undone [. . .] was born in Cádiz[8] [. . .]. The third estate grew by driving a wedge between the clergy and the nobility. Disdainfully pushing aside these two atrophied, lifeless forces, the middle class came to rule over all things, forging out of its strengths and weaknesses a new nation (vol. 2, p. 111).

This being the case, what would have been the point of depicting conflicts like the one which placed Doña Perfecta (and her local priest) in violent confrontation with Pepe Rey? Gilman is surely right when he says that the novels of Galdós's abstract period 'still portray [. . .] the tormented concerns of the previous decade'.[9]

Furthermore, if in 1879, four years after the start of the Restoration, Galdós believes that a 'new nation' has already been born in which the clergy and nobility no longer dominate, how is he to link the end of the action of *Un faccioso más y algunos frailes menos* (1834) with this new reality, without again turning to the *National episodes* he has vowed to give up for ever? A lot has happened between 1834 and a Restoration which by 1879 appears stable enough to be 'identified' by the novelist. And it was precisely in the years Galdós had not yet written about (the end of Isabel II's reign in particular) that – 'disdainfully pushing aside [. . .] the clergy and the nobility' – the Spanish bourgeoisie implacably forged its way ahead. Particularly important for the financial and industrial development essential to the Restoration are the years between the 1854 Revolution and 1866,[10] plus the years 1868–75: Galdós will not treat this long key period in his *National episodes* till the very end of the fourth series, some thirty years later. The dissatisfaction I mentioned stems from the fact that, if on the one hand the exploration of 'origins' ('the past as past') proved insufficient for an understanding of this 'new' age, the fleeting references to a few relatively contemporary historical events typical of the novels of Galdós's 'second period' proved equally inadequate.

It is true that – as Casalduero has shown – *La familia de León Roch*, while thematically related to *Doña Perfecta*, *Gloria* and *Marianela*, is much less abstract, if only because the events described do not take place in fictitious, symbolic locations like Orbajosa and Ficóbriga; this is what makes it a novel of transition, as both Casalduero and Montesinos point out. But a transition to what? The answer may be clear to us, with our retrospective overview of Galdós's career, but we must remember that in 1878–9 Galdós had before him nothing more than a theory, the reality from which he had derived that theory, his talent, and an immense capacity for work. What was he to do? How was he to find a way out of the impasse caused by his decision not to continue the *National episodes* and the discovery that he needed to be much more concrete in his description of the contemporary world – which anyway had by his own admission moved on from the concerns of his earlier novels?

It must have been questions such as these, together with disappointment at unfavourable reviews, that in 1879 caused Galdós to fall silent until, definitively leaving the *National episodes* behind, he picked up his pen to write *La desheredada* in 1881. From that point on and for many years to come, he would write only contemporary novels, an apt term if we accept that what was 'contemporary' in the Spain of 1879–81 was a new social structure that was 'identifiable' but incomprehensible without reference to its immediate antecedents: the key political and economic events of 1865–1875.

To go back to the beginning. As early as 1870 Galdós had stated that the novel should explore the 'manners' of its time, insisting that in contemporary Spain the new 'middle class' had produced enough 'personalities' for novelists to be able to find in it characters and ways of behaviour worthy of their attention.[11] He also insists in this famous piece that he is writing in an age very different from that of Mesonero Romanos.[12] If this is how he felt in 1870, how much clearer things must have seemed by 1879: by that time the 'middle class' or 'third estate' was at the height of its powers.

For Galdós, nineteenth-century Spain is a continuum ('born in Cádiz [. . .] today it is the dominant force'), but to look back in 1879 over the first half of the century was to realize that the outcome of that long turbulent period of history was a new and very different society. The new social structure was created not only out of continuity but also by a series of decisive breaks. In order to represent this new structure in his novels, Galdós had to turn to the years when those key breaks occurred, without of course losing sight of the fluctuating continuity of certain ideological tendencies and institutions. Within continuity there is always change. Which is why, years later, the key word – at the level of both plot and ideas – in the *Torquemada* series will be that of 'metamorphosis'.[13]

But this intuition could not have been confirmed till well into the Restoration when, as we all know, everything was in 'metamorphosis'.

For in the early days of the Restoration there was no overwhelming confidence in its stability and continuity, nor was it completely clear that the newly implemented political system was appropriate to the new kind of society. The prevailing mood of the time, ranging across a wide spectrum of groups and tendencies (Galdós included), was one of weariness after seven years of crisis, and the feeling that revolutionary movements drawing their inspiration from the Cádiz Parliament of 1812, the Liberal triumph of 1820–3 or the Revolutions of 1854 and 1868 were doomed to failure. Rather than gratuitous optimism or outmoded revolutionary impulses, what was needed was a determined effort on the part of the newly dominant class to make the Restoration work. And although Cánovas's first term as Prime Minister lasted only from January–September 1875, his second term of office lasted from December 1875 to March 1879, and his third term till February 1881, after which the parties alternated peacefully, with Sagasta becoming Prime Minister till October 1883, Cánovas taking over from 1884–5, and Sagasta again from 1885–90: the so-called 'Long Parliament'. This growing political stability was partly due to the exhaustion of popular and radical movements, the conservative Constitution of 1876, a King who unlike Fernando VII did not go back on his word, the end of the Third Carlist War in February 1876 and the Peace of Zanjón (signed 10 February 1878); but a more important factor was the spectacular economic growth which had begun, despite the Revolution, back in 1869 and after 1877 took off to become what Carr has called a 'boom', lasting, despite a setback in 1884, till at least the end of the 80s.[14]

It is logical that Galdós should not have been able to form a clear picture of this new structure till the years 1878–81. *La familia de León Roch* gives us a glimpse of what this new view will be: not for nothing is this the first novel in which he explores the Madrid of his time, and the first in which we are introduced to the world of finance which will come to dominate Madrid society under the Restoration. This is surely why, although *La familia de León Roch* is still a novel with a 'thesis' (or 'theme'), its portrait of contemporary society is so much more convincing than that of the three other novels in the cycle. But this glimpse of something of major significance forced Galdós to pause and reconsider his literary production. When in 1881 he ended what was to be the longest silence of his entire career by publishing *La desheredada*, he had definitively come down on the side of the contemporary, in the sense of a new social structure created by its immediate history. This required Galdós to embark on a new kind of novel.

Any reasonably thorough reader of Galdós will realize that *La desheredada* marks a decisive change. 'With *La desheredada*,' Casalduero writes, 'the novelist takes possession of reality.'[15] And since in fiction reality depends on narrative technique, the first and probably chief impression created by this 'possession of reality' is that of an impressive narrative ease. We all remember the novel's extraordinary opening in the middle of a parliamentary speech that turns out to be by an inmate of Leganés lunatic asylum; and further on, the two chapters written in dramatic form; or the beginning of Part 2 of the novel, when a chronicler takes us racing through the years 1873–5, mixing 'historical' events with those of Isidora Rufete's private life; or the virtuoso chapter also in Part 2 in which we are told, in a grotesque sermon, of Spain's 'big fish'. And, throughout the novel, the presence of a narrator who is also a minor character, leading – given the occasional use of free indirect style – to a blurring of the traditional boundaries between first and third person narrative voices.[16] Of course none of this is radically new, either in the European novel or in Galdós's own work; but never before had Galdós employed these devices so freely and systematically. It is true that there are moments when all this produces a feeling of clumsiness (or hesitancy) in the narration; but the dominant impression, as critics have variously noted, is one of controlled ease or freedom.

At the same time, readers familiar with Galdós's work will immediately notice not only that the novel's scope is wider and more complex, but also that a number of things are missing: no thesis, less insistence on symbolic representation and, more important still, unlike *Doña Perfecta, Marianela* etc., no 'theme'. What exactly is *La desheredada* about? (Or, later, *El amigo Manso, Tormento, La de Bringas*?) We could if pressed define *La desheredada* as the story of a young woman from a poor family who is deceived by her father and a pseudo-uncle into believing she is a marchioness, and so on. While *El amigo Manso* deals with x, *Tormento* with y, *La de Bringas* with z. . . . But this is to talk of plots, which is very different from the 'themes' that dominated the earlier novels (the dead weight of religion and/or intolerance in Spain; the Spirit/Matter dichotomy, etc.). Casalduero observed that the abstract 'has now become individual', rightly so for what *La desheredada* and its sequels depict is, quite simply, the various ways in which various people try to make something of their lives.[17] No more, but no less. At the same time, as Bly has shown so well, we also find in most of these novels of Galdós's 'third period' a virtual obsession with socio-political dates and events, all more or less from the period 1865–76.

What has happened for us now to encounter so little abstraction, so little symbolism, so few 'themes', so much narrative freedom and so much chronological precison with regard to the events immediately preceding the Restoration? We are familiar with the most plausible explanations, which to my mind complement one another. Galdós has reacted to negative criticism from himself and others, re-assessed Balzac and Cervantes (as he would do continually), been newly influenced by

Zola, taken further what Gilman termed the 'betrothal' of biography to history (meaning that the characters see themselves as the product of contemporary history),[18] and is well on the way to maturity. But why did this happen in 1881 and not two or five years earlier?

It is perfectly reasonable to suppose that the determining factor may have been Zola, for Galdós could hardly have had access to his influential work before 1879–81: although Zola had been publishing since the 1860s, his two key novels *L'Assommoir* and *Nana* appeared only in 1878 and 1880 respectively. If we bear in mind that Pardo Bazán published *Un viaje de novios* in 1881 and *La cuestión palpitante* in 1883, it seems logical to conclude that naturalism first made its impact in Spain in those years, precisely the period when Galdós was silent. Is Zola then the decisive factor which led him to break his silence and embark on his 'second or third period'? If we are using the term 'influence' in the sense proposed by Amado Alonso,[19] I see no reason to doubt that Zola was decisive at this key moment in Galdós's career.

The point I have been groping towards in the previous pages should however, I think, also be taken into account over and above the various 'literary' factors that come together here: if Galdós's critical dissatisfaction, his re-reading of Cervantes and Balzac, and his discovery of Zola lead him to change his way of writing, it is because of his clear sense that what he wanted to write about was the daily life ('manners') of a new historical structure which was only just beginning to become visible.

If we see this historical awareness as a determining factor that functions as a cause mechanically producing a particular fictional effect, we shall of course fall into the conceptual trap of associating 'causes' and 'effects' of a different nature: as I have tried to clarify elsewhere, socio-historic determinants do not necessitate the appearance of specific 'forms' (literary or political).[20] The connections are clearer when we talk, for example, of Galdós's change of style being the result of his having borrowed from Zola the technique of free indirect style.[21] Which is why it is convenient – if something of a stock ploy – to talk of literature as a dialogue with other literature. But if texts reach each other it is not in isolation, as the Russian formalists pointed out long ago: factors intimately related to non-literary phenomena can often spark the dialogue.

Even if all of this is accepted, it may help my argument to view this key moment in Galdós's career from a negative angle, as follows. Between 1878–9 and 1881 Galdós clearly understood that he could not write novels as he had been doing till that point; he could not write about the same things and consequently could not write in the same manner. But this negation, as in every dialectical process, has to be set against something, and here that something is the by now irrefutable existence of a society that has changed from the one Galdós was writing about before. It is therefore important to consider the nature of Restoration society, as Galdós saw it, some four or six years after 1875 as it starts to acquire stability.

Its three pillars were: order (alternation of power; 1876 Constitution; repressive state apparatus); economic take-off (railways, industry and, in Madrid, banking); and, given the middle class's new access to power, the consequent chance or hope of upwards social mobility (the mythical 'confusion' of classes that several Galdós narrators talk of). With the failure, exhaustion and jettisoning of all extremisms and extremists, the ideology uniting and cementing these three pillars could be said to be built on the famous phrase uttered by Alfonso XII: 'a good Catholic, like all my forebears; a true liberal, like a man of my century'. In other words the claim to have achieved ('in the English manner', as several of the contemporary novels will say ironically) the difficult marriage, or at least balance, of historical factors previously opposed to one another.

It was, therefore, a society in which the only issue was that of surviving by moving with the times. Máximo Manso will say as much, so will Agustín Caballero, and so will several Galdós narrators. In a passage of *Fortunata and Jacinta* written in 1886, the former Carlist Juan Pablo Rubín will rationalize his situation in similar fashion when he realizes, at the end of 1874, that Alfonso XII is going to acceed to the throne: 'Nothing for it . . . we'll have to grin and bear it. A supporter of Alfonso I'll be . . . like it or not. What a bind! . . . Jesus, what a bind!' (vol. 3, p. 57). As late as 1907–8, the narrator of *España sin rey* can describe that period as 'a patching up or muddling through' (vol. 2, p. 822). For although it may be true that, as Juanito says to Fortunata, 'expediency, my child, is stronger than we are' (vol. 3, p. 104), it is equally true that, once earlier extremist positions have been thrown out of the window (almost all of them had by this time 'bowed to the yoke'),[22] such expediency, exemplified at the centre of power by the alliance between a traditional but down-at-heel aristocracy and a new-rich bourgeoisie, consists precisely in adopting a 'proper' course of action so as to shore up the newly established compromise order. So for example – and it is an absolutely central point in the first major series of contemporary novels – adultery is permitted despite hymns of praise to the family, but only so long as appearances are maintained (which often does not even mean relegation to clandestinity, but hypocrisy on the part of those who commit the adultery and those who, being in the know, comment on it discreetly and usually ironically). Families, like the King, are performing a balancing act, as too are politicians and bankers, often the same people.

The reason for all this is that, the moment of capitalism having finally dawned for Spain with the Restoration, everything necessarily revolves around the fetishism of goods (the omnipresent representation of which is, of course, money). And given this fetishism, everything is inevitably 'disguised' as something it is not, as alienated individuals find they cannot transcend their individuality (there is no longer a grand socio-political historical scheme they can participate in or collective aspirations they can share), while – logically, despite the apparent paradox – their survival and social success depend on how well they can manipulate the prevailing conventions and ideas: everyone, including Alfonso XII, Cánovas and Sagasta, is forced to go in for what Galdós called 'sticking your finger in the pie' ('pasteleo').[23] A society, in other words, in which – as has often been said with reference to Golden Age concerns that have little or nothing to do with the Restoration – 'Being' becomes confused with 'Seeming', both of them fuelled by a 'Desire to Be' founded primarily on speculation and credit, since only money offers the possibility of climbing the social ladder (though one can also climb the social ladder to get money, as in the case of Isidora Rufete).

Of course there are always notable exceptions (Galdós always keeps the idea of freedom, even when most influenced by Zola's narrative techniques): Fortunata, Camila in *Lo prohibido*, 'Miau', Amparo in *Tormento;* in the later series of novels Nazarín. But Fortunata – after being forced into prostitution – dies without Juanito's love and is deceiving herself when she entrusts her son to Jacinta (which does however mean a step up socially for the future 'dauphin'). 'Miau' commits suicide. Camila does reject adultery and the novel gives us to understand that, despite her unyielding principles, she and her husband Constantino will succeed; this is however largely due to the fact that José María has used his influence on behalf of Constantino in the War Ministry . . . after giving him a horse that enables him to satisfy his most infantile obsessions. Amparo does not end up in prostitution like her sister Refugio, thanks to the love and financial security offered her by Agustín Caballero; but their happy ending, worthy of a popular melodrama, is not only an exception in Galdós's work but is highly ironic, since in order to live together Agustín and Amparo have had to accept the 'bind' of not marrying and having to go and live in France, for, as the many references to Paris imply, Spain still has a lot to learn from France as far as keeping up appearances goes. This is therefore a world in which, with these few exceptions, and as Steve Gilman has succintly put it with reference to *La desheredada,*[24] it is not for most people a matter 'of suicide, or death, but of prostitution'.

How could Galdós possibly write about 'manners' like these, which as early as 1878/9–1881 he could see represented something new, using the same techniques as in his 'second period'? As we have pointed out, the novels begun after 1881 have no central thesis, shy away from abstraction, etc. At the same time, in keeping with the 'personalities' offered him by society, his new fictional characters have to be lacking in something that was an essential ingredient of his novels prior to 1881.

The characters of Galdós's 'second period' – whether in *El audaz*, the *National episodes* or *Doña Perfecta* – have a tendency to the heroic (and even have an assortment of Achilles's heels: Pepe Rey's impatience, for example); in other words, on a political and ideological level they act as though they were makers (agents) of History. It is no coincidence that Pepe Rey is an engineer; Martín Muriel a conspirator who is 'inexorable, as revolution was in those days' (vol. 4, p. 241); Teodoro Golfín, a scientist ready to challenge the unknown; Doña Perfecta, a landowner and political boss defending traditions under threat, and so on. By contrast, with the sole exception of Torquemada (and among the minor characters a few businessmen such as the Santa Cruz family), the central characters of the contemporary novels, from Isidora to Fortunata, from Manso to 'Miau', however endearing and fascinating they may be as individuals, however free they may be (or rather however free they may consider themselves to be), are totally lacking in heroism. That is, they appear to us not as the makers (agents) of History, but as made/unmade by it. Even those who triumph like the politicians and Torquemadas (Villalonga, Manolito Peña, the protean Peces . . .) lack this dimension. This should not surprise us since, as Galdós will tell us in *Tristana* (written in 1896), the Restoration was 'a paper rather than an iron age' (vol. 5, p. 1543); an age which, as Rafael complains in the *Torquemada* novels, could only produce 'Médicis' made of 'papier mâché' (vol. 4, p. 1110).

If Galdós's characters are like this because that is what the 'personalities' thrown up by the newly emergent society are like, and if Galdós – as a good realist writer – was above all a creator of characters, it is logical that the loss of that energy previously seen as a central ingredient of Spanish history should be accompanied by the disappearance of abstraction, 'theses', etc. This 'negative' starting-point left the way open for Zola's narrative techniques, as also for certain aspects of his naturalist determinism. Apart from which the particular solution Galdós would find to this prolonged silence – the elaboration of what would be his 'third period' – was obviously the combined outcome of his talent plus a host of likely 'random' factors operating within the limits of the possible.

In this new novelistic mode not only is the dialectic between characters and history vital (as Gilman has convincingly shown), but so too is the dialectic between 'immediate formative past' and 'new social structure' (as indicated at the start of this article, and by Bly).[25] In fact, out of the first eight novels of this 'third period', only two (*El amigo Manso*, 1882; *Lo prohibido*, 1884–5) can be called strictly contemporary in the sense that the events described take place at the time of writing. The other six are situated between 1863 (*El doctor Centeno*, written 1883) and 1878 (*Miau*, written 1888), though the majority take us (in chronological order of period treated: *Tormento, La de Bringas, Fortunata and Jacinta, La desheredada, Miau*) from the end of 1867 (*Tormento*) up to 1878 (*Miau*), with particular emphasis on the years 1867–9 (*Tormento, La de Bringas, Fortunata and Jacinta*) and 1872–6 (*Fortunata and Jacinta*, Part 2 of *La desheredada*). This makes clear the formative importance Galdós attached to the seven or eight years between the crises that precipitated the 1868 Revolution and the start of the Restoration.

So much so that some of the fundamental characteristics of established Restoration society (living on credit, hypocrisy, adultery, prostitution, 'sticking your finger in the pie') – represented contemporaneously in *Lo prohibido* – are already present in novels such as *Tormento, La de Bringas* and *La desheredada*, set between 1867–76. Here it is worth recalling the description made in 1887 by the narrator of *Fortunata and Jacinta* (Part 3, Chapter 1) of a social gathering that took place in 1874:

> It was a luminous example of that particular Spanish kind of fraternity which allows Carlists to shake hands with Republicans, entrenched progressives with inveterate moderates, as bosom friends (vol. 5, pp. 294–5).

If we consider some of the well-worn clichés about the Spanish character, this is an astonishing statement. What has happened to that terrible, bloody Spanish intolerance, represented time and time again in the irreconcilable confrontations portrayed by, among others, Galdós ('The map of Spain is not a geographical chart but the military plan for an endless battle'); the violence that Unamuno would talk of in *En torno al casticismo*, that would again be the subject of sombre meditations under the Second Republic, and in the post-Civil-War period would obsess not only historians like Américo Castro but no less a figure than Franco? Galdós offers as full an explanation as one could hope for:

> In the past, parties which were separate in public were also separate in private; but progress in our social behaviour brought a relaxation in personal relations, which in turn led to a dilution. Some believe we have gone from one undesirable extreme to the other, without finding a point of equilibrium; they see this fraternity as a weakening of character. Everyone being a personal friend of everyone else is a symptom of the fact that ideas have become a mere pretext for making or maintaining a living (vol. 5, pp. 294–5).

At this point we are introduced to Feijoo, of whom we are told: 'he too had had his wild moments but had recovered his reason, and reason in politics was, in his view, the total absence of belief'. The kinds of social behaviour mentioned earlier are the inevitable outcome of this view of mental health and the 'drop-out' mentality (to use an apt current term) that inevitably results.

It is worth noting that another member of that social gathering was Ramón de Villaamil, 'Miau', protagonist of a novel which ends depressingly in 1878, that is exactly ten years after the 'Glorious Revolution', the date when Galdós fell into the lengthy silence that ended with *La desheredada*. These are the opening lines of *Miau*:

> At four in the afternoon, the crowd of children from the school in the Plazuela del Limón rushed out of class, kicking up a din like a thousand demons. None of the many hymns to liberty penned in the various nations of the world is as joyous as that sung by the prisoners of primary education as they throw off the shackles of school discipline and take to the streets shrieking and cavorting. The insane fury with which they launch themselves into the most dangerous acrobatics, the damage they often cause unsuspecting passersby, the orgiastic display of individual freedom which often ends in blows, tears and bruises, is like a rough sketch of those revolutionary parades which engage men's energies in less fortunate times (vol. 5, p. 551).

With this start to a novel about an 'invalid tiger' (vol. 5, p. 555), written in 1888 but with the action going back to 1878, the narrator makes it abundantly clear that nowadays, unlike in 1868, the only eruptions of freedom that can be found – and tolerated? – are those of schoolchildren, who anyway will next day return to the 'shackles of school discipline' and later in life (this is a state school) to the shackles of earning a living, in whatever form. By then they will have no great inclination to 'take to the streets' (as can be deduced from the contrary examples of Mauricia la Dura and Fortunata), because life is not like that any more, and *Miau* is above all the appalling story of an honourable, slightly dotty bureaucrat (like Torquemada he is obsessed with converting the foreign debt into a domestic one) who, despite his long years of service (he is two months short of retirement age) is not even allowed to 'defend' his rights of service. 1888 sees the end of the dialectic between 'immediate formative past' and 'new social structure' that characterizes the first eight contemporary novels. From now on, with the sole exception of *Torquemada en la hoguera*, all of Galdós's other novels from *La incógnita* (1888–9) to *Halma* (1895) will be strictly contemporary (in the sense that none of the events are given dates).

Does this mean that from now on Galdós is going to write 'ahistorical' novels, as Bly has essentially proposed?[26] This conclusion is possible if one believes, as Bly appears to, that in Galdós's novels 'History' can be reduced to political and military events and dates, and that it plays a purely allegorical and/or symbolic function in his writing; but not if one holds that, as I have tried to show in my earlier work, it is Galdós's view of historical reality that determines the basic structure of his texts. Nowhere is this clearer than in *Lo prohibido*, one of the two novels prior to *La incógnita* which is strictly contemporary,[27] or in the *Torquemada* series where, after the first novel, nearly all the historical events or dates found in the novels prior to *Miau* have disappeared.

Bly seems surprised that in *Lo prohibido* and the *Torquemada* series the main characters, who no longer 'have a history', should devote themselves exclusively to seeking, earning or exchanging money (and other goods), even when they are supposed to be engaging in politics.[28] The fact is that the whole political and economic development of the nineteenth century, particularly in the period 1865–75, has led to the creation of a kind of society in which the only significant activity is speculation and 'sticking one's finger in the pie'. What else could an intelligent, sceptical, energetic man like Torquemada devote himself to? The same is true, in different ways, of poor Villaamil, Rosalía, Villalonga, Refugio, Eloísa . . . (I have already mentioned some of the exceptions). If by 'History' we mean 'events' of the kind that characterized the period prior to 1875–6, we can say that in the dominant ideology of the Restoration there will be no more 'History' until 1895–8 (with the wars of independence in Cuba, Puerto Rico and the Philippines) and until a new social class impresses its presence on the collective consciousness.

For the money which justifies the activities of so many characters could not have existed without the prior existence of railways, industry in the Basque provinces and Catalonia, foreign investment, etc.: the 'boom' of which Carr speaks. The convergence of all these forms of economic development under the Restoration not only brought to power the bourgeoisie whose rise Galdós traces back to the Cádiz Parliament of 1812, but also saw the first major emergence of a new working class, without whose exploitation there would have been no money to put into circulation. They will determine the socio-political 'events' that comprise Spanish history from now on, and are already starting to become visible in 1893–5 (*Torquemada en la cruz, Torquemada en el purgatorio, Torquemada y San Pedro*) for as early as 1890 the first May Day celebrations had taken place, accompanied by strikes and demonstrations, while in 1892 Jérez had been occupied by anarchist peasants. Galdós, always keenly aware of social matters, wrote a short but significant article on the May Day celebrations of 1890. This explains why Torquemada feels the stirrings of revolution within himself, a future intuited by his brother-in-law Rafael del Aguila. Many years later in 1912, when Galdós returns to the Restoration period with *Cánovas*, these new historical 'events' will be clear and he will be able to write (with the benefit of hindsight) that the 'giddy days' of the Restoration 'will not create a Nation [. . .] will not pacify the unrest of the proletariat' (vol. 4, p. 876). But Galdós is the novelist of the history of the Spanish bourgeoisie, and these new 'events' and 'dates' come too late for him.

Inevitably limited to his own time and class, Galdós nevertheless managed to overcome them both ideologically and politically. One cannot ask for more; there is no reason why he should have been able to create a new kind of novel based on new class conflicts and their impact on the private lives that interested him so much. However he could, and did, go on making novels out of a world in which the 'middle class' was no longer a positive force but, while continuing to be an agent of History, used its energies to put a final stop to History (which is why Galdós uses the phrase 'giddy days'), seeing such (political) immobility as proof that it had definitively consolidated its position in power, a position it obviously wished to maintain.

So the few attempts at radical opposition which occurred once the Restoration was established, such as the 1886 uprising in which Angel Guerra takes part at the start of the novel named after him, were absurd from the perspective of a class which was already enjoying the power it had sought. The differences that existed within that class should and could be resolved in other ways: 'in the English manner' we might say, not through nostalgic pseudo-revolutionaries 'taking to the streets'. Angel Guerra is quick to understand this and abandons History at the instigation of the dreadful, sanctimonious Leré. But it is Angel Guerra rather than Galdós who abandons History, and Galdós goes on to narrate here, in *Nazarín* and in *Halma*, the confusion and sense of defeat of those who are unhappy with the situation they find themselves in, who feel unidentified with the interests of their class, who are unable to foresee the fresh conflicts that are fast approaching, and who are completely powerless as a result. It was impossible for them to feel, as Prim had done thirty years earlier, that it was necessary to 'destroy in the thick of the raging battle' everything around them. By way of conclusion, I should like to hazard what might seem a paradoxical assertion: that it is in this prolonged final period when political 'events' and 'dates' disappear from Galdós's novels that we can most clearly see to what extent his deep awareness of the historicity of all human activity determined the 'form and content' of his fiction, here as always.

Notes

1. Galdós, 1950, *Obras completas*, ed. F. C. Sainz de Robles, Aguilar, Madrid, vol. 3, p. 1280. All quotations from Galdós's works are taken from this edition.

2. Blanco Aguinaga, C., 1978, *La historia y el texto literario: Tres novelas de Galdós*. Nuestra Cultura, Madrid, pp. 109, 91, 16.

3. Casalduero, J., 1970, *Vida y obra de Galdós (1842–1920)*, 3rd edn, Gredos, Madrid; Montesinos, J. F., 1968–72, *Galdós* 3 vols, Castalia, Madrid; Gilman, 1981; Hinterhäuser, H., 1963, *Los 'Episodios nacionales' de Benito Pérez Galdós* trans J. Escobar, Gredos, Madrid; Regalado García, A., 1966, *Benito Pérez Galdós y la novela histórica española 1868–1912*, Insula, Madrid; Rodríguez Puértolas, J., 1975, *Galdós: Burguesía y revolución*, Turner, Madrid; Gogorza Fletcher, M. de, 1973, *The Spanish historical novel 1870–1970*, Támesis; Bly, P. A., 1983, *Galdós's Novel of the Historical Imagination: A Study of the Contemporary Novels*, Francis Cairns, Liverpool.

4. Casalduero, J., 1970, p. 43.

5. See Montesinos, J. F., 1968–72, vol. 1, pp. 28–9.

6. See Montesinos, J. F., 1968–72, vol. 2, p. 1.

7. The inscription on Marianela's tomb reads: 'RIP María Manuela Téllez. Heaven took her back on 12 October 186 . . .' (vol. 4, p. 755).

8. *Editor's note*: The Cádiz Parliament (cortes de Cádiz) of 1812 drafted Spain's first Liberal constitution in protest against the Napoleonic occupation.

9. Gilman, S., 1981, p. 87.

10. See Tortella, G., 1970, 'Ferrocarriles, economía y Revolución', and Nicolás Sánchez-Albornoz, 1970, 'El trasfondo económico de la Revolución', in Lida, C. E. and Zavala, I. M. (eds) *La Revolución de 1868: Historia, pensamiento, literatura. La Revolución de 1868: Historia, pensamiento, literatura*, Las Américas, New York, pp. 126–37 and 64–79 respectively.

11. It is worth remembering that Galdós speaks of the 'personalities' that society offers, and the 'characters' the novelist creates out of those personalities. *Editor's note*: Blanco Aguinaga here refers to Galdós's article 'Some observations on the contemporary novel in Spain' printed in this volume.

12. Montesinos, J. F., 1968–72, vol. 1 p. 31.

13. Blanco Aguinaga, C., 1978, pp. 95–124.

14. Carr, R., 1966, *Spain 1808–1939*, Oxford University Press, Oxford, p. 390.

15. Casalduero, J., 1970, p. 69.

16. Gilman, S., 1981, pp. 98ff.

17. Casalduero, J., 1970, p. 69.

18. Gilman, S., 1981, pp. 101–2.

19. Alonso, A., 1955, 'Estilística de las fuentes literarias: Rubén Darío and Miguel Angel', in *Materia y forma en poesía*, Gredos, Madrid, pp. 381–97.

20. Blanco Aguinaga, C., 1978, pp. 49–94.

21. See Gilman, S., 1981, p. 121.

22. Blanco Aguinaga, C., 1978, pp. 5–16.

23. See Blanco Aguinaga, C., 1985, 'Positivismo y pasteleo de personajes y

narradores de las Contemporáneas', in *Homenaje a Koldo Mitxelena*, Universidad del País Vasco, Vitoria, pp. 835–41.

24. GILMAN, S., 1981, p. 121.
25. GILMAN, S., 1981; BLY, P. A., 1983.
26. BLY, P. A., 1983.
27. See BLANCO, A., 1983, 'Dinero, relaciones sociales y significación en *Lo prohibido*', *Anales Galdósianos* **18**: 61–73.
28. BLY, P. A., 1983, pp. 77–8.

14 *Angel Guerra*, or the Monster Novel*

NOËL M. VALIS

This second metafictional piece, published in 1988, has been chosen out of many recent alternatives (for example, Tsuchiya 1988, 1989a, 1989b, 1990) partly for its brilliance, and partly because *Angel Guerra*, arguably Galdós's most interesting novel after *Fortunata and Jacinta*, has been neglected. (Gratifyingly, an English translation – 1990, Edwin Mellen Press, Lampeter – has recently appeared.) Valis's stress on the monstrous aspects of the novel highlights Galdós's fascination in his later work with different forms of the abnormal, under the influence of Lombroso's theories. Her definition of the monstrous as the impossible juxtaposition of opposites again reminds us of Urey's analysis of the blurring of oppositions in Galdós's work. Valis relates such ironic juxtapositions to Freudian theories of the creative process: this is virtually the only critical article on Galdós to use psychoanalytical theory imaginatively. The essay provides an interesting gloss on the Spanish phrase 'the madwoman in the house', used to refer to the imagination; this could usefully be related to Sandra Gilbert and Susan Gubar's classic study *The Madwoman in the Attic* (1979, Yale, New Haven). Feminist critics may also want to develop Valis's discussion of the novel's curious gender reversals, whereby the woman thinks and the man conceives; and of the link established between formlessness and the family. The view of Galdós's writing that emerges here could not be further removed from our traditional view of the nineteenth-century novel as the culmination of bourgeois rationalism. Valis's thesis that the monstrosity of the novel's characters functions as a metaphor for the monstrosity of the creative imagination, as manifested in the novel's structure, fits the heteroge-

* Reprinted from 'Angel Guerra o la novela monstruo', 1988, *Revista Hispánica Moderna* **41.1**: 31–43. Trans. Nick Caistor, 1991.

neous elements of this hallucinatory text into a coherent theory without diminishing its strangeness.

Critics of Galdós's novels acknowledge that *Angel Guerra* (1890–91) is one of the most thought-provoking works of this writer from the Canary Islands, and that it is full of acute perceptions about the process of spiritual conversion and the psychology of revolt. Despite this, until fairly recently these same critics have dealt harshly with the book, accusing it of the archetypal Spanish fault of being long-winded (see Clarín, 1912, p. 244), or of the peccadillo, to some extent excusable in Galdós, of piling up so many episodes and secondary characters that in the end we are left dizzy from the sheer effort of reading (see Pardo Bazán, 1973).[1] This latter critic is surely right when she concludes her subtle appreciation of the novel by saying that 'Galdós's method creates the same problem as the horizontal flickering of Leré's eyes: it makes one giddy and distracts one's attention' (pp. 1104–5).

It is precisely this capacity that Galdós has to make his readers *giddy* that is worth re-examining in the light of aesthetic values less influenced by the mimetic criteria dominant until recently. There must have been something in this huge novel of over a thousand pages that did not fit in with the notions of just proportions which, according to Clarín and others, were part of the organic structure of the novel genre.[2] While they could admit the idea of the open novel, in which the frame for the picture painted was left out, paradoxically they could not conceive of a non-constructed novel, whose shape was so out of proportion and unbalanced that the principles of its construction were incomprehensible, or rather improbable. It was not natural. These critics implicitly stuck to the idea of a norm in art, that of not going against Nature. By conceiving the novel in biological terms as a living, imperfect organism always awaiting completion (but which in the end always dies), they were including in the canon everything that could be explained according to (and as part of) the vital processes of all living beings. This means that for writers like Galdós and Alas, Flaubert and Tolstoy, life itself had a latent, perceivable shape. So Clarín could use to his own ends the argument put forward by the most hostile critics of the realist-naturalist movement when he wrote: '"How dreadfully it is constructed!" the idealist reader cries. "Exactly, just like the world, which is very badly constructed . . ."' (1912, p. 112). As inheritors of the last vestiges of the great rationalist tradition, writers such as Galdós and Clarín could not deny the formal qualities of the universe; what they criticized were the faults in the construction of our world, not the absence of any form at all. It can be argued that what Galdós was doing – like every other artist before and after him – was to impose a shape on external reality, but it is clear that the model he was following was the great printed book of nature.

What room then is there for all that does not conform to this norm of the natural? Whatever goes against nature is, quite simply, monstrous. Or as Gilbert Lascault says in his stimulating book on the monstrous in Western art: 'L'imitation par l'art des formes est également, par définition, en opposition avec les formes *m* [the monsters] qui sont . . . contre nature' (1973, p. 23). It is worth noting that biological monsters are excluded from this idea of the monstrous because they are not *voulus*, since they are created by factors outside human control. I mention this point here because, as is well known, the realist-naturalist novel is full of such sorry creatures; we have only to think of Valentín in the *Torquemada* series, or the freak known as 'the monster' in *Angel Guerra* itself. The importance of these abnormal creatures lies more in the creative possibilities they are deemed to possess than in their physical aspect, whether this is determinist or not. It might even be said that 'the resurrection of the monsters' is a basic part of modern art, beginning with Goya and Blake and ending in anti-rationalist movements like Surrealism (see Lascault, 1973, pp. 59–60; Abel, 1966, p. 198).

In the pages which follow I should like to suggest an interpretation of *Angel Guerra* which places it in this teratological context, seeing it ultimately as a monster-novel. It is a transitional novel in Galdós's output, and consequently reveals the contradictory impulses of its creator, impulses which could be classified as *biological* and *imaginative* modes respectively. Marthe Robert has used neo-Freudian terms to speak of the novel genre as a kind of 'foundling', whose real parents are imagined to be other, much grander and more splendid procreators who are idealized – and created – by the infantile mind in the face of its first disappointments at its protectors' imperfections and lack of sensitivity. This aesthetic use of a Freudian myth – which also serves to explain the creation of neuroses – is a good illustration of the ever-present tension between the ideal and the real in what is the bastard genre par excellence (Robert, 1980, pp. 21–40). In other words, the world of the imagination is born out of human dissatisfaction with inescapable biological reality. In Galdós, this generic conflict is shown in an almost deterministic way in a novel such as *La desheredada* (1881), where the heroine Isidora Rufete duplicates in her own life the same antagonism between procreator (biology) and procreated (imagination) which created the novel form in the first place. In this case, the character stands in a synecdochic relationship to the work of which it is part, creating a kind of *mise en abyme* or interior duplication, with a close identification between the two levels.

As well as novels, this union of biology and imagination can produce monsters. In the naturalist realm, one of its products was, in fact, the biological monster, which was perfectly natural since it could be explained in the context of hereditary laws and the mimetic norms of direct observation. But there was always the problem of being able to distinguish clearly and unequivocally between a human being classified as normal and his mis-shapen, grotesque photographic negative. This is the difficulty we find in the rationalist thought of someone like Diderot when he writes: 'L'homme n'est qu'un effet commun, – le monstre qu'un effet rare; tous les deux également naturels, également dans l'ordre universel et général . . . Et qu'est-ce qu'il y a d'étonnant à çela? . . . tous les êtres circulent les uns dans les autres, par conséquent toutes les espèces . . . tout est en un flux perpétuel' (1966, p. 269). By giving validity to the monstrous as simply another expression of the natural, Diderot manages to negate monstrosity; if there are no norms, 'man and monster,' as Emita Hill has shown, 'are equal' (1972, p. 195). When the nineteenth century substituted the law of heredity as it was then understood for the law of reason, the problem grew rather than being resolved; only in this way could someone like Zola see a prostitute as the symbol of a whole corrupt, decadent order while at the same time attributing to her attributes such as 'man-eater' and 'golden fly'. In other words, a human monster whose hereditary flaws are hidden beneath a healthy, gilded carnality.

In *Angel Guerra* however, this *biological mode* clashes with the *imaginative mode* to produce various levels of the monstrous, from the crudest, most horrifying physical aspect to a concept of the monstrous that is a paradigm for the creative imagination. To put it another way: it is as though Galdós had given birth to a creature that is a cross between Cervantes and Goya, for the monstrous in *Angel Guerra* is 'the madwoman in the house' (as the imagination is called in Spanish), at the same time both creative and created. 'The sleep of reason produces monsters,' as Goya claimed in his *Capricho* 43. Even taking into account the fact that 'sleep' here could equally read 'dream', as Paul Ilie and others have noted, and the lack of definition of the term 'reason', it is clear that what is referred to in the etching are all those deeply irrational forces which govern our psyche and imagination.[3] These monsters may symbolize our anguish and our terror as well as our capacity for invention, since the unconscious is the source of all these phenomena. It is curious to note in Goya's etching exactly how he represents this creation of the monstrous: the central figure is that of the artist asleep (it looks in fact as if he is lying prostrate) with his implements scattered on the table, while the background is occupied by a host of winged creatures – owls and bats, which as they recede become increasingly shapeless – and a cat or lynx of some sort. If what we are seeing here is among other things the creative act, this birthgiving is striking not only for being purely mental but also for being anti-natural.

It is the artist's privilege to create anti-natural forms, or in other words to call on the imagination in defence of artificiality and of itself. If we ask ourselves where these monsters came from originally, the answer must be: from nowhere, since the monstrous as a form constructed from the remains of previously existing forms has no forebears in the biological sense of the term. As Descartes suggested, the monstrous, like art, is often the extravagant, fantastic outcome of a kind of *bricolage* or combinatory activity (Lascault, 1973, pp. 102–4).[4] This leads one to the logical and perfectly defensible view of 'art in general as a deformation of perceivable reality', as proposed by Lascault (p. 27) and others, that is, art seen as a monster of monsters. Nor should this be regarded as wholly negative, for we have only to think of the exuberance with which the hideous, threatening shapes of Romanesque monsters were sculpted from the shapeless mass of our unconscious, to be convinced not only of art's power to exorcize but also of its power of invocation.

Consider for example the protagonist's name Angel Guerra (literally 'Angel War'), which provides the novel's title. The first thing to note is its composite nature, since Galdós has joined together two usually incompatible nouns, suggesting traditional dualities such as negative/positive, peace/war, life/death and so on. They are terms which should not be placed on the same level since in Western thought they represent irreconcilable opposites, yet there they are. A real tension is created in the phonic cluster as well, juxtaposing initial soft sounds that end imprecisely ('Angel') with subsequent harsher ones ending with a definite vowel sound ('Guerra'). But it is precisely the sense of contained antagonism that joins the two words, despite their tendency to pull in opposite directions. What we are aware of, right from the outset of the novel, is the ability of Galdós's imagination to hold in check the winged creatures of his unconscious, forcing them to inhabit this earth: to be, in other words, a 'warlike angel'. By yoking together two mutually hostile entities, Galdós has denaturalized them in both senses of the word. Since they find themselves on the one hand exiled and on the other transmuted into alien form, 'angel' and 'war' occupy fresh territory, neither heaven nor earth but both at once, plus something else: the title *Angel Guerra* creates a third category that the fictional space (which is also real) will fill, thereby transcending the initial binary opposition.

It is this third reality created by the text itself that I call the monster-novel. Since it is a combination of disparate elements – a kind of *bricolage*, if you like – fused into one by the author's will, this textual monstrosity is particularly noteworthy because it contains within itself all possible and relevant terms, negating them and creating them at the same time in a crucible of deconstructionist *différance*. If Angel Guerra is monstrous –

as novel and character – it is precisely because the figure encompasses its opposite, the angelical. We should remember, for example, that in Gothic sculpture the angels, who along with heroes and saints are considered the enemies of demons and other monstrosities, triumph over those same monsters (Abel, 1966, pp. 130–1, 144–6). But in this novel Angel Guerra – an 'angel' in the sense that he is the hero – is also a monster; thus each extreme supports the other, simultaneously destroying and affirming the traditional dialectic between devils and angels. (Incidentally it is worth noting how the term 'angel' becomes an obsessive leitmotif in the novel.) The same ambiguous status can be seen in the character of Leré, who is often referred to as 'the saint' but whose aversion to the sexual act makes her, as she herself says, as much of a 'monster' as her brothers, who are monstrous in the physiological sense (Pérez Galdós, 1970, p. 1280).

This is an inversion of values which ultimately represents a subversion of the hierarchy of angels and monsters. In fact, creating angels who are monsters and monsters who are angels is not in itself so important, since both are the expression of a greater creation, that of the text itself: that angel which is war and that war which is angel. How can one imagine a text whose birth cannot come out of biological norms, precisely because of its monstrous otherness? How does one create monsters? They are conjured up by the arts of magic, whose secret key resides in the appropriate ritual usage of words themselves. Monsters have to be invoked. Think of the opening words of *Angel Guerra*: 'It was already dawning.' From the very start, it is as though one were reading a kind of novelistic invocation in which Galdós, literally and figuratively, was calling on his text to create itself. Think also of how the figure of Angel Guerra, hammering on his lover Dulcenombre's door, enters so suddenly and forcefully into the life of the reader. We can hear the blows as the morning light steals into the room. Before Dulcenombre can even open the door, 'he was already pushing it open, anxious to seek refuge in that cramped, out-of-the-way dwelling' (p. 1198).

The narrative voice also propels the action – and our enthusiasm – forward by continuing a moment later: 'Let us hasten the narration by saying that the person who went to open the door was called Dulcenombre, and the person who entered Angel Guerra . . .'. It is as though the narrator cannot wait any longer before dropping his characters into the reader's lap. This produces a kind of giddiness in the narrator himself, so that he goes on to check himself, adopting a more measured pace of narration, asking 'But why such haste?'. The narrator is seemingly disturbed by the creative energy he has unleashed, the movement that could be likened to the nervous flickering of Leré's miraculous eyes or the drunken reeling of the sealess sailor, Don Pito. This novelistic giddiness is in reality the incarnation of the Holy Spirit invoked by Galdós in his text, the spirit which informs the creative act and governs the lives of his characters.

Angel Guerra is a book which defies origins. By which I mean – without forgetting that this is in many ways a transitional novel – that its main characters, Angel and Leré, seem to make an immense effort to negate their past, to go beyond what they once were and make themselves anew, *ex nihilo,* in the same way that the irrational impulse to create seems to be born with the 'dawning' with which Galdós begins the novel. It is surely significant that the novel's action begins with a failed revolution, that is, a failure in an attempt to radically redefine historical reality. As a result of this frustrated attempt, the novel's hero arrives wounded at the house where his lover Dulce has been waiting for him the whole night through (this is emphasized by Galdós), as though the 'incorrigible night-owl's' hammering on the door were needed to galvanize the novel's human occupants into action, at a single stroke. The protagonist's energy and impatience, dramatic examples of the creative breath that impels and gives birth to the whole novel, in this first scene adopt the frenetic form of the buzz of an annoying bumblebee.[5] Or as the narrator has it: 'To Guerra's agitated imagination, the buzzing insect almost came to represent a monstrous animal filling the whole room with its vibrating wings' (p. 1200). Finally – following the absurd, unequal battle between the beast and its pursuer Dulce – 'the monster', the narrative voice tells us, 'without so much as uttering a moan, fell to the floor with its legs folded, its wings broken'. 'It's dead', Dulce says. As if to drive home the point, we then read: 'In its death throes it seemed as though it were eating its own feet, digging its head into its protruding stomach' (p. 1200).

From the first pages of *Angel Guerra*, the ideas of the imaginative and the monstrous are linked in a close, possibly inseparable union, since here as elsewhere it is hard to distinguish between the creative faculty and the product of that faculty.[6] Angel's powerful imagination – shown to the full on other occasions as well – by increasing the size of a creature that initially is a real one uses a procedure similar to Goya in his *Capricho* 43, where he multiplies the winged forms, filling more and more of the space in the artist's room. That is, replacing external, visible reality with the reality of the imagination. So Galdós's real bumblebee has to die, because its true nature as such no longer interests him.

Also noteworthy is the way the narrator describes the extinguishing of life in the insect, as if its physiological turning in on itself were a kind of return to the self, a return to origins. There is nothing surprising in this, since the concern for origins is a constant not only throughout Galdós's work, but in nearly all naturalist-realist novels. What is more remarkable in *Angel Guerra* is a half-hidden, potentially conflictive element created and intensified by this interest in origins. In other words Galdós here unites the concept of origins with that of non-origins. The bumblebee's death reminds us of the inevitable circularity of our biological self; the return to our origins which is at the same time the unavoidable encounter with death. We should not forget however that the bee dies at least twice: first, when Dulce actually squashes it; and second, when in his fevered imagination Angel believes he can hear the annoying buzz again, and to soothe her lover's hallucinations Dulce pretends to kill it once more. Even then, 'just wait and see how it comes back to life . . .,' the revolutionary mutters in his delirium (p. 1209).

This resurrection – which in reality is a second reappearance, as the first one was equally fictitious – shows by its very repetition something essential about the functioning of the imaginative faculty. The first thing we can observe is the ease with which one imaginative element is added to another; in other words, how from one element a whole series can be produced that in theory stretches to infinity. This is what Angel himself suggests when he declares that he is capable of resurrecting the 'bumblebee of the imagination'. To reproduce here is to magnify, as in the *Capricho* 43, because each new repetition carries with it the previous one, and so on an *ad infinitum*. In this sense the artist is caught in his own chain of subterfuges, of inventions that paradoxically threaten in the end to become independent of their own creator. One has only to think of the nightmare atmosphere of Goya's etching where the figure of the artist is chained to his table while the creatures of his imagination fly out, with ambivalent gestures that alternately threaten their creator and suggest they will make good their escape from him. Galdós's bumblebee works in the same way, providing the reader with a visible representation of what is perhaps the fundamental problem for all writers and artists: the impossibility of returning to one's origins, a desire that all too readily becomes transformed into a hideous fear. This is because to return to the first reality is to die. Thus the artist is condemned to perpetual repetition, because he can never create something from nothing: there will always be 'another bumblebee'. And each bee is a kind of metaphorical *bricolage*, manufactured from the remains of another winged being. There is no way we can escape our own imagination.

This desire to escape from the realm of the imagination which can be called primordial, a desire that is at the same time a feeling of terror, turns the treatment in *Angel Guerra* of the previously mentioned tension between biology and imagination into an apology for procreation or a defence of genius: of pro-creation. For example, according to the narrator in the first chapter: 'Humanity does not yet know what comes before it nor what will follow it, which forces create and which forces conceive' (p. 1207). This dichotomy between creating and conceiving – which in fact, as Galdós himself shows here, is a false dichotomy – or rather, the confusion between the two, will be an extraordinarily intense concern for the novel's protagonist, in his continual attempts to found a new spiritual order. He will even reach the point where he transforms the traditional (biological) roles of man and woman by endowing Leré with the ability to beget and himself with the ability to conceive. Leré's 'winged imagination', as shown in the flickering of her pupils, represents to Angel 'the wingbeats of the Holy Spirit, who has set up his dovecote in her eyes' (p. 1372). It is Angel's mind which will give birth to Leré's ideas. 'Their organisms reversed,' the narrator writes, 'Leré's work was that of the father, and Guerra's the passive, laborious work of gestation' (p. 1366). Further on, there is also mention of the protagonist's 'laborious giving birth' as he constructs section by section the various parts of the building that will house his new religious order (p. 1369). (It is no coincidence that all this takes place in a city such as Toledo, whose architectural appearance shows all the whimsical irregularities that come from being built in disparate bits and pieces, in other words as a kind of *bricolage*.) Towards the end of the novel, when Don Juan Casado asks Angel if he is not afraid of the 'vertigo' that Sister Lorenza (Leré) seems to produce, Guerra replies: 'I no longer have ideas, no longer have plans. She has taken it on herself to think for me. In the realm of thought I am not myself, I am her. As you can see, she gives me shape, as though I were a liquid and she the vessel containing me' (p. 1508).

Whilst it would be wrong to dismiss the barely controllable motive of passion which often inspires Angel's decisions and acts, it is clear that the desire to found something new points to a deeper, more all-encompassing motive, of which love is a significant but secondary expression. Angel is driven to be the way he is by the same impulse that the author feels: the irresistible urge to create. If any one thing characterizes Angel Guerra it is his imaginative capacity, or as he himself says: 'I must warn you I have an incredible faculty for bringing ideas into being . . .' (p. 1454). Think for example of the ecclesiastical *doppelgänger* he invents, giving him shape in the same way that he projects his image of the 'new man' on to the future: 'They were, if the expression is acceptable, two selves, one facing the other; one the spectator, the other the spectacle' (p. 1420). One can sense how surprised Guerra must have been at the sudden apparition of what appears to be a fully-fledged *alter ego*; 'the confusion and giddiness that he felt,' the narrator tells us, 'defy definition' (p. 1437).

This splitting into two, which functions in a similar way to the episode of the bee, again shows not only a duplicating capacity but also the imagination's power of invocation. Angel partially explains it to himself in terms of his thirst for the supernatural: 'One of the yearnings that most beset me is a longing for the supernatural, the urge to experience sensations which go beyond the laws of physics as we know them'

(p. 1454). But 'bringing into being' the ideas and images his brain creates is simply another way of 'making them Word'; this miraculous gift shows us that Angel is a sort of exorcist, in the same sense that this holds true for Goya or Galdós himself, for the magic is purely aesthetic, be it expressed in words or in pigment.

An outstanding example of Angel as magical creator is the terrible scene of the lost goat kid which becomes transformed into 'the most hideous, vicious he-goat imaginable, with mis-shapen, twisted horns and filthy strands of beard'. It seems to me significant that Angel should invoke supernatural aid against the evil creature that is trying to devour him: 'Invoking all the forces of his spirit, the man was at last able to draw sound from his crushed chest, and shouted in terror: "Away with thee, hound of hell. Thou shalt not tempt the son of your God"' (p. 1480). At this Leré appears on the scene; she tears a chunk of white flesh from her own breast to placate the beast, then slowly moves off, leaving Angel at the mercy of a whole host of 'fearsome, repugnant creatures, snakes with the heads of greedy swine, dragons with dust-covered wings and emerald eyes, dogs with beards and crocodile skins; all the foulest, most dreadful beasts that could occur to the delirious fantasy of a condemned man. All these incredible creatures were biting him, tearing his flesh, smearing him with their pestilent drooling; one of them snatched out his eyes, and wore them on its belly; another ripped out his intestines and stuffed them in its own brain, or with a single bite left him with no heart' (p. 1481).

I have quoted this long description, which in its combination of literary and pictorial realities recalls a whole series of *Temptations of St Anthony*, because it is here that the concepts of imagination-invocation-monstrosity are most clearly related. Not only are unnatural and clearly fabricated beings brought to life but Angel, who creates them, himself becomes a monster, made up of displaced bits of his own body. Displacement and reassembly – two key elements of *bricolage* – produce both monsters and art. The fact that the origin of this monster/art replicates its features demonstrates, first, the difficulty of distinguishing between the faculty of invention and the thing invented. And second, the interior nature of the process, since the call for these beings of the imagination to show themselves is a call made to the innermost self. To in-voke therefore means to create life by use of the voice, life which fluctuates between seeking to struggle free from its creator and remaining his slave. Once again, we can recall Goya's *Capricho* 43.

Invocation also means, according to Covarrubias, 'the aid requested before beginning a work of art, used by orators and poets'; while the Dictionary of the Spanish Royal Academy gives 'part of a poem in which the poet invokes a true or false divine or supernatural being'; in a more general sense, it means to ask for help. So Angel calls on the Virgin Mary or God at several critical moments in the book. And Leré advises him to 'invoke, incessantly invoke the Holy Virgin . . .', to which Guerra fervently replies, 'I will invoke her, I will' (p. 1392). But, as we have seen, in his nightmare Leré is the fantasmagorical presence that Angel invokes, and it is she who produces ideas in his mind. It also seems significant to me that the narrator describes her as a being 'totally freed from the laws of physics' (p. 1341), recalling Angel's attitude towards the supernatural and everything which defies such physical laws. We should not forget however that Leré's eyes (in which the Holy Spirit is lodged) are those of a freak.

The narrative voice tells us that 'her green-tinged eyes with their golden striations were affected by an inbuilt mobility, a horizontal oscillation like that of those clockwork dolls which mechanically move their pupils from right to left . . . as if this were not enough, in adulthood she acquired the tic or nervous habit of constantly blinking . . .; and the combination of this horizontal oscillation and the opening and shutting of her long black lashes produced such a tangled confusion of flashes and shadows that, when talking to her, it was impossible to keep looking at her without feeling giddy' (pp. 1229–30).

This defect is partly blamed on biological factors, since the elder children in the family 'became monsters soon after birth', but Leré tells us, 'in my case the only mark of monstrosity was this thing in my eyes . . .' (pp. 1256–7). We are also told, however, that it was the result of a big shock her mother received while pregnant. This means that Galdós offers us two possible explanations for Leré's grotesque eyes: one of them biological, the other purely imaginative. In any case, the result is a phenomenon which is clearly unnatural and as such perturbs the senses, causing this deeply disconcerting giddiness and confusion. I previously mentioned how traditional roles are reversed in the novel, since it is Leré who begets and Angel who conceives. Is it not possible to see here as well that it is the imagination which begets and biology which conceives? In this sense Leré, or rather her flickering eyes standing as a synecdoche for her, represents a new version of the muse of inspiration, since in this context the creative faculty is seen as feminine. But the product of this fusion is of course androgynous, or in the final instance monstrous, because what is created out of the spiritual union between Angel and Sister Lorenza – a true Galdós heroine, if at first sight an unlikely one – is precisely the text called *Angel Guerra*.

I would suggest that the 'new man' invented by Angel's and Leré's only half-conscious desires is the incarnation of a biological imagination in which dark forces come together in a desire both to transcend and to repeat the birth-giving impulse of all human beings. Both of them had previously rejected their forebears; Leré, out of disgust for the sexual act and marriage as a result of the evil brutality of first her father and then her stepfather; and Angel, in his revolt against his mother's tyrannical authority. Psychologically, they have both undertaken a fierce struggle to free themselves from their immediate procreators. This desire to start again from nothing, to get rid of one's personal history (parallel to the attempt to rewrite the political history of the country) is a way of affirming individual consciousness without having to confront others, or take intersubjectivity into account. It stresses the subjectivity of the individualizing imagination which appears capable of rewriting the universe on its own. But even so the pressure of the family is felt by its very absence; in other words, this rejection of the family contains within it the same procreative impulse represented by the latter. This also means that it is impossible for the children of the imagination to have a spontaneous birth that would overcome the baseness of our unspeakable origins. For the imaginative faculty would appear to be deeply rooted in our biological being.

Why then does this imaginative faculty disturb us so? Precisely because it is monstrous. The flickering of Leré's eyes which so unsettles Angel is a hereditary defect, a biological consequence that neither of her brothers has managed to escape. Even the youngest Sabas, who was born without deformities and is apparently a musical genius, is called the new Mozart, the new monster of music, while her brother Juan is called 'the monster' *tout court*. 'From the waist down,' as Leré describes him, 'his whole body is withered and flabby as if he had no bones; he's got a man's head, a child's body, arms and legs like empty pillowcases . . . if you saw him on the table where he's kept, his arms and legs all mixed up and his head in the middle, you'd not think this could be a human being.' Yet, surprisingly, this being who never does more than grunt can 'repeat whatever snatches of music he hears in perfect tune' (p. 1257). By presenting us with one of those rare, pathetic cases of what we would perhaps today call an *idiot savant*, it is plain that Galdós was well aware of the existence of a mysterious link between genius and idiocy. What are the properties of genius? And if it has something monstrous about it, how do we distinguish between the two? Sabas can also imitate the musical notes he hears and reproduce perfectly, for example, 'the flute, bassoon and flageolet stops' of the cathedral organ (p. 1258). This capacity to imitate is simply the symptom of a much deeper, more complex link between imagination, art and something which appears to reside in the interstices of our biological being, intertwined with our imaginative faculty: the monster living within us.

In this sense, it might be more appropriate when referring to the imagination to call it, not the 'madwoman', but the 'monster in the house'. What is most striking about the case of Leré's brother Juan are not only the abnormal proportions of his body but the fact that he does not really have a proper human form. He appears in fact to lack all form, and this inspires horror in any observer. But he is also a domestic monster, sheltered in the bosom of his family. This fusion between lack of form and the family can further be seen in the Babels, Dulcenombre's family. Their name itself immediately suggests a link with chaos. Dulce is described as a woman without a proper background (p. 1231). According to the narrator, the whole family is 'improbable' ('which does not prevent them from being true', p. 1213). By offering us the history of the Babels (chapter 2, part 1) in the form of a list of its members as if it were a descriptive catalogue of a rare species of human insect, the novelist not only reveals his realist inclinations, but at the same time the absurdity of such techniques, because this is such an extraordinary, crazy family there is no way it can be convincingly conveyed by a naturalist's rational explanations. We have only to think of the example of Dulcenombre's mother, Doña Catalina de Alencastre, a genuine madwoman whose obsession with her lineage (non-existent, it goes without saying) produces in her 'an epileptic quiver, the rictus of a laugh mixed with tears . . . and such a waving of arms and nervous jigging of her body that she seemed the living image of perpetual motion' (p. 1214). In mocking the family origins of the Babels, their improbability, Galdós neither completely accepts nor rejects the force of the laws of heredity, which leads him both to a subversion of such norms and a constant oscillation between the biological and imaginative which, it seems to me, structures the whole narrative of *Angel Guerra*.

One illustration of this basic oscillation is the narrator's attitude to the task of narrating. The cumbersome dimensions of the novel are mainly due to the narrator's obvious delight in straying off into the description of secondary episodes and characters. Galdós, in the guise of the narrative voice, cannot refrain from giving us the individual biography of each and every character, even when this is not absolutely necesssary to the development of the plot. He is ruled by the biological urge to show himself the father of his own creation, in much the same way that Angel Guerra feels the need to duplicate himself in the shape of a clerical *alter ego*. But at the same time this realization of the 'ideas' fermenting in the protagonist's mind is, as we have seen, a function of his imaginative faculty. The idea of a biological impulse implicitly carries with it its opposite; and this applies equally in reverse. More importantly for us, the fusion of both terms suggests a third category which is as unstable as its components, that biological imagination I have already referred to, hinted at in the title of the novel itself: *Angel Guerra*, a monster/invention born of an improbable delivery/*bios*.

This urge to create stories is repeated in a way I would call unconsciously obsessive, forming an integral part of the human activity depicted in Galdós's novels. Angel, for example, feels on the night of his revolutionary adventure a 'need to talk [that] bordered on the frantic', and he will effectively recreate for Dulcenombre all that happened – whether he saw it or not – during the failed uprising. His precocious daughter Ción, with her 'mouselike curiosity', has the peculiarity of 'spinning lies and inventing stories with a thousand realistic details that made them seem true to life' (p. 1255). Shortly before her death, the narrator tells us, she is anxious 'to hear her father tell of tremendous, fabulous things, and to relate them herself with a display of imagination that astounded everyone' (p. 1270). In the case of Don Pito, the sailor beached on dry land, drunk on nostalgia as much as on gin cocktails, 'the words spilled out of his mouth before thought had ordered them' (p. 1299), leading to increasing incoherence. Later on, during the nights in the country house outside Toledo, this 'chronicler of himself' (p. 1217) tells tale after tale of his adventures at sea, in what is perhaps a literary echo of the short stories within a frame of the seventeenth century. The fabulous nature of his story-telling is pointed up by Galdós, who uses the anaphoric repetition of the phrase 'you should hear . . . how' to introduce each new tale. The culmination of Don Pito's narrative art comes with the jumble of reminiscences about Brigham Young's Mormon sect (p. 1424). One final example: Don Francisco Mancebo, who is nothing more than a ranting gush of words, creating dialogues with a phantom interlocutor.

Every reader of Galdós will have noted the important role the imagination plays for these characters, but what has not been sufficiently emphasized is the genuine enthusiasm with which many of them launch into talking and narrating. Their equation of telling with living leads one to suspect a mania for invention that supplants purely biographical fact. In effect what is imagined has here the force of a biological event, and this is what leaves both the reader and the other characters feeling so giddy. Galdós uses expressions like 'to make dizzy', 'giddiness', 'flickering', 'perturb', 'confusion', 'vertigo', etc. on countless occasions. There is a constant toing and froing in the novel, a tremendous vitality and mobility which expresses itself in Leré's flickering eyes, the bumblebee's annoying buzz, Ción's feverish energy and Doña Catalina's epileptic fits. It is to be found in Don Pito's alcoholic dizziness at seeing 'the world in a spin, maps upside down, water becoming dry land . . .' (p. 1301). In the 'vertigo of the lottery' which will produce a 'giddy feeling the whole day through' for Don Francisco Mancebo (p. 1334). Or in the '*maremagnum* of repairs, resurfacings and patchworks' displayed by the idiosyncratic architecture of Toledo (p. 1336); the streets which after a fall of snow 'at every step presented stumbling blocks, obstacles and dangers' (pp. 1348–9). Or the music of the *Dies irae*, 'so danceable' that 'the children started bobbing up and down . . . and the altar boy began a frenzied dance . . .' (p. 1387). Or again, in an echo of this, the 'pupils [of Leré, which] danced in a frenzy, as they had never danced before'

(p. 1418). The text of *Angel Guerra* forms an unstable universe, which has lost its equilibrium and is governed by a mounting series of oscillations and disruptions; one can easily see why this world of disturbed beings should have created such a feeling of giddiness in an eminently reasonable mind like that of Emilia Pardo Bazán.

In this sense, what is most disturbing about a work like *Angel Guerra* is precisely its monstrosity. In its outlandish proportions, its tens of thousands of words which in a way anticipate the horrors of today's taped books (see Hardwick, 1985, p. 6), the novel already contains the seeds of its genetic deformity. But in a much deeper sense the connections outlined here between art and the monstrous point towards a new kind of novelistic creation, one which is seriously top-heavy. Like the disproportionately large head of Leré's brother known as 'the monster', *Angel Guerra* is typified by its feverishly active brain, which imagines at the expense of all else. And like that same outsize head, it does so from a central position. To put things slightly differently, we could say that Galdós has created an encephalic novel (encephalitis being an inflammation of the brain tissues), in which the encephalon (the brain) is called on to substitute for the phallus. In this displacement from the phallic to the encephalic, the imagination acts as the supreme creator, defying the natural biological laws that govern our existence. By going against nature, the imaginative faculty becomes a way of defeating the fear of death, a way of proclaiming our fragile human individuality. What we invoke with our silently recited words is pure invention, pure monstrosity, made up of already existent parts which we unknowingly repeat endlessly, since we cannot reach back to the origins of our being (witness the bumblebee). However this invocation inevitably leads us further into our inner selves than we would perhaps wish to go. In creating his double, the protagonist of *Angel Guerra* is announcing his own death, though he takes it for an omen of someone else's, that of the priest Don Tomé. Creation is always an attempt to discover origins, which ultimately means a return to nothingness. That is why the death of Angel is a logical, perfect finale, because only by death can the dilemma be resolved.

The hybrid that Angel Guerra represents, as work of art and as character, is the monster-novel, or art as deformity.[7] But in the end this creation disturbs us, and we try to dispel its implications in the same way that Leré tries to placate the kid transformed into demonic he-goat by throwing it a chunk of her own breast. The irony here is that when we act against nature in art we fall back into the biological trap, as the bits of flesh torn from our imaginative faculty return us once more to the biological realm, to the breast as sexual and reproductive organ (a repeated image in the novel). Because if the monster is art, this monster also resides within us. And if we are reproducing anything in art, perhaps it is those monstrous – or animal – origins we are always trying to forget, to exorcize by conjuring them up aesthetically: hence *Angel Guerra*'s biological imagination. Galdós, by intuiting that art appears to have a biological basis, a basis which at the same time it tries to overcome, is also suggesting that we ourselves are 'the monster in the house'.

Notes

1. See for example Lowe, 1975; Hafter, 1969; Scanlon, 1973; Sinnigen, 1977 and Montes Huidobro, 1971.
2. Clarín could write, for example, that there must be a 'generic sense' of the construction of a novel, in which 'literary symmetry' should be evident from 'the just proportions between the effort spent on the main and secondary themes, a clear sense of the key moments in the plot . . .' (1892, p. 84). He was specifically referring to the disproportion of the various parts of Pereda's *La Montálvez*.
3. See Ilie, 1984; Cirlot, 1971, pp. 213–4; De Vries, 1976, pp. 325–6.
4. Concepts possibly related to this are the 'capricho' and the 'grotesque', both highly ambiguous terms capable of many interpretations. See Dowling, 1977; Ilie, 1976; and Kronik, 1976. The notion of *bricolage* I am using here comes from Lévi-Strauss via Derrida, Lascault and others. It is of course important to remember that one should not limit oneself to the Cartesian position, for although it gives a fair description of the mechanics of the monstrous, it does not explain how it comes into being (see Lascault, 1973, p. 177–95). As an antidote to Cartesianism, Lascault (p. 185) insists on 'la recherche de caractère herméneutique, que provoque la forme monstreuse'.
5. Montes Huidobro (1971, p. 55) makes an intelligent analysis of this scene, stressing the multiple transformations of reality which occur in it. 'The bumblebee,' he writes, 'seems to be born out of Angel (interior), become reality in the room (exterior), and then return to the man's subconscious (interior)'.
6. Ilie discusses a similar double and confusing use of the term 'capricho' (1976, p. 241).
7. 'Guerra was one of those ugly men who reveal by I know not what mysterious ethnographic stamp that they were born of good-looking parents. His features clearly showed the combination of two distinctive, beautiful natures' (p. 1210). Similarly Leré's face has the irregular, asymmetrical features of a 'capricho' (p. 1229).

References

Abell, W., 1966, *The Collective Dream in Art*, Schocken, New York.
Alas, L. see Clarín.

CIRLOT, J. E., 1971, *A Dictionary of Symbols*, 2nd edn, Philosophical Library, New York.

CLARÍN, 1892, *Ensayos y revistas 1888–1892*, Manuel Fernández Lasanta, Madrid, pp. 81–102

CLARIN, 1912, *Galdós*, in *Obras completas*, vol. 1, Renacimiento, Madrid, pp. 95–112, 241–50.

DE VRIES, A., 1976, *Dictionary of Symbols and Imagery*, 2nd edn, North Holland Publishing Co., Amsterdam.

DIDEROT, D., 1966, *Le Rêve de d'Alembert*, in *Le Neveu de Rameau, suivi de six oeuvres philosophiques*, Paris, pp. 238–47.

DOWLING, J., 1977, 'Capricho as style of life, literature and art from Zamora to Goya', *Eighteenth-Century Studies* **10**: 413–33.

HAFTER, M. Z., 1969, 'Bálsamo contra bálsamo in *Angel Guerra*', *Anales Galdosianos* **4**: 39–48.

HARDWICK, E., 1985, 'The teller and the tapes', *The New York Review of Books* **31.9**: 3–6.

HILL, E. B., 1972, 'The role of "le monstre" in Diderot's thought', *Studies on Voltaire and the Eighteenth Century* **97**: 239–55.

ILIE, P., 1976, 'Capricho/caprichoso: a glossary of eighteenth-century usages', *Hispanic Review* **44**: 239–55.

ILIE, P., 1984, 'Goya's teratology and the critique of reason', *Eighteenth-Century Studies* **18**: 35–56.

KRONIK, J., 1976, 'Galdós and the grotesque', *Anales Galdosianos* (supplement): 39–54.

LASCAULT, G., 1973, *Le Monstre dans l'art occidental: Un problème esthétique*. Klincksieck, Paris.

LOWE, J., 1975, 'Structural and linguistic presentation in Galdós's *Angel Guerra*', *Anales Galdosianos* **10**: 46–53.

MONTES HUIDOBRO, M., 1971, *XIX. Superficie y fondo del estilo*, North Carolina University Press, Chapel Hill, pp. 53–68.

PARDO BAZÁN, E., 1973, 'Angel Guerra' (1891)', in *Obras completas*, vol. 3. Aguilar, Madrid, pp. 1093–105.

PÉREZ GALDÓS, B., 1970, *Angel Guerra*, in *Obras completas*, 7th edn, vol. 5. Aguilar Madrid.

ROBERT, M., 1980, *Origins of the Novel*, Indiana University Press, Bloomington, Indiana.

SCANLON, G., 1973, 'Religion and art in *Angel Guerra*', *Anales Galdosianos* **8**: 99–105.

SINNIGEN, J. H., 1977, 'The problems of individual and social redemption in *Angel Guerra*', *Anales Galdosianos* **12**: 129–40.

15 Galdós's *Gloria*: A Re-vision*

CATHERINE A. JAGOE

Jagoe's work on Galdós, although in its early stages, has established a solid basis for feminist analysis. This article has been chosen in preference to her excellent piece on *Fortunata and Jacinta* (in press) to avoid over-representing that novel, and because *Gloria* was Galdós's best-selling novel during his lifetime and up to the Spanish Civil War, owing to its polemical indictment of religious intolerance (which made it anathema to the Franco regime). Jagoe's feminist reading reveals a very different novel in which the female protagonist is the victim rather of Galdós's hesitant attitude towards women's emancipation, which undermines the text's overt political liberalism. (This piece compares well with Pardo Bazán's analysis of *Tristana*, see Chapter 5.) The article provides a short but useful introduction to nineteenth-century Spanish views of the domestic woman as 'angel of the house' and 'caged bird', giving further bibliographical references for those interested. Jagoe's observation that Gloria comes to see female creative powers as monstrous connects interestingly with the previous article by Valis (Angel Guerra is a masculine 'angel', something feminist critics might like to think about). Jagoe's article is firmly within the historically oriented Anglo-American strand of feminist criticism. French feminist theory, with its psychoanalytic bias, has not yet penetrated Galdós studies; Jagoe's demonstration of the importance of the father–daughter relationship in *Gloria* offers possibilities for the application of Freudian theory.

Galdós's *Gloria* (1877) has traditionally been interpreted as a thesis novel about religious intolerance. José Montesinos, Gustavo Correa, Eamonn Rodgers, William Shoemaker and Walter Pattison have convincingly

* Reprinted from 1991, *Crítica Hispánica* **13**: 31–43.

illustrated the centrality of the religious aspect.[1] More recently, there has been some questioning of the traditional approach. Brian Dendle argues that *Gloria* should not be seen as a 'thesis' novel at all.[2] Thomas Lewis reminds us that it was received by the Spanish reading public as a liberal manifesto rather than simply as an affirmation of the need for religious freedom. Both he and Benito Varela Jácome point to the political theme contained in the novel's dramatization of the conflict between two rival religions.[3]

The present study of *Gloria* is offered as a further and more radical 're-vision', an attempt to see the novel through the prism of gender and to ask different questions of it than have been asked hitherto.[4] Particularly interesting is what Nancy Miller terms 'the heroine's text', that is to say the ideology of gender informing the characterization and the trajectory of the heroine.[5] From a feminist critical perspective, *Gloria* offers a striking example of the way that nineteenth-century ambivalence about gender roles became inscribed in the fiction of the period. *Gloria*'s eponymous protagonist is indeed the site of religious conflict, but she is also the site of conflicting ideologies of gender in the text. In order to comprehend the significance of the recurring patterns of imagery used to represent her, it is necessary to read the novel in terms of the historical and literary context in which it was written, particulary the powerful late nineteenth-century stereotype of the Angel in the House (*ángel del hogar* in Spanish), around which the characterization of the heroine revolves, although in a contradictory way.

The concept of the Angel in the House emerged in Spain in the middle of the nineteenth century, and its appearance has been interpreted as the most visible symptom of the bourgeois project to map out a new set of gender roles for both sexes.[6] Interestingly, it coincided in its inception with the mid-century 'Catholic revival' or neo-Catholicism, the effects of which Galdós depicts in *Gloria*.[7] By the time Galdós wrote *Gloria* in the late 1870s, the preoccupation with equating the feminine with the angelic had exerted an enormous influence upon the literary production of the period. Bridget Aldaraca and Alicia Andreu have illustrated how the Angel in the House or 'woman of virtue' is found across the literary spectrum, in a wide variety of different forms of writing – pamphlets, speeches, part works, medical texts, novels, poetry and conduct manuals.[8] The model angelic woman depicted in this plethora of texts was meek, passive, middle-class, asexual and innately moral. She was defined in terms of her 'place' both physically (confined to the domestic sphere) and emotionally, in terms of her triple family role as 'daughter, wife and mother'.

There was a significant amount of feminine resistance to the new bourgeois definition of womanhood, from a quarter that Galdós was particularly likely to encounter: middle- and upper-class intellectual women. Important figures such as Pardo Bazán and Concepción Arenal explicitly protested that the new ideal of femininity entailed the confinement and figurative mutilation of women.[9] Their use of the language of slavery and confinement drew on the writings of an earlier tradition of Romantic women authors, whose protest about women's lot is seen in the metaphor they used: that of Woman as a caged bird.[10] Once the Angel in the House became established in the 1850s as the norm for respectable women, the caged bird image became even more apt. For, as Nina Auerbach has pointed out, nineteenth-century society had redefined the metaphor of the winged and mobile angel, traditionally associated with martial power and masculinity, in order to represent a feminine ideal of stasis, subordination and domestic confinement.[11]

Aspects of the nineteenth-century feminist discourse which represented women as painfully confined by domesticity are insistently present in Part 1 of Galdós's *Gloria*. In the opening pages the narrator introduces two images which are to be central to the first half of the novel: that of the home as prison, and that of the heroine as at once angel and caged bird. Early scenes involving Gloria, for example with Caifás, the villager to whom she plays a ministering angel, suggest that she is a model heroine, for they establish her domesticity, purity, piety and nurturing skills. Yet, significantly, our first introduction to the Lantigua household is an ironic reference to the joys of living in a 'prison' (1, 1, 516), and the narrator from the outset suggests that the heroine is metaphorically a bird prevented from flying: 'even when birds walk you can tell they've got wings' (1, 2, 517).[12] The reason for this evocation of the heroine as caged bird becomes clear when the narrator introduces another aspect of her character: she is a woman of considerable intellectual stature, and therefore doomed to dissatisfaction. The narrator frequently directs the reader's attention to the conflict between the heroine's desire for mental freedom and exercise, represented in the text as the desire to use her 'wings', and the familial injunction to be an immobile and enclosed Angel in the House. The metaphors used in the characterization of Gloria at the outset contain clear feminist overtones. As the novel progresses, the ideal feminine role for which Gloria is being trained is increasingly associated with a negative state of constraint and mutilation: like a domestic bird the heroine, says the narrator, 'has her wings clipped' to prevent her from flying (1, 6, 525).[13]

Numerous small details confirm the association between Gloria and the figure of the Angel. The names of Gloria's relatives suggest their intimate involvement with the process of making an angel out of her, for example, Don 'Angel' and 'Serafinita'.[14] The diminutive used of Serafina, and Don Angel's characterization as a 'child', contribute to the negative association between angelicity and artificial childishness or stunted growth. Gloria's father's name, Lantigua, can also be interpreted symbolically, for the ideology of domesticity constantly harked back to a mythical past, what Andreu (1982, p. 19 [see note 8]) calls a 'return-to-the-values-of-old', while his second name, Crisóstomo, links with the Church Father who advocated the silencing of women. All three of the heroine's relatives take part in the process of containing, confining, and intervening with her that goes on throughout the novel.

The relationship portrayed between the heroine and her father is a particularly clear example of the intertwining of feminist and liberal discourse in Part 1. Lantigua's general philosophy as a 'neo-Catholic' is coercive: he believes that 'perverse, dispossessed Humanity needs a straightjacket' (1, 4, 520). The link between his authoritarian religious and political stance and his espousal of patriarchal sexual politics is laid out for the reader in Part 1. The narrator points out that Lantigua's main criterion in the education of his daughter is containment, rather than growth: 'he believed that to shut his daughter up in school was enough' (1, 5, 521). Lantigua tells her that she must apply a 'brake' to her thoughts and praises her for submitting to the 'yoke of authority' (1, 11, 5320). When Lantigua confronts his daughter with his choice of a suitor, she remains silent, incapable of words, but with the point of her parasol she draws in the sand. While her future is being discussed, the thing that she is drawing is gradually revealed, without comment, by the narrator. It provides a visual metaphor for the sensation of imprisonment which Gloria is presumably experiencing in her mutism, for it is a 'metal grille' (1, 11, 532). Having symbolically completed her picture with arrows, like the door of a castle keep, Gloria announces her acquiescence: 'All right, papa; I'll always do what you tell me' (533). Later, Gloria envisages this proposal as a mutilation of wings: 'Several times my father has told me that if I don't clip my mental wings I'll be very unhappy . . . So, bring on the scissors' (1, 12, 534).

Chapters 5 and 6 of Part 1 deal with Gloria's reading and the markedly heterodox development of her intellect. She displays a startling capacity for independent thought, and on more than one occasion contradicts canonical interpretations of history and literature. Each time she is either dismissed or else severely reprimanded by her father: 'What do you know of such things? Go and play the piano' (1, 5, 521). Lantigua limits his daughter's mental travels by barring her access to the novels in his library, citing the cultural commonplace that novels represented a particular danger to women's morals: 'they inflame the imagination, they ignite wishes and desires in the pure hearts of young girls, showing them things and people in a false and dangerous poetic light' (1, 5, 522). Lantigua has his daughter read aloud to him from religious and moral works. However, in the intervals while he is writing, Gloria secretly devours forbidden picaresque works such as *La Celestina* and *El buscón*.[15]

In chapter 5 Gloria embarrasses her father by voicing in male company her opinion that the society and literature of the Golden Age are not the pinnacles of achievement her father believes them to be. Lantigua's response deserves quoting in full because it shows the tension between his own patriarchal viewpoint and that of the narrator, who takes pains to distance himself from Lantigua at this point. Lantigua's reaction is to state categorically that religion, politics and history are male preserves upon which she, as a woman, has no right to intrude or offer judgement. He qualifies the use of her mind for independent thought as criminal and sinful. The narrator is so openly sarcastic about Lantigua's august companions that we are not tempted to conflate Lantigua's judgement of his daughter, evidenced in words such as 'absurd', 'blunders and abominations' and 'obviously', with that of the narrator:

> Later on, when his learned friends had deprived the house of their majestic presence, Don Juan de Lantigua, who was in somewhat of a bad mood due to his daughter's absurd opinions, shut himself in with her and gently reproached her, advising her in future to keep to correct interpretations of History and Literature. He asserted that a woman could never understand such weighty matters, because they involved far more than toiling over books, as many serious-minded men with sharp critical faculties had found. He also told her that all the things written by illustrious men about diverse aspects of Religion, Politics and History made up a worthy canon before which one should bow one's head; and concluded with a sarcastic repetition of all the blunders and abominations Gloria had committed, which would obviously lead her, if left unchecked, to loss of reason, heresy, perhaps even sin (1, 31, 579).

Montesinos, puzzled by this chapter, which clearly does not fit the notion of the novel as religious thesis, pronounces it 'completely unnecessary' (1968, p. 208). From our perspective, however, it shows the author explicitly bringing the reader's attention to the fact that 'correct' ways of reading texts were defined by men, and that women's potential for creative thought and free exposure to different kinds of writing were severely limited by the gender roles of a patriarchal society which prescribed the ideals of submissiveness and chastity for women. Lantigua invokes a patriarchal canon, the 'worthy canon before which one should bow one's head', produced by 'illustrious men' who define the correct ways to interpret history and literature. Gloria acquiesces to this curtailing of her mental horizons. Crucially, she vows never to read anything but the things read by an Angel in the House: 'she made a vow never again to read anything written or printed, apart from her missal, the household accounts, and her uncle and aunt's letters' (1, 6, 525). In trying to limit her mind to the pattern set for the angelic woman, Gloria begins to incorporate the patriarchal notion of female creative powers as monstrous: 'her faculty of discernment was like a fertile monster she carried within herself, which kept on producing ideas at all times' (1, 6, 525). But her vow of obedience is shortlived. After the introduction of Daniel Morton into the household, Gloria begins to question her father's ideas about religion, falling as she does so into a sin whose very name reveals her longing for space and freedom: 'latitudinarianism'. Again the heroine's desires are figured in terms of flying: the narrator comments at the end of Part 1 that 'Gloria beat ever more strongly the ill-fated wings of her latitudinarianism' (1, 31, 579).

Images of flight as revolt against the feminine role occur repeatedly in chapter 26. In this chapter, appropriately entitled 'The rebel angel', Gloria's Satanic or Promethean rebellion against her father's religious creed is also a rebellion against the special requirements for the female angel. The use of interior monologue constructs a heroine tormented by contending impulses on the one hand to obedience and immobility and on the other to self-assertiveness, power and flight. The description of her struggle is presented in such a way as to thwart moral condemnation, for the hubristic inner voice urging Gloria to rebellion speaks not as the devil but as an echo of Christ: 'Rise up, be not afraid. You have a great and powerful understanding. Give up your deadening submission, the cowardliness that has so oppressed you . . . You are capable of great things. You are an adult: do not strive to be a child. You can fly to the stars; do not crawl on the ground' (1, 26, 569). Gloria imagines her hidden strength to be such that, released, it would destroy the myths of male authority around her: 'I know more than my father, more than my uncle. I listen to them talking and talking . . . and in my heart of hearts I tell myself: "I could demolish this whole pile of words with a single phrase"' (1, 26, 569). Her fantasies of power and destructive revolt are accompanied by a clear intuition that she has acquiesced to the mutilation of her own wings:

> 'I've been a hypocrite; I allowed my wings to be clipped, and when they grew back again I pretended I didn't have any . . . I pretended to subordinate my thoughts to someone else's, and to allow my soul to shrink, shutting it into a narrow confine. But no. Heaven is not the size of a mirror glass! It is immense. I'll emerge from this cocoon I'm wrapped in, because it's time for me to do so, and God is saying to me: "Come out, I created you to give off your own light, like the Sun, not to reflect someone else's, like a pool of water"' (1, 26, 569).

We continually witness indications of her strong impulse to rebel against the gender role urged upon her. She wishes to be like the 'masculine' principle of the sun, an independent source of light, rather than the 'feminine' principle of reflection. The choice that Gloria faces, besides being a choice between religious orthodoxy and heterodoxy, is also one of conformity to or rebellion against the model of femininity.

In Part 1, then, intertwined with the critique of neo-Catholicism, we can read a critique of patriarchal sexual politics and their effect upon the heroine. Scenes such as those we have discussed subvert the ideology of domesticity by positing a relation between the angelic feminine role and confinement and mutilation. Galdós provides a strikingly modern analysis of the way that women were excluded from the historical and literary discourses of his time. The novel does not, however, consistently maintain the feminist critique of gender roles which it undertakes at the outset. It consists of two parts, which were published separately, and in which we can trace fundamentally opposing ideologies of woman's place. Part 1 details the rise but also the end of Gloria's rebellious stance. Halfway through the novel, with Gloria's fall, there is a radical shift in the characterization of the heroine. In the early descriptions of Gloria, before the appearance of Daniel, and up until her union with him, the tragedy we are invited to consider is the destruction of Gloria's free mind because of the requirements placed on women by a society whose central icon is that of a confined, domestic angel. This theme is not pursued further, for the subject of Gloria's struggle to use her mental powers is abandoned once she loses her chastity to Daniel Morton, at the end of Part 1. The results of this fall are so catastrophic that she no longer fights to use her mind for herself. The choice which had faced her earlier, of 'rebellion or resignation', is translated into the emblematic feminine dilemma of love of a man versus duty to family, rather than a rebellion against the feminine role-model.

The sexual union between Gloria and Daniel in Part 1, chapter 36 is staged in a storm and flood of gothic proportions, signalling the disturbance and disorder of the entire cosmos. Even though, like Tess of the d'Urbervilles, the heroine is passively propelled by circumstance and her lover into succumbing, her loss of chastity is still symbolically invested with earth-shaking implications: 'then the wind blew again furiously; the branches of the trees, in their whirling frenzy, seemed to be lashing one another, and in the midst of all this turmoil it seemed that the sound could be heard of the broken wings of a falling angel that had been cast out of Paradise' (1, 36, 592). The storm indeed presages dire consequences for the heroine, for after consummating their love, Daniel reveals that he is not, as Gloria has assumed, a Protestant, but a Jew. Gloria's sexual initiation is furthermore figured as striking at the very heart of the patriarchal order, for upon discovering the lovers in Gloria's bedroom her father falls dead instantly of a heart attack. Gloria's disobedience has rendered her nothing less than a parricide.

At this central point of the novel, the metaphor of breaking wings is employed for the heroine's loss of chastity. In context the metaphor bears an important second meaning, which is that Gloria's powerful, independent thought-processes are now broken. From this point on, her path is one of submission and obedience, not free flight. She uses all her energies to punish herself and to try to conform to the angelic mould which, in the eyes of contemporary society, has been irreparably shattered by her extra-marital sexual initiation. Ironically, at the point at which Gloria becomes in conventional terms a 'fallen' angel she in fact starts to be characterized by Galdós as most angelic. The latter half of the novel traces Gloria's decline, during which she demonstrates two main characteristics of the angel figure: woman as redemptive sacrificial victim, and woman as mother. In so doing, the narrative foregrounds the image of woman as angel rather than as caged bird, and the latter image is largely left behind. Thus the domestic ideology of the middle classes, which was subverted in the opening pages of the novel, is in the end reaffirmed. The angelic values of purity, piety, submissiveness, martyrdom and motherhood displace the earlier transgressive, intellectual, rebellious stance of the heroine. After her fall Gloria begins a long process of atoning self-effacement which culminates in her death. Far from completing the process of rebellion against the injunction of her societal environment to 'suffer and be still', she now concurs with it completely. The silencing and confinement imposed on her by her father in Part 1 she now imposes on herself: her 'confinement' in order to give birth to an illegitimate son has become the reason for a perpetual confinement with the ultimate 'limit' of death.

In Part 2 the patriarchal gender codes which were formerly imposed on Gloria by the male characters are taken up and endorsed by women: by Gloria herself, by the women in Ficóbriga, and by her aunt Serafina. All of them combine to uphold the Angel in the House as the model of womanhood and to punish Gloria's departure from it. The narrative stance here is contradictory, for although the narrator displays a good deal of dislike for the punitive zeal of these women, Gloria is nevertheless presented as admirable for submitting to them. As a result of her fall, Gloria becomes almost totally submissive, focussed obediently on the need for penitential suffering. Christ-like, she 'drained the chalice without a murmur' (2, 7, 617). She is tutored by Serafina in remorse and self-sacrifice, and has become desperate to conform: '"What must I do not to be rebellious? I'll do anything," the young woman said, casting out of her the last atom, so to speak, of free will' (617). Her acceptance of suffering, her resignation and self-prostration are clearly intended to be construed as signs of nobility of soul. Her self-offering is made in the language of the female mystics: 'I accept a dreadful expiation . . . I'll not say a single word in my defence, because I know I merit it, and that my sins are great; I'll drink to the depths, to the foulest dregs of this bitter chalice. I offer God my lacerated heart dripping with blood, which will never for the rest of my life give a beat that is not full of pain' (2, 7, 617). By the end of the novel Gloria has dedicated herself to becoming the instrument of her family's will, in obedience to nineteenth-century culture's injunction to women: 'I have no will' (2, 22, 662).

In accordance with the ideology of domesticity, maternal sentiment is invoked in Part 2 as a central value. Motherhood is presented as an irresistible biological and moral instinct in both Gloria and Esther Spinoza, Daniel's mother. Since loose and fallen women were typically imagined to be 'bad mothers' or 'unnatural', Gloria's overwhelming love for her child acts as a sort of moral shorthand signalling that, despite her fall, she remains a pure 'woman of virtue' rather than a 'whore'. Gloria refuses to give up seeing her son, despite Serafina's exhortations, for although 'I despize myself as a woman,' she declares, 'as a mother I can't do it' (2, 19, 653). It is this maternal instinct which causes her to flout prohibition and to overcome her own intense physical weakness in order to visit the child alone, at night. She describes the bond with her son as 'noble', 'holy', 'divine', all conventional nineteenth-century epithets for a mother's feelings. She now defines herself as a mother before all else: 'I am a mother!' (653), and puts the difference of views between herself and Serafina down to the fact that Serafina is childless: 'You're a saint . . . but you've never been a mother' (2, 19, 655). Chapter 21 of Part 2, in which Gloria makes her final *via crucis* to the child's cradle, is entitled 'Mater Amabilis', that is, 'mother worthy of love'. She is described by the narrator as 'the mother' (691), and 'the unhappy mother'. The immensely painful effort of her last journey, undertaken while in a state of near-collapse, is intended to show how she is now, like an ideal woman, entirely devoted to the child's welfare rather than her own. In this final journey, the parallel between Gloria and the Mater Dolorosa is very clear. Love, marriage and the family have replaced individual self-affirmation as the central dynamic in the heroine's character.

After her fall Gloria continues to manifest the same strength of character she demonstrated in Part 1, but it is turned inwards against herself. In Part 1, Gloria's inner voice tells her that she should emerge from her 'cocoon' and exercise the 'wings of her spirit'. But she makes a penitential return to the cocoon in Part 2, deliberately arresting her own growth and development. She submits herself to a long process of atonement and tries to conform to the image of the angel woman. She has interiorized the angelic ideal of selflessness and self-sacrifice. Like the angel, she is now represented as an icon of passivity. This is in strong contrast to the restlessness and movement with which she was characterized at the outset. In the opening chapters she was described as 'extremely lively', 'impatient' and as showing signs of 'constant restlessness': 'inside her there was a lively and energetic spirit, which she had to keep constantly occupied' (1, 2, 517). By Part 2, she has become virtually lifeless. In chapter 26, entitled 'Prisoner', Gloria is ambushed by Daniel on her way home from a clandestine visit to her son. The clichés of style seen here are linked to clichéd gender attributes (for example his 'arms of steel' versus her 'pretty, grieving face'). Feminine fragility, beauty and suffering are contrasted to masculine strength, action and energy in this vignette of ideal manliness and womanliness:

> Daniel sat down on a large boulder by the side of the pathway, still holding the girl in his arms, then set her on his knees, as if she were as light as a feather . . . He enfolded her in his arms of steel . . . Held prisoner in his loving arms, Gloria sat still, and the cloak covering her, leaving only her pretty, grieving face free, made the prison she was enclosed in even smaller (2, 15, 646).

The trauma of admitting to Daniel the existence of their son (2, 16, 647) causes Gloria to lose consciousness and to have to be transported home in an invalid state. Her moral sense is so acute that voicing the secret that she has borne an illegitimate child causes her to begin to die of shame.

The heroine's decline into invalidism and death demonstrate a 'dysphoric' plot as analysed by Nancy Miller (1980, p. xi [see note 5]), and we can trace marked links between this novel and the popular literature of Galdós's time, in which, as Andreu has remarked, a fall from virtue on the part of the heroine was typically followed by social ostracism or death (1982, pp. 65–6 [see note 8]). Galdós ostensibly uses the sentimental plot of the woman dying of a broken heart because she cannot marry her true love in order to illustrate a tragedy caused by religious antagonism. But the subtext of this drama, the terms in which it is framed, are dictated by cultural notions of womanhood. Gloria's death scene, for example, is suffused by a characteristically nineteenth-century predilection for transfigured and visionary fallen women, seen at its most spectacular in operas such as *La Traviata*. Gloria's death is represented as a sort of obedient suicide: 'Imagining that her person was no more than a written name, she said, "I hereby erase myself"' (2, 30, 688). Galdós's representation of the moribund Gloria repeatedly evokes the image of the Angel in the House which is treated as a positive value throughout Part 2. She speaks with an 'angelic smile' (2, 32, 694), declaring that 'my husband and my son will ascend with me to find rest in the shade of the heavenly tree in whose branches the angels sing' (2, 32, 695). Daniel calls her his 'poor angel' (694), and when she finally dies, having wrung a promise of conversion from Daniel, she is, according to the narrator, carried off to heaven by the angels (697). Significantly, Gloria dies at the very moment on Easter Sunday when the priest is intoning the *Gloria in excelsis Deo*, just after she has uttered the words 'tomorrow you will be with me in Paradise' (2, 32, 697). Since she has also produced a son called 'Jesús' Gloria has come, by the end of the novel, to fulfil the ambiguous spiritual function of the Angel, identified at once with the Virgin Mary and, thanks to her obedient self-erasure, with the redemptive powers of Christ, the supreme sacrificial victim.

As we have seen, the representation of Gloria changes direction halfway through the novel, creating an odd combination of reaction against and reiteration of the patriarchal construction of woman as Angel in the House. The very power of this cultural stereotype is attested by the way it resurfaces in a novel whose initial premises had been overtly opposed to it. The figure of woman as suffering, redemptive victim, living only for her relations with man, is resoundingly restated. In Part 2 the Promethean rebel is replaced by a woman whose entire being is concentrated upon doing penance for disobeying her father, whilst suffering because she cannot marry her natural mate or care for her son. In the place of the lively, spirited, rebellious adolescent girl of Part 1 we see a debilitated, fragile, spiritualized angel woman who struggles painfully to a visionary death. Gloria's acquiescence to the cultural code embodied in the angel woman becomes the index by which we are invited to judge her morally worthy. The nineteenth-century dictum that 'woman cannot live without man', since 'the end of woman on this earth, her evident vocation, is love'[16] is upheld in this narrative by the contrast in the fates of the heroine and hero: while the former dies, the latter survives, albeit tortured and, in later years, insane. In obedience to the ideal of femininity, the heroine destroys her physical and mental self.

In contrast to the traditional view of *Gloria* as a one-sided novel, our study has highlighted its paradoxical complexity at the ideological level of gender, thanks to its espousal of two radically conflicting sets of cultural values. The author himself was, according to Clarín, dissatisfied with the second half, pronouncing it 'contrived and *tourmentée*' (Alas, 1912, p. 28). There is no doubt that he provides a conservative resolution of the questions about gender roles raised in the early part of the novel. The narrative recoils from the rebellion against prescriptions of femininity implied in Part l. In depicting the heroine's evolution into a suffering angel, the novel reaffirms the very ideology that it had challenged earlier, thereby manifesting at a submerged level an unresolved ambivalence about nineteenth-century society's model of womanhood.[17]

Notes

1. Montesinos, J. F., 1968, *Galdós* 3 vols, Castalia, Madrid, vol. 1, pp. 193–233; Correa, G., 1974, *El simbolismo religioso en las novelas de Pérez Galdós*, Gredos,

Madrid, pp. 49–62; Rodgers, E., 1966, 'Religious conflict and didacticism in *Gloria*', *Anales Galdosianos* **1**: 39–51; Shoemaker, W. H., 1976, 'A note on Galdós's religion in *Gloria*', *Anales Galdósianos* **11**: 109–18; Pattison, W., 1969, 'The manuscript of *Gloria*', *Anales Galdosianos* **4**: 55–61 and 1979, *Benito Pérez Galdós: Etapas preliminares de 'Gloria'*, Puvill, Barcelona.

2. Dendle, B., 1980, 'Perspectives of judgement: a re-examination of *Gloria*', *Anales Galdosianos* **15**: 23–43.

3. Lewis, T., 1979, 'Galdós's *Gloria* as ideological *dispositio*', *Modern Language Notes* **94.2**: 158–82; Varela Jácome, B., 1985, 'Bipolarizaciones ideológicas en *Gloria*, de Galdós', *Boletín de la Biblioteca de Menéndez Pelayo* **61**: 237–57.

4. The term 're-vision' has become emblematic of the agenda of Anglo-American feminist scholarship, since its use by Adrienne Rich in 1972 ('When we dead awaken: writing as revision', *College English* **34.1**: 18–30).

5. Miller, N. K., 1980, *The Heroine's Text: Readings in the French and English Novel, 1722–1782*, Columbia University Press, New York, p. x.

6. Discussed most recently in Susan Kirkpatrick, 1989, *Las Románticas: Women Writers and Subjectivity in Spain, 1835–1850*, University of California Press, Berkeley.

7. Carr, R., 1966, *Spain, 1808–1939*, Oxford University Press, Oxford pp. 285–7.

8. Aldaraca, B., 1982, '"El ángel del hogar": the cult of domesticity in nineteenth-century Spain', in Mora, G. and Van Hooft, K. S. eds, *Theory and Practice of Feminist Literary Criticism*, Bilingual Press, Ypsilanti Michigan; Andreu, A. 1982, *Galdós y la literatura popular*, SGEL, Madrid.

9. See Arenal, C., 1893, *La mujer de su casa*, 1881, 1st edn, Gras y Compañía, Madrid, pp. 10, 14, 82; Pardo Bazán, E., 1976, *'La mujer española' y otros artículos feministas*, ed. L. Schiavo, Editora Nacional, Madrid, pp. 74–5. The theme of Woman as captive is a common one in nineteenth-century literature by women. The Spanish tradition, to which Arenal and Pardo Bazán belonged, dates back at least to the 1830s (Kirkpatrick, S., 1989, p. 85), and is echoed elsewhere in Europe and America. Sandra Gilbert and Susan Gubar (1979), for example, illustrate how images of enclosure recur throughout the literature produced by women in nineteenth-century England in *The Madwoman in the Attic: The Woman Writer and the Nineteenth-Century Literary Imagination*, Yale University Press, New Haven.

10. The image of the caged bird has a long history as a political metaphor. Lorenz Eitner has shown that it was originally a symbol for the liberal cause during the French Revolution (1978, 'Cages, prisons and captives in eighteenth-century art', in Kroeber, K., Walling, W. (eds) *Images of Romanticism: Verbal and Visual Affinities*, Yale University Press, New Haven, pp. 13–38). The bird image was adopted by Hispanic women writers during the 1840s such as Coronado and Gómez de Avellaneda as a feminist metaphor for the self (Kirkpatrick, 1989, pp. 187–8, 196–9). For further discussion of its feminist significance in Galdós, see Lisa P. Condé, 1990, *Stages in the Development of a Feminist Consciousness in Pérez Galdós (1843–1920): A Biographical Sketch*, Edwin Mellen, Lampeter, pp. 48–70, which appeared when this essay was in press.

11. Auerbach, N., 1982, *Woman and the Demon: The Life of a Victorian Myth*, Harvard University Press, Cambridge, pp. 71–2.

12. This and all further citations from *Gloria* refer to the following edition: PÉREZ GALDÓS, B., 1981, *Novelas*, 3 vols, ed. Sainz de Robles, F. C., Aguilar, Madrid. I will give part, chapter and page numbers in that order.

13. The sustained metaphor of the caged bird was noticed by Clarín, who described the heroine as an 'eagle caged like a miserable songbird' (Alas, L., 1912, *Obras completas*, 4 vols, Renacimiento, Madrid, vol. 1, p. 55). Interestingly, in comparing Gloria to an eagle, Clarín employs an image typically used to describe the *male* subject in Romantic discourse (KIRKPATRICK, S., 1989, p. 232).

14. In the creative evolution of *Gloria* we can trace the gradual heightening of the theme of conflict between angel-makers and a young woman. Don Angel is introduced in the second draft of the novel and Serafina in the final one. The heroine's name is changed from Rosalía to Gloria in the third draft. WALTER PATTISON (1969, pp. 56, 61) contrasts the meek, submissive heroine of the early versions of the novel to the spirited, independent and rebellious character of the final version.

15. *Editor's note: The Celestina* (1499) by Fernando de Rojas, and *El buscón* (1626) by Francisco de Quevedo are notable for their bawdiness and scurrilous humour.

16. MICHELET, J., 1860, *Woman*, trans. J. W. Palmer, New York, pp. 50, 81.

17. Galdós came under pressure to change course during the writing of *Gloria*. When Part 1 appeared in January 1877, the author was accused by Pereda of anti-Catholicism, a charge repeated later by MENÉNDEZ PELAYO in his *Historia de los heterodoxos españoles* (1881, Librería Católica de San José, Madrid, vol. 3, pp. 812–2). Galdós was sincerely distressed by Pereda's attack and extended considerable effort refuting it in his letters (Bravo-Villasante, C., 1970–1, 'Veintiocho cartas de Galdós a Pereda', *Cuadernos Hispanoamericanos* **250–2**: 9–51). Galdós consciously set out to make Part 2 more acceptable (Bravo-Villasante, p. 15). One of Pereda's specific complaints was that Galdós's characterization was morally unacceptable (Ortega, S., 1964, *Cartas a Galdós*, Revista de Occidente, Madrid, p. 51). Since the figure of the Angel in the House was such a central part of the Catholic traditionalists' view of what should be presented in literature (a point illustrated by Menéndez Pelayo's violent objection to Gloria, whom he described as an immoral 'blue stocking, garrulous and querulous'), it is feasible to attribute the change in the characterization of the heroine to Galdós's desire not to be seen as undermining Catholicism. To reverse the novel's liberal feminist ideology by having the heroine develop into a loving, suffering, angelic victim, was perhaps Galdós's way of mitigating the novel's challenge to religious orthodoxy.

Glossary

The entries below explain terms used in this volume, and give information on Spanish cultural figures mentioned who are relevant to Galdós's work.

Alas, Leopoldo de (penname **Clarín**) (1852–1901) Best known in his day as an influential literary critic, Alas is the author of a large number of short stories and two novels: *La Regenta* (1884–5; 1984, Penguin), a major contribution to the nineteenth-century European novel of adultery; and *Su único hijo* (1890), whose strange gender reversals and sensual spirituality echo fin-de-siècle decadentism. The pre-Freudian psychology of *La Regenta*, together with its relation of female frustration to mysticism and hysteria, offer enormous scope for feminist criticism.

Buñuel, Luis (1900–83) Buñuel's two film adaptations of Galdós novels (1958, *Nazarín*; 1970, *Tristana*) are among his best work. *Nazarín*, filmed in exile in Mexico, curiously omits the extraordinary hallucinations that occur towards the end of the novel, and over-Freudianizes the psychology, but captures the irony of Galdós's depiction of his Christ figure superbly. *Tristana* makes several changes to Galdós's plot that bring out the heroine's sadistic enjoyment of the power that is the other side of female submission, thus skewing the novel's feminist potential but producing some brilliant insights into emotional perversity.

Caballero, Fernán (penname of **Cecilia Böhl de Faber**) (1796–1877) Daughter of the German scholar who claimed Spanish Golden Age literature for Romanticism, Cecilia Böhl de Faber was a collector of Andalusian folk tales and poetry, which she started to work into fictional form (originally in German and French) in the 1820s. They appeared as magazine supplements from 1849 (*La gaviota* [The Seagull]) onwards. Moralistic and conservative, her fiction celebrates female resignation and a static rural order.

Carlism Named after the rival pretender to the throne Don Carlos, brother of Ferdinand VII, Carlism represented the counter-revolutionary reaction of clerical absolutism to attempts at liberal reform. Capitalizing on regionalist resentment at the imposition of central state control, it had its stronghold in the Basque Country and Navarre (with some support originally in Catalonia and Valencia). The three Carlist Wars of 1822–3, 1833–40 and 1870–5 saw the northwest of Spain (and in the first two cases parts of the east) torn by civil strife: a number of Galdós's *National episodes* describe the military campaigns.

CERVANTES, MIGUEL DE (1547–1616) The acknowledged influence of Cervantes's *Don Quixote* (1605, Part 1; 1615, Part 2) on Galdós's work is manifest in his love of obsessive characters (obsessed with books they have read or with an idealized Dulcinea) and his use of unreliable narrators. Like Cervantes, Galdós often makes use of mock historical documentation, and exploits the ironic potential of intertextual references that blur the boundary between reality and fiction. It is from Cervantes's work that Galdós's novels derive their conscious self-reflexivity, as in *Nazarín* and its sequel *Halma* where his quixotic Christ figure (the Bible here plays the role of the romances of chivalry in the *Quixote*) is in the second novel given the first to read and comment on, just as in Part 2 of the *Quixote* the hero reads and comments on his own story as told in Part 1.

CONDUCT LITERATURE The generic term given to the various kinds of instruction book for women, including manuals of etiquette, medical treatises, and women's magazines. While these had always existed, the nineteenth century saw a proliferation of literature aimed at bourgeois young ladies, which stressed the ideal of domesticity. In Spain, where the middle classes attained social prominence late, these developed from the 1850s onwards: Pilar Sinués de Marco's classic conduct manual *El ángel del hogar* (The Angel of the Hearth) was published in 1859. Galdós contributed to two women's magazines: *La Guirnalda* (whose editor became his publisher) and *La Madre y el Niño*; and to the luxury volume *Las españolas pintadas por los españoles* (1871–2, Spanish women painted by Spanish men). His library contained key English, French and Spanish treatises on women, including one by his Krausist teacher Fernando de Castro. *La desheredada* has been shown to be a critical reworking of the moralistic novel *La cruz del olivar*, published in the women's magazine *Correo de la Moda* (Fashion Post) in 1867, by the writer of conduct literature Faustina Sáez de Melgar. Catherine Jagoe (in press), from whom most of this information is taken, has convincingly argued that *Fortunata and Jacinta* should be read as a critique of the concept of the 'angel of the hearth' that constituted the key ideal of nineteenth-century instruction books for women.

CONTEMPORARY NOVELS The term Galdós originally gave to his novels (excluding the ***National episodes***, see entry below) from *Doña Perfecta*

(1876) onwards. Subsequently, Galdós referred to the novels from *La Fontana de Oro* (1870) to *La familia de León Roch* (1878) as 'the novels of my early period', as opposed to the novels from *La desheredada* (1881) onwards (again, excluding the *National episodes*) which he termed 'the novels of my second or third phase' (second phase, if one takes the early novels in a block; third phase, if one divides them into pre- and post-*Doña Perfecta*). The term 'contemporary novels' is generally used by critics to refer to the novels from *La desheredada* onwards, since the contemporaneity of the novels from *Doña Perfecta* to *La familia de León Roch* is somewhat tenuous (see Carlos Blanco Aguinaga's essay, Chapter 13). To avoid confusion, I use the term 'contemporary novels' to refer – as in Galdós's original definition – to all the novels from *Doña Perfecta* onwards that deal with present, as opposed to past, history. The novels prior to both the 'contemporary novels' and the *National episodes* (that is, *La Fontana de Oro, The Shadow, El audaz*) are referred to as 'the early novels'.

Costumbrismo The mid-nineteenth-century vogue for sketches of popular customs, which constitute the genre of 'costumbrismo', derives from the Romantic stress on local colour. It was disseminated through a series of magazines specializing in 'cuadros de costumbres' from the late 1820s to the 1860s. Unlike the Romantic writer Mariano de Larra's 'artículos de costumbres', which satirize traditional attitudes, the 'costumbrista' writers cultivate the aspects of low life that are threatened by modernity. Apart from **Mesonero Romanos** (see below), the main 'costumbrista' writer was Estébanez Calderón, who depicts a folkloric Andalusia. The genre had a lasting influence on the regional novel and on Galdós's novels of urban life, encouraging writers to observe contemporary social manners. A more negative legacy was its tendency to reduce popular culture to the picturesque: even Galdós succumbs to this at times.

Free indirect style A cross between direct and reported speech (a better translation of the original French term 'style indirect libre' would be 'free reported speech'), in which a character's thoughts are presented in the form of interior monologue, but in the past tense and third person. This produces a superimposition of character's and narrator's point of view that can be exploited for ironic purposes. Flaubert is generally credited with being the first writer to make extensive use of this technique; Alas, who was greatly influenced by Flaubert, developed its potential to the full in his novel *La Regenta* (1884–5). Galdós's use of free indirect style precedes that of Alas, first occurring in *La desheredada* (1881), but it appears only sporadically in his work.

Generation of 1898 Named after the historical disaster of 1898 in which Spain lost her last significant colonies Cuba, Puerto Rico and the

Philippines, the Generation of 1898 (Ganivet, Unamuno, Baroja, Azorín, Maeztu) undertake an analysis of what has gone wrong with national history. Their conclusion that Spain is suffering from a loss of energy and will (in a word, from decadence) is anticipated by many of Galdós's novels from *Fortunata and Jacinta* onwards, whose protagonists develop a single-minded ideal that has a regenerative impact on a sterile society. Like the 1898 writers, Galdós will (despite his late flirtation with socialism) reject state solutions for an anarchistic individualism. It was in 1898 that Galdós opportunistically turned back to writing his historical *National episodes*, after a nineteen-year break. Baroja, Azorín and Maeztu were responsible for turning the first night of Galdós's play *Electra* (1901) into an anticlerical riot; Baroja accompanied Galdós on his excursions round working-class Madrid. Unamuno, who had political contacts with Galdós in his last years, rejected the descriptive basis of his realism but modelled his own Pirandellian experiments on the metafictional aspects of Galdós's work.

Krausism The leading intellectual current among liberal and republican circles in Spain from the 1860s to the 1880s, Krausismo was a freethinking alternative to institutionalized religion, that sought to reconcile oppositions through its doctrines of 'harmonic rationalism' and what, in a typically vague neologism, it called 'panentheism' (an attempt to marry idealism and materialism). Krause (1781–1832) was a minor post-Kantian German philosopher belatedly discovered in the 1840s by Sanz del Río, who in 1857 started teaching his thought at Madrid University. Krausist lecturers would dominate Madrid University in the 1860s and 1870s (Galdós studied there from 1862–3), being twice dismissed from office – and in some cases imprisoned – for refusing to accept state control. Their concern for academic freedom led them to set up the Institución Libre de Enseñanza in 1875 (Galdós had close links with it through his friendship with its founder Giner de los Ríos), which would be praised in a famous editorial in *The Times* for its progressive educational techniques. Their emphasis on ethics made them take an active interest in the education of women (traditional transmitters of morality), in the course of the 1870s founding a number of female training colleges. Their concern with marrying the spiritual and the physical led them to institute the study of psychology as a discipline. In retrospect, Krausism can be seen as an exercise in intellectual fence-sitting, as would be tragically illustrated by the Second Spanish Republic of 1931–6, many of whose ministers were educated by the Institución Libre de Enseñanza. The Krausists' contribution to education was nonetheless real.

Melodrama All Spanish realist novelists complain about the flood of imported French serialized novels that shaped popular taste in the mid-nineteenth century (see also **serialization**). Particularly popular with the new working-class public were the socialistic novels of Eugène Sue, first translated in the 1840s, and Hugo's *Les Misérables* (1862). These were imitated with great popular success by Wenceslao Ayguals de Izco, whose bestselling *María o la hija de un jornalero* (1845–6, translated into French with a prologue by Sue) dramatizes a working-class girl's resistance to a wealthy suitor; and Enrique Pérez Escrich, who made a fortune with his sensationalist exposures of upper-class immorality, notably *La mujer adúltera* (1864). Also popular were historical romances à la Walter Scott: over 300 of these were written by Manuel Fernández y González. Their reduction of class conflict to private moral dramas, centred on the family, places these popular serialized novels firmly in the category of melodrama. One of Galdós's favourite returning characters is the writer of serial novels José Ido del Sagrario, who attempts to impose his melodramatic plots on to the characters of *Tormento* and *Fortunata and Jacinta*. Melodrama is to Galdós's fiction what the romances of chivalry are to *Don Quixote*: while parodying its excesses, Galdós will also imitate its forms (as in the plot of *La desheredada*, whose heroine's head is turned by her reading of popular novels). The melodramatic representation of class conflict via the family romance underlies much of Galdós's literary production.

Mesonero Romanos, Ramón de (penname **'El Curioso Parlante'**) (1803–82) An extremely popular writer from the 1830s to the 1860s of short, humorous journalistic pieces describing typical Madrid lowlife customs, known as 'cuadros de costumbres' (see **Costumbrismo** above). As founder of the magazine *Semanario Pintoresco Español* (1836–57, Spanish Picturesque Weekly), which was the main organ of 'costumbrismo', Mesonero Romanos illustrates the close links between journalism and fiction in the nineteenth century. His best known collection of 'cuadros de costumbres' is *Escenas matritenses* (1836–42, Madrid Scenes). His celebration of life in the capital was decisive in shaping Galdós's literary project: the gossip Estupiñá in *Fortunata and Jacinta* is affectionately modelled on him.

Metafiction The term given to fiction that comments on its fictional status or on the nature of the fictional process (also known as 'self-reflexive fiction'). The classic example is Cervantes's *Don Quixote* (see entry on **Cervantes** above), which leaves its traces throughout Galdós's novels. Metafiction necessarily undermines the illusion of realism by drawing attention to the work's constructed nature; it has thus held an immense appeal for many twentieth-century novelists concerned to break with their realist predecessors.

NATIONAL EPISODES The title Galdós gave to his five series of historical novels spanning the history of Spain from the battle of Trafalgar (1805) through to 1880. The first two series (written 1873–9) remain among his best-selling work with the Spanish reading public, for obvious patriotic reasons. He discontinued the project in 1879 to devote himself to what he called his **contemporary novels** (see entry above), which despite critical success sold less well. For commercial reasons, he resumed the enterprise with the third series in 1898, capitalizing on the rash of national soul-searching provoked by Spain's loss in that year of her last major colonies. The fifth and last series was left unfinished in 1912, by which date Galdós had gone completely blind (worsening eyesight had obliged him to employ an amanuensis since 1907).

NATURALISM This can be defined only as the body of literary theory expounded by the late-nineteenth-century French novelist Emile Zola, for in practice no novels (even those by Zola) conform entirely to its tenets. Naturalism is the logical extension of nineteenth-century realism, in its application to literature of the positivistic medical belief in causal diagnosis. Zola will insist that everything is governed by a physical determinism that makes the moral concepts of good and evil irrelevant. This, together with his insistence on including working-class subjects in his 'human comedy' (or tragedy, given the lack of free will), made Zola's novels deeply shocking to his public, who for that reason consumed them avidly. From 1880 onwards his work was translated into Spanish almost immediately on publication, and between 1881 and 1884 Madrid intellectual life was dominated by discussions of the new literary trend. While no major Spanish novelist produced works that can be called naturalist, the influence of naturalism on Spanish fiction from 1881 (Galdós's *La desheredada*) to 1887 (Pardo Bazán's *La madre naturaleza*) is evident. Both Galdós and Pardo Bazán will make documentary studies of working-class environments. Hereditary neurosis is suggested in several Galdós novels, and the importance of physiology in determining human behaviour is crucial to the work of Galdós, Pardo Bazán and Alas, all of whom however shy away from adopting an entirely materialist position. Naturalism enjoyed a belated flowering in Spain in the late 1890s and early 1900s with the Valencian novels of Blasco Ibáñez (see **Regional novel** below).

PALACIO VALDÉS, ARMANDO (1853–1938) A friend of his fellow Asturian Leopoldo Alas, he wrote over twenty novels that were immensely popular in their day. Some of his works touch on working-class subjects (miners and fishermen) while others attack a decadent aristocracy, but he is best known for charming, lightweight love stories like *La hermana San Sulpicio* (1889, Sister San Sulpicio).

Galdós

Pardo Bazán, Emilia (1851–1921) A woman of extraordinary energy, Pardo Bazán was at the head of every new intellectual current, being responsible for sucessively popularizing in Spain the ideas of Darwin (which she opposed), Zola's naturalism, the Russian novel, and in the 1890s the criminological theories of Cesare Lombroso (on which she based her novel *La piedra angular* [1891, The cornerstone]). She went further than any other Spanish writer in her attempts to write a naturalist novel (*La Tribuna* [1883] documents workers in a tobacco factory; *La madre naturaleza* [1887] is a re-write of Zola's *La Faute de l'abbé Mouret*), but the endings of her novels undermine her materialist premises by imposing a moral, often overtly Christian, solution. A sincere Catholic, she nevertheless led an unconventional life, separating from her husband because of his opposition to her writing and having a number of affairs with leading intellectual figures, including Galdós. An active feminist, she campaigned for women's education, founded a women's publishing house, wrote a series of articles on Spanish women for foreign and Spanish magazines, and in 1916 became Spain's first woman university lecturer. Her major work *Los pazos de Ulloa* (1886, *The House of Ulloa*; 1990, Penguin) uses the Gothic format to dramatize women's tragic subordination to fathers and husbands.

Pereda, José María de (1833–1906) Writing, like Galdós, mainly from the 1870s to the 1890s, Pereda was the main exponent in late nineteenth-century Spain of the **regional novel** (see entry below), concentrating on his native Asturias. A close friend of Galdós, whom he first met in 1872, he nevertheless opposed the anticlericalism of the latter's early novels. His first work *Escenas montañesas* (1864, Cantabrian Scenes) consists of 'costumbrista' pieces. Pereda's work forms a bridge between 'costumbrismo' and realism, the regional novels of his mature period continuing the nostalgic conservatism of the earlier genre. A prolific writer, his major works are *Sotileza* (1884) and *Peñas arriba* (1895, Rugged Heights); the landscape descriptions in this last novel are among the finest in Spanish literature.

Positivism The belief that the only valid form of knowledge is that based on the observation of phenomena that can be verified empirically through the senses; in other words, that reality consists solely of physical phenomena. First elaborated in the early nineteenth century by Auguste Comte (1798–1857), its influence was particularly strong in the necessarily empiricist discipline of medicine; it was Claude Bernard's positivist notion of 'experimental medicine' that formed the basis of Zola's theories of literary **naturalism** (see entry above). In Spain, positivism was briefly influential in progressive medical circles in the period 1876–84, but few Spanish thinkers – even those who, like Galdós, were opposed to the Church – were prepared to renounce all belief in the spiritual (see the quotations from Galdós in Goldman's article in this volume). Perhaps the chief legacy of positivism in Spain is the repeated presence of doctors in the novels of Galdós, Pardo Bazán and Alas, where they represent 'the voice of reality'.

RATIONALISM In its original seventeenth-century philosophical usage, rationalism represented the belief that reality could be established *a priori* by non-empirical reasoning. In the course of the eighteenth-century Englightenment, rationalism became associated with the questioning of religious authority, and the attribution of all phenomena to natural rather than supernatural causes. By the nineteenth century, the term had taken on the general meaning of the rejection of all beliefs founded on anything but the rational analysis of experience, thus coming close to being synonymous with **positivism** (see above), to whose empiricism the original seventeenth-century meaning of the term had been opposed. In everyday nineteenth-century usage, rationalism not only had strong connotations of atheism but was also closely linked to economic pragmatism.

REGIONAL NOVEL The mid-nineteenth century saw the beginnings of organized regionalist movements in Spain as elsewhere in Europe, particularly in the Basque Country, Galicia and Catalonia. A major theme in the late-nineteenth-century Spanish novel is the problematic relationship between city and country, examined with regard to Galicia by Pardo Bazán, Asturias by Pereda (and to a lesser extent Alas, who writes about the provincial capital Oviedo), and Andalusia by Valera (like Fernán Caballero before him). Palacio Valdés sets novels in Cantabria, Valencia and Andalusia. (Catalan regionalist sentiment was given literary expression in the Catalan language.) While all writers express concern about the effects of urbanization, only Pereda's work can be seen as a direct expression of regionalist sentiment. In his 1897 speech welcoming Pereda to membership of the Royal Academy, Galdós claimed that his own work constituted a regional novel of the city, but his interest in social change represents a reaction against the conservatism of the genre. The regional novel would in the late 1890s and early 1900s be revived by Blasco Ibánez, whose Valencian cycle dissociates the genre from its traditionalist roots through recourse to a blend of naturalism and political radicalism.

SERIALIZATION From the 1840s onwards, two forms of serialization developed: instalments in magazines (the 'novela por entregas') and part publications in booklet form, often as a magazine supplement (the 'folletín'). These made fiction available cheaply to a wide public, including the illiterate for the instalments could be read out loud; and created a new form of popular print culture. Serial publication encouraged sensationalist plots and the manipulation of suspense (see also **melodrama**). Galdós occasionally had advance excerpts of his novels printed in the press for publicity purposes, but the only novels he had published in serial form were the early *The Shadow* (1870, *El Debate*), *El audaz* (1871, *Revista de España*), *Doña Perfecta* (1876, *Revista de España*), and – curiously, given its attack on serialized fiction for women – *La desheredada* (originally issued in 'folletín' form from January 1881, prior to its publication in two volumes in the course of the same year). Several of his novels were, however, published in several volumes issued over a period of one to two years. Despite his hostility to publication by instalments, Galdós frequently imitated the cliffhanger chapter endings of the serial novel.

Valera, Juan (1824–1905) A distinguished diplomat, Valera wrote a number of novels set in his native Andalusia. His lyrical evocations of nature are a vehicle not so much for regional sentiment as for a kind of pantheistic mysticism, which is the expression of religious scepticism at the same time as of a profound distaste for contemporary materialism. His best known novels are the immensely popular *Pepita Jiménez* (1874), *Doña Luz* (1879) and *Juanita la larga* (1895): the first two describe the love affairs of a seminarist and priest respectively.

Notes on authors

CARLOS BLANCO AGUINAGA has since 1967 been Professor of Spanish at the University of California (San Diego). Born in Spain, he has lived in the United States since the Spanish Civil War. The author of a wide range of studies on modern Spanish and Latin American literature, he is particularly noted for his work on Galdós.

PETER BLY, a graduate of the University of London, has since 1971 been Professor of Spanish at Queen's University, Ontario. The current Editor of *Anales Galdosianos*, he is author of four books and numerous articles on Galdós, and editor of a critical anthology devoted to his work.

GERALD GILLESPIE is Professor of German and Comparative Literature at Stanford University. His wide-ranging publications include several articles on Spanish literature.

STEPHEN GILMAN was, from 1957 until his recent death, Professor of Spanish at Harvard University, and a distinguished Hispanic scholar. Particularly outstanding are his contributions to scholarship on the *Celestina* and Galdós.

PETER GOLDMAN is Professor of Spanish at Syracuse University, New York, author of a long list of articles on Galdós and editor of a volume on his work.

CATHERINE JAGOE recently completed her PhD on Galdós at the University of Cambridge, and is currently Assistant Professor at Northern Illinois University. She is preparing a book on gender in the novels of Galdós, and is co-editing an anthology of writings on women in nineteenth-century Spain.

JOHN KRONIK is Professor of Romance Studies at Cornell University, and a former Editor of *Anales Galdosianos*. He has produced many distinguished studies of Galdós's fiction.

JOHN SINNIGEN teaches at the University of Maryland, Baltimore, and has published a number of articles on Galdós's work plus a book on the postwar Spanish novel.

DIANE UREY is Professor of Spanish at Illinois State University. She has published on nineteenth- and twentieth-century narrative, including two books and numerous articles on Galdós.

NOËL VALIS has recently moved from the University of Michigan to take up the post of Professor of Spanish at Johns Hopkins University. She has written and edited numerous critical studies on modern Spanish literature, including three books on Alas, and has also edited a volume on Hispanic women writers.

Bibliography

This bibliography consists of the following:

- Works by Galdós
  1. Early novels
  2. Contemporary novels
  3. National episodes
  4. Plays
- English translations of Galdós's works
- Selected critical works on Galdós in English
  1. Books
  2. Articles

Works by Galdós

For explanation of the categories used here, see **contemporary novels** and **National episodes** in the Glossary.

1. Early novels

La Fontana de Oro, 1870
La sombra, 1870
El audaz, 1871

2. Contemporary novels

Doña Perfecta, 1876
Gloria, 1876–7
Marianela, 1878
La familia de León Roch, 1878
La desheredada, 1881
El amigo Manso, 1882
El doctor Centeno, 1883
Tormento, 1884
La de Bringas, 1884
Lo prohibido, 1884–5
Fortunata y Jacinta, 1886–7
Miau, 1888
La incógnita, 1888–9
Torquemada en la hoguera, 1889
Realidad, 1889
Angel Guerra, 1890–1
Tristana, 1892
La loca de la casa, 1892
Torquemada en la cruz, 1893
Torquemada en el purgatorio, 1894

Torquemada y San Pedro, 1895
Nazarín, 1895
Halma, 1895
Misericordia, 1897
El abuelo, 1897
Casandra, 1905
El caballero encantado, 1909
La razón de la sinrazón, 1915

3. National episodes

First series

Trafalgar, 1873
La corte de Carlos IV, 1873
El 19 de marzo y el 2 de mayo, 1873
Bailén, 1873
Napoleón en Chamartín, 1874
Zaragoza, 1874
Gerona, 1874
Cádiz, 1874
Juan Martín el Empecinado, 1874
La batalla de los Arapiles, 1875

Second series

El equipaje del rey José, 1875
Memorias de un cortesano, 1875
La segunda casaca, 1876
El Grande Oriente, 1876
El 7 de julio, 1876
Los cien mil hijos de San Luis, 1877
El terror de 1824, 1877
Un voluntario realista, 1878
Los apostólicos, 1879
Un faccioso màs y algunos frailes menos, 1879

Third series

Zumalacárregui, 1898
Mendizábal, 1898
De Oñate a la Granja, 1898
Luchana, 1899
La campaña del Maestrazgo, 1899
La estafeta romántica, 1899
Vergara, 1899
Montes de Oca, 1900
Los ayacuchos, 1900
Bodas reales, 1900

Fourth series

Las tormentas del 48, 1902
Narváez, 1902
Los duendes de la camarilla, 1903
La revolución de julio, 1903–4
O'Donnell, 1904
Aita Tettauen, 1904–5
Carlos VI en la Rápita, 1905
La vuelta al mundo en la Numancia, 1906
Prim, 1906
La de los tristes destinos, 1907

Final series

España sin rey, 1907–8
España trágica, 1909
Amadeo I, 1910
La primera república, 1911
De Cartago a Sagunto, 1911
Cánovas, 1912

4. Plays

Realidad, 1892
La loca de la casa, 1893
Gerona, 1893
La de San Quintín, 1894
Los condenados, 1894
Voluntad, 1895
Doña Perfecta, 1896
La fiera, 1896
Electra, 1901
Alma y vida, 1902
Mariucha, 1903
El abuelo, 1904
Bárbara, 1905
Amor y ciencia, 1905
Pedro Minio, 1908
Casandra, 1910
Celia en los infiernos, 1913
Alceste, 1914
Sor Simona, 1915
El tacaño Salomón, 1916
Santa Juana de Castilla, 1918

English translations of Galdós's works

Angel Guerra, 1990, trans. K. O. Austin, Edwin Mellen Press, Lampeter.
Doña Perfecta, 1960, trans. H. de Onís, Barrons Educational Series, New York.
Fortunata and Jacinta: Two Stories of Married Women, 1985, trans. A. M. Gullón, Penguin, Harmondsworth.
Miau, 1963, trans. J. M. Cohen, Penguin, Harmondsworth.
Nazarín, (in press), trans. J. Labanyi, Oxford University Press, Oxford.
Our Friend Manso, 1987, trans. R. Russell, Columbia University Press, New York.
The Shadow, 1980, trans K. O. Austin, Ohio University Press, Columbus.
The Spendthrifts (*La de Bringas*), 1951, trans. G. Woolsey. Weidenfeld and Nicholson, London.
Torquemada, 1988, trans. F. M. López-Morillas, André Deutsch, London.
Torquemada in the Fire, 1985, trans. N. Round, University of Glasgow, Glasgow.
The Unknown (*La incógnita*), 1991, trans. K. O. Austin, Edwin Meller Press, Lampeter.

Selected critical works on Galdós in English

1. Books

Berkowitz, H. C., 1948, *Pérez Galdós: Spanish Liberal Crusader*, University of Wisconsin Press, Madison.
Bly, P. A., 1981, *Pérez Galdós: 'La de Bringas'*, Grant and Cutler, London.
—— 1983, *Galdós's Novel of the Historical Imagination: A Study of the Contemporary Novels*, Francis Cairns, Liverpool.
—— 1986, *Vision and the Visual Arts in Galdós: A Study of the Novels and Newspaper Articles*, Francis Cairns, Liverpool.
—— 1991, *Pérez Galdós: 'Nazarín'*, Grant and Cutler, London.
Dendle, B. J., 1980, *Galdós: The Mature Thought*, University Press of Kentucky, Lexington.
Engler, K., 1977, *The Structure of Realism: The 'novelas contemporáneas' of Benito Pérez Galdós*, North Carolina Studies in the Romance Languages and Literatures, Chapel Hill.
Eoff, S., 1954, *The Novels of Pérez Galdós: The Concept of Life as Dynamic Process*, Washington University Press, St Louis.
Gilman, S., 1981, *Galdós and the Art of the European Novel: 1867–87*, Princeton University Press, Princeton.
Goldman, P. B. (ed.), 1984, *Conflicting Realities: Four Readings of a Chapter by Pérez Galdós ('Fortunata y Jacinta', part III, chapter IV)*, Támesis, London.
Nimetz, M., 1968, *Humor in Galdós: A Study of the 'novelas contemporáneas'*, Yale University Press, New Haven.
Pattison, W. T., 1975, *Benito Pérez Galdós*, Twayne, Boston.
Ribbans, G., 1977 *Pérez Galdós: 'Fortunata y Jacinta'*, Grant and Cutler, London.
Rodgers, E., 1978, *Pérez Galdós: 'Miau'*, Grant and Cutler, London.
—— 1987, *From Enlightenment to Realism: The Novels of Galdós, 1870–1887*, no publisher given, Dublin.
Santaló, J., 1973, *The Tragic Import in the Novels of Pérez Galdós*, Playor, Madrid.
Scanlon, G. M., 1988, *Pérez Galdós: 'Marianela'*, Grant and Cutler, London.
Schraibman, J., 1960, *Dreams in the Novels of Galdós*, Hispanic Institute, New York.
Shoemaker, W. H., 1980, *The Novelistic Art of Galdós*, 2 vols, Albatros/Hispanófila, Valencia.

—— 1988, *God's Role and His Religion in Galdós's Novels: 1876–1888*, Albatros/ Hispanófila, Valencia.
TSUCHIYA, A., 1990, *Images of the Sign: Semiotic Consciousness in the Novels of Benito Pérez Galdós*, University of Missouri Press, Columbia.
UREY, D. F., 1982, *Galdós and the Irony of Language*, Cambridge University Press, Cambridge.
VAREY, J. E. (ed.), 1970, *Galdós Studies*, Támesis, London.
WEBER, R. J., 1964, *The 'Miau' Manuscript of Pérez Galdós: A Critical Study*, University of California Press, Berkeley.
—— (ed.), 1972, *Galdós Studies*, vol. 2, Támesis, London.
WHISTON, J., 1983, *The Early Stages of Composition of Galdós's 'Lo prohibido'*, Támesis, London.

2. Articles

(articles which form chapters in this volume are not listed here)

ALDARACA, B., 1983, 'The Revolution of 1868 and the rebellion of Rosalia Bringas, *Anales Galdosianos* **18**: 49–60.
ANDERSON, F., 1985, 'Ellipsis and space in *Tristana*', *Anales Galdosianos* **20**: 61–76.
BLANCO AGUINAGA, C., 1968, 'On "The birth of Fortunata"', *Anales Galdosianos* **3**: 13–24.
—— 1984, '"Having no option": the restoration of order and the education of Fortunata', in Goldman, P. B. (ed.), 1984, pp. 13–38, (see Books section).
BLY, P. A., 1977, 'Fortunata and N 11, Cava de San Miguel', *Hispánofila* **59**: 31–48.
BOWMAN, F. P., 1987, 'On the definition of Jesus in modern fiction', *Anales Galdosianos* **2**: 53–60.
BRAUN, L. V., 1970, 'Galdós's recreation of Ernestina Manuel de Villena as Guillermina Pacheco', *Hispanic Review* **38**: 32–55.
—— 1977, 'The novelistic function of Mauricia la Dura in Galdós's *Fortunata y Jacinta*', *Symposium* **3**: 277–89.
CARDWELL, R. A., 1972, Galdós's '*Doña Perfecta*: art or argument?', *Anales Galdosianos* **7**: 29–47.
CASTILLO, D. A., 1985, 'The problematics of teaching in *El amigo Manso*', *Revista de Estudios Hispánicos* **9**: 37–55.
CHAMBERLIN, V. A., 1981, 'The first annotated, illustrated edition of *Fortunata y Jacinta*', *Anales Galdosianos* **16**: 133–6.
CHARNON-DEUTSCH, L., 1975, 'Inhabited space in Galdós's *Tormento*', *Anales Galdosianos* **10**: 35–43.
—— 1985, '*La de Bringas* and the politics of domestic power', *Anales Galdosianos* **20**: 65–74.
—— 1990, 'Galdós: the power of the role and powerful roles', in Charnon-Deutsch, L., *Gender and Representation: Women in Spanish Realist Fiction*, John Benjamins, Amsterdam, pp. 123–62.
COLIN, V., 1967, 'A note on Tolstoy and Galdós', *Anales Galdosianos* **2**: 155–68.
—— 'Tolstoy and *Angel Guerra*', in Varey, J. E. (ed.), pp. 114–35 (see Books section).
DENDLE, B. J., 1974, 'Point of view in *Nazarín*: an appendix to Goldman', *Anales Galdosianos* **9**: 113–21.
DURAND, F., 1974, 'The reality of illusion: *La desheredada*', *Modern Language Notes* **89**: 191–211.
ENGLER, K., 1970, 'Notes on the narrative structure of *Fortunata y Jacinta*', *Symposium* **24**: 111–27.

—— 1970, 'Linguistic determination of point of view: *La desheredada*', *Anales Galdosianos* **5**: 678–73.
—— 1977, 'The ghostly lover: the portrayal of the animus in *Tristana*', *Anales Galdosianos* **12**: 95–109.
FOLLEY, T., 1972, 'Clothes and the man: an aspect of Benito Pérez Galdós's method of literary characterization', *Bulletin of Hispanic Studies* **49**: 30–9.
FRIEDMAN, E. H., 1982, 'Folly and a woman: Galdós's rhetoric of irony in *Tristana*', in Mora, G., Van Hooft, K. S. (eds), *Theory and Practice of Feminist Literary Criticism*, Bilingual Press, Ypsilanti Michigan, pp. 201–28.
GILLESPIE, G., 1966, 'Dreams and Galdós', *Anales Galdosianos* **1**: 107–14.
GILMAN, S., 1966, 'The birth of Fortunata', *Anales Galdosianos* **1**: 71–83.
—— 1970, 'The consciousness of Fortunata', *Anales Galdosianos* **5**: 55–65.
—— 1982, 'Feminine and masculine consciousness in *Fortunata y Jacinta*', *Anales Galdosianos* **17**: 63–70.
GOLD, H., 1986, 'Problems of closure in *Fortunata y Jacinta*: of narrators, readers and their just deserts/desserts', *Neophilologus* **70**: 227–38.
GOLDMAN, P. B., 1974, 'Galdós and the aesthetic of ambiguity: notes on the thematic structure of *Nazarín*', *Anales Galdosianos* **9**: 99–112.
GORDON, M., 1972, 'The medical background to Galdós's *La desheredada*', *Anales Galdosianos* **7**: 67–77.
GULLÓN, A. M., 1974, 'The bird motif and the introductory motif: Structure in *Fortunata y Jacinta*', *Anales Galdosianos* **9**: 51–75
HAFTER, M., 1961, 'Ironic reprise in Galdós's novels', *PMLA* **76**: 233–9.
HALL, H. B., 1970, 'Torquemada: the man and his language', in Varey, J. E. (ed.), pp. 136–63 (see Books section).
JAGOE, C. A., (in press), 'The subversive angel in Fortunata y Jacinta', *Anales Galdosianos*.
KING, S. E., 1983, 'Food imagery in *Fortunata y Jacinta*', *Anales Galdosianos* **18**: 79–88.
KIRKPATRICK, S., 1982, 'More on the narrator of *Fortunata y Jacinta*', *Revista de Estudios Hispánicos* **9**: 143–50.
KRONIK, J. W., 1978, 'Galdós and the grotesque', *Anales Galdosianos* (supplement): 41–54.
—— 1981, '*Misericordia* as metafiction', in *Homenaje a Antonio Sánchez Barbudo: Ensayos de literatura española moderna*, University of Wisconsin Press, Madison, pp. 37–50.
—— 1982, 'Galdosian reflections: Feijoo and the fabrication of Fortunata', *Modern Language Notes* **97**: 272–310. Also in Goldman, P. B. (ed.), 1984, pp. 39–72 (see Books section).
LABANYI, J., 1988, 'The raw, the cooked and the indigestible in *Fortunata y Jacinta*', *Romance Studies* **13**: 55–66.
—— (in press), 'The problem of framing in *La de Bringas*', *Anales Galdosianos*.
LAMBERT, A. F., 1973, 'Galdós and Concha-Ruth Morell', *Anales Galdosianos* **8**: 33–49.
—— 1976, 'Galdós and the anti-bureaucratic tradition', *Bulletin of Hispanic Studies* **53**: 35–49.
LEWIS, T. E., 1979, 'Galdós' *Gloria* as ideological dispositio', *Modern Language Notes* **94**: 258–82
—— 1981, '*Fortunata y Jacinta*: Galdós and the production of the literary referent', *Modern Language Notes* **96**: 316–39.
PARKER, A. A., 1967, '*Nazarín*, or the Passion of Our Lord Jesus Christ according to Galdós', *Anales Galdosianos* **2**: 83–101.
—— 1969, 'Villaamil – tragic victim or comic failure?', *Anales Galdosianos* **4**: 13–23.

Ramsden, H., 1971, 'The question of responsibility in Galdós's *Miau*', *Anales Galdosianos* **6**: 63–78.
Ribbans, G. R., 1970, 'Contemporary history in the structure and characterization of *Fortunata y Jacinta*', in Varey, J. E. (ed.), pp. 90–113, (see Books section).
—— 1980, '*Historia novelada* and *novela histórica*: the use of historical incidents from the reign of Isabella II in Galdós's *episodios* and *novelas contemporáneas*', in England, J. (ed.), *Hispanic studies in honour of Frank Pierce*, University of Sheffield, Sheffield, pp. 133–47.
—— 1981, 'The portrayal of Queen Isabella II in Galdós's *episodios* and *novelas contemporáneas*', in Paolini, G. (ed.), *'La Chispa '81': Selected proceedings*, Tulane University Press, New Orleans, pp. 277–86.
—— 1982, '"La historia como debiera ser": Galdós's speculations on nineteenth-century Spanish history', *Bulletin of Hispanic Studies* **59**: 267–74.
—— 1986, 'Galdós's literary presentations of the interregnum, reign of Amadeo and the First Republic (1868–1874)', *Bulletin of Hispanic Studies* **63**: 1–17.
Rodgers, E., 1968, 'Religious conflict and didacticism in *Gloria*', *Anales Galdosianos* **1**: 39–51.
—— 1968, 'Galdós's *La desheredada* and naturalism', *Bulletin of Hispanic Studies* **45**: 285–98.
—— 1970, 'The appearance-reality contrast in Galdós's *Tormento*', *Forum for Modern Language Studies* **6**: 382–98.
Round, N. G., 1971, 'Rosalía Bringas' children', *Anales Galdosianos* **6**: 43–50.
—— 1971, 'Time and Torquemada: three notes on Galdosian chronology', *Anales Galdosianos* **6**: 79–97.
—— 1986, 'Villaamil: three lives', *Bulletin of Hispanic Studies* **63**: 19–32.
Russell, R. H., 1967, 'The Christ figure in *Misericordia*', *Anales Galdosianos* **2**: 103–29.
Rutherford, J., 1975, 'Story, character, setting and narrative mode in Galdós's *El amigo Manso*', in Fowler, R. (ed.), *Style and Structure in Literature: Essays in the New Stylistics*, Blackwell, Oxford, pp. 177–212.
Sackett, T. A., 1976, 'Creation and destruction of personality in *Tristana*: Galdós and Buñuel', *Anales Galdosianos* (supplement): 71–90.
Scanlon, G. M., and Jones, R. O., 1971, '*Miau*: Prelude to a reassessment', *Anales Galdosianos* **6**: 53–62.
—— 1973, 'Religion and art in *Angel Guerra*', *Anales Galdosianos* **8**: 99–105.
—— 1976, 'Torquemada: "Becerro de oro"', *Modern Language Notes* **91**: 264–76.
Sinnigen, J. H., 1976, 'Resistance and rebellion in *Tristana*', *Modern Language Notes* **91**: 277–91.
—— 1977, 'The problems of individual and social redemption in *Angel Guerra*', *Anales Galdosianos* **12**: 129–40.
—— 1979, 'Literary and ideological projects in Galdós: The Torquemada series', *Ideologies and Literatures* **3**: 5–19.
—— 1980, 'Galdós's *Tormento*: political partisanship/literary structures', *Anales Galdosianos* **15**: 73–82.
Smith, G., 1975, 'Galdós, *Tristana*, and letters from Concha-Ruth Morell', *Anales Galdosianos* **10**: 91–120.
Terry, A., 1970, '*Lo prohibido*: unreliable narrator and untruthful narrative', in Varey, J. E. (ed.), pp. 62–89 (see Books section).
Tsuchiya, A., 1988, 'Maxi and the signs of madness: reading as creation in *Fortunata y Jacinta*', *Hispanic Review* **56**: 53–71.
—— 1989a, 'The struggle for autonomy in Galdós's *Tristana*', *Modern Language Notes*, **104**: 330–50.
—— 1989b '*La incógnita* and the enigma of writing: Manolo Infante's interpretive struggle', *Hispanic Review* **57**: 335–56.

TURNER, H. S., 1980, 'The control of confusion and clarity in *El amigo Manso*', *Anales Galdosianos* **15**: 45–61.
—— 1983, 'Family ties and tyrannies: a reassessment of Jacinta', *Hispanic Review* **3**: 1–22.
—— 1984, 'The shape of deception in *Doña Perfecta*', *Kentucky Romance Quarterly* **31**: 125–34.
ULLMAN, J. C. and Allison, G. H., 1974, 'Galdós as psychiatrist in *Fortunata y Jacinta*', *Anales Galdosianos* **9**: 7–36.
UREY, D. F., 1985, 'Repetition, discontinuity and silence in Galdós's *Tormento*', *Anales Galdosianos* **20**: 47–63.
VALIS, N. M., 1984, 'Art, memory and the human in Galdós' *Tristana*', *Kentucky Romance Quarterly* **31**: 207–20.
VAREY, J. E., 1970, 'Charity in *Misericordia*', in Varey, J. E. (ed.), pp. 164–94, (see Books section).
—— 1978, 'Man and nature in Galdós's *Halma*', *Anales Galdosianos* **13**: 59–72.
WHISTON, J., 1979, 'The materialism of life: religion in *Fortunata y Jacinta*', *Anales Galdosianos* **14**: 65–81.
—— 1980, 'Determinism and freedom in *Fortunata y Jacinta*', *Bulletin of Hispanic Studies* **57**: 113–27.
—— 1984, 'The struggle for life in *Fortunata y Jacinta*', *Modern Language Review* **79**: 77–87.
ZAHAREAS, A., 1965, 'The tragic sense in *Fortunata y Jacinta*', *Symposium* **19**: 38–49.

Index